Therapy with Couples

A BEHAVIOURAL-SYSTEMS APPROACH TO MARITAL AND SEXUAL PROBLEMS

MICHAEL CROWE
DM, FRCPsych

AND

JANE RIDLEY
BA (Hons), PQSW

FOREWORD BY
ROBIN SKYNNER
DPM, FRCPsych

b

**Blackwell
Science**

© Michael Crowe and Jane Ridley 1990

Blackwell Science Ltd
Editorial Offices:
Osney Mead, Oxford OX2 0EL
25 John Street, London WC1N 2BL
23 Ainslie Place, Edinburgh EH3 6AJ
238 Main Street, Cambridge
  Massachusetts 02142, USA
54 University Street, Carlton
  Victoria 3053, Australia

Other Editorial Offices:
Arnette Blackwell SA
  1, rue de Lille, 75007 Paris
  France

Blackwell Wissenschafts-Verlag GmbH
  Kurfürstendamm 57
  10707 Berlin, Germany

  Feldgasse 13, A-1238 Wien
  Austria

DISTRIBUTORS

Marston Book Services Ltd
PO Box 87
Oxford OX2 0DT
(*Orders:* Tel: 01865 791155
          Fax: 01865 791927
          Telex: 837515)

North America
  Blackwell Science, Inc.
  238 Main Street
  Cambridge, MA 02142
  (*Orders:* Tel: 800 215-1000
            617 876-7000
        Fax: 617 492-5263)

Australia
  Blackwell Science Pty Ltd
  54 University Street
  Carlton, Victoria 3053
  (*Orders:* Tel: 03 347-0300
            Fax: 03 349-3016)

First published 1990
Reprinted 1992, 1996

Set by Best-set Typesetter Ltd., Hong Kong
Printed and bound in Great Britain
by Hartnolls Ltd., Bodmin, Cornwall

British Library
Cataloguing in Publication Data

Crowe, Michael
Therapy with couples.
1. Married couples. Psychotherapy
I. Title   II. Ridley, Jane
616.89'156

ISBN 0-632-02375-9

Contents

feelings of helplessness;   **12.11** Training in the appropriate use of empathy in the context of a more active therapeutic approach;   **12.12** Thinking about a relationship systemically; **12.13** Formulating messages or tasks;   **12.14** Training in dealing with sexual issues;   **12.15** Conclusion of the training section;   **12.16** Supervision.

Foreword

Robin Skynner, FRCPsych, DPM

It is a great pleasure to be asked to write a foreword to this excellent book, and for me a special enjoyment that it derives so strongly from work with families and couples at the Maudsley Hospital.

At the time of my own training at the Maudsley (together with its sister hospital the Bethlem Royal and its training arm the Institute of Psychiatry) Professor H.J. Eysenck and his colleagues in the Department of Psychology were actively developing the new behavioural methods of treatment of psychological disorders, and applying them in suitable cases with promising results. Around this time, also, the first reports were arriving in American journals about exciting experiments in treating patients with mental disorders by interviewing them together with their families.

The psychodynamic approaches were already well-represented there, and when the behavioural methods were promoted in an adversarial style which attacked their validity, the two schools of thought became polarised in a way that made mutual exchange and learning difficult. However, as a trainee I could draw upon both forms of understanding and experimented with both approaches, finding them to be complementary and combinable once the different languages and philosophies were taken into account. I felt the rivalry between these schools of therapy impeded a search for more effective psychological treatments, and hoped that one day I, and others similarly minded, might help to bridge them and also find links to the new work with whole families.

In the years that followed, while I was trying to develop more effective treatment approaches within child psychiatry, some modest steps were taken in this direction. A limited integration of psycho-analytic and behavioural methods, linking the different concepts of 'model' developed by Bowlby (internal object) and Bandura (modelling as learning by example), and applied within an understanding of the family system, appeared to promise quicker and more effective results (Skynner, 1976).

In 1971 the opportunity arose to return to the Maudsley with the brief of teaching and supervising work with couples and families, in the adult departments of the hospital. I found there was already much active interest in couple therapy, and was invited to lead what had been until then a self-help peer-group of senior registrars. (For those unfamiliar with these medical titles, this means doctors in the final stages of their training for consultant posts). I was delighted to do so, and enjoyed meeting with this lively, active group until the teaching developed other forms.

A key figure in this group, who took responsibility for the organisation of its meetings and later of the video demonstration seminars which followed it, was one of the authors of this volume, Dr Michael Crowe. His basic orientation was then, and remains now, essentially behavioural, influenced particularly by his personal contact with Isaac Marks and Robert Liberman, and by the work of Masters and Johnson. But throughout he has had an open and questioning mind and I found him to be clearly more interested in seeking the truth, and serving the best interests of patients, than in defending a position. We found we could learn from each other, and if he gained from my formal teaching, my own understanding certainly also broadened and grew in the process of my contact with him. I am sure this sharing of knowledge and skills was all the greater because we also appeared to share an enjoyment of exploration, and a sense of humour which is put to service in our professional work.

When in 1973 I set up the Introductory Course in Family Therapy under the auspices of the Institute of Group Analysis, designing it to bring together both psychiatrists and social workers and including representatives of psycho-analysis, group analysis, behavioural methods and action techniques, Crowe was a natural choice for the staff group. In the lectures we each provided specific input to the participants according to our favoured model, and also all learned from each other's work in our staff meetings, to broaden our knowledge and improve our teaching. Crowe was a major source of the input on behavioural approaches, and when this course developed into the Institute of Family Therapy in 1977, he and I worked closely together in guiding its early growth, I as chairman, and he as honorary secretary.

Since that time he has become one of the main leaders in the field of family therapy, in particular the treatment of marital and sexual problems. He carried a major responsibility for the Family and Marital Diploma course at the Maudsley Hospital, where his influential position as chairman of the Medical Committee must have helped to enhance respect for and acceptance of family and systems methods. He has also played leading roles in the formation of the Association of Sexual and Marital Therapists, and of the Standing Committee for Couples in Trouble, being a past chairman of the former and present chairman of the latter.

His co-author, Jane Ridley, brings to this book the different perspective of social studies to complement the medical view, having worked in almost all areas of social work. Her approach to marital therapy has derived particularly from an early interest in social anthropology, the group work of Bion and the family techniques of Satir. She also has had a deep interest in, and much experience of, psycho-analytic techniques, together with a commitment to furthering the integration of systems, behavioural and psycho-analytic ideas. Like so many of us in the field of family therapy, she was strongly influenced early on by the observation that brief interventions were often more effective than extended casework.

After she became a therapist at the Maudsley Hospital in 1983 she joined Dr Crowe in his work in the Marital and Family Clinic and the Sexual Dysfunction Clinic, participating in both the research and therapy programmes.

Not least, though little is mentioned explicitly in the text, I know both authors to have a strong commitment to, and enjoyment of their own marriages and families, and I am sure that this contributes greatly to the strength and the common-sense, convincing quality of the material.

Clearly, a collaboration between two such authors, bringing together yet respecting each other's different professions and orientations, is work after my own heart. And their aim is admirably realised. Most striking of all is the extraordinary range and inclusiveness of the ideas, which are nevertheless embodied in very specific and detailed recommendations. Few books deal with sexual problems in the context of the marital relationship as a whole, or both of these in the context of the dynamics of the whole family, but this book must be added to the select few that take that comprehensive view.

In a review of the literature on behavioural marital therapy I wrote (Skynner, 1987) that.

> 'the behavioural approach has unique value in the way in which it has developed the *detail* of interviewing or treatment procedures in a way that beginners can easily learn, a task that the other perspectives in general neglect and leave students to learn all over again for themselves'.

Though this virtue is exemplified here by the whole volume, the reader who turns to Chapter 5 on Reciprocity Negotiation will find it a marvel of clarity, simplicity and good sense, conveying the essence of a long accumulation of skills through a number of principles that are easily absorbed.

In the above review I also noted that.

> 'behavioural approaches require an alliance with reasonably mature and adult aspects of the spouses' personalities, and are difficult to implement when there are primitive, psychotic or borderline aspects in the functioning of the couple that produce unrealistic expectations that are difficult to modify; an incapacity to understand the need for reciprocity; a lack of commitment, or an extreme vulnerability'.

No such criticism could be made of the methods advised here, because modifications to the straightforward behavioural interventions, drawing upon systemic and psycho-analytic understanding, are advised where such complications are met with. Also, these interventions are clearly graded in a hierarchy according to assessment of the level of pathology, degree of rigidity/flexibility, capacity for objective self-awareness or insight, and degree of honesty and co-operativeness.

Similar flexibility is shown in the authors' acceptance, in appropriate cases, of the value of other forms of treatment – individual psycho-therapy, medication, etc. – either independently or in conjunction with couple interviews. All this, together with the focus on brief therapy and the clear guidance offered towards making decisions in each case, makes this book of particular value to those working within a medical system like our own National Health Service, or in the Social Services, where the full range of pathology has to be coped with, including patients who are psychotic, potentially suicidal, addicted, brain damaged or suffering from other organic conditions.

Throughout, there are excellent, detailed case-examples, structured to enable others to understand and replicate the interventions. And as might be expected, there is a good outline of important statistics and other relevant background information, as well as a succinct but com-prehensive review of research findings, assessment and rating scales, observation measures, and outcome studies. I hope that my own enthusiastic response will have whetted the reader's appetite. I could say much more, but any further words would only delay the reader's opportunity to fall upon this feast.

Preface

Introduction

The field of couple therapy is an expanding one at the present time, with a number of institutions in Britain now offering both therapy and training in this kind of work. Couple therapy was for a long time thought of as an offshoot of individual or family therapy. Now, however, there is an increasing recognition that couple relationships both in and outside marriage are important in themselves and can contribute to the development of, or the prevention of, psychiatric problems.

This book presents a particular way of working with couples, the behavioural-systems approach. It is essentially a practical book, which is however based on a firm foundation of theory, research and clinical experience. In it we combine an understanding of the nature of couple relationships with clear guidelines for effective therapy to help couples in difficulties.

The foundation of our experience is the work of the marital and family clinic at the Maudsley Hospital. Here we have been working together as a team for the past ten years, seeing couples in therapy and using the one-way screen for observation and live supervision. As might be expected, this setting provides the opportunity for a great deal of creative experimentation in therapy, and a lively exchange of ideas and hypotheses.

We have been influenced by many different theories in our ideas, but we have mainly drawn from behavioural and systems theories in developing our therapeutic approach. While relying on research literature, including work carried out in our own unit, the majority of our original ideas and techniques (such as the use of timetables, Chapters 9 and 10, and decentred negotiation, Chapters 4 to 8) have arisen by a process of distillation from the discussions in the therapeutic team.

Finding your way around the book

The behavioural-systems approach invites the therapist to be flexible and choose interventions which suit each couple, ascending or descending the hierarchy of alternative levels of intervention (ALI) according to the particular difficulties of each couple (see Chapter 3). The reader may also wish to use this book flexibly and select from different chapters those elements which fit his or her own particular interest. We are therefore suggesting some alternative ways of approaching this book.

The behavioural-systems approach

For those readers who are anxious to learn about the behavioural-systems approach you may wish to begin with Chapter 3 where the ALI hierarchy is introduced. We use this when making decisions about the level at which it may be most effective to work. Chapter 4 introduces the process of our work and Chapters 5, 6, and 7 go on to describe the basic building blocks of the behavioural-systems approach. The following chapters either give specific examples of interventions such as encouraging arguments over trivial issues (Chapter 8) or the use of messages (Chapter 9), or describe case material in some detail.

Treating couples with specific problems

For those readers who are anxious to solve particular problems it may be useful to select from different parts of the book using the Contents and Index as reference points. For example, if you wish to help a couple develop the ability to talk and listen to each other more effectively you may like to select sections such as 6.5 (encouraging mutual exchange of 'emotional messages'). If you are working with couples where one partner is depressed or jealous or reluctant to have sexual intercourse you may wish to read Chapter 10 in some detail to see whether the interventions suggested there would help you with such couples. If your clients have other sexual difficulties, Chapter 11 gives an overview of some of the more useful interventions which are available.

If more familiar techniques have been tried without success, it would certainly be useful to consult Chapters 7, 8 and 9 to explore some of the systemic options available including the use of paradox (Section 9.12).

Training issues

Trainers or supervisors may wish to explore Chapter 12 or specific sections such as 12.6 which shows how role-play can be used to help trainees think in terms of interaction and learn to use the behavioural-systems approach.

Using the total approach or being selective

The reader may wish to understand the totality of this approach or may wish to select specific interventions which seem to be helpful for particular difficulties. We find that in much of our work, whether it be at the behavioural or systemic level, we often include messages as described in Chapter 9. Such messages can, of course, be either direct or paradoxical in their intention, and if they embody timetables these can suggest many different activities, from outings together to heated discussions or homework for sexual problems.

One specific area we cover which is not usually included in the couple-therapy literature is that of sexual problems (Chapter 11). This more specialised chapter is, however, well integrated with the rest of the book and could be used by therapists who already see themselves as competent in working with couples but wish to extend their knowledge and skills in dealing specifically with the sexual difficulties which couples encounter.

The pressures couples face

For those readers who wish to consider what pressures may be experienced by couples in Britain today we have included an introductory chapter (Chapter 1). It is of necessity a rapid overview of some of the social, economic and psychological factors which may impinge upon a couple, and attempts to suggest reasons why couples may increasingly look to professional therapists for help in overcoming difficulties with which they are faced.

Chapter 2 is part of this same exploration of the nature of couple relationships, the difficulties they may encounter and the alternative resources available to assist them. We hope to have shown how behavioural-systems couple therapy fits into the spectrum of therapies available and what it specifically offers to the couple in trouble. We have also tried to demonstrate in Chapter 3 that the behavioural-systems approach can successfully be used alongside other forms of treatment such as psychiatric care or family therapy.

Case material

For those readers who find they are most interested in case material, an alternative way to use this book might be to begin by reading the cases described in Chapters 8, 9 and 10. We have chosen to present the case material in some detail (with names changed and any recognisable characteristics of the partners disguised to preserve confidentiality) and have drawn the cases from the clinic, with verbatim extracts from case files or videos wherever possible. We hope that this will help the reader to understand the more practical aspect of therapy, and show how the theory relates to practice.

We have also tried to show in our case reports how important it is in this work to relate therapy to the everyday aspects of people's lives. For example, in Section 8.2.1 we have described Edith and Robert who we suggest hold a quite widespread belief that 'good couples do not argue': this the therapist successfully challenged. In Section 8.4.4 we describe the difficulty that Samuel and Diana had in finding a subject for argument and how they eventually argued successfully about whether the toilet seat must always be left down after use, and thereby began to resolve their long-standing problem over sex. We hope in this way to show how the ordinary everyday difficulties which couples face may often be symbolic of their total relationship, which can be improved by focussing on these trivial (yet powerful) issues.

Beginning with the summary

In Chapter 13 we summarise the main ideas discussed in this book and the innovations which the behavioural-systems approach offers to therapy with couples. Another alternative approach to the book might therefore be for the reader to begin with this chapter and then pursue any of the interventions which raise the reader's particular interest.

Our general aims in this book

We hope therefore to have produced a book which can be dipped into at various points, used as a resource when seeking alternative interventions or read from cover to cover. In doing so we hope to have met some of the needs of therapists and trainers who seek to extend their therapeutic repertoire, and also that by describing the ALI hierarchy we will have provided a framework which can make decision making in therapy a little simpler.

Chapter 1

Who are the clients and what pressures lead them to seek therapy?

1.1 Introduction

In this chapter we describe some of the social pressures currently influencing marriages and similar relationships, and suggest some of the reasons why people decide to share their lives together. Factors which seem to sustain successful or 'non-distressed' relationships are explored and on the other hand the pressures which appear to be causing an increasing number of couples to seek therapy are discussed.

1.1.1 The social matrix: changing social roles

Intimate relationships are talked about very openly and are the subject of much interest at the present time. It is as though, as the ties of the extended family or close community weaken, and the associated social, religious or economic sanctions and supports diminish, so the couple has become the focus of heightened expectations, experimentation or despondency. The media exhibit this fascination, as discussion programmes and news stories revealing the intimate relationships of public figures reflect back to society its own preoccupation with the nature of couple relationships. None of this is new. Poetry, literature and the arts have fulfilled this role in the past; what is perhaps a modern phenomenon is the widespread interest in experimentation and a readiness to challenge past assumptions about relationships between men and women.

We have deliberately chosen to focus on couples, rather than on the marriage as we wish to acknowledge the changing pattern of society. We use the term marriage infrequently, because we wish to include not only married couples in our discussion but all men and women who are sharing their lives together and maintaining and developing a long-term relationship, with or without children. The term couple is also used to refer to partners of the same sex, who seek to develop a long-term relationship together. In this particular book, same-sex couples are not dealt with specifically, mainly because of the rarity of these couples among referrals to our clinic. However, we should acknowledge here that we believe that the ideas and approaches presented are equally relevant to these relationships.

We believe that at the present time pressures exist which both tend to idealise the couple relationship and at the same time undermine it, and together have perhaps contributed to the increasing demand for couple therapy. Two things seem to be happening at the same time. There is a growing interest in exploring the nature of couple interactions, and there is a parallel process which questions and undermines the stability of long-term relationships between couples.

1.1.2 Statistics on marriage and divorce

Statistics on marriage and divorce are an indication of the fluid patterns of present society. The Family Policy Studies Fact Sheet (1985) presents this picture.

> 'Looking at the family today, we need to be aware of both continuity and change.
>
> Change is reflected in the pace of marriage breakdown, and the increase of lone parenthood. The divorce rate in England and Wales has increased sixfold in the last twenty years. If present trends continue one marriage in three could be expected to end in divorce. One child in every eight currently lives in a one parent family. One child in five could see their parents divorce before they reach 16. Continuity is also evident as nine out of ten people will marry at some time in their lives. Nine out of ten married couples will have children. Two out of every three marriages are likely to be ended by death rather than divorce. Eight out of ten people live in households headed by a married couple.'

If the figures for 1983 for marriages are examined, a further interesting feature emerges.

> 'In 1983 the total number of marriages in England and Wales was 344,000, just ½% higher than in 1982 which was the lowest annual figure since 1959. About 64% of all marriages were first marriages for both parties: a further 19% were first marriages for one partner only, while in 17% of cases both partners were remarrying. This compares to 15% of all marriages involving remarriage for one or both partners in 1961.'

One might therefore conclude that whilst the divorce rate stays at a high level, marriage itself has lost little of its appeal, and remarriage is on the increase.

A further factor, evident amongst the changing patterns of couple relationships, is that of cohabitation. To quote the Family Policy Studies

Fact Sheet again,

'It is sometimes suggested that cohabitation is replacing marriage. Certainly living together before marriage is becoming more common. In 1979–82 about one quarter of women marrying under the age of 35 had cohabited with their husband before marriage where the marriage was the first for both partners, and this was true of about two thirds of those women where one or both partners had been married before. The corresponding proportions for women in the period 1970–1974 were 8% and 42% respectively.'

So we have a picture of a more fluid society, couples no longer beginning marriage with a virgin bride, nor necessarily staying together 'till death us do part'. Cohabitation, single-parent families and second marriages are all becoming more prevalent.

1.1.3 The changing roles of men and women

Much of the confusion felt by men and women in permanent relationships may be linked to the debate about their respective roles. The women's movement has drawn attention to the unequal burden placed upon women within the marital relationship. Childbearing, child-rearing and lack of equal opportunities for work outside the home have been a main thrust of concern (Rowbotham 1983, Oakley 1974).

Other writers wish to draw a distinction between childbearing and child-rearing in an attempt to redefine the nature of child-rearing, and to reallocate part of the responsibility to the male partner (Chodorow 1978; Walsh 1987). Questions have been raised as to whether women have any greater inherent nurturing ability than men, and a preference seems to be growing amongst the women's movement for the concept of parenting rather than mothering, in which the responsibilities and skills of nurturing and caring for children are seen as being shared more equally between men and women. In this way parenting is redefined as a skill which can be learned, rather than inherently a female characteristic (Chodorow 1978). Whilst these issues have been raised for discussion, there is little real consensus (Rossi 1981; Gilligan 1982). This may however be one of the pressures which contributes to the present uncertainty about relationships.

The use of contraception, and even abortion, has enabled women to take greater control of the number of pregnancies they have. Social attitudes and social changes such as the availability of childminders, nurseries or the use of au pairs play a part in the movement to free women from the inevitability of the housewife's role. In 1980–82 the proportion of married women with dependent children working outside the home full-time was 15%, and part time was 36%.

These changes provide both opportunities for a more 'symmetrical' relationship to develop (Young and Wilmott 1973), and for greater tension, uncertainty and disagreement to exist within the couple. Burgess and Locke (1953) suggested that there was a detectable wish within society to move from what they called 'institutionalised marriage' to a 'companionate marriage' with greater sharing of duties. Bott (1971) however suggested that marital patterns developed according to the different class and network structure surrounding the couple.

Regardless of what ideology is currently being discussed within society, the reality seems to be that women often find themselves freed from the routine of housework and child-rearing during part of the day, only to have to carry the major burden of these tasks when they return home (Henwood *et al.* 1987). Resentments that expectations and reality do not match can rapidly build up within such couples.

1.1.4 Employment and finances

Allied to the question of greater equality for the woman at home is that of whether she is in full- or part-time employment, what effect this has upon the couple, how they manage their finances and whether this gives either or both of them greater independence.

The Women and Employment Survey (Martin and Roberts 1984) showed that in 57% of couples, both husband and wife were working; only 31% of couples were in the one-earner category, that of the husband working and the wife economically inactive. The question of how couples manage their finances has been examined by Pahl (1980). He studied issues such as whether couples pooled their resources if the woman was an earner; whether the woman had a separate account if she did not earn; whether the husband declared all of his income to his wife; and who paid which bills. The patterns which emerged were variable. Observable trends were, however, that when incomes were low the whole wage was usually pooled. An allowance arrangement for the wife was likely as incomes rose and more particularly if the husband was the sole earner. Where both partners worked, pooling of some proportion of the incomes and independent money management was likely. Although these were discernible statistical trends, individual couples are still faced with making their own separate choices about declaring and managing their finances. In a situation of such fluidity of options it is not surprising that the management of finances can become the focus for discord in some couples.

1.1.5 Caring for dependants

Another less publicised aspect of the male/female balance of responsibility is that of caring for elderly or disabled family members. The Equal

Opportunities Commission found 75% of carers of elderly or handicapped persons were women (EOC 1980). Parker (1985) reviewed research data and said:

> 'The evidence then, is unequivocal. While the family, where it exists, still cares for its elderly members within the family, it is the wives, daughters, daughters-in-law and other female relatives who shoulder the main burden of responsibility.'

The role of care of dependants creates an additional stress upon the woman and when she is unsupported by her spouse in this role the issue can become a source of marital discord.

The changing expectation of women may then be part of a stimulating ongoing dialogue between partners who develop their own particular flexible solutions; for others these issues simmer with little recognition of their relevance, or remain unresolved, as unspoken resentments and power struggles.

1.1.6 The impact on the male partner

The male partners are often placed in an equally ambiguous situation, no longer being able to rely upon their traditional role, often being asked to be both a caring and sensitive father (a 'new man') as well as being the authority figure in relation to their children and the main wage-earner. Additional uncertainties relating to employment opportunities, redundancy or retirement often make the male feel defensive or undermined. Solace may be sought in greater involvement with work or activities outside the home, leaving the woman to feel yet more isolated and burdened.

The women's movement in its various facets has become a mouthpiece for women's issues, giving women at least the sense that someone is enunciating their concerns. Consciousness-raising groups, assertiveness groups and women's therapy centres are appearing, giving women some structure for exploring these questions.

An equivalent men's movement has not yet developed. No doubt the 'stiff upper lip' and 'men don't cry' philosophy can make it difficult for men to be responsive to the mounting pressures for a re-evaluation of their roles in the family. Such questions as those of male expressiveness and male ability to nurture and parent are potentially of equal importance to men as to women (Metcalf and Humphries 1985). Exactly how couples negotiate their own particular response to these dilemmas is one of the elements needed to produce a satisfactory relationship (Burgess and Locke 1953; Bott 1971; Beavers 1976, 1985; Olson *et al.* 1983).

1.1.7　Sexual expressiveness

Today's greater freedom for sexual exploration with a variety of partners can bring confidence into a couple's sexual life, or create greater resentment and jealousy. Current anxiety about AIDS, however, adds extra pressure upon couples who have explored or wish to explore sexuality with other partners. It may be that in response to this pressure couples are increasingly trying to achieve sexual and emotional satisfaction within a monogamous relationship. The woman in particular may be looking for a different level of sexual satisfaction with her partner and may no longer be so satisfied to 'lie back and enjoy it', regardless of the approach of the partner, or her own prior experience of sex (Comfort 1972; Jehu 1979; Kaplan 1981).

1.1.8　Stress and developmental phases

Some evidence suggests that stresses upon marriage are greater at certain periods. These tend to be the early phase of adjustment and negotiation between one and three years of marriage, the developmental phases of parenting with adolescent children and the phase when the children leave home. This latter phase is often called the leaving home period or the 'empty nest' (Chester 1973; Rappoport *et al.* 1977; Haley 1980).

(See also Section 1.6 for a discussion of the family life cycle.)

1.1.9　Help-seeking behaviour: gender differences

Important questions are being asked about gender differences in seeking help for psychological and physical illness, as well as the greater incidence of mental illness in women (Briscoe 1982, 1987). The suggestion that women are more susceptible to illness as a result of their biological destiny is being challenged, and instead the environment in which women are expected to survive is being investigated as an explanation for the higher incidence of women's greater susceptibility (Clare 1985; Jenkins 1985).

Marriage in particular has been explored as the source of women's greater vulnerability to mental illness, especially depression (Brown and Harris 1978; Briscoe 1982). The nature of the relationship between husband and wife and whether it is sufficiently close to be described as a confiding relationship has been identified as an important factor in whether women become depressed. Brown found that women looking after children at home and who are working class and lack both outside employment and a confiding relationship are most at risk to depression in the inner city.

It seems that in addition to the documented differences between men and women in the incidence of psychiatric problems there is a sex difference in help-seeking behaviour. It is sufficient here to note that women by-and-large seek more help for minor psychiatric illness (women between the ages of 18 and 44 years consult at the rate of $2\frac{1}{2}$ women for every man), and that by-and-large men are reluctant to seek help.

Briscoe suggests that one should conclude that

'this difference is probably due to sex differences in the ability to communicate psychological distress. As one of the potential sources of emotional support is the G.P., women are more often diagnosed as suffering from poor mental health. Conversely, men's difficulties are much less likely to surface.

Perhaps the major question facing G.P's is therefore, not so much how to discourage women from consulting as how to encourage men to consult more frequently.'

Briscoe was of course talking about consultation for minor psychiatric disorders. However the same question may be asked about distress in marriage; who notices and who consults? Evidence suggests that women are usually aware of relationship distress before men, seek help more often and are also more likely to seek a divorce (Thornes and Collard 1979).

The converse of these findings, which is rarely stated, is that men are often insensitive to the relationship difficulties of their partner, are reluctant to seek help and increasingly find themselves in situations where the partner has made unilateral choices about the future of their relationship. This might be moderated if men were prepared to accept a more expressive and interactive role in relation to their partner; this however is in opposition to much of male conditioning.

(See also Chapter 10 on depression in women and Chapter 8 on sexual reluctance in men.)

1.1.10 Generation differences

It is probably less possible than in the past for couples to turn to the older generation for advice. The question 'what did you do in these circumstances?' may be irrelevant, as increasingly couples find themselves in situations not faced by their parents. Couples are nowadays exposed to a multitude of pressures and choices about which they often have had little experience, and for which they have few role-models to follow (Kiely 1984).

Additional factors such as what material standards are possible, the adequacy of family or friendship networks, the pace of life, sickness, employment or unemployment, mobility and the needs of dependants all add to the choices and pressures upon couples. The absence of clear guidelines regarding almost all these aspects of life provides couples with areas of fruitful collaboration or potential discord. It is not surprising that many couples seek therapy to assist them with some of the difficulties they face in their relationship, within the fluid matrix that is modern Britain.

1.2 'Falling in Love'

None of the above takes into account the notion of 'being in love', a concept which is difficult to define and understand, and yet is often given as the reason why couples joined together in permanent relationships. Mansfield and Collard (1988) investigated a group of couples marrying for the first time in church in two London suburbs. They suggest that this selected group of couples marrying in the 1980s are pragmatic, choosing to marry because they are 'ready for marriage', a somewhat vague concept which seems to include within it the notion that couples see marriage as primarily an initiation into adulthood and are therefore ready to settle down.

In spite of this apparent pragmatism in the young of today, we would like to explore here the concept of being in love, as we find it still a prevalent concept. It may help us to understand some of the reasons for, and expectations of, couples who join together in permanent relationships.

According to Bergmann (1987)

> 'The first to find words for love were the Egyptians who 3,500 years ago wrote poems of love. They discovered the metaphor as the vehicle to express love. Some of their metaphors, such as comparing love to sickness, and a sickness that only the presence of the beloved can cure, have remained with us. The Egyptians also created the metaphor of love as a sweet entrapment.'

Bergmann selects from philosophers and poets their definitions of love such as 'from the Platonic fable: the yearning to be forever united with another person' or a paraphrase of Schopenhauer's definition of love as 'endless bliss associated with the possession of one particular person, and unutterable pain associated with the thought that the possession is unattainable.'

Although falling in love has been a recurring theme throughout written history, it has only become an acceptable reason for marrying in the late nineteenth and twentieth centuries, and is associated only with marriages where Western influences prevail. In much of India, Africa, many parts of Latin America and Asia marriages are still decided for primarily economic, social or status reasons. Consideration for the other and the possibility of a love relationship may develop later. Love is not a *sine qua non* of such marriages.

Falling or being in love, this shared state of feeling understood and cared for by the other and a longing to be in the presence of the other when separated, is usually accompanied by idealisation of the loved one, during which phase the loved one can usually do no wrong. Not only is the partner idealised, but the couple usually find it very difficult to explain what made them fall in love. These two elements of idealisation and irrationality, or inability to explain, provide the basis for optimism and anxiety about the future of relationships based upon the state of being in love. Optimism because the element of being in love, though irrational, seems to propel couples towards finding solutions to difficulties encountered later in their relationship. Anxiety because as the idealised phase passes, as it usually does, so an inevitable struggle emerges for the couple, that of working out a relationship based on a greater sense of the reality, separateness and vulnerability of each partner.

Some of the behaviour patterns of couples in the early stages of being in love are particularly pertinent to this book. The picture of a couple gazing steadily into each other's eyes, their need to touch and be close physically, and to whisper 'sweet nothings' to each other is familiar to us all, either from our own experience, from observations of those we know or from descriptions or portrayals in novels and drama.

1.2.1 Mother/child interaction

Scharff (1982) suggests that

> 'The adult need for kissing, smiling and physical caring or lovemaking have their origins in the shared gaze, touch, holding and vocal "conversations" of infant and mother.'

Pines (1989) explores the literature and research data on mother/child interaction described variously as mirroring, social fittedness or state-sharing and suggests that it is a significant early experience of inter-subjectivity in which the mother and child have moments of shared pleasure.

> 'In mental state sharing, the infant and the mother share similar experiences. State-sharing covers such events as vocalising together, games such as pat-a-cake, interactional synchrony, mutual gazing, and interaction between mother and infant such as smiling, where the smile of one evokes the smile of the other, which in turn increases the pleasure and the intensity of the smiling response, acting as a positive feedback loop.'

We cannot discuss here the evidence of Papousek and Papousek (1974) and Stern (1983) supporting the above statement from mother/child observational studies. For our purposes it is sufficient to draw attention to the similarity between the interaction between the mother/child dyad described by Stern as 'interactional synchrony' and the behaviour of the couple who are 'in love'. Whether the adult state of being in love is an attempt to recreate the mother/child shared mental state (Winnicott 1965, 1971) can only be hypothesised; it might however be a useful indicator of the level of understanding and empathy which is craved by adults seeking an in love relationship. It may also help us to understand the irrational element of being in love.

1.2.2 Distressed and non-distressed couples

The work of Schaap and Jansen-Nawas (1987) may also help us to understand the nature of falling in love and what individuals seek in a couple relationship. Schaap compared the problem-solving behaviour and effect of nine non-distressed and nine distressed couples to investigate whether differences could be clearly identified between the interaction of the different categories of couples. The results of this study, summarised below, add weight to the hypothesis which links adult intimacy needs to those of the mother/child shared mental state as described by Winnicott, Scharff and Pines.

The factors which discriminate between the non-distressed and distressed couples are eye contact, synchronous non-verbal interaction and positive attention to the other person. For example 'not tracking' (when the listener does not look at the speaker for at least three seconds) was highly discriminating for both frequency and duration. 'This means that in the non-distressed couples listeners looked at their spouses much more than the distressed listeners did.' Eye contact, facial expression, gestures and voice quality were all highly significant as discriminators, as the distressed couples judged these behaviours of spouses more negatively than the non-distressed couples. Of all the non-verbal interactions rated, the authors judge eye contact to be most relevant.

These findings stand on their own as important to the ability to discriminate between non-distressed and distressed couples. Whether there is a direct link between the behaviour of non-distressed couples, those who are in the idealised phase of being in love and the early mother and child relationship is impossible to answer. What is relevant is the level of satisfaction found in these relationships and what we might learn about the relationships being sought by couples. It is clear that the non-verbal aspects of eye contact, touch and attentiveness (listening) are important correlates of marital satisfaction, and may set the scene for 'good enough' relationships between spouses (borrowing Winnicott's phrase which originally described parenting).

The Munich Marital Therapy study found that ratings of what they called the 'emotional-affective quality of the relationship' (these were tenderness, communication and sexual intercourse) were predictive of successful outcome of therapy. Hahlweg et al. (1984) write

'The second scale (tenderness) includes verbal and nonverbal behaviours indicating tenderness and intimacy. ("He/she caresses me tenderly" and "He/she tells me that he/she loves me"). The third scale (Togetherness/ Communication) includes items like "We talk to each other for at least half an hour every day" and "We make plans for the future together".'

This study supports the hypothesis that the 'emotional qualities' of a relationship are predictive of relationship satisfaction and may form part of the core requirements of an enduring relationship. The factors identified by the Munich study do seem to be very similar to those identified by Schaap and deduced by Winnicott, Stern and Pines to link with early mother/child nurturing needs.

1.2.3 Negotiating a transition

Since the statistics for separation and divorce indicate a clustering in the first three years of marriage, one might hypothesise that for these couples the transition from the irrational state of being in love to a more reality-based current relationship has not been adequately negotiated. One might also suggest that, since the expectations of the couple were irrational and over-idealised, falling in love on its own is an unstable foundation for a long-term relationship. As we have seen, unless an adequate degree of intimacy is maintained (expressed through the non-verbal levels of eye contact, voice tone and attention) beyond the in love phase, then the relationship is likely to become distressed. Or to put this more positively, the couple should expect the in love phase to diminish and the work of establishing a long-term relationship to begin during the early years of their marriage. This will mean that many problems may arise which require open discussion between the partners so that joint decisions can be made. When choices are made without the full agreement of one partner then resentments, power struggles and arguments are likely to ensue and as Skynner (1976) suggests

'Non-verbal exchanges which are less under conscious control often give the secret away first, and we should always be alert to these, particularly movements of the eyes which say more than anything else about the real pattern of emotional bonds.'

1.2.4 Male/female variation

The discussion so far has concentrated upon the similarity between the mother/child experiences and the adult's search for a state of being in love. Clinical experience suggests that there may be significant differences between men and women in their expectation of the couple relationship. One pattern which we often observe is where the woman is constantly seeking an empathic relationship while the man is nonplussed by this. The man for his part seems to need the woman to 'be there' but does not seem to be seeking a close and empathic relationship. He may want an active sexual life but seems easily overwhelmed by the woman's wish for more love and understanding.

Little research has been carried out into this area, although Mansfield and Collard (1988) seem to suggest that such differences exist. Such evidence raises the question of whether men's experiences of being nurtured and nurturing give rise to different expectations of a couple relationship from those of women. Until recently, few men have had intimate experiences of caring for and nurturing babies and infants; they therefore have had little opportunity to savour this interaction and to build a reservoir of knowledge and experience of intuitive nurturing (intuitive because the baby cannot speak about his/her needs.) Eye gazing, eye contact and mutual interaction between father and baby has usually been time-limited, occurring as and when father was available after work. Some men (and some women) have few opportunities to experience the touch and tenderness of this intimate exchange between baby and adult. In the absence of such experiences as part of the natural nurturing of children, one wonders whether physical touch and tenderness is therefore mainly experienced by men as sexually arousing.

Again, does this mean that for some men the experience of being left alone to care for their children, either by choice because the woman is out or while the man is unemployed and his wife is the main bread-winner, puts them into a situation where the unaccustomed contact with their children may potentially become sexualised?

This is in the main conjectural, but suggests that some men may need much more assistance and guidance than they are currently being given in order to develop tenderness and appropriate nurturing skills apart from the sexual situation. Women may therefore need to pay more attention to assisting men (and their sons) to learn nurturing skills which are non-sexualised in relation to children and are more empathic in the adult male/female relationship. Otherwise there may be a continued risk that the more susceptible men will tend to sexualise nurturing relationships with their children and fail to appreciate the needs of their wives or partners for non-sexual affection.

1.2.5 The concept of closeness and distance

The concept of closeness and distance is seen by many workers and therapists as central to relationship struggles (see Section 1.3). Whilst acknowledging that this concept is a constructive development in understanding the nature of the search for more intimate relationships, it may be that the concept itself is too simplistic.

From clinical observation it would seem to us that the concept of closeness/distance may not be a unitary concept as described by Byng-Hall (1985) but may revolve around several different factors. Feldman (1979) suggests five different types of intimacy anxiety which he feels may contribute to interpersonal difficulties and Birtchnell (1989) describes a yet wider range of alternatives.

We think that the general concept of closeness/distance may have several different facets which together or separately may form part of the couple's relationship difficulties. Clinical experience so far suggests at least four key variables which tend to parallel those described by Hahlweg *et al.* (1984) as predictive of the successful outcome of therapy (see Section 1.2.2). These might be described as:

(1) *Sexual closeness*: This might be characterised by the ability to be comfortable with sexual intercourse and with levels of sexual closeness which are acceptable to both partners; differences in needs for sexual closeness are very common within couples.

(2) *Physical and non-verbal closeness*: This would include the whole spectrum of giving and receiving of affection through non-verbal interaction such as being comforted by being cuddled; needs for this and the ability to accept and tolerate it may vary widely from individual to individual, and it would therefore often be necessary to develop a compromise level of physical closeness acceptable to both partners.

(3) *Emotional empathy*: This would include the ability to relate empathically to the feelings and experiences of the partner which may vary from individual to individual and may therefore become an area of distress within couples when the level of empathy is either too close or too distant for one or both partners.

(4) *Operational closeness*: This rather clinical term is used to describe those aspects of a relationship which are about the daily life of the couple. This would include the sharing of tasks, their wish to know where the other person is and to plan and organise their life together and separately by being aware of and supporting each other's activities. It might also include a different need in each for privacy or togetherness, and the issue of whether to have separate and individual interests or share most activities and interests together.

Although the concept of closeness and distance is useful it may be a more satisfactory tool for the understanding of couple relationship if it is subdivided into categories such as those described here.

It may also be that at different stages in the life cycle of the individual or family each partner may be looking for different elements or degrees of distance or closeness; or different life events may evoke quite separate responses from each partner. For example a mother of a new-born baby may seek a greater degree of physical and non-verbal closeness at this time, whilst the father may be seeking a renewal of sexual closeness, and the two different needs could be in conflict. Or after the death of his brother a man may be feeling the need for greater emotional empathy with his wife whilst she may wish to comfort him through sexual closeness, and again these two may be in conflict.

Clinical evidence also suggests another aspect which may be of central significance in couple relationships, and that is the level of comfort or discomfort with which individuals and couples are able to engage in 'fighting'. This fighting or arguing is verbal and involves some degree of emotional arousal. Perhaps the fear of this kind of exchange, by one or both partners, may form another facet of the general concept of closeness/distance regulation.

(Several examples of this problem are included in Chapter 8: see Examples 8A, 8B and 8C.)

1.3 *Marriage as a process of negotiation of appropriate levels of emotional sharing*

The Institute of Marital Studies has developed the notion that many couples seek, in marriage, 'the opportunity this committed adjustment to a person of the opposite sex will give them for personal development' (Pincus 1960; Dicks 1967).

This theme is picked up by the Working Party on Marriage Guidance (1979) as follows:

> '2.30 Our evidence and experience confirms the thesis that personal development and satisfaction are core values underlying contemporary expectations of marriage.'

These conclusions are usually drawn from within a psychoanalytic view of human development, and as such are an extension of that theoretical perspective.

Whilst not denying the individuals' search for greater development of their potential, we would not necessarily accept the premise that couples enter into marriage or permanent relationships with personal growth as part of their main declared agenda. What seems to us as more relevant, although in some ways related to the concept of personal growth, is whether the couple can develop the ability over time to negotiate with each other appropriate levels of emotional sharing, as well as a flexible approach to problem solving. This starts from the premise that each partner may initially seek different levels of sharing and in the process of adjusting to marriage have to make suitable compromises (see also Section 2.2.4).

Byng-Hall (1985) describes the conflicts which may arise when resolving intimacy/distance differences between partners. He describes the two thresholds 'too close and too far' and suggests that 'symptoms' may remove a distance conflict, since anxiety is created by the 'too close, too far conflict'.

Feldman (1979) explores

'repetitive cycles of non-productive marital conflict which are a major cause of psychological distress, physical injury and violent deaths and are frequently a major impetus for the initiation of marital therapy'.

He outlines both the fear of and the wish for intimacy and suggests that the conflict arises as a result of the anxiety provoked in the struggle to maintain an adequate level of intimacy.

He writes

'In the adult, the desire for intimacy is a major motivation for forming and maintaining a marital relationship. However, existing side by side with the wish for intimacy is fear of intimacy.'

He conceptualises five main types of intimacy anxiety, 'fear of merger, fear of exposure, fear of attack, fear of abandonment, and fear of one's own destructive impulses'.

This tension between partners' need for, and fear of, intimacy can provoke painful conflict, and often must be negotiated and a compromise reached which respects each partner's individuality (see also Birtchnell 1986). We suggest therefore that couples may need to negotiate their mutually acceptable level of emotional sharing, rather than use marriage as a forum for personal growth. Spouses may well have to accept compromises, which curtail some aspect of each individual's personal development. Indeed Helen Franks (1988), surveying the use women are making of counselling directed towards personal growth, suggested that if the individual uses marriage solely as a basis for personal growth, then many women would choose to separate or divorce as they develop greater autonomy and seek greater freedom of expression free from the domination of men (Orbach & Eichenbaum 1983; Briscoe 1987; Graaf 1988; O'Brien 1988).

The complementary aspect, from a man's perspective, might be that he too must accept a compromise between his autonomy as a single man and the responsibilities of being the main wage earner, a father and being affiliated to one woman.

In the case of both partners, some giving up of personal potential may be a necessary and acceptable compromise in order to negotiate a permanent satisfactory relationship. Part of this negotiation is directed towards attaining appropriate levels of emotional sharing. We suggest that satisfactory levels of intimacy and mutual empathy develop as a result of acceptable and empathic negotiation. This may be a painful and difficult process, but as the couple share together their different needs and fears, so their understanding of each is likely to grow. At the same time, a respect for each other's individuality and separateness may emerge as they support each other through these negotiations.

However a couple who acknowledge each other's differences are also likely to come up against the need to compromise. In our experience many couples come to therapy deeply distressed that 'things are going wrong' when they each still feel a strong commitment to each other. One wonders if part of their fantasy had been that their individuality would find complete expression and support within marriage. Therapy is often about helping such couples to make the necessary adjustments, and to accept that a relationship can be 'good enough' (see Section 1.2.2) while still falling short of their original ideals.

1.4 Children and marriage

Nine out of every ten children are born within marriage, although illegitimate births as a proportion of all births have risen from about 6% in 1961 to 11% in 1979 (OPCS). Illegitimate births are highest in the younger mother age group and have been increasing in this group. In 1979 two out of five births to women under 20 were illegitimate, as were one in eight of those to women who were between 20 and 24 years. West-Indian-born mothers are most likely to have an illegitimate child and Indian-born mothers are the least likely (OPCS 1979).

A proportion of these mothers will either be cohabiting with, or subsequently will marry, the father. Statistics are not available but it seems reasonable to suggest that because of these high rates of illegitimacy in the under-20 age group, a proportion of women will be taking into their first marriage a child by another man. Lesley Rimmer (1985) suggests that

'Nowadays when a child is conceived outside of marriage, women are more likely to resort to abortion, or failing that to an illegitimate birth, than they are to marry in order to legitimise their child.'

Since divorce is increasing this means that there are many one-parent families, and nearly 60% of couples divorcing in 1983 had children under 16 years of age. The National Council for One Parent Families has estimated that there are about one million one-parent families in the UK with the care of 1.6 million children. With the increase in both divorce and remarriage it is not surprising that more children are growing up in stepfamilies, with 7% of children under 18 years living with their natural mother and a stepfather. Many couples are no doubt well able to integrate into their family children from previous relationships and previous marriages. However, we know from the evidence emerging about child physical and sexual abuse that proportionally more of these incidents occur between steprelations than blood relations.

These are the extreme examples of problems which might be encountered when children are integrated into a new relationship. Naturally a certain degree of tension is bound to exist between the members of the new family unit. Unless the couple are prepared to work together patiently to develop a coherent relationship towards the children, such families are likely to experience some difficulties.

Some couples may hope to have children, but remain childless; for others adoption, fostering of children or intense work with fertility clinics are all available as potential sources of fulfilment for couples who wish to parent, but may also be the cause of stresses and disappointments. The handicapped or disabled child, the child who develops a severe illness, or is crippled by an accident or dies, brings to couples added sources of distress, or perhaps eventual deeper commitment to each other and their dependants.

The following brief excerpt from a poem by Tony Harrison (1970) written on the morning of his daughter Jane's traffic accident describes a father's torment.

> Down corridors, a shadow man,
> I almost sleepwalk, float past An-
> aesthesia, X-Ray, Speech
> Therapy and, come full circle, reach
> again the apparatus where you lie
> between the armless and the eyeless boy.
> I sicken. Jane! I could cut off
> your breathing with a last wet cough,
> break the connections, save you from
> almost a lifetime's crippledom, . . .

. . .

Parenting and the developmental tasks associated with parenting demand of the couple a resourcefulness and ability to work together which will inevitably cause some anxieties and stresses to their relationship as a couple.

Childbirth and the 'primary maternal preoccupation' (Winnicott 1956) of the wife may make the father feel rejected or useless, while the child's first major separation from the mother when school starts may lead her to feel no longer needed. The tension between being too distant as parents as against being over-involved (too close) with one or more children keeps parents in a continuous process of re-evaluation and change, as the children pass through each developmental phase. Each phase with the adjustments required brings its stresses and its pleasures. How the couple jointly or separately negotiate these life stages will enable them to grow close together or develop an often hidden agenda of resentment. The bearing and raising of children, so often taken for granted as a desirable outcome of a permanent relationship, is very demanding and will make a significant impact upon this relationship. The couple must slowly develop adequate ways to agree how to share the burden and the joys of parenting, and it is not surprising that many couples increasingly seek outside help with this task.

1.5 Ethnicity and marriage

The term 'ethnic group' is offered by the anthropologist Ashley Montague as an alternative to race. An ethnic group may also be defined as a group of people sharing a common cultural heritage. The *Encyclopaedia Britannica* defines minorities or ethnic groups as

> 'aggregates of people who are distinct in race, religion, language or nationality from other members of society in which they live and who think of themselves, and who are thought of by others, as being separate or distinct'.

Britain is increasingly a multi-racial society containing a rich variety of language, customs, education, class, status and wealth, and providing an abundant source of fascination and divergence amongst couples who seek therapy. Skin colour and place of birth seem to figure prominently in the public mind regarding ethnic issues; but from our perspective we do not subscribe to the view that ethnicity of itself is necessarily a cause of marital tension.

Ethnic issues are often a smoke screen for lack of commitment, sensitivity or awareness of interpersonal difficulties the couple face. For example: a couple living in London, whose first language for the woman was Turkish and for the man was Greek, communicated with each other in a mixture of English, Greek and Turkish. There certainly were ethnic issues which faced this couple; however far more pressing was their inability to communicate with and listen to each other, to respect the other's feelings and to develop a common approach to a daughter who had become the scapegoat for their lack of sensitivity to each other. We do not therefore feel it necessary to highlight ethnic issues throughout the book, except to restate that where ethnic issues are presented as a reason for distress, we suggest that the therapist focus on the specific interpersonal difficulties faced by the couple rather than upon ethnicity itself. (See Example 10A, Nelson and Abigail.)

For some ethnic groups the couple's relationship may be intertwined with the extended family. Conflicts regarding the responsibility of parents or extended family for child-rearing may be presented by the couple as ethnic difficulties. Again we recommend that these issues are best approached as the interpersonal difficulties of the clients, rather than accepting the label of ethnicity, which can carry with it an unfortunate sense of inevitability and hopelessness regarding change.

Many couples have very real difficulties in making joint choices about how they wish to live in multi-cultural Britain, what social/cultural/religious values they themselves hold in a changing sociocultural environment. These concerns are however shared by most couples who seek therapy, and it is a matter of degree as to how much they should be focussed on in any particular couple.

1.6 The time dimension: the family life cycle and life events

When considering what pressures may lead couples to seek therapy we would constantly wish to bear in mind the question of the impact of time, the family life cycle and life events on the couple's relationship. Whilst acknowledging their complexity we believe that the family life cycle and how the family responds to its experience of life events may well have a fundamental impact upon the couple and the family's ability to cope successfully with their ongoing relationship.

Time is implicit in most aspects of a couple's relationship. Their ages, how long they have known each other, the ages of their children and their parents, previous relationships and the length of time these existed in relation to the present marriage, affairs and when they occurred may all have some influence upon the couple's present relationship.

It is not simply the passage of time which is of such importance, the life cycle of the family and how various life events have affected families and their members may be crucial elements. By the life cycle we mean the development of the nuclear family through the various stages into old age and death. These can be described as beginning in courtship and progressing through the phases of establishing a marriage or long-term relationship, pregnancy and childbirth, followed by the stages of development of the child (or children) through infancy, schooling, the first job and leaving home. All these make demands of the parent/s to be responsive to the children's changing needs (Rutter 1980; Campbell 1982; Dare 1982; Elton 1982; Skynner 1982). (See also Section 1.4.)

The departure from the home of the adolescent children brings a new phase for the couple, sometimes called the 'empty nest', in which the couple may be thrown together in a way they have not been since their early relationship (Dare 1982). (See also Section 9.7.) This phase may be closely followed by the physical and emotional changes experienced in middle age, with grandparenting being another aspect of this period. Retirement and old age bring accompanying changes in physical well-being and pace of life until the death of one spouse brings to a natural close the life cycle of the couple (Byng-Hall 1982).

Life events may of course interrupt the life cycle in a fundamental way so that illness, accident or divorce may cut short the cycle as described above or have a profound effect on the couple's relationship. Some of these have already been touched upon (Sections 1.1.3 to 1.1.5) and include a wide variety of experience, some very pleasurable and others full of grief and stress. The promotion of a husband to a new job may bring increased financial reward but may involve a change of home for the family and schooling for the children which can bring added stress into a relationship. How couples negotiate such life events may have a powerful impact on their adjustment. Life events such as the birth of a handicapped child, the death or injury of a family member, redundancy, imprisonment, accident or illness all bring with them accompanying stress upon the couple as well as an opportunity for greater shared intimacy (Lask 1982; Lieberman & Black 1982).

Child physical or sexual abuse place demands upon the couple which may be difficult to overcome. One or both partners may have experienced either physical or sexual abuse themselves as a child and hence may feel that this is how life is. Others may find the demands of both the partner and the child/ren are in conflict with their own needs to be cared for and loved, particularly where they themselves may have been inadequately cared for as a child. Where a step-parent is involved the rivalry for affection and attention may escalate. Problems such as how to establish the role of the step-parent within the family or the fear of losing the partner may make it difficult for either partner to function as a protective parent.

The life experiences of each spouse may have given them little preparation for the emotional demands of parenting and there may be a need to seek additional help. Seeking such help can however add to the uncertainties and some couples may be very reluctant to admit their need for help because of legal and social consequences.

Where separation or divorce occurs but there are children of the marriage, there is likely to be a need to continue their shared parenting responsibilities which again brings demands that are difficult to fulfil (Robinson 1982).

Time, the developmental phases and life events come together in a complicated pattern which may often be difficult to disentangle. Time may have been significant in choosing to marry; for teenagers it may have been part of wishing to leave the parental home; or for a woman entering her late 30s a wish to bear children. The break-up of a first marriage of 6 years may be relevant to stress in a second marriage at the same interval; concern for the physical health of a husband of 56 years may be stimulated by memories of the death of a father at the same age. Anorexia in a teenage girl is probably related to both her own personal development as a teenager and that of her parents, who may be unable to face their separate future as a couple without her; thus the appearance of such symptoms may be directly related to a time factor in the life cycle of this particular family (Minuchin *et al.* 1978; Crisp 1980; Kraemer 1986).

The onset of the menopause and middle age for a couple is often accompanied by the illness or death of aging parents and the leaving home of children, which presents such a couple with multiple simultaneous stresses at a time of greater vulnerability of each partner. Later again the aging process and the approach of old age with its accompanying hazards may be met by the couple with equanimity or distress (Byng-Hall 1982).

These many facets cannot be ignored as a source of pleasure, stress or challenge to couples, and may be involved in leading couples at the time of such events to seek therapy ('why now?': see also Sections 4.3.1.1 and 7.4.2).

1.7 Successful marriages or long term relationships

It is curious that so little research has focussed on successful relationships. One wonders whether we are afraid to destroy some of the myths surrounding male/female relationships, preferring fantasy tales of drama and tragedy to the reality of developing interpersonal relationships which last.

Beavers (1985) builds on his work as a researcher to develop six aspects of observable behaviour which he suggests are present in 'healthy families'; these are:

(1) A modest overt power difference.
(2) The capacity for clear boundaries.
(3) Operating mainly in the present.
(4) Respect for individual choice.
(5) Skill in negotiating.
(6) Sharing positive feelings.

He suggests that some attitudes are healthier than others, and sees such 'health-promoting beliefs' as being conducive to good and stable family relationships. He writes that

'The qualities of healthy couples found in formal research and clinical study begin with attitudes and thinking patterns, the most important being a benign view of one's own and the spouse's basic nature, and an awareness that human truth is always subjective.'

Beavers and Olson have developed theories of family adaptability which are recognised as useful in both research and clinical work. There is a fairly general agreement that successful relationships seem to have three key elements: an ability to be flexible enough to adapt and change

when faced with changed circumstances or problems, an ability to communicate together effectively and an ability to empathise with each
other at an emotional level.

A conceptual disagreement has emerged which focusses upon the
vexed issues regarding adaptability and whether it should be seen as
linear (as in the Beavers model) or curvilinear as in the Olson model (Lee
1988). The details of these models need not trouble us here, save to
acknowledge that central to the discussion is the question of balance.
Difficulties have arisen in trying to develop a model which is able to
accommodate all the multi-faceted elements of interpersonal relationship in itself.

The Olson model has two main dimensions, those of high or low
cohesion and high or low adaptability. Within this model the healthy
couples are said to be balanced in the central area, that is, midway
between the extremes of high or low levels of cohesion or adaptablility
(Olson *et al.* 1983). According to Olson the position the family occupy on
the model will be facilitated by good communication skills; thus it is
hypothesised that balanced families will have more positive communication skills than extreme families (Olson *et al.* 1983; Barnes and Olson
1985).

The question of adaptability is taken up by Beavers *et al.* (1988) who
remind the reader that adaptability is not defined by them but is
itemised under several discrete headings (Hampson *et al.* 1988). These
are

'The observed/rated ... dimensions that relate to this adjustment and regulatory property include goal-directed negotiation, clarity of communication, power structure and flexibility, and general affective properties of the
system.'

The debate has served to underline the strengths and similarities of
these two research tools which provide a useful if rudimentary framework for the assessment of couples. They also provide a starting point
for decisions about which therapeutic interventions may be helpful for
each couple as they seek therapy. The two models are compatible with
behavioural-systems couple therapy, and although they and the behavioural-systems approach developed separately, they share some
important ideals as to the goals of therapy (see also Chapters 2 and 4).

1.8 Who seeks therapy?

We have so far been examining the different factors which either bring
stress to a relationship or contribute to the success of relationships. As
already stated, approximately one in three marriages currently ends in
divorce. It is also clear that not all of those who choose to divorce

actively seek help with their relationship before divorcing.

Who then does seek help? We have already cited some evidence to suggest that women are most likely to seek help for minor psychiatric illnesses and that women are usually aware before men of some distress in their relationship (see Section 1.1.9). Women also seem to sue for divorce more often than men. Does this mean that women are more likely than men to seek help with a relationship difficulty?

Brannen and Collard (1982) are quite clear on this issue:

'We wish to argue that any consideration of the process of problem definition must take account of gender, and that there is a socially structured bias which on balance appears to favour the position of the husband in these processes.'

1.8.1 Relate Marriage Guidance

Patricia Hunt (1985) examined a sample of clients who referred themselves to Relate Marriage Guidance in 1980. The aim of the study was to understand more about the clients' responses to marriage counselling.

The study was undertaken in Manchester Marriage Guidance Council and used a two-month sample of clients. The sample population consisted of 84 couples and 57 single clients (where one spouse only came into counselling). After a further drop out over six months, the final sample group comprised 51 people from 42 marriages, and of these 17 were men and 34 were women. There is not much more information regarding the gender of those interviewed but if one takes the rather flimsy evidence already presented one might assume that, for both counselling and research purposes, women more often than men are prepared to attend to the distress within their relationships.

This study also highlighted several significant factors about those who seek help for their relationship difficulties.

'In the majority of cases, couples had been married for ten years or less, and a third of those interviewed had been married for less than five years and were accordingly at a particularly vulnerable stage in their marriage.'

'Only four of the clients interviewed were childless, although several of the others had grown up children who no longer seemed to be a factor in the current relationship.'

With regard to class the author states that

'the sample did include a much wider range of people than the professional middle class clientele that is commonly attributed to the M.G. Agency.'

1.8.2 A local authority social work setting

Mattinson and Sinclair (1979) undertook their research in a local authority setting and examined all the referrals for one year, a total of 1198 cases. They had hypothesised that a significant proportion of initial referrals would be couples with relationship difficulties; they were somewhat disappointed however to discover that only 265 clients or 22% were in fact married. They then examined the cases which were said by social workers to be demanding or high-priority cases, and of these slightly more than four out of ten cases on which the social workers said they were spending most time and to which they gave priority involved marital problems. These high priority cases fell into two distinct categories: young mothers under stress with children at risk and problem families. Of these two groups, over two-thirds shared the following characteristics

(1) Ambivalent marital bonds.
(2) Lack of success in parental roles.
(3) Lack of constructive support from family of origin.
(4) Continual threat of separation from one or other family member.

   Mattinson and Sinclair report that not only did these couples take up a significant part of the social workers' priority time, but also 'these cases had a quite disproportionate effect on the agency in terms of the work and anxiety created'. They suggest ways in which local authority social work teams might work with this client group, by providing a safer work environment and more specialist skills for workers. Their study is important for having pointed to the very significant need in local authority for work with couples who represent about 30% of the high-priority case load of local authority social workers.

1.8.3 Maudsley Marital Therapy Clinic

The Maudsley Marital Therapy Clinic is set within a psychiatric hospital which is also a major teaching centre for psychiatry. This no doubt influences both the source and character of referrals to the clinic. In any one year about 61% of referrals are direct from general practitioners, about 15% are from psychiatrists and 15% from social services; the rest are self referrals and occasional other referrals such as from a priest.

   The couples tend to fall into two groups: those who see themselves as having a 'relationship difficulty' and those who enter therapy having been sent, usually by the GP, because one partner is considered to be 'ill'. The 'illness' will vary from vague pains and constant attendance at the doctor's surgery to quite severe symptoms such as depression, phobia or intense jealousy. Another small group of couples are referred because of the impact of physical illnesses such as epilepsy or multiple sclerosis on the relationship.The policy of the clinic is to work with both spouses, and although we sometimes find that one partner may come alone we can usually find ways of helping the other partner to attend, even if initially it is only in order to help us understand the problem.

Some couples who have accepted an appointment do not in fact attend. So far we have not been able to follow up these non-attenders in any systematic way; one must however allow for the fact that some may not attend because only one partner is willing to do so. Our impression is that men seem to be as prepared to attend as women, and this may have something to do with the 'medical' setting.

The psychiatric and medical setting is both a help and a hindrance to couples work. Many couples find it extremely difficult to come to a psychiatric hospital, and this may be connected with the meaning of such a setting in terms of 'madness' for the couple. Others come content in the notion that the 'illness' is firmly implanted in one partner and the other is a 'ministering angel in attendance'.

Such issues are taken up in the body of the book when considering what help can be given to such couples. However we feel that the 'medicalising' of relationship difficulties has a profound impact on couples and, as will be seen in later chapters, we spend considerable amounts of time and effort trying to remove unhelpful medical labels in therapy. Much of our initial work is to assess how much of a change in perception the couple can make towards seeing the problem as part of the relationship.

Although these three settings, Relate Marriage Guidance, social services and a marital therapy clinic within a psychiatric hospital, are quite different, from the data available it does seem that couples present with similar problems in each setting. These can be seen generally as either problems accepted by both partners as relationship difficulties or alternatively symptoms which have become 'medicalised' and are felt by both partners to reside in one member of the couple.

1.9 Conclusion

In this chapter we have tried to indicate some of the current pressures upon couples. We have suggested some of the factors which may be present in couples who are not distressed and who have a stable and lasting relationship.

We have also tried to understand why some couples seek therapy or are seen by professionals as in need of marital therapy.

The figures are not available for direct comparison, but it is likely that there are significantly more couples seeking divorce than those seeking help with their relationship. Where couples feel that they cannot themselves find a solution to their problems an appropriate next step would be to seek the advice of a couple therapist who could use his/her expertise to assist them.

In the rest of the book we outline some of the options available to couples when faced with difficulties in their relationships. We suggest ways in which problems can be ameliorated, moderated or accommodated, rather than shattering a relationship which was entered into with some degree of commitment.

Chapter 2

Relationship problems and the goals of therapy

2.1 Introduction

What is a good marriage or couple relationship? How can we distinguish good relationships from the less good? In view of the complexity of human nature and the profound influences exerted on people by their relationships and other aspects of their environment, it might seem presumptuous even to ask this sort of question. However, in offering to carry out couple therapy the therapist is making an implicit statement about satisfactory and unsatisfactory relationships, if only to say that he or she knows how to improve them. We must therefore try, however imperfectly, to assess the quality of a relationship, and we will begin by looking at a variety of criteria which might be used.

2.1.1 Biological criteria

One of the crudest criteria by which to assess a marriage or couple relationship is the biological one, which could be applied equally to most forms of pairing in the animal kingdom. This is simply to judge a relationship on whether the couple are sufficiently competent at home-making, providing and protecting to bring up children, who are then able to repeat the process themselves and continue reproducing the species. If these basic abilities are missing in a couple who have children, then biologically the children will be at risk, and in most societies the community will take some responsibility for them. However such couples may be quite content with their relationship, and most social workers and psychiatrists are familiar with couples who produce children in just these circumstances, and who resent any interference with their rights as parents.

2.1.2 Socio-cultural expectations

Beyond these simple biological considerations, marriage can be seen as a legal, social and economic institution, usually underpinned by religious sanctions, and representing the public ratification of the pairing of two individuals for the purpose of cohabitation and procreation (see Chapter

1 for further discussion).In any society there are many rules and cultural expectations as to the behaviour of wives and husbands, for example how they should present themselves together and separately and how they should organise their life together. In these respects marriage is supposed to be stable and lasting ('till death us do part') and to be unaffected by the vicissitudes of life ('for better, for worse, for richer, for poorer, in sickness and in health').These criteria for a 'good' marriage would be widely supported, especially by the traditional religious authorities of many belief systems, but in many couples who satisfy the religious and social obligations placed upon them, there is nevertheless a great deal of unhappiness and dissatisfaction with their relationship and even symptoms or other ill-effects from the stress involved.

2.1.3 Self report and marital adjustment measures

If one is seeking a more relevant criterion of satisfaction with a relationship, it might be appropriate to ask a couple whether they are in fact satisfied with their relationship. This is the approach used by most of those who have applied self-report questionnaires to assess relationship satisfaction, and they have shown in most cases satisfactory reliability in their results (Locke and Wallace 1959; Spanier 1976; Gurman and Kniskern 1981; Rust *et al.* 1986).

Some marital adjustment scales which are completed by self-report, such as the Locke-Wallace MAT (Locke and Wallace 1959) and the Spanier DAS (Spanier 1976), have become very well known and are frequently used. They are reliable and simple to use, but have the disadvantage for use in this country that they were standardised on American populations. These and other measures of marital and family adjustment have been recently assembled in a single volume (Fredman and Sherman 1987) which is of great value to those wishing to carry out research in the field.

Perhaps the best rating scales available in this country are the Golombok-Rust Inventories of Sexual and of Marital Satisfaction (GRISS and GRIMS, Rust and Golombok 1985, Rust *et al.* 1986). The GRIMS is a measure of marital satisfaction, psychometrically constructed using British couples, with a unidimensional score on the single factor of marital satisfaction. The GRISS performs a similar function in the area of sexual satisfaction, but the scores are recorded separately for such factors as male satisfaction, female satisfaction, impotence, anorgasmia, communication and overall satisfaction. The results are often shown graphically as a profile on these and on other dimensions. Both the GRIMS and GRISS are excellent research instruments and are sensitive to the changes brought about by therapy.

A more extensive method to evaluate marriage and family interaction has been developed by Olson *et al.* (1983) using self-report (the FACES questionnaire) and therapist assessment of interaction. The two criteria which emerged as the most important in distinguishing between successful and unsuccessful families were labelled 'cohesion' and 'adaptability', and as we will be mentioning later in this chapter (Section 2.4.2) these factors seem to coincide with our own clinically-based ideas that the increase in flexibility and the reduction of over-involvement are important goals in couple therapy (see also the discussion on successful marriage in Section 1.7).

Another British-based measure which has been widely used in the field of research in child psychiatry is the interview rating developed by Quinton and Rutter (1976). This was shown to be reliable, and to be able to predict future marriage breakdown at a statistically significant level over a four-year period.

There are other measures of couple interaction which are based on direct behavioural observation and analysis. The MICS (Hops *et al.* 1972) and the KPI (Hahlweg *et al.* 1984) both depend on detailed analysis of couples' videotaped interaction divided into categories for rating. They are very time-consuming to score, and are useful only in detailed behavioural research.

However, the results of these measures, whether self-report or observational, are not accepted by all couple therapists as the best way to determine whether a relationship is really satisfactory or not. Some would reject such methods as being biased by social desirability factors and other sources of error. More subtle ways of deciding whether a relationship is satisfactory will vary according to the theoretical orientation of the person making the judgment. We will in the next section be exploring the ways in which psychoanalytical, behavioural, systems and rational-emotive therapists assess how good or bad a relationship is, and what changes they would like to bring about in improving it.

2.2 The main theoretical formulations of marriage and the goals of therapy

2.2.1 Psychoanalytical ideas

Psychoanalytical ideas have been reviewed by Daniell (1985) and Meissner (1978). A central concept is that it is the inner world of the partners and the nature of their interaction which determine their responses to changing circumstances. It is as though each partner is using a kind of internal blueprint of both the relationship and their partner's personality, and in some more disturbed individuals these blueprints will have little in common with what others perceive as external reality.

From this perspective, the marriage is said to exist on at least two levels, the conscious and the unconscious. The unconscious aspects of the relationship are usually assumed to derive from the partners' infantile and early childhood experiences. The baby's and young child's experiences of being loved and cared for by parent figures are said to be central to the unconscious blueprint carried by each individual into a two-person relationship (see Section 1.2.1). Motivations which underlie the choice of partner are as much unconscious as conscious, and in the relationship a system of shared fantasies and defences develops which moulds the nature of the relationship. Such formulations are interesting and thought-provoking and can lead to creative hypotheses in individual cases but are in the last analysis difficult to verify.

Since these concepts are usually presented with great certainty they give the therapist a powerful sense of being in control, and the belief that s/he understands where to search for the 'root cause' of the problem. Our doubts about the existence of such a root cause for relationship problems will be discussed later.

The therapeutic strategy is clear and involves elucidation of those unconscious processes in both partners which are perpetuating the problem. The remedy for the impasse is to offer the couple either individual or conjoint sessions exploring these shared fantasies and defences, helping them in the process to understand both themselves and each other.

In the sessions, transference issues (Scharff and Scharff 1987) may be used to assist with the process of therapy, if the therapist judges this to be helpful. Interpretations of the interaction between the patient(s) and therapist can be used in order to enable the development of greater insight into the source of the difficulties encountered.

Where major difficulties arise between the partners, the therapist may spend much time with the couple, either together or separately, helping them to recall events, situations or experiences with parents (or parent figures) which had a similar impact upon them to the current relationship difficulty with the spouse. By becoming aware of the links between past and present experiences, the partners are helped to disentangle fact from fantasy, and to learn to relate to their spouse without the added burden of uneasy past feelings being transferred into the present relationship.

It is thus expected that personal insight will, in a successful case, enable the individual to make more mature decisions, unencumbered by the unconscious pressures from infantile experiences.

An intriguing aspect of this way of working is the relationship between co-therapists. Co-therapists report that they find themselves reacting to each other in unfamiliar ways, in sessions and between sessions with different couples, which are thought to represent the projected feelings and fantasies which they have absorbed from the clients (see Chapter 12).

The process of change within this theoretical orientation is related first to the couple feeling safely contained within the therapeutic setting. Gradually through the development of a creative transference relationship they will become more aware of the sources of interpersonal difficulties. This awareness, or insight, will then enable the individual to give up compulsive and repetitive patterns of behaviour and withdraw damaging projections.

Psychoanalytical literature has contributed much to the debate regarding the development of personality and the individual's search for intimate long-term relationships, and we find some psychoanalytical notions very creative in informing discussions about symptoms and their significance. However, concepts including transference, projection, unconscious processes and shared fantasies as developed within psychoanalysis are at the same time helpful and unsatisfactory. They are helpful because they provide many alternative ways of understanding a couple's attraction, interaction and inability to change without outside intervention. They are unsatisfactory because these assumptions are difficult to test. They also rely heavily upon the unproven hypothesis that insight necessarily brings with it some ability to change one's behaviour.

The pace of change where it does occur is usually slow, and some critics of the psychoanalytical approach feel this to be a weakness. It is clear from descriptions that therapy may continue for months or even years of weekly or twice weekly sessions. Changes that do occur, and which are amenable to measurement, are not necessarily any greater than those changes which result from the shorter behavioural or systemic methods.

The question as to which form of therapy has most long-lasting results is still open to debate and, in the present state of knowledge, the combination of the long duration of therapy and the difficulty in testing both the outcome and the underlying assumptions of the psychoanalytical approach mean that this approach to therapy remains, in our view, of uncertain value.

2.2.2 The behavioural viewpoint

The 'pure' behavioural view of marriage is in some ways diametrically opposed to the psychoanalytical. The main emphasis is on the practical aspects of the relationship, such as the sharing of rights and duties, the ability to negotiate with each other, the existence of clear and unmistakable communication and the efficient management of the relationship. In his pioneering work Stuart (1969) emphasised the need to substitute positive reinforcement for coercion in dealing with partners, and from this beginning the behavioural approach has developed and diversified (Mackay 1985). In one respect the behavioural approach has perhaps become a degree closer to the psychoanalytical in recent years, with the inclusion of the cognitive concepts of 'inappropriate beliefs and perceptions' as a focus for work, although, as might be expected, the behaviourists prefer to modify such beliefs rather than to understand their origins.

In behavioural terms marriage is a contractual situation in which both partners have expectations and duties. The early stages of a relationship are seen as being characterised by a high level of rewards (for example sex, mutual communication and recreation) and a low level of costs (such as the demands of children). In this phase the couple expect the same level of reward to continue, and may resort to mutual blame and coercion if it is found not to continue into the later stages of the relationship (Jacobson and Margolin 1979). In the evolution of a relationship, there may be many factors which cause it to seem unrewarding and marital disharmony results when the costs exceed the rewards in a relationship.

In the behavioural approach to help disturbed relationships, the emphasis is on trying to modify the observed behaviour of the partners, rather than trying to understand the underlying causes. The modification is in two basic areas, those of communication and negotiation. The thoughts and feelings of each partner are left largely out of the discussion, and the focus of therapy is very much more on the next few days than on the past. The therapist is trying to help the couple to change their interaction directly by the use of rational and cognitive means. In this way it is hoped that the couple will find new and more rewarding ways to interact and thus improve the whole relationship.

The use of this approach implies dependence on one important item of faith, namely that a change which the couple have brought about will last because they both see the advantage to themselves of the partner's rewarding behaviour. This faith seems to be justified, however, in that follow-up studies (such as that of Crowe 1978) have shown that the gains achieved at the end of therapy continued for up to 18 months thereafter.

The problems with the behavioural approach are partly due to its very simplicity, in that the clients themselves may need some further persuasion that an approach as rudimentary as this is going to make an impression on the apparently intractable problems they are presenting. Some couples will also object to the idea of 'bargaining' as a means of solving their problems, and in practice it is often necessary to use more sophisticated methods of treatment in couples showing resistance to the approach or presenting problems labelled as psychiatric or individual (see Chapters 4 and 10). However, the behavioural approach has many advantages, among which could be included that of a clear indication of whether it is working session by session and the fact that, being short-term in its application, not too much time is lost by the couple if it proves ineffective. Another advantage of the behavioural approach is that, as shown by Crowe (1978), it is most effective with those couples who are not highly educated. Such couples have been found to be dissatisfied with the less structured and more theoretical approach of the insight therapies (Hunt 1984).

In practice, this is the approach which has most consistently been shown to be effective in treating relationship problems, especially in couples who are mildly to moderately distressed (see Section 13.4 and Jacobson and Weiss 1978).

2.2.3 Rational-emotive and similar approaches

These approaches to marital and relationship problems have been reviewed by Dryden (1985). In this formulation there seem to be some features of the behavioural approach and other features which are reminiscent of the psychoanalytical approach. A distinction is drawn between marital 'dissatisfaction' and marital 'disturbance', the former being similar to the kind of problems dealt with by the negotiation methods of the behaviourists, and the latter referring to anger, hostility, depression, etc., which can be traced to the relationship. In the situation in which disturbance has been superimposed on dissatisfaction the couple may not be able to 'communicate' their way out of the problem without help in sorting out their emotional disturbance.

The rational-emotive solution to the problem involves using different types of phrase to describe the difficulties. The words 'awful' and 'intolerable', for example, are replaced by 'bad' and 'difficult to put up with', and couples are encouraged to find ways of expressing desires rather than commands. There is an analysis of the repetitive cycles of cognitive and behavioural disturbance, in which each partner attributes the other's behaviour to a negative motive and assumes that there is nothing that can be done to alter the situation. These distortions of reality are corrected with both the individual and the couple together, and there are specific indicators for using individual sessions, for example when arguments hinder the course of therapy or one partner is so inhibited by the conjoint situation as to be more or less silent. The therapy can be divided into two main phases, that of overcoming marital disturbance and that of enhancing marital satisfaction. The rational-emotive approach is quite near to the behavioural-systems approach described in this book in its willingness to move from one technique to another according to the stage of the therapy, and many of the other methods described by Dryden, such as how to develop a therapeutic alliance, how to deal with intractable arguments, secrets or hostility are in the same area as many of the systemic techniques described here. The problems treated in this approach seem, however, to be milder and less psychiatrically focussed than those which we are able to tackle using the behavioural-systems approach.

Transactional analysis is another type of therapeutic method which may be applied to relationship problems. The concepts of adult/adult and parent/child types of relationship are very relevant to the ways in which couples interact, and unlike the psychoanalytic notions mentioned above, they are near enough to everyday experience to be acceptable to couples and therapists without undue suspension of disbelief. In our own clinic we use these concepts quite freely, whilst not accepting the whole theoretical basis of transactional analysis.

2.2.4 Systems approach to couple relationships

The general area dealt with by systems theory is that of family interaction, of which the couple's relationship is seen as an important part. Often, as in the approach of Minuchin (1974), the couple is termed the 'parental pair' and the therapeutic efforts are designed to help them to let go of a teenager or take firmer control of a younger child. Sluzki (1978) has outlined a systemic approach to the couple, which is of considerable practical value. Systemic concepts are sometimes difficult to grasp, and we will be attempting to give a fuller description of those we find most useful in Chapter 7. At the present stage the aim will be to outline the main aspects of systems thinking about what constitutes a good or bad marriage.

One of the chief concepts used by Haley and Minuchin in thinking about families systemically is that of 'enmeshment', which could be paraphrased as excessive involvement by other family members in what should be the business of the individual. They suggest that the parental couple should be reasonably close, with the capacity to act as the 'decider sub-system' for the other members of the family. They also acknowledge that when children are very young a high degree of enmeshment is appropriate. However, as children grow up, a degree of autonomy should exist, which allows them to live increasingly separate lives without deferring to their parents, and it is in families with older children that they identify enmeshment as a family problem.

Closely associated with enmeshment is another concept, that of boundaries (Section 7.3.6). The intergenerational boundary is one which can be too rigid (e.g. where the children have no say in the family decisions) or too weak (where they are asked to be more-or-less parent substitutes). Other boundaries are relevant, for instance the degree to which matters which might be seen as confidential to the couple are shared by one or other partner with their own parents or others (see 'triangles', Section 10.13). It is often found in couple therapy that there are disputes and arguments about boundaries, and the resolution of these can lead to much greater harmony.

The question of hierarchies is less important in couple work than in family therapy, but at times the therapist is asked to help to sort out hierarchical issues between partners, for example over rights and responsibilities.

The concept of homeostasis is further expounded in Chapter 7, and all that needs to be said here is that it is a hypothetical mechanism which is thought to act to keep a family or relationship functioning in the way in which it habitually or traditionally does. Various negative and positive feedback mechanisms are hypothesised which tend to counteract changes feared by the family in that they might undermine stability. The symptoms which some partners develop can thus be seen as a homeostatic influence tending to stabilise the system, for instance because they might reduce the amount of argument or hostility and evoke instead a sympathetic response from the other partner.

Another useful concept in thinking about relationships systemically is that of 'distance regulation'. Here we are referring to the way in which people in a relationship use tactics to create a greater emotional distance from each other, and thus avoid what is seen as the discomfort of too great an intimacy (see Section 1.2.5 for a further discussion of the separate components of distance and closeness). An example might be that a husband moves to another room when his wife begins to talk about their relationship, or that when a husband begins to ask probing questions his wife stirs up an argument about something trivial which sidetracks the discussion. Ideally couples should be able to change from intimacy to distance without effort and without a struggle or any avoidance on either side. In some couples, however, the process of distance regulation has reached the level of a problem in its own right, and may be contributing to the symptoms presented by the 'patient'.

Another important area, which is related to systems theory but not always included in its theoretical discourse, is the concept of the developmental family life cycle (Skynner 1982). This is further discussed in Sections 1.6 and 7.4.2, and its great value in systemic couple therapy is that it provides a basis for understanding the current pressures on couples in relation to their stage in the cycle. Knowing what stage a couple has reached (e.g. first baby, empty nest or retirement) will help the team to develop hypotheses as to why the problem might be helping at this time to stabilise the relationship.

Underlying all systems thinking is the concept of circular causality. This assumes that in a relationship things happen not because one person is sick, wicked or irresponsible, but as a result of a complex cycle of interaction in which both partners participate. In more general terms, people's actions are assumed to occur not because of a single cause, either in the recent or more remote past, but as the result of a continuous chain of causation to which all members of the family and outside persons and events are contributing. Thus, when seeking the solution of a problem, systems therapists do not usually try to alter one of the participants, e.g. by medication or by individual psychotherapy, but rather seek a change in interaction in which each partner has a changed role, or the status quo is reframed as being of some benefit to both or all those concerned.

The systems approach does not have such clear guidelines for what is a good or bad relationship as some of the other approaches, but in general most systems therapists would agree that flexibility in the face of new challenges in life, such as the maturing of children or the illness of one of the partners, is a sign that things are reasonably well with the relationship. The other issues such as enmeshment, boundaries, hierarchy, homeostasis and distance regulation are less easy to use as criteria for improvement, because in some couples one may need to strengthen these, while in others they may be too rigid.

In some ways the systems concepts outlined here are self-evident, and need no defending. We refer especially to the idea of circular causation, which simply states that in a relationship between two people it is a mistake to see one or other as the initiator of a sequence of interaction, but one should rather think of each contributing equally to the ongoing cycle of the relationship. Other concepts, such as homeostasis, are more speculative, and may or may not be adequate explanations for the symptoms or other behaviour observed. Boundaries, enmeshment and hierarchies are probably intermediate in having some fairly universal validity, but at the same time being open to alternative interpretations in individual cases. For more detailed descriptions of these terms used in systems approaches see Chapter 7.

The strengths of systems approaches are still relatively unproven as the critical outcome studies, especially in relation to couple problems, have not been done. However, both this and the psychoanalytical approach have had a strong influence on the development of the method we are describing in this book, and in the process of formulating cases we would be considerably less flexible and creative without them.

2.2.5 Mixed or eclectic approaches

Most couple therapists actually use a mixture of techniques, and it might be said that to use a single approach for all cases is too rigid and also may deprive some couples of the sort of interventions which could help them. We do not wish to describe in detail all the possibilities for mixed and eclectic ways of working, but perhaps three such methods could be mentioned.

The first is the psychodynamic-behavioural approach of Segraves (1982) in which the basic underlying cause of marital disturbance is assumed to be the partners' conflicting internal schemas (or blueprints, see Section 2.2.1) of themselves and each other. Intervention is directed both at helping them to understand these and to increase the direct, reality-based communication which will improve negotiation and also disconfirm many of the faulty schemas which cause the problems. The approach is interesting, but somewhat limited by the necessity for belief in the still untestable assumptions of psychoanalysis.

A more comprehensive form of eclectic marital therapy is presented by Weeks (1989) in which the 'intersystem' approach is described. This tries to take account of the individual, interactional and intergenerational aspects of couple relationships and combines them in what is probably closest to a systemic model (Section 2.2.4 and Chapter 7). The therapy described seems very comprehensive and quite long in duration, and may involve both couple and individual sessions. One frequent intervention is that of decentring (see Sections 4.6.9 and 6.4.1.2) and much of the work also makes use of paradox (Section 9.13). There are thus many aspects of this approach which are similar to the one we are describing in this book, although we perhaps have more to contribute to the management of mixed psychiatric and relationship problems.

The third eclectic approach which must be mentioned is 'behavioural-systems marital therapy' (Spinks and Birchler 1982). They use predominantly a more traditional behavioural approach, with the therapist in a central position training the couple to communicate and negotiate more effectively, and when 'resistance' emerges they move to the use of paradoxical interventions and other strategic techniques. Again, the similarities between this approach and the one we are advocating are greater than the differences, and the only major components in our approach which differ radically from theirs are our greater integration of behavioural and systems techniques and our method of treating problems with a psychiatric or sexual component with specific combined techniques (see Chapters 10 and 11).

2.3 Differentiation of couples by the type of problem presented

There is no really adequate way of differentiating the couples who present to our clinic, on the analogy of a medical or psychiatric diagnosis. In describing them and trying to distinguish those which might respond to different types of intervention, we, in common with most couple therapists, tend to rely on a somewhat crude classification according to the type of problem or symptom presented.

It might be argued that the exercise has little point, and that the therapist should take each new case on its merits and treat them by whatever approach seems most appropriate at the time. In our setting, however, and using behavioural-systems therapy, we believe that we can help different problems with different methods, and we have necessarily developed a form of classification which helps us to think about the case in terms of such a matching of method to problem.

The process of matching our therapeutic approach to the problem presented (the ALI hierarchy) is dealt with in detail in Section 3.4, and will not be described any further here. However, the existence of the hierarchy makes the use of some classificatory system quite important for the work of the clinic.

2.3.1 Problems of communication and negotiation

It is now so common as to be arguably the cliché of the decade to say 'We have problems of communication'. It is certainly a very common introduction by couples in our marital therapy clinic. While in some couples this may mean just what it says, there are some variations in presentation. For example, one couple might hardly exchange a word from one day to another, while another might talk to each other a great deal but frequently experience misunderstandings. In a third couple it might mean that they talk very easily on everyday problems and plans, but there are some subjects of great importance to the relationship that they find impossible to talk about, and find that true empathy with each other is very hard to achieve.

When the couple present themselves at the clinic with problems of communication or with inability to negotiate, this makes it easy in some ways for the therapist. There is no argument with them about where the main problem lies, and the therapist can go ahead and treat the relationship problem without any 'reframing' (see Chapter 7). The goals of therapy are clear, and it should be easy for all those involved to know when they have been reached. It is not always as easy as it seems, however, as in some couples with these problems one partner may be expecting the other to do all the changing, even though both recognise that the main problems are those of communication. (See Chapters 5 and 6 for guidelines for the treatment of these problems.)

2.3.2 Infidelity and other 'triangles'

We are referring here firstly to the situation where one partner has had an affair which is known to the other, but they both feel that this does not mean the end of their relationship. Obviously there will at times be some doubt (a) whether the affair is really over, and (b) whether both partners are equally sure that they want the marriage to work. A therapist faced with this kind of couple should try to establish as clearly as possible what each partner wants of the therapy, but sometimes one has to take a good deal on trust in the early stages and continue to be aware of possible ambivalence on both sides throughout the therapy. The goals of therapy will, of course, be greatly modified if either the affair continues or if one or other partner stops working for the marriage and seriously contemplates divorce.

Secondly we refer to couples where a third person is involved in the couple's relationship difficulty. This can be a parent of one or the other, a child who is enmeshed with one or both partners (as may be the case with young anorexic clients) or even the over-involvement of one partner in their work or other relationships which are seen by the other as interfering with the couple's interaction. The goals of therapy will usually be to help the couple draw more effective boundaries around themselves. (For further discussion of this issue, see Section 10.13.)

2.3.3 Arguments and violence

Here the therapist's goal is rather similar to that in couples with a lack of communication. They are usually presenting the arguments as the problem, and it may be that if they can simply find a better way of negotiating, the problem will be solved to their satisfaction. However, in most cases it is not so simple, and more work will be needed in improving understanding of each other's feelings, in learning better ways of self-control, in altering other aspects of the system or in accepting that rows can sometimes be good and constructive rather than dangerous (see Sections 8.2.1 and 8.3.1).

2.3.4 Divorce and separation

It is not unusual for couples to come to therapy having decided that the marriage is over, or at least wishing to have help in making such a decision. We are still in the area of declared relationship problems rather than individual symptoms arising from the relationship, and although the goals are rather different from those where the couple wish to continue and improve their relationship, the approach we would use is not dissimilar from that used for communication problems (Section 2.3.1). Goals of therapy will often be those of deciding whether to continue the relationship or not, and if it is to end the question of custody and access to the children may have to be negotiated. One very effective way of facilitating this decision-making process is to ask the couple to talk directly together in the session while the therapist helps the communication process without biassing the outcome.

A complete new form of counselling has grown up around these issues, called conciliation counselling (Parkinson 1986). The aims are quite limited, and include the encouragement of divorcing couples to take joint responsibility for deciding questions of custody, care and access, and matters of property and maintenance. They do not replace the legal process of divorce, but help to expedite it, with less adversarial conflict and, it is to be hoped, less residual bitterness.

Conciliation counselling can be carried out in court, either by specialist counsellors (as in the experimental services in some county courts) or more frequently by probation officers. Alternatively, conciliation can be provided in other settings such as private marital or family clinics or in marriage guidance agencies. Whichever setting is used, it is always necessary for the conciliation counsellors to communicate with the legal advisors to both partners, and with those who might represent the children, to ensure that the legal process is complemented rather than hampered by conciliation. Preliminary results appear to indicate considerable benefit to both the divorcing partners and to any children involved, but the long-term value has yet to be assessed.

For further discussion of the issues round divorce, separation and 'reconstituted families' when one or both partners remarry, see Section 10.16.

2.3.5 Psychiatric symptoms in one partner

This is a more difficult type of presentation, although it is a very common one in our setting. The problem is that the two partners are probably both expecting a solution which may be medical, and in that case will result in major changes in the 'patient' and no change in the partner. The task of the therapist is to try to reframe the problem as being in the relationship rather than the individual, and then to work on changing the relationship so as to enable the couple to work together to remove the problem. The kinds of problem which can be dealt with in this way include depression, anxiety, fears and phobias and other forms of neurosis.

An important point needs to be made here, one which will recur in different forms throughout the book. It is that the way a problem is formulated is in the last analysis a matter of choice. A woman may be depressed, and at the same time feel resentful towards her husband: the therapist can choose to focus on the depression, using cognitive therapy or antidepressants, or on the relationship, using conjoint therapy with the couple. Neither approach is more correct, and both may be successful by different means. Thus, the reason for the therapist reframing the problem as in the relationship is only because there is perceived to be a better chance of helping the patient and also the partner by means of conjoint therapy rather than by treating the individual.

Thus, in treating psychiatric and dysfunctional patients and their partners by conjoint couple therapy, the goals of therapy will include the resolution of the symptoms, an improvement in the relationship and possibly various changes in perception leading to the symptoms being seen as a stabilising factor in the relationship or in other ways less dangerous or frightening than they seemed at first. (See also Section 4.6.1 and Chapter 10.)

2.3.6 Couples where one partner is abusing alcohol or drugs

The couples presenting with these problems can be quite similar to those presenting with psychiatric symptoms (Section 2.3.5), but the problems of motivation for change are likely to be more troublesome, and perhaps the willingness to see the problem as one of relationship rather low on both sides. In some cases it is possible to work on the relationship, but in general the level of dependence on the drug must be fairly mild, and the problem recognised by both partners as connected to the relationship, before the decision is made to embark on couple therapy with such couples.

See Section 10.15 for further discussion of the management of problems of substance abuse within couples.

2.3.7 Problems of sexual functioning

It is quite common for couples to present with problems of sexual functioning within the relationship, and in many cases they are quite ready to accept that they have a joint problem. In that case we can go ahead and offer them conjoint therapy with the clearly stated goal of improving the sexual life for both of them. Whether this sexual therapy takes place within the marital clinic will depend on how much the problem is seen as one of motivation and how much of the problem is a technical one (see Section 11.2). In the latter situation it is preferable for the couple to be referred to a sexual dysfunction clinic, where more specific behavioural or physical treatments are available.

In any case, even if the technical dysfunction takes precedence, there is much that can be done to improve communication and thus help sexual motivation in the couple. The sexual side of a relationship is in many ways a reflection of the non-sexual side, and it would be quite inappropriate to treat the sexual aspect without respecting the rest of the relationship.

2.3.8 Other behavioural problems

In a similar way to psychiatric problems, problems in the behaviour of one partner may present to the couple therapist. They may include such behaviour as compulsive lying, gambling, general irresponsibility, or other patterns nearer the psychiatric field , such as jealousy, possessiveness or impulsivity. In a similar way to that in which we deal with the more clearly psychiatric problems, we tend to try to reframe the problems in terms of the relationship, to look for ways in which the partners can help each other to solve the problems and, failing that, to help them to accept that the problem is in some way stabilising the relationship. (See examples in Section 9.8.1, 9E and Chapter 10).

2.4 *The goals of therapy in the behavioural-systems approach*

The goals of therapy are not always spelt out in a clear way in descriptions of other approaches, but in the behavioural-systems approach we feel that it would be inconsistent with our general philosophy not to do so. There are obviously risks involved in this exercise, in that research could prove that we are not in fact achieving our stated goals, but we feel that it is right, in a field where there are so many unsubstantiated assertions, to state clearly what we hope to achieve in therapy.

The type of therapy we are advocating is limited both in time and in scope. The goals are therefore also limited, and we put the emphasis more on improved behavioural adjustment than on any radical change in attitudes or insight in either partner. We would go further and say that we doubt whether it is realistic to expect the changes produced by psychotherapy of any sort to do more than improve adjustment. Given the enormous complexity of brain function and of personality, and the even greater complexity of an ongoing relationship between two people, any theory of human interaction which does more than summarise the observable aspects of interactional behaviour must go well beyond the bounds of what can be known with any certainty.

Thus, in our approach to therapy and its goals, we intend to keep the discussion as simple as possible and remain as close as we can to the kinds of goal that the couples themselves choose to work on.

One exception to this is when couples come to us in an attempt to find the 'cause' of their problem. It is, in our view, more useful and more fruitful to experiment with different kinds of communication and inter-action, rather than to chase an illusory 'cause' of the trouble in the hope that understanding the cause will lead to the problem going away. The most unhelpful aspect of cause seeking is when the cause of the trouble is pinned on one partner only. This leads the labelled partner to accept the total responsibility for changing his or her behaviour, and leaves the other partner feeling justified and self-satisfied. We find in practice that it is easier for two people to 'give' a little, rather than for one to adapt radically while the other hardly changes.

2.4.1 The general philosophy of behavioural-systems couple therapy

We are presenting to the reader an approach to couple problems which is predominantly one in which the therapist is attempting to alter the process of interaction. This is based on our belief that such alterations will in the end be helpful towards the couple being able to solve their own problems.

The approach is therefore more like a process of training for athletic performance or to play a musical instrument than the sort of detec-tive work involved in the diagnosis of a medical disease. We make no apology for this, in that, at this stage of our knowledge of relationships and what makes them good or poor, we feel that the fruits of our own and other workers' efforts in improving relationships have more to offer than theories about why the couple are disturbed.

One clear preference in our work is for the couple to communicate and negotiate as far as possible on small, often trivial, everyday issues. These are less threatening to the couple than many of the more serious problems that they face, and we believe that in finding a solution to such minor issues they are both laying the foundations for fruitful discussions on the major ones and even partly solving them as they go. This is because, just as the couple's sexual relationship is in some way a micro-cosm of their general relationship, the trivial issues they argue and compromise about in the sessions are also often representative of the larger issues that divide them.

Thus we respect the larger issues that a couple may be concerned about, such as worry about their children, troubles with the extended family, redundancy, bereavement, infidelity or the shattering of mutual ideals. Our major form of intervention, however, is at the level of negotiation about much smaller areas, and we hope by this means to give them the tools to be able to deal with the major issues later in therapy or even at home in between sessions. In one way the fact that we use the 'decentred' position in therapy much of the time prepares the couple for continuing to work in this way without the therapist's intervention, both between sessions and after the therapy is over. To put it another way, we are providing them with a model of self-help under direction which should be 'transportable' to the home situation.

2.4.2 The overall goals of therapy

The major goal of therapy is an improved interaction between the partners, which generally implies increasing their flexibility and repertoire of alternative ways of interacting. This might be at a verbal level or in the ability to solve problems, and it could involve any aspect of their relationship from dishwashing or budgeting to providing each other with support through bereavement.

We would often expect, as a result of this, that some symptoms or behavioural problems in the individual might improve as well. The symptoms themselves might resolve, or they might remain the same but no longer be seen by the couple as a serious problem. For example, a man's obsessional checking of gas taps and door locks might be relabelled in therapy as his taking responsibility for the family's safety, and his wife's lack of such checking might be understood as undue risk-taking.

At the lower end of therapeutic ambition we might decide with the couple that it was preferable for them to agree to live with a problem, and thus lower their expectations of solving it. This would obviously be advisable when, after a good deal of therapy in a couple presenting with mainly relationship problems, it became clear that things were not changing. It is important for the therapist to avoid blaming the individual or the couple for such a failure. In our view (and that of many behaviour therapists) there is no such thing as patient 'resistance', but only therapy which is not yet adequate to solve the problem. Thus we would rather blame ourselves or our therapy than a mysterious unconscious or systemic factor in the individual or couple for the failure. This is partly a genuine belief in the sincerity of couples seeking our help, but partly a therapeutic strategy to minimise any conflict between couple and therapist. If a couple or individual begins to feel that the therapist is acting in an omnipotent way, or arrogating too much power or responsibility to him/herself, they may begin to oppose the therapist, and we feel that a therapist who adopts a modest and collaborative approach is more likely to avoid this pitfall and gain the couple's cooperation.

The overall goals in therapy may be summarised as follows:

(1) Improved marital adjustment (communication, negotiation and satisfaction).
(2) Increased flexibility of interaction in the relationship.
(3) Reduction of any symptoms or individual problems.
(4) Decrease in labelling one partner as the 'problem'.
(5) If the relationship or the individual problems cannot be improved, reduce expectations and 'live with it'.

(6) Any improvement should be able to last without further thera-
    peutic help.

(It is interesting to note how similar these clinically derived goals are to
the criteria which Beavers used, as quoted in Section 1.7, to distinguish
'healthy families' from others.)

2.4.3 More specific and intermediate goals

In the process of helping couples to reach these overall goals, it is of
course necessary to have in mind some intermediate goals. These will be
mainly related to numbers (1) and (2) above, the goals of improving
adjustment and flexibility within the relationship, although some will be
more relevant to the other overall goals.

2.4.3.1 *Clarifying the goals of therapy*
The first intermediate goal is to clarify what agenda each individual
brings to therapy, and if possible to agree with the couple what the joint
goals should be. This may not be an easy task: sometimes couples come
to therapy with incompatible goals.
   A wife, for example, may wish that sex could be quietly forgotten, the
couple living as brother and sister, while the husband may see an
increase in the frequency of sex as the major goal. In this sort of case the
therapist should make it clear at the outset that it will be impossible to
achieve both goals, and that one priority in therapy will be to try and
reach a compromise between the two.
   In another example, both partners may agree that the husband's
gambling is the main issue to be dealt with, but the therapist may decide
to be cautious in accepting this as the primary goal, since it may be that
the gambling is helping to stabilise a relationship which needs excitement and risk to survive, and removing the source of excitement might
mean a greater chance of the relationship ending.
   This discussion on goals should take place at a relatively early stage
(see Chapter 4) as the setting of realistic and agreed goals brings several
benefits. Firstly it clarifies the direction which therapy ought to take;
secondly it gives the therapist an idea of how flexible the couple are at an
early point in therapy; and lastly it is in itself a useful exercise in couple
therapy and communication, especially if it can be done from a decentred position.
   In the process of agreeing the goals of therapy it is important to maintain a realistic and practical approach. As mentioned above, couples
often come to therapy with unrealistic expectations of the outcome, and
are prone to put too much responsibility for producing change on to the
therapist (see Chapter 4). A therapist faced with this situation should
maintain a helpful attitude, but continually emphasise that the couple
must themselves take responsibility for changing their own behaviour
with the therapist's advice.

A third aspect of the establishment of therapeutic goals, and one which is more specific to our own approach, is related to our belief that it is better to treat individual problems by changing the relationship than by changing the individual. Thus, as discussed more fully in Chapter 4, one may need to reframe the problem as one of interaction in order to get the couple to work on it together.

An example of this is a case where the husband was depressed and unable to get on with his writing. The therapist invited the wife to the first session as an informant and as someone who might be able to help the husband to overcome his depression. Quite soon, however, they were able to focus on the relationship, and the way in which the wife's protective and dominant approach was maintaining the husband's help-less attitudes. Eventually she realised that taking less responsibility for him would release his initiative, and he then became more effective and productive.

We can summarise the process of clarifying the goals of therapy as follows:

(1) Ensure a consensus on the goals of therapy.
(2) Set realistic and practical goals, without the therapist accepting too much responsibility for producing change.
(3) Prefer interactional goals, rather than expecting one individual to do all the changing.

2.4.3.2 *Improving communication and negotiating ability*
The second subsidiary goal has to do with communication and negotiation. This will be dealt with in detail in Chapters 5 and 6, but it may be useful at this point to summarise what we hope couples will achieve in improving the quality of their communication.

One of the most important aspects of communication is the ability to empathise with one's partner. A therapist can make a rough assessment of this by simple questions such as: 'Can you say how you think your wife feels at this moment?' or 'How do you think this affects your husband?'. However, it may take much longer to reach an adequate understanding of the degree of mutual empathy in the couple, and throughout therapy in many couples it will be necessary to continue checking whether the partners are in touch with each other's feelings. For some couples improvement of empathy and understanding may be the main goal of therapy.

A case will illustrate this point. The couple, both intelligent profess-ionals, had had marital difficulties for almost the whole five-year dura-tion of their relationship. In one session the wife, who suffered from phobias and depression, was asking why she became so anxious when entertaining friends, and the husband began to lecture her (with the best of intentions) on how silly it was to become anxious at such a trivial issue. He did not notice her tears until the therapist pointed them out, and then he was encouraged to ask her more about how she felt, rather

than telling her what to do. The improved understanding which re-
sulted made the rest of the therapy much easier.

A closely related issue in the field of communication is the ability
of the couple to communicate together on an emotional level. Many
couples have quite good ability to communicate about mutual interests,
household duties or what to buy on shopping trips, but become tongue-
tied when trying to express feelings. At times, too, the feelings
expressed are not appropriate to the situation: the aggrieved wife who
dissolves into helpless tears instead of expressing justified anger, or the
husband who, in attempting to show sympathy, blames his wife for her
lack of self-control. (See also the discussion in Section 1.3 on negotiation of appropriate levels of emotional sharing.)

Another goal in the communication area is to reduce repetitive sequences of argument or similar unproductive interactions. Some arguments are healthy, and it often does good to an inhibited couple to have
an unaccustomed argument or heated discussion. But for many couples
arguments are almost rituals, and represent a retreat from constructive
interaction into mindless repetition of old grudges with no hope of
resolution. Such 'blame/blame' sequences need to be modified if possible, and interventions may either take the form of trying to increase the
constructive side of the discussion or at times escalating the argument,
leaving it to the couple to see the futility of it and move on to other areas.
One of the most useful ways of getting away from unproductive arguments is to help the couple to negotiate effectively for a change of
behaviour over the coming week or two (see Chapters 5 and 6) using
positive, specific, reciprocal and repeatable tasks.

Non-verbal aspects of communication are an important and sometimes neglected area in therapy. Eye contact is almost non-existent in
some couples (see Section 1.2.2), and it has been shown by Schaap &
Jansen-Nawas (1987) that distressed couples look at each other less than
non-distressed couples. Another observation which may give information about the quality of a relationship is to note which partner looks at
the other more often. There may be several interpretations of this in
different couples. The partner who looks more often may be concerned
about the other's state of mind (e.g. looking for signs of anxiety or
depression), or may be looking to the other for approval or confirmation
or may simply be relying on the other to be the spokesman in therapy.
Whatever the explanation, we usually feel that more equal sharing of
eye-contact is preferable to very unequal looking. (See also Sections 1.2
and 8.6 for further discussion of eye contact and non-verbal interaction
between partners.)

There are other forms of non-verbal interaction which are sometimes
relevant: the way a person sits, for instance, whether on the edge of the
seat or leaning back, with legs crossed or open, and whether the arms
are held down by the side, folded across the chest or raised with the
hands behind the head. The significance of some of these postures is
largely speculative, and may differ between individuals. However, it

has been shown, again by Schaap, that couples in distress interpret their partners' postures more negatively than contented couples.

The subjects which couples can talk about may be an important aspect of the goals of therapy. Too much dwelling on the past can cause problems, both because of the repetitive nature of the interaction and because it prevents the couple talking about more constructive issues. Similar problems arise when couples spend too much time dwelling on current resentments, on plans for future activities or even on agreeing how happy they are. In general, the goal of therapy should be to increase the repertoire and variety of subjects which the couple can discuss freely.

On the whole, it matters less what couples discuss than how they discuss it, giving due consideration to each other's views and wishes. Some important issues, however, should not be left out, and one vital point to discuss early in therapy is their views on the future of the relationship. If it seems that separation is likely, it is often a good idea to see each partner separately early in therapy, to ascertain their separate views on the value of therapy and the goals with which both are entering it.

One important aspect of communication, which is dealt with in detail in Chapter 5, is the couple's ability to negotiate. As we emphasise there, negotiation should be constructive, positive and future-orientated, and should be kept fairly strictly to the point. Those who bring a lot of irrelevant issues in when negotiating about specific points may drift off the topic altogether, and it is up to the therapist to help them to develop the ability to remain single-minded in negotiation.

In summary, then, the goals related to communication are as follows:

(1) Mutual empathy between the partners.
(2) Ability to communicate emotionally as well as factually.
(3) Reduction of repetitive arguments or complaints.
(4) Improved eye-contact and other non-verbal aspects.
(5) Ability to talk freely about a wide range of subjects, for example painful past experiences and the future of the relationship.
(6) Ability to negotiate.

2.4.3.3 Boundaries and responsibility (see Section 7.3.6)
The concept of boundaries is a fundamental one in thinking about family systems (see Chapter 7 and Hoffman 1981). It has to do with how much people are involved in each other's lives. If one partner in a relationship acts in a parental way to the other (who is perfectly fit), helping him to dress, opening his mail, planning every detail of his life and speaking for him in therapy, one would say that there is an insufficiently firm boundary between them, and they are enmeshed with each other. Such weak boundaries are often seen when the protected partner is psychiatrically ill, and sometimes it is not clear whether the illness has caused

the enmeshment or the active partner's 'need to be needed' has prolonged the illness.

Boundaries between individuals can be strengthened in therapy by various techniques such as encouraging assertiveness in the weaker partner, or setting tasks which demand independent action from that partner. The issue of responsibility is also important, and one general rule which is common to both behavioural and systems approaches is that each person should be held responsible for his or her own actions. One frequently hears partners in therapy saying such things as: 'He made it impossible for me to go' or 'She drove me to it'. We try to counter such comments by asking each partner to take responsibility for their own behaviour, and may even ask them to rephrase their own comments, as for instance: 'I decided not to go because of the difficulties I thought he would raise'.

Although the question of individual boundaries and responsibility is not usually among the couple's stated goals in therapy, we feel that the issue is important enough to be one of the fairly frequent subsidiary goals in the behavioural-systems approach to therapy.

In addition to boundaries round the individual, there are also legitimate boundaries round the couple which should be respected, and which should not be too weak. The phrase 'shutting the bedroom door' can connote more than simply keeping children out of involvement in the parents' sexual relationship: there should also be a certain degree of privacy surrounding the discussion between partners of important and intimate issues, such as threats of separation, jealousy, finance or the welfare of young children. These boundaries should be erected not only against the couple's children, but also to exclude others such as friends or relatives from discussions which ought to be kept confidential within the relationship.

In summary, the goals relating to boundaries and responsibility are:

(1) Partners should respect each other's 'personal space'.
(2) Each partner should accept responsibility for all his/her own actions.
(3) The partners should respect each other's confidences and avoid discussing with others intimate matters concerning the relationship.

2.4.3.4 *Increasing flexibility and repertoire*
Most couples with relationship problems could be characterised as being too inflexible in their interactions. It is possible at times to observe the repetitive responses that lead to communication difficulties. It often feels as if a knee-jerk reflex is triggered, for example if a husband apologises for something and his wife repeatedly ignores the apology and continues her criticism; or if during an argument the husband regularly raises his voice and the wife regularly becomes silent and withdrawn. Often the partners have a sense of helplessness over the inevitability of these sequences, and often too each will feel that it is the other who is being inflexible.

An example of increased flexibility in behaviour might be if during an argument, instead of always criticising, a husband could develop a variety of options such as expressing sadness, walking out of the room or giving his wife a hug.

Such interactions are by no means confined to verbal exchanges. Sexual approaches often lead to similar repeated misunderstandings and difficulties. The wrong kind of touch can trigger a whole sequence of negative interaction which leads to repeated failure, in which each partner may blame the other. The sense that each partner has in these sequences of being out of control of the situation makes it useful to devise methods in therapy to give the couple alternative strategies for dealing with these repetitive patterns of negative interaction.

This intermediate goal of increased flexibility can be achieved in different ways, of which some of the most useful are training in different means of communication (Chapter 6), encouraging different ways of arguing (Chapter 8) or giving strategic, often timetabled, tasks (Chapter 9). In all these approaches the goal is to achieve greater flexibility of response, whether verbal or physical, and to get away from the stereotyped interaction which is found in so many couples with relationship problems.

Some couples complain not so much of active disputes and arguments as of boredom and a lack of purpose in the relationship. For them one useful subsidiary goal may be to encourage them to do more things together: for instance to go out to cinemas or restaurants or to plan weekend trips as a couple. In a suitable relationship these timetables for enjoyment (see Chapter 9) or developing the ability to play together may have quite a good effect on the couple, and also act as a catalyst for improved communication, empathy or sexual pleasure.

In summary, the goals related to flexibility and increased repertoire are:

(1) To increase flexibility of response, both verbally and behaviourally.
(2) To enlarge the couple's repertoire of alternative responses, especially in 'stuck' situations.
(3) To plan joint 'fun' activities together which will increase the couple's ability to enjoy things and to play together.

2.4.3.5 Decisions which ought to be left to the couple

Although our approach is quite directive, we like to think that this directiveness is limited to altering the process of interacting in the relationship. There are many other aspects of the partners' life on which we as therapists should expect to have no influence at all, beyond encouraging them to discuss the issues together in the session. These include any matter to do with religious belief or observance. They also include most questions of employment, unless one partner's employment seems in itself to be putting a strain on the relationship. We feel, too, that questions of whether to remain together or to separate are the business of the couple alone, and the therapist should have no influence on these, even when the couple are insistent that he or she should decide the issue for them. This does not mean that the question should not be discussed in therapy, but simply that the therapist should remain separate from the decision-making itself, preferably in the decentred position while the couple discuss the issues.

A similar caution applies to the question whether a couple should try for a pregnancy: they will often almost beg for the therapist to pronounce on the future stability of the relationship, and therefore whether it would be a good thing for them to have a child. This is another challenge the therapist would be wise to avoid taking up.

In our setting patients are very used to asking the psychiatrist about medication, and we often find ourselves asked that sort of question in the course of therapy. The best solution is for the general practitioner or the referring consultant to take the responsibility for medication, but in exceptional circumstances we have occasionally used another member of the team to write prescriptions for the 'patient'. Another, more difficult, area for the therapist to remain neutral over is the question of who is right or wrong in an argument. The couple will frequently treat the therapist as if he or she were the judge, and they were putting their cases before the court. Again it is necessary for the therapist to avoid making the decision or taking sides, but various other therapeutic moves are possible (see Chapter 4) and the argument can provide a fruitful field for modifying the relationship.

To summarise, decisions to be left to the couple include issues of religion or employment, decisions about separating or remaining together, decisions about pregnancy and the question in an argument as to who is right. Matters of medication and other types of medical treatment are best dealt with by a doctor outside the therapeutic team.

2.4.3.6 The goals of therapy: conclusion

Our behavioural-systems approach to couple therapy is one which aims at better adjustment of the partners to each other and greater flexibility in their interaction as the main goals. We do not aim to analyse unconscious conflicts in our couples, or produce 'personal growth', nor do we attempt to give them insight into what we might hypothesise are the 'causes' of their problems. However, we do hope that they may develop a kind of 'behavioural insight', whereby, faced with a problem they have solved with help during therapy, they will remember the approach they used before and apply it again.

The improved adjustment which we hope the couples will achieve will include better communication, both on an emotional and a practical level, greater ability to negotiate and, where necessary, to argue successfully; better acceptance of personal boundaries and individual responsibility and a greater repertoire of responses leading to a more flexible and tolerant relationship. We also hope that any individual symptoms will abate as the relationship improves, but we would prefer not to speak of 'cure' in connection with either relationship problems or symptoms. In such a complicated field, involving the personalities of both partners and the complexities of the relationship, we feel that the concept of cure is too grandiose and simplistic, and becomes almost meaningless in contrast with the more modest but practical aim of improved adjustment.

Chapter 3

The overall strategy of therapy

3.1 Introduction

Couple therapy using a behavioural-systems approach is in our view an effective form of therapy for a wide variety of problems. This includes not only the more obvious relationship difficulties but also problems often seen as individual, such as depression or impotence (see Chapters 2, 10 and 11).

We are not, however, advocating that the behavioural-systems approach is a universal remedy for all problems occurring in people who are married or living in a similar close relationship. It is an approach to therapy which should be used with discrimination for those problems which are suited to it.There are many difficulties experienced by individuals which are best dealt with by individual approaches such as behaviour therapy, dynamic psychotherapy, medication or admission to hospital. There are also some couple problems which can best be helped by alternative forms of couple therapy, perhaps of a longer-term nature.

What this chapter attempts to address is firstly the basis on which we would choose to offer couple therapy rather than refer to another form of therapy or treatment. The choice to offer couple therapy having been made, in the second part of the chapter we go on to outline the different types of interventions available within the behavioural-systems approach, using the hierarchy of alternative levels of intervention or ALI (see Section 3.4).

3.2 The indications for couple therapy

In describing the indications for couple therapy we hope to avoid giving the impression that there is certainty about the right or wrong approach for particular problems. Many problems, both in individuals and in relationships, can be helped in several different ways, and ultimately in many cases the choice of therapeutic approach is arbitrary. Some relationship problems may be helped equally well by couple therapy or individual therapy and some individual problems may be dealt with better by modifying the relationships in which they occur.

We do believe, however, that when both partners have compromised a little in producing a solution to a problem, that solution is likely to be more durable than one in which one partner has changed a great deal and the other not at all. This may be particularly true in relation to life events to which both partners need to adapt, and if one of the two fails to adapt this failure may put an undue strain on both partners and on the relationship.

When an individual, couple or family seek help how can we decide what type of problem is suitable for couple therapy?

3.2.1 Information from research

There is unfortunately very little research available on this question either in couple or family therapy. The field was reviewed by Crowe (1988) and several possible reasons were suggested for the lack of research. The first reason suggested was that many 'radical' family and couple therapists are so committed to their own way of working and thinking that they view this as the only logical solution to almost any problem and therefore are not concerned to distinguish between those problems which are suitable or unsuitable for that form of therapy. Needless to say, we do not share this view and feel the exercise to find criteria for suitability is a worthwhile one.

Other therapists would see the necessity for such a distinction but would feel that more clinical experience is necessary in such a new field before embarking on research to find which problems are suitable for its use.

The main drawback, however, is probably the inherent difficulty of doing such research. In order to distinguish the presenting problems which are suitable for a particular form of therapy, we would need:

(1) An agreed method of labelling what sort of problems we are treating (a sort of diagnosis for relationship problems).
(2) A reliable measure of outcome, both for individual problems and for the relationship.

Although measures of outcome are becoming available (see Chapter 13) there is still no very good classification for relationship problems. In the absence of a good classification method, there are at present virtually no research findings on the indications for couple or family therapy.

3.2.2 Some factors affecting suitability for couple therapy

In the absence of research evidence, probably the best way to approach the question whether to use couple therapy or some other treatment is to look back on cases we have seen and attempt to identify those which seemed to do well with such therapy. We will look at various aspects of the cases to try to find criteria, admittedly rather rough ones, to decide whether to offer couple therapy.

3.2.2.1 *How are the problems presented?*
Problems to do with arguments and marital tension seem to be an obvious starting point for couple therapy. Another clear indication (as

pointed out by Ackerman in 1966) is where one partner in a relationship spends much of the individual session complaining about the other's behaviour. A third indication is when one partner experiences increased stress following the improvement of the other as a result of individual therapy.

In addition to this type of problem, which is more or less obviously a relationship one, there are many individual problems with a relationship aspect to them and in many of these we would choose to offer the couple therapy together. A wife with a phobia of sex, for example, might feel that the problem is all on her side, and we might in fact suggest some individual help for her during therapy. However, the problem would almost certainly cause some frustration to her husband and for most of the therapy we would want to see the couple together, both to explore the impact the phobia has on the relationship and to look at the part both partners may be playing in maintaining the problem.

At a slightly greater remove, some other psychiatric problems such as depression, low self-esteem or psychosomatic symptoms may be closely associated with the relationship, and may be perceived by one or both partners as being caused by the relationship. In one such case, for example, the depressed husband requested that his wife might accompany him to the first session 'because she is my memory'. In fact, the wife was very protective to her husband, and her 'good memory' was almost all in relation to his problem behaviour, which he tended to forget. We acceded to this request and began a most fruitful series of marital sessions, as a result of which both the marriage and the depression were greatly improved. In such cases it would seem a wasted opportunity not to see the couple together, and it is in such cases that we often seem to be most successful in therapy (see Chapter 10).

In contrast, there are problems presented by individuals which seem to be much less suitable for couple therapy. Some phobias, for example, occur mainly in the workplace or during travel, and may be quite successfully treated behaviourally without involving other family members. In one research study, Cobb *et al.* (1980) showed that behavioural treatment for married women who were phobic was more successful in reducing their phobias than marital therapy. On the other hand, a combined approach is often helpful (as shown by Hafner 1984) in which the husband of an agoraphobic woman may help her to carry out her behavioural 'homework' between sessions. Here the husband is acting more as a therapist in collaboration with those treating the phobia, rather than being involved in couple therapy as such.

Other psychiatric problems may also need to be dealt with by a combination of treatments. For example, married patients with depression, especially if there are biological symptoms (e.g. loss of appetite, sleep and energy, loss of sexual interest and physical slowness), will probably need to be treated by antidepressant drugs in combination with some individual and/or couple therapy. Some more severe anxiety and panic states can also be well treated by seeing the individual and giving relaxation, anxiety management training and possibly medication. Patients with schizophrenia and psychoses would probably not be treated best by couple therapy alone (Falloon and Liberman 1983) but are better helped by a combination of medication, individual support and a form of educational and problem-solving therapy with the couple to prevent relapses and maximise the benefit of treatment (see Sections 3.3.3, 3.4.14 and 9.10.1).

The abuse of drugs or alcohol may often, like schizophrenia, be best treated with a mixture of individual and couple or family therapy. The necessary amount of each will depend very much on the degree to which the habit has become self-sustaining and all-absorbing. In the earlier and milder cases, frustration with family members may be playing a major part in keeping the habit going, but more severe cases will be impervious to family influences and therapy (see Section 10.15).

3.2.2.2 *Does the problem seem to be connected with the relationship?*
Some of the above problems are seen to be on a kind of borderline between suitability for individual or couple therapy. One question which might help to decide this is: does the problem seem to be closely bound up with the relationship? For example, a man's depression may be mainly experienced away from the home, whether at work or in social activities, and his partner may perceive him as relatively normal at most times. He would be less suitable for couple therapy than a man who attended the clinic mainly on the initiative of his partner who was more worried about him than he was about himself.

This raises a related question. How much difficulty does the problem cause the partner? In some cases this may not be very serious at all. For example, with some types of phobia the partner may be at most slightly inconvenienced. However, in other cases the problem may of its nature cause great difficulties for the partner. Some examples of this might be alcoholism, gambling, violent behaviour, morbid jealousy or suicidal behaviour. The more the problem affects the partner, the greater the indication to include both partners in therapy, at least for part of the time. (Where drinking, gambling, suicidal or similar behaviour is serious and seems out of control, the individual may need to be given treatment for some time before couple work is commenced: see Section 3.2.2.5.)

A third question to ask, though of less importance than the preceding two, is whether the problem antedates the beginning of the relationship itself. If it did not begin earlier, then the strong probability is that there is a connection between the two. Even if the problem was there earlier, however, this does not necessarily mean that couple therapy is inappropriate. The relationship may still be maintaining the problem to some extent, and the couple may have sought each other out in the first place partly because of the problem or something connected with it.

3.2.2.3 *Will they attend together?*
This practical issue can affect therapy fundamentally, and may be the deciding factor as to whether we undertake couple therapy or not. Partners can give various reasons for not attending, from the more

mundane ones, such as inability to obtain time off work or to arrange baby-sitters, to more psychologically relevant ones, such as fear of the therapy or unwillingness to be labelled as part of the problem.

We usually make efforts to involve a recalcitrant partner (see Chapter 4), especially if the only communication we have from them is via the other partner (who may for their own purposes be misrepresenting the situation to avoid couple therapy). With such couples therapists may have to spend some time helping one partner find ways of including the other in therapy. However we may have to accept at the end of the day that conjoint therapy is going to be impossible to organise and individual help may have to be given.

In some cases it may be possible to provide couple therapy by seeing only the partner who attends for sessions. Bennun (1985) showed that if both partners were willing to co-operate one could obtain just as much improvement in marital adjustment whether both partners were actually seen for therapy or only the 'patient' attended, taking home to the other partner instructions for homework exercises. This would, of course, apply more to those who were prevented from attending for practical reasons than to those who were unwilling to be involved.

3.2.2.4 Is the relationship continuing?

Another reason for deciding to see only one partner is if the relationship is virtually at an end because of separation or divorce. Often the partner who comes for help is going through the equivalent of a bereavement in this situation, and needs to mourn the loss of the relationship (see Section 10.16).

A related problem is where the partner who is not attending is in another relationship which he or she is unwilling or unable to terminate. This too makes it difficult to do more than support the partner who attends the sessions and try to help them through the crisis (see Section 10.13). An ongoing affair is, of course, not always a complete block to therapy, but even if the involved partner will attend the sessions, the divided loyalty and strong ambivalent feelings involved can make therapy much more difficult, and the therapist is often uncertain which of the shifting and conflicting goals the couple will pursue.

3.2.2.5 Is the problem too acute for couple therapy at present?

When the couples present with one partner who is severely symptomatic and the symptoms are acute or present too great a danger to self or others it is usually better to avoid couple therapy in this phase. It may then be undertaken only when the crisis is over and there is then a chance that the couple can use the greater stability of remission to practise homework tasks and improve communication and mutual understanding.

During the acute phase couple therapy may not be appropriate because of the slow pace of couple therapy, with its intervals of at least two weeks between sessions and its emphasis on relationship issues and homework exercises. Some cases of depression can present in this way, with suicidal threats and attempts, the risk of neglect of self or of a dependent young baby etc. In such cases it is important to stay in touch with the other agencies involved so that couple therapy can still be considered after the acute phase has passed.

3.3　Combining behavioural-systems couple therapy with other forms of therapy.

In many cases it is useful to combine behavioural-systems couple therapy with other treatments. These cases are likely to fall under three general headings: family problems, sexual difficulties or individual psychiatric problems.

3.3.1　Family problems

A fairly common problem we encounter is where a couple present with a marital problem, but in addition one or both of them has a difficult relationship with one or more of their children. In these circumstances it is our practice to mix family sessions with those where we see the couple alone, and work simultaneously or alternately on both problems. An example of this is a family in which the son of 13 had been in juvenile court for drawing graffiti on underground stations at a time when he was truanting from school. The father was insisting that his son paid him back the money he had paid in settlement of the boy's fine, but it seemed to the team that this did not really represent an adequate degree of parental control and responsibility. Indeed, both parents seemed to be very laid-back in their attitudes to their children and seemed to argue mainly about whose fault it was that the son was misbehaving. The parents mentioned in passing that their sex life was not good, but for the first few family sessions they worked on achieving a greater parental authority and a stronger generation boundary, as a result of which the son did much better in school and stopped truanting, The couple then needed a good deal of further work on their emotional and sexual communication, since in both areas they had major difficulties. In the outcome, the sexual problem (the wife's refusal and total lack of enjoyment) was not much improved, but they showed considerable improvement in their parenting and their mutual understanding.

As a general rule we do not see the whole family together throughout a course of therapy, even if the main problem seems to be with the children. We prefer at times to see the couple alone, partly because the couple's inconsistency and lack of communication are often contributing to the children's problems, and partly to ensure that the couple (the 'decider sub-system') have a chance to discuss the family problems as a couple without the children present. It is striking how often after such sessions the couple report that the children have been behaving better, thus confirming that the 'sub-system' can influence the children without the latter being present in therapy. (See also Section 7.5, and Section 10.12 where therapy with couples and families in relation to child abuse is described.)

3.3.2 Sexual problems
(see also Chapter 11)

Another situation in which couple therapy can be combined with other work is that of sexual dysfunction. Some problems of sexual function, particularly those of impotence and dyspareunia (painful intercourse), may have an organic element in their causation. It is therefore necessary to do what we can as therapists, both through history-taking and through physical examination and blood tests, to determine how much of the problem is organic and how much is part of the relationship. Even if there are major relationship aspects to the problem, there are usually some aspects of treatment that are best carried out with the individual, such as the early stages of the control of orgasm in premature ejaculation and the use of vibrators in female anorgasmia. On the other hand, there is in most cases a good deal of work needed on communication and on relationship aspects. As with other problems we treat, we try to keep the couple's goals paramount, but if there seems to be a block in the sexual treatment due to poor communication, we will work with them on their communication, even if they have not identified this as a goal.

In some couples there is an additional presenting complaint of sexual deviation in one partner (usually the male), for example a couple in which the husband admitted to his wife after twenty years of marriage that he had always had homosexual fantasies and more recently had become actively involved in a relationship with another man. Here too we will do a considerable amount of work with the couple on communication, but we may also need to do individual therapy with the partner involved in the outside sexual activities to assess his or her own goals, and if these include reduction of the competing urges we may work also on self-control techniques, orgasmic conditioning or aversion to attempt to modify the sexual urges of the affected partner. It is often more at the initiative of the other partner than that of the patient that the couple are trying to reduce the strength of the deviation, but we do not want to bias the therapy too far in the direction of there being only one labelled as patient, and would therefore insist on some conjoint work.

Sexual dysfunction can present in women who have had earlier experience of sexual abuse either from a family member or from a stranger. In these cases it can be helpful to combine work with the couple and individual counselling for the woman, looking at the past experiences preferably with a female therapist (see Sections 10.11 and 11.3.3). Again, the main goal in both types of session is on what the couple are seeking in therapy, but in the individual sessions it may become necessary to work quite intensively on the past experiences in order to be able to make progress with the couple problem.

3.3.3 Individual psychiatric problems

We pointed out in section 3.2.2.2. that the presence of individual psychiatric problems in one partner may be a contra-indication to offering couple therapy. In some such couples, however, it may be possible to give both individual and couple therapy at the same time.

Example 3A
An example is given by a couple in which the wife was agoraphobic and depressed. The symptoms had been present for a number of years and at the time of presentation at the clinic she had been also suffering from anorgasmia, a problem which proved to be due to the drug phenelzine, which happens to have this side-effect in addition to its antiphobic and antidepressant qualities. The drug was stopped and the sexual problem disappeared, but we were left with the wife's depression and phobia, and the long-standing marital difficulties.

These centred round the husband's long hours at work, his bringing work home and the wife's feeling that she was the only one taking responsibility for the family. He felt, in contrast, that she was over-anxious and did not need to worry so much about their two sons.

Therapy included work with the couple together on communication, the prescription of a different antidepressant for the wife, behavioural treatment for the wife's phobia (in some of which the husband acted as the therapist) and general support for both the wife and the husband. There were conjoint sessions, particularly at the beginning of therapy, but there were also a number of individual consultations for the wife and one or two individual sessions for the husband. After about a year of combined therapy (14 sessions) the wife was travelling more freely, she was free from depression and the couple were communicating very well (see also Section 10.8).

Such combined therapy is quite acceptable to the couple as a rule, and if the therapist can remain in touch with both the relationship and the individual problems, without letting one obscure the other, it is reasonable to attempt both approaches at the same time. However, if therapy cannot be done by the same person, or with the active co-operation for example of an informed general practitioner, it may be better to leave one approach until after the other is finished.

Example 3B
An example of this is given by a second couple with an agoraphobic wife. They had been referred by the behaviour therapy unit, where she had had some unsuccessful treatment for her phobia and depression. Despite the full consensus of our unit and the behaviourists that the marital difficulties were mainly responsible for maintaining the phobia, the couple kept returning to the other unit in emergencies and were quite uncooperative with the couple therapy.

Only after a joint meeting between the teams on both units, which formulated a policy as to who the couple should contact in an emergency, did they begin to make some progress in couple therapy. After a year of therapy, in which the husband became much less protective to his wife and she improved in her phobic behaviour, they decided to discontinue couple therapy, but it was felt both by them and the therapeutic team that the wife could now benefit from some dynamic psychotherapy, for which she was referred after the last couple session.

These two cases illustrate the ways in which it is possible to combine couple therapy with individual therapy, either concurrently in the same clinic or consecutively in different settings. The two cases happened to involve phobias and behaviour therapy, but it is quite possible to combine couple work with many other forms of therapy for individual problems. Some of these, for example depression and drug and alcohol dependency, are dealt with in Chapter 10. With these, as with most other psychiatric problems occurring in people living in a close relationship, the therapist has to make an assessment as to how great a part the relationship is playing in causing or maintaining the psychiatric symptoms. On this basis it will then be possible to decide whether to offer couple therapy, individual therapy (which may be with medication or with cognitive, behavioural or dynamic psychotherapy) or a combination of the two.

3.4 The hierarchy of alternative levels of intervention (ALI): matching interventions to problems

We describe at this point a clinical guideline which we will be returning to in many other sections of the book. We have developed it in order to simplify the process of making choices about which intervention may be most effective with which couple. We have called this clinical guideline the ALI hierarchy. In a simplified diagrammatic form (see Section 3.4.3) it shows how a therapist may select interventions which are appropriate to the different levels of complexity and rigidity in a couple's interaction. The use of the ALI hierarchy gives the therapist the option of ascending the hierarchy where symptomatology or rigidity is very evident or descending the hierarchy and working with more straightforward interventions where couples present with less complex difficulties and greater flexibility in their interaction.

3.4.1 Following the ALI hierarchy throughout the book

The hierarchy is introduced to the reader in this chapter and is expanded in the following pages. The general format of the book then follows the structure of the hierarchy. Chapter 4 describes our general way of working and the process of both the initial interview and later sessions, and describes interventions at several ALI levels. This is followed in suc-

ceeding chapters by descriptions of work at different levels of the hierarchy, beginning with the simpler interventions of reciprocity negotiation
in Chapter 5 and communication training in Chapter 6. Chapters 7, 8
and 9 move up the hierarchy into both structural and strategic systems
interventions. Chapters 10 and 11 show how the behavioural-systems
approach can be used for specific difficulties including psychiatric and
sexual problems, and Chapter 12 describes the training of therapists
who wish to use it. The hierarchy is thus a rather simple guide as to
what types of intervention to use and when to use it.

We use the word hierarchy here as the best way to describe our
approach, even though we recognise that it may carry inappropriate
connotations of greater purity and authority which we would not wish
to convey in the context of our theoretical system. The structural and
strategic approaches are not in our view superior to the behavioural
approaches, but simply more appropriate to the greater degree of
rigidity shown by some couples. An analogy is the way in which, when
driving a car, one changes gear to ascend hills compared with driving on
the flat. The use of the term ALI hierarchy thus refers to the matching of
greater levels of therapeutic ingenuity to higher levels of rigidity and
symptomatology in the couple, and the reader should remember that
in the hierarchy higher does not necessarily mean better, but only
different.

3.4.2 Moving up and down the ALI hierarchy in behavioural-systems couple therapy

In our clinical experience with couples it has become clear that different
problems respond to different interventions. The approaches of behavioural marital therapy usually called reciprocity negotiation and communication training (see Chapters 5 and 6) are very effective for couples
who present problems of power struggles, arguments and inability to
negotiate, and have the advantage of being the best researched and
validated form of couple therapy available. However, for some couple
problems, particularly those which involve an individual who has specific symptoms, the behavioural marital therapy techniques do not seem
to offer enough. In fact, such couples will often deny any relationship
problems as such, and present no disputes to resolve by negotiation.
Systems techniques, on the other hand, were developed partly in
response to the presence of such symptoms in families and couples. We
have therefore developed the behavioural-systems approach, which
combines the most effective elements of behavioural marital therapy
with some systems techniques such as reframing, evoking arguments
and intensifying (Chapter 8) and the setting of various systems tasks
(Chapter 9). The purpose of the present section is to indicate the general
principles for choosing which intervention to use in which situation and
to present a general framework, the ALI hierarchy, for using behavioural and systems techniques within couple therapy.

3.4.3 General principles of the ALI hierarchy

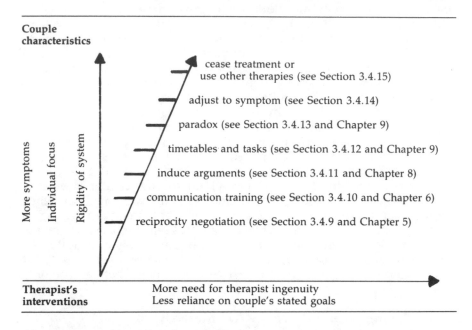

Couple characteristics

cease treatment or
use other therapies (see Section 3.4.15)

adjust to symptom (see Section 3.4.14)

paradox (see Section 3.4.13 and Chapter 9)

timetables and tasks (see Section 3.4.12 and Chapter 9)

induce arguments (see Section 3.4.11 and Chapter 8)

communication training (see Section 3.4.10 and Chapter 6)

reciprocity negotiation (see Section 3.4.9 and Chapter 5)

More symptoms   Individual focus   Rigidity of system

Therapist's interventions

More need for therapist ingenuity
Less reliance on couple's stated goals

As we can see from the diagram there are some fairly clear guidelines as to which level of intervention to use for various types of presenting problem. The vertical axis of the diagram represents the couple, and as one ascends the hierarchy there is an increase in three main areas:

(1) the symptom,
(2) individual focus,
(3) rigidity of the system.

The horizontal axis represents how the therapist can intervene according to the intensity of symptom, the degree of individual focus and rigidity in the couple. As these increase the therapist can choose interventions which rely less on the stated goals of the couple and require more ingenuity from the therapist. Alternatively, as the symptomatology, individual focus and rigidity of the couple lessen so the therapist can vary the intervention style by moving down the hierarchy to a less complex form of intervention.

The hierarchy is therefore of assistance to the therapist throughout the process of therapy and not just in the initial assessment phase.

3.4.4 Greater degree of individual symptomatology

In general the greater the severity of individual symptoms complained of (often psychiatric symptoms), the more ingenuity the therapist has to use to get the couple involved in conjoint therapy. This higher degree of ingenuity has to be applied when the couple seem to be uniting to put blame for the problem on only one partner (as, for example, in a case of low sex interest, see Sections 8.3.1 and 10.10).

3.4.5 Rigidity in the system

Similarly, in couples who seem to be resistant to change in therapy, more therapeutic ingenuity and flexibility is needed to overcome their inflexibility. In general, when we talk about using more ingenuity this implies a use of systemic interventions and therefore treating the couple's stated goals as being temporarily overridden by the need to understand and modify the system. In these cases the assumption is that the couple will be more able to achieve those stated goals, or perhaps to alter them to more realistic ones, once the system has been unlocked. This means using interventions at the upper levels of the hierarchy.

If, for example, the couple present with a problem defined as the husband's gambling, and both partners try all along to exonerate the wife from any kind of part in it, the therapist may decide to see how far the problem can be relabelled as a relationship difficulty. S/he may therefore ask a lot of circular questions about the wife's contribution to the difficulties, rather than asking the couple to negotiate around the gambling, and will probably end the first session with a strategic task rather than an instruction for an equal exchange of desired behaviour (see Section 8.12 and Example 8E).

3.4.6 Later stages of therapy

Later in therapy, however, when the couple have become more flexible as a result of a systems approach, the therapist may decide to use negotiation for what by then may be recognised as relationship problems, thus moving down the hierarchy.

3.4.7 Flexibility of the method

The first thing to say about this method is that it is a very flexible and practical one. The therapist does not decide in advance that the couple are going to be treated by one or other particular approach, but responds to the problem the couple come with by using the most appropriate intervention. Thus in a single session the therapist may ask the couple to negotiate, to have a focussed argument and to communicate more clearly, and may end the session by giving a paradoxical task, thus taking interventions from different parts of the hierarchy in the one session.

These interventions are made in response to the way the couple are interacting at the time and are designed to increase the flexibility of response in the couple, which is one of the main goals of therapy (see Chapter 2).

3.4.8 Assessment of the couple's flexibility

In Chapters 5 and 6 we suggest that behavioural marital techniques can be used early in therapy, partly to assess the rigidity or adaptability of the couple's interaction. Having said that, it often happens that a couple seen in our setting will prove unresponsive to the behavioural approach early in therapy and will need systems interventions rather than behavioural marital therapy as the main thrust of therapy. At later stages of therapy the more straightforward behavioural marital therapy will be needed. This may be a peculiarity of our clinic setting, in that we see a high proportion of couples with a psychiatric dimension to their problems, whereas in other settings more clearly acknowledged relationship problems are seen. This does not, however, invalidate the approach, which is equally useful in many different settings.

3.4.9 When to select reciprocity negotiation from the ALI hierarchy
(expanded in Chapter 5)

Reciprocity negotiation is a well-tried and validated method for the management of relationship problems. It has, however, been mostly used in the context of either couples attending marriage counselling or couples replying to advertisements to take part in research studies. It has been much less widely used in couples with problems which might be labelled psychiatric. The one exception to this is the study by Jacobson (1979) in which reciprocity negotiation made some improvement in distressed couples. In our clinic reciprocity negotiation has been found to be particularly useful for couples complaining of problems recognised by both partners as being marital or relationship difficulties, in which neither partner is labelled as a patient. It is therefore less valuable in the early stages of therapy where there are problems such as sexual dysfunction or psychiatric symptoms. The problems which respond best are those involving arguments, fights, bilateral complaints, nagging and threats of violence.

Example 3C
To take a typical example where reciprocity negotiation was useful, a couple in their fifties were referred by their general practitioner with a complaint that the husband had become rather withdrawn and silent, while the wife was described as hostile and aggressive. The couple were thinking of separation, and the husband had also become sexually uninterested in his wife, a fact which tended if anything to increase her hostility. In the first session some tasks were worked out which both agreed would be practicable and which each had requested of the other. The husband was to try to be home within 20 minutes of the time he

had predicted, and if he was delayed he would telephone his wife to let her know. The wife was to spend the first 10 minutes after his arrival home listening to his news of the day, not interrupting, and giving him a 'soft answer' rather than challenging or criticising what he said.

As a result of these initial tasks the couple greatly improved their interaction and the husband found, to his surprise, that he was finding his wife much more attractive in her new approach, so much so that the couple had sexual relations for the first time in several months.

In other cases of apparently uncomplicated relationship problems it soon becomes clear that the picture is not as simple as had first appeared. One may be faced with resistance to negotiate reciprocal changes or to communicate effectively; or a failure to complete homework tasks or an increase of focus on an individual. If these characteristics emerge the therapist may find that s/he needs to move to another therapeutic approach. In such a situation reciprocity negotiation may be used as an effective aid to assessment.

3.4.10 When to select communication training from the ALI hierarchy
(expanded in Chapter 6)

There are a number of couples who have relationship problems which are admitted and clearly defined, but whose communication style is such that they cannot keep to the point for long enough to negotiate a behavioural exchange. There is nothing wrong with their motivation for change, nor are they labelling one partner with a problem which would be better handled as a relationship issue. Such couples are suffering from problems of communication in the purest sense, and may well respond to communication training. This is also a behavioural approach, and like its opposite number reciprocity negotiation, it has been subjected to fairly extensive evaluation in couples who present for marital counselling, and has been shown in many couples to improve the quality of communication and to enhance marital satisfaction.

Couples particularly suited to this approach are those who have difficulty in keeping to the point in arguments, who tend to misunderstand each other and who cannot negotiate well. Their negotiations can be interfered with by getting off the point, by continual mutual blaming, by long monologues, by not hearing what the other says, by putting requests in a negative way or by disqualifying the other's requests.

Example 3D
A good example of the indications for communication training is given by a couple in their late twenties. The wife was quite psychologically minded and wanted to find explanations for everything in life, especially her husband's behaviour which she found difficult to accept. He was in the Territorial Army and would go off on weekend exercises, rather than spend time with her. In their communication, with the therapist in the decentred position (see Section

4.6.9), they experienced quite marked difficulties: she would ask him to explain something he had said or done, and he would smile and make a joke of it, whereupon she would become angry and frequently tearful as well. In communication training the therapist pointed out this sequence, and whenever it occurred he asked the husband to take his wife's request seriously and the wife to expect less in the way of explanation.

Communication training is successful as long as the couple are prepared to be flexible enough to accept that kind of advice. Where it fails, however, is in those couples who cannot be co-operative with each other long enough to accept that they must both make an effort to change. Couples who are unlikely to respond to communication training are usually continually hostile towards each other or stick firmly to their individual views that the problem lies in one partner only. By introducing communication training in the early sessions of therapy it becomes possible to make a rapid assessment of how flexible the couple are currently (see Section 6.2.2).

Once again we are faced with the three reasons for ascending the hierarchy of therapeutic interventions, namely individual focus, psychiatric or other symptoms and rigidity of the system. Equally reasons for moving down the hierarchy in later stages of therapy would be a lessening of the individual focus, a greater acceptance of relationship difficulties and a greater flexibility and preparedness to work together either on communication difficulties or reciprocal changes.

3.4.11 When to select the inducement of arguments from the ALI hierarchy
(extended in Chapter 8: structural therapy)

This approach can seem rather strange to some couples, in that they come to therapy to improve their interaction and are effectively asked to argue with each other as a part of therapy. This is a good example of the way in which, at the upper levels of the behavioural-systems approach, the therapist, in trying to help the couple, may have to pursue goals which are some way from those which the couple say they want to deal with. (Therapists may also have some difficulties with this intervention: see Chapter 12 for advice on how to deal with the problem in trainees.)

The kinds of problem for which this approach is suitable are those in which one partner in a couple is unassertive while the other, at least on the surface, is competent and confident. As a rule, the unassertive partner presents a symptom, which is not a major psychiatric disorder, but rather one of minor depressive reaction, anxiety or sexual dysfunction. It is unusual for the other partner to present a symptom, but an understandable frustration is often seen.

If the unassertive partner is not symptomatic as such, they may be behaving in a passive and perhaps manipulative way in the relationship. Sulky silences and unspoken resentments are not uncommon in this type of relationship, the competent partner apparently doing their best to smooth things over and reduce embarrassment, while the other partner finds it hard to explain what the trouble is.

As mentioned above, one of the common symptoms in these couples is sexual dysfunction (see Chapter 11) and a frequent type of dysfunction is loss of sexual interest on the part of the unassertive partner (see Sections 8.1 and 11.4.3).

3.4.12 When to select timetables and strategic tasks from the ALI hierarchy
(extended in Chapter 9: messages, formulations, tasks and timetables)

The strategic approach is one which we often use at the end of the first session. As already suggested, this may be partly because we work in a psychiatric hospital in which many of our referrals come from other units in the hospital, and those who do not have been selected by their general practitioner for referral to a marital therapy clinic at a psychiatric hospital. As mentioned in the introduction to this section, the more psychiatric symptoms are present, the higher we need to ascend the hierarchy to find a suitable intervention.

The couples who need strategic interventions, and seem to do well as a result of using them, have a fairly high level of symptoms and individual focus. Such symptoms include the less serious (i.e. non-psychotic) cases of morbid jealousy, really intractable arguments, more severe cases of depression and anxiety and some cases of sexual refusal (particularly when the woman is the reluctant partner).

Many other problems, too, can be treated this way (see Chapter 9 for more details of the therapy), and the only prerequisite seems to be either some small task which can be set as homework (for example finding time to 'do nothing together', see Section 9.8.2.6) or a piece of repetitive symptomatic behaviour which can be prescribed on a timetabled basis (see timetables for jealousy, Section 10.4).

It would probably be quite difficult to carry out a strategic task on couples with a declared relationship problem because of the difficulty of finding a suitable piece of repetitive symptomatic behaviour to use in the timetabled task. In any case, as we have already discussed, reciprocity negotiation is quite successful on these more basic problems, and the strategic approach is only necessary for those for whom reciprocity negotiation and communication training has been ineffective (that is those who for the moment show rigidity in the system). Several good examples of cases suitable for this approach are reported in Chapter 10, in particular the two cases of jealousy (Sections 10.3 to 10.6).

If we usually opt for a strategic task at the first session of therapy we often move to another form of intervention at later stages of therapy. In some cases we will move down the ALI hierarchy in the later sessions, as the couple become more flexible, and use either arguments or behavioural interventions. In others, particularly those who seem not to be

responding to tasks, we will move up the hierarchy to paradox or split-
team messages, in the hope that this will unlock the system sufficiently
to allow us to use techniques lower in the ALI hierarchy later.

3.4.13 When to select paradoxical injunctions from the ALI
      hierarchy
(extended in Sections 9.12 to 9.17)

Quite frequently we encounter cases in which there appears to be no
chance of improvement with the types of approaches above. We recognise this either because they have been unable to carry out the homework exercises or they have done them and there is no noticeable
improvement in their interaction. Alternatively, it might become clear
after the initial session that the problem presented to us is so intractable
that no simple homework tasks will move it. In addition, problems
of this severity usually have the characteristics mentioned above (in
Section 3.4.1), namely a strong individual focus or an emphasis on psychiatric symptomatology.

Whether we reach this consensus by the failure of the approaches
(Section 10.5) or by our first session assessment (Section 10.4), these
cases are the ones for whom we usually choose to work paradoxically.
We do not make this choice lightly because, like Perrotta (1986) in the
field of family therapy, we feel that paradox is a technique of last resort
and like to use it as sparingly as possible. Our objections are partly that,
more than the other systemic approaches above, it diverges a long way
from the couple's own stated goals. It also leaves it more obscure as
to what an improvement is: should the couple be considered to have
responded well to the paradox if they obey it literally and increase their
symptomatic behaviour, or if they reject it and become more normal
in their interaction? Lastly a paradox can put the therapist in a false
position to the couple, in that s/he has to take an opposite attitude to
their problem from what they would expect, and if the paradox follows
other forms of therapy, an opposite attitude from that which s/he has
taken before.

Having said this however, there are some couples for whom the paradox is probably the only effective approach, and the only alternatives to
its use are to continue with ineffective therapy or discharge the couple
(see Section 9.12.2). The problems which are most likely to need paradoxical therapy are couples in which one partner is quite severely
depressed, couples with one partner markedly jealous (although we
would prefer to use timetables or other tasks first in such cases) and
couples in which one partner is suffering severe neurotic symptoms
such as phobias, panic attacks or obsessional neurosis. Apart from
psychiatric difficulties, other problems needing paradox are those where
there seems to be a rigid holding on to any unhelpful attitude. In one
couple, for example, it seemed impossible to stop them bringing other
family members into their discussion, and after one session in which the

therapist tried unsuccessfully to get them to talk about themselves, she gave them the instruction to practise at home talking about everyone but themselves.

Sometimes when a couple has been given a paradox the therapist will continue working paradoxically the next time they are seen, and if they have rejected the paradox they will be cautioned not to change too quickly. Alternatively, the therapist may move in the next session to work in a different way, for example giving timetabled tasks, or even working through negotiation and thus rapidly moving down the hierarchy to a lower level. The decision will rest, as always, with the therapist's (or the team's) assessment of the couple's flexibility at the time.

3.4.14 When to help the couple to adjust to the symptom

Up to this point we have been making the assumption that the symptoms that people have can be modified by couple therapy. These are the symptoms which might be seen as arising from the sick role, and as such may be considered as optional or under the control of the system or the individuals in it. There are, however, some conditions, including the major psychoses and organic psychiatric conditions, as well as much physical illness, which appear to have a course unaffected by most of the relationship factors we have been referring to (see Section 7.4). Here, when doing couple therapy, it is as if there is an immovable block around which we are obliged to work, and which will remain despite all our efforts.

It has been shown by Leff *et al.* (1983) and by other workers such as Falloon and Goldstein that in schizophrenia, family and marital factors can play a part in affecting the outcome. If families can take a low-key attitude to the psychotic member, showing low expressed emotion and not being critical or domineering, the likelihood of relapse and the need for readmission to hospital is less. This may seem to be a rather modest goal, but if it can lead to a better quality of life for a psychotic patient and his or her family, it is worth while pursuing. It is, in its way, no more modest than the goals outlined in Chapter 2, in which we pointed out that adjustment to each other in a relationship can be one of the main goals of couple therapy.

Faced with a schizophrenic or manic-depressive patient in our marital clinic, we would first of all respect the treatment being given for the psychotic condition. In the approaches of Leff and Falloon, much emphasis is placed on the importance of medication for the psychosis, and on educating the relatives in the nature and progress of the illness. Having said that, however, we would seek for any problems of interaction which the couple are experiencing in addition to the illness in one partner. These would be tackled in their own right, by whatever approach seemed to be most appropriate (see Example 9D). Problems recognised as those of the relationship would be dealt with by reciprocity negotiation, for example, and we might certainly ask the couple to carry out various timetabled tasks if this was felt to be useful. Induced arguments, however, which would be very appropriate in other sorts of couple, might be avoided in couples with a psychotic partner because it would be feared that the criticism involved in the arguments might prove too much for the psychotic member and lead to a relapse. However, discussions focussed on developing simple and straightforward problem-solving skills can be encouraged. Once again we should re-iterate that we do not claim to treat the psychiatric illness as such by this kind of approach, but would hope to delay relapse and improve the relationship.

We have in fact treated a number of such couples in the clinic, and the outcome for their relationship problems has been certainly no worse than that for other types of couple. Whether the problem has been a psychiatric or a physical illness, it seems perfectly possible to carry out good couple therapy with them.

3.4.15 When to cease treatment or to use other therapies

Sometimes we are faced with a couple who, despite our best efforts, do not seem to be making any progress in therapy, and it is then important to assess whether to cease treatment or refer to another agency.

One older couple had hoped to find an explanation for the husband's fascination with younger women, and his tendency to fantasise about relationships with them, which deeply upset his wife. They made no progress in couple therapy, and were told that therapy was not helping them and that they would do better without therapy. They seemed relieved that they did not have to do any further work on this question and happily left therapy. Others choose to end their long-term relationship and hence also leave therapy, perhaps having used therapy to help make the decision to end their relationship (see Section 10.16).

Others may continue to see the individual as the ill or symptomatic person and seek individual treatment, or we may ourselves consider the symptom to be too acute for couple therapy and refer to individual treatment.

Whatever the circumstances, if treatment after a number of sessions without progress does not seem to be having any significant impact it is necessary to assess the situation and, where no change has occurred, either end treatment admitting that therapy has failed or refer on to another agency (see Section 4.8).

3.5 *Summary*

In this chapter we have introduced our readers to two levels of decision making in couple therapy. The more fundamental one is when to offer couple therapy as opposed to other forms of treatment; the more detailed one is what type of therapeutic techniques to use within our hierarchy of alternative levels of intervention within behavioural-systems couple therapy. We are trying in this way to help therapists to become orientated and therefore more confident within the somewhat confusing variety of presenting problems and alternative treatments within couple therapy.

This way of choosing different therapeutic methods for different problems, which might be termed a 'horses for courses' approach, is particularly suitable for short-term focussed therapy. In particular, it indicates to the therapist when it is appropriate to change the therapeutic style from behavioural approaches (for problems of communication or negotiation) to more systemic approaches (for individually focussed or more intractable problems) and vice versa. Equally, it suggests how to judge when it may be necessary to cease therapy or to refer on to alternative forms of treatment. The therapist with a repertoire of skills can be more flexible, and using the ALI hierarchy of behavioural and systems interventions can change gear when necessary to overcome a more resistant problem.

The remaining chapters, especially Chapters 5 to 10, make continual use of this model and present in greater detail the component parts of the behavioural-systems approach.

Chapter 4

The process and structure of therapy: beginnings and endings

4.1 Source of referral and expectations

Many agencies and clinics providing marital counselling and marital therapy may see couples or individuals who are self-referred, but at the Maudsley Hospital Marital Therapy Clinic, in the majority of cases, the first contact is by a letter from another agency. In most cases the letter comes from the general practitioner (61%) but we also receive referrals from other psychiatrists (15%), from social services (15%) and from probation officers (4%). About 5% are self-referred.

The source of referral affects the prognosis. We found that those couples who came via their general practitioner did significantly better in therapy than those sent to us by hospital psychiatrists (Crowe 1978). The reasons for this were not explored in detail, but could have been connected with the process of labelling problems as psychiatric which might make the couple referred by a psychiatrist more resistant to our reframing of the problem as a relationship issue. These couples might therefore be less likely to respond to therapy. This question of expectation seems to us to be very important in assessing the likely response to therapy and the overall strategy to be used (see Chapter 3). Briefly, the more a couple are wedded to the idea that one partner is psychiatrically ill, addicted or delinquent and that this is the only real problem they have, the more indirect and subtle the therapy must be and the greater the ingenuity required by the therapist to carry out successful conjoint treatment. On the other hand, the couples who present with a stated problem of the relationship are likely to respond better to a more direct therapeutic approach such as working on negotiation or communication skills.

4.2 The process of engagement

4.2.1 The referral letter

This can vary from two lines of the 'please see and treat' variety to detailed descriptions of the problem in its various aspects. The letter tells us a good deal about the kind of discussion that has gone on between the referrer and the couple (or quite often the partner who has consulted him or her). Some of the more detailed letters contain information about previous medical approaches to the problem and very little about the relationship, while others go into great detail about the couple's interaction and even about attempts by the referrer to carry out counselling. We welcome this last type of letter because the referrer has obviously prepared the couple for the idea of conjoint therapy, and they are likely to be more receptive to it. On the other hand, those who come with a brief or a heavily medical letter may not even realise that the referrer thinks there is a relationship problem, and may be quite surprised to receive our explanatory letter (see Appendix).

One ominous sign in a referral letter (see Example 9A) is when the writer goes into great detail medically or biographically about one partner and not the other. This probably indicates a large amount of therapeutic effort directed at the labelled partner and a corresponding difficulty for the therapist in trying to focus on the relationship rather than the individual.

4.2.2 Biographical history sheets

We prefer not to spend too long in the first session of therapy taking a biographical history from each partner, as this reduces the momentum of the session and inhibits the therapist from focussing on the presenting problem. On receiving the referral letter, therefore, the clinic secretary sends out to the couple one history sheet for each partner for them to record details of their families of origin, previous medical and psychiatric health, present and/or previous marriages and children and current state of mind (see Appendix).

When we receive these sheets back from the couple, they are then sent their appointment. The information on the sheets is invaluable, not only in saving time in the first session, but in giving a more systematic life history for each partner than most therapists could obtain in a conjoint session. Often the therapist looks through the completed sheets with the team just before seeing the couple, and can develop hypotheses from them which assist the process of therapy.

The sending of sheets to both partners also helps to emphasise our view that the problem can be most fruitfully tackled by the couple working on changes in their interaction rather than taking a medical approach to one partner alone.

If the referrer has concentrated on the individual aspects of the problem, then receiving a letter requesting biographical history from both partners can help the couple to begin to think about their relationship, and thus perhaps begin the process of reframing the problem in those terms.

We are not, however, uniformly successful with the history sheets. Sometimes neither partner fills them in and in this case we usually go ahead with the therapy, but with the assumption that the non-completion of the history sheets may predict a somewhat lower level of co-operation with therapy. Sometimes only the referred patient fills them in, and again we usually go ahead. In both these cases we are then forced to obtain some historical details from one or both partners in the first session, which slows it down and causes an unfortunate individual focus at the beginning of therapy.

4.2.3 Explanatory letter

In order to prepare the couple for the possibly intimidating setting of the clinic, the secretary sends out an explanatory letter at the same time as the history sheets. This describes the setting, including the one-way screen, the team of colleagues observing the therapy, the duration and frequency of sessions and the possibility that some sessions may be recorded on videotape. (See Appendix for example of letter.)

There are obviously two views on the desirability of this letter. It may deter some couples from coming for therapy, but for those who do come it can diminish the surprise they may experience when faced with the rather unusual setting. We have found that this surprise can sometimes interfere with the therapy and reduce the therapist to a defensive attitude in the first session, which again reduces the therapeutic value of the session. On balance, therefore, the letter seems to have more of a positive than a negative effect.

4.3   Preparing for the case

4.3.1   Forming hypotheses

In our setting we have a seminar before seeing the new case, and this often takes the form of a team discussion about the case to be seen. It is important to go into the first session with an idea of what to look for, otherwise the session can be very unfocussed and amount to no more than a sympathetic but casual conversation with the couple.

Although the behavioural-systems approach involves two components, the simpler and more fundamental behavioural approach and the more complicated systemic approach, we do in fact work mostly in a combination of the two. We will often begin to work with a couple behaviourally, but at the same time be thinking in systemic terms from the outset and not just when the going becomes difficult. It therefore seems appropriate to begin our work on a case by developing hypotheses about the origins of their problem even when we may start the actual therapy by using behavioural negotiation.

There are many ways of attempting to understand a couple's problems, from the simplest, most common-sense approach to more speculative systems or psychodynamic formulations. The main trap to be avoided, whichever way is chosen, is that of excessive reliance on one's own hypotheses, and the belief which some family and dynamic therapists appear to hold that a hypothesis about a family functioning can in any way be the 'true' explanation of the symptom. Our position is that many hypothetical ideas which emerge in discussion or in therapy are interesting and can lead to creative interventions. However, such hypothetical ideas can never be confirmed (as, for example, suggested by Selvini Palazzoli *et al.* 1978) but will always remain hypothetical and at best useful hunches as to the direction which therapy might take.

Some therapists are reluctant to allow themselves to be sufficiently flexible to consider hypotheses from a variety of theoretical viewpoints because of this tendency to see truth as belonging within discrete theories. Anxieties arising from this conflict in the therapist can also slow down the momentum of therapy and need to be discussed in the supervision break (or with the supervisor if working alone) (see also Chapter 9). It is often helpful for the therapist to bear in mind the need for the therapy to be as creative, flexible and innovative as possible to help change some of the very rigidly stuck clients who come to the clinic.

4.3.1.1 *Hypotheses relating to the family life cycle and life events*
(see also Sections 1.6 and 7.4.2)

Some of the common factors which we tend to find in the couples we see, and which form the basis of our hypotheses, are to do with the family life cycle and family life events. As already stated, we believe that difficulties in negotiating the various life stages or adjusting to life events are often crucial elements contributing to the couple's present problems. It is, for instance, not unusual for couples to come for therapy either when they have very young children or when their children are in their teens, and the strains imposed on both parents at such times can be easily understood. Similarly the 'empty nest', when the children are distancing themselves from the parents either by leaving home or by becoming socially independent, puts a different kind of strain on the marriage.

Other events in life can precipitate relationship problems. Bereavement of either partner can lead to an increased dependence on the part of the bereaved partner, which may be rejected by the other. Change in work circumstances, including loss of job, can also put strains on both partners. Other possible life cycle factors which may need to be taken into account include the similarities between the present situation and previous experiences each partner has had, either in earlier relationships or in their family of origin. For example, if a couple have been married for five years and the husband's first marriage broke up after five years, this could be one of the factors undermining the security of the present relationship. Again, if in the wife's family the mother forced the father to leave when she herself was nine years old, and her own daughter is now nine, this may be adding to the strains she feels in the marriage now.

4.3.1.2 Hypotheses relating to the function of the symptom
(see also 7.3.5 and 8.4.2)
Another way of looking at a couple's problem is to ask what the possible advantage or function of the symptom might be. For example, one partner's depression may be drawing attention away from his dissatisfaction with the marriage and thus protecting the stability of the family. In another case the irresponsible behaviour of one partner may be giving the other a chance to have someone to protect, and thus enriching his or her life. In a third case the self absorption and withdrawal of one partner may be creating a safe distance between them and preventing the hypothesised risk of too much intimacy (Byng-Hall 1980).

It should be reiterated that these hypotheses are not thought of in any way as true explanations for couples' problems; it is simply that they provide a framework for thinking about them, and extend the range of perspectives from which the team, and eventually the couple, can look at the problems (see Chapter 7).

4.3.1.3 Alternative hypotheses
(see also Sections 10.3, 10.7 and 10.10)
In a team which contains members of different theoretical orientations, the variety of explanations can add to the richness of discussion, and thus to the number of different perspectives available for understanding the system. In such a team the contributions to the discussion of the case referred to above might include the following:

MARY (*analytically orientated*)
It seems to me that she has been looking for a father figure in Tom and perhaps her sexual difficulties are because she is still subconsciously thinking about him as her father.

SUSAN (*behaviourally orientated*)
Tom needs to be helped to approach her more caringly, and Philippa needs to be helped to be more assertive.

JANET (*systemically orientated*)
Perhaps Philippa's symptom of sexual reluctance is helping Tom to avoid worrying about his inability to satisfy a really demanding woman.

4.3.2 Planning behavioural interventions

Such discussions, however, form only one aspect of the team's discussion of the case. The major part of the pre-therapy session is taken up with helping the therapist to handle the first interview, and in particular to focus on the problem as presented from a behavioural angle. This means helping to observe the couple's communication and their ability to negotiate and find ways of altering their interaction in the session and subsequently at home (see Chapters 5 and 6). The hypotheses are retained, but in many cases it is the behavioural work which occupies the first session.

This movement backwards and forwards between behavioural and systemic work is an integral part of the approach, and although it may be difficult for new therapists to grasp, it finally gives them a firm foundation for flexible responses within the session.

Sometimes the discussions at this stage become quite lively, and individual team members may find themselves siding with one or other of the partners. This can lead to useful understanding for the therapist as he or she prepares to try and empathise with both partners.

4.3.3 General plan of approach in the interview

The key points for the therapist to bear in mind in the first interview are:

(1) joining with each partner,
(2) remaining in control,
(3) keeping the momentum going, and
(4) maximising the opportunities for the couple to change their interaction.

The interview is necessarily a complicated and unpredictable sequence of interactions, and considerable experience and/or assistance from the observation team may be needed to keep the therapist and the therapy on course. When working alone, or in a different setting, the therapist will need to use his/her supervision sessions, a silent observer, or tape or video recordings of sessions to assist with this process.

It is important for the therapist to 'touch down' with each partner at the beginning of therapy (point (1) above and Section 4.6.2), but this only needs to take a brief time, and then the relationship work can begin.

The therapist will also have to show a considerable degree of flexibility in order to combine the three key elements of therapy (points (2), (3) and (4) above), and at the same time to show respect for the partners as individuals, for their problems in the relationship and for their wishes in relation to each other. In addition it is vital for the therapist to remember the general rules of therapy and counselling, which include non-possessive warmth, empathy and genuineness, as without these it may be impossible to maintain the co-operation of the couple.

4.3.4 A light touch and a sense of humour

Although couples may bring into therapy many difficulties, often accompanied by great pain and distress, experience teaches us that a light touch and a sense of humour can frequently soften a difficult session and help couples engage more quickly with the therapist.

It is sometimes about those topics which couples are most hesitant to speak that a sense of humour can be helpful. For example, when a couple are somewhat embarrassed to describe an unusually emotional argument they have had, a therapist may quietly enquire with a grin 'so you had something of a screaming match?' and find the couple suddenly amused at their own behaviour, admitting that they did indeed shout and scream at each other. They may then describe the argument with enthusiasm and gain pleasure in the telling of their emotional outburst. An alternative reaction might be for the couple to relax and say, 'no it didn't get that bad, but we did feel like hitting each other'.

It is as though the appropriate use of humour can cut through embarrassment and allow a greater degree of freedom for the couple to express their feelings or describe experiences. It is a difficult skill to describe and it is clear that some therapists will feel more comfortable than others in introducing humour or lightness into the session. Of course the therapist must judge the sensitivities and metaphor with which the couple are most familiar. One middle-aged couple were extremely agitated and upset that the wife had helped the husband to escape by car from an irate shop assistant who was correctly accusing him of shop-lifting. It was only when the therapist suggested that they had been rather like Bonnie and Clyde that they relaxed and animatedly described the incident as though they were indeed bank robbers in a film.

A light touch may be particularly required when the therapist is being persistent in helping the couple to stick with a topic or when encouraging one partner to be more assertive, but as a general rule there is no need to be heavy handed. A gentle but firm approach from the therapist coupled with a sense of humour may be one of the less recognised but more useful resources available to therapists.

4.3.5 Taking each other seriously

Paradoxically, although we have just suggested that humour is a useful skill for a therapist, we often find that couples may use humour destructively by joking or teasing in a way which shows that they are not taking each other seriously. One of our general approaches throughout therapy is to help the couple learn to listen to and take each other seriously at many different levels. By doing so couples learn that they are indeed separate individuals who may each respond quite differently to similar circumstances. Many couples make assumptions that they understand the other partner without ever checking this out.

A general aim is then to help couples notice the impact of different experiences on their partner and to be attentive to this and not to diminish or undermine the partner's experience. Teasing and joking as well as simply not noticing can all amount to ways of discounting the other person (see Penny and Paul, Example 9A, and Nelson and Abigail, Example 10A). It is sometimes quite difficult for a therapist to switch from the light touch suggested in Section 4.3.4 to getting the couple to take each other seriously as in this section, but it is worth while acquiring the skill, not only because it helps to run a good session but also because the therapist can thereby model flexibility for the couple.

4.4 The tasks of the first interview and of the whole course of therapy

The first interview is not simply a time for the therapist and couple to become acquainted, but is seen by us as a time in which to initiate the process of change. In doing so we need to keep the momentum going, and it is often useful to find some small area of conflict or of other sorts of problem in which the couple can have the experience of altering their interaction, and so begin the process of change from the beginning.

The following sections (4.4.1 to 4.6.12) refer primarily to the first interview, but in fact most of what is said is relevant to the whole of therapy, and should be understood in that way.

4.4.1 Focus on the interaction

One of the main difficulties a therapist will face at the beginning of therapy is to keep the focus on the interaction. Sometimes the problem is presented by both partners, or at least by the spokesperson, as being only in one partner, for example excessive drinking, violent behaviour or depression. At other times each partner will be blaming the other exclusively in an adversarial fashion, and addressing the therapist as if he or she were a judge. There may be some validity in this way of presenting the problem, and one would be foolish and disrespectful to deny it altogether. However, changing attitudes and behaviour is almost always easier if there is a focus on the interaction, and whatever the cause of the difficulties, the increased flexibility of the interactional focus will facilitate change.

It is the balance between accepting the couple's point of view of the problem as individual and encouraging an interactional view of how to overcome the problem that is the key to the success of the first interview. If the therapist moves too fast in the direction of an interactional view s/he may lose the couple's co-operation and they may drop out; if s/he accepts their view exclusively s/he will also accept the intractable nature of the problem which their seeking therapy implies, and no improvement is likely to occur. Minuchin (1974) has termed these two tactics 'accommodation' (taking the couple's viewpoint) and 'restructuring' (altering the interaction in the session) and he too advocates a balance between the two, especially in the first interview. The balance which is reached should usually shift during the first interview from almost complete accommodation at the beginning to fairly strong efforts at restructuring towards the end. (See Section 12.8 for further training in focussing on the interaction.)

4.4.2 Restructuring the relationship

The means used to restructure the relationship in the interview will vary considerably according to the type of problem presented, the degree of openness and the degree of flexibility of which the couple is capable. The details of the kind of interventions used will be discussed in Chapters 5 to 10, and they may involve attempts to persuade the couple to negotiate, attempts to alter their communication by detailed instructions, attempts to induce arguments or the use of circular questioning.

In many of these restructuring manoeuvres, it will be necessary for the therapist to become decentred, that is to insist that the partners talk directly to each other without addressing the therapist. For inexperienced therapists this is a very difficult thing to do and a good deal of courage is needed to step out of the expected role as an active participant and to insist on being left out of the discussion. (See Section 6.4.1 for a fuller discussion of decentring).

4.4.3 Observation

Whether participating or decentred, the therapist needs to be highly attuned to the verbal and non-verbal aspects of the couple's communication. The use of words can be very revealing: phrases like 'It's as if he's one of the children' or 'She can't help her temper outbursts' lead one to be alert to the likelihood that the speaker feels the other partner to be not fully responsible for him/herself. Similarly, when one partner says 'I just have to tread carefully when she's like this' or 'I can't trust him even with the house-keeping money' the therapist should be looking for opportunities to emphasise the shared responsibilities and to help the spokesman to appreciate some of the ways in which the 'irresponsible' partner is, in fact, pulling his or her weight.

Non-verbal cues may be important. In one couple the 'responsible' wife was sitting upright on the edge of her chair and complaining about the husband's laziness, while he was sitting back and sinking lower and lower in his chair. When the therapist brought him out and established that he had kept the family in regular contact with their church and that he took pride in this, he began to sit more upright and the wife began to relax for the first time.

Tone of voice can be important, too, as with the husband who reported how he habitually withdrew from discussions with his wife when she 'increased the decibels'. It took considerable efforts on the therapist's part to persuade him to remain in the room and continue the discussion in spite of the crescendo. Other aspects of gesture can be important in this observational exercise in therapy. A partner who sits defensively with folded arms, or a partner who puts his hands behind his head (usually interpreted as an aggressive gesture) can tell the therapist and observers a good deal about habitual attitudes and interactions.

In a therapeutic method such as this, in which the therapist takes a directive role, another aspect to observe carefully is the response of the couple to any intervention. This may tell the therapist and the observation team a good deal about the couple and their potential for flexibility, and may help to decide the next move, especially what kind of task to prescribe at the end of the session.

(See also Section 6.4.2.1 for further discussion of non-verbal communication.)

4.4.4 Eliciting and using information

The use of the couple's description of the problem is an important consideration for the therapist. Again a balance needs to be created between taking the information at its face value (accommodating) and using it in terms of behavioural or systems principles (reframing).

A process of active listening should be going on, the therapist being very selective about what he or she pays attention to, and steering the discussion round to these aspects which will contribute to the conjoint therapy. Thus if one partner wants to spend a long time talking about past traumatic experiences the therapist should pay sufficient attention at first to assure the speaker that he or she has the therapist's attention and empathy, but should soon open out the discussion to include the other partner. This may take several forms:

(1) Asking the other partner if he or she has had similar experiences.
(2) Asking if the other partner knows how the speaker feels.
(3) Asking how the experiences seem to be affecting the relationship now.
(4) Asking questions of either partner which are related, but gradually leading away from the discussion of the past, for instance relating these events to the present relationship.
(5) Getting the couple to discuss the matter together, but making sure that they both contribute.
(6) In extreme cases insisting that discussion of the past is off-limits for the moment.

It is usually necessary to strike a balance between several different considerations in this part of the therapy:

(1) Between each partner's input and interests.
(2) Between respect for the individuals and the need to focus on interaction.
(3) Between exploring how things have been and planning how they might be changed.
(4) Between what happens within the marriage and outside considerations – children, parents, work, schools, friends or neighbours.

The key considerations in drawing the balance between the above factors is the need to keep up the momentum of change without risking antagonising the couple (or one of the two partners) who might then reject therapy and drop out.

4.5 *Difficulties and pitfalls*

For those who are new to this way of working there are many opportunities for things to go wrong. Some of these have already been mentioned above: for example, not being empathic to both partners, trying to change things too quickly or losing momentum. There are, however, some particular ways in which the unwary therapist can be trapped into unproductive interaction with a couple, and many of these derive from what in other settings (e.g. social work, counselling or supportive therapy with individuals) would be good practice. Two examples are set out below.

4.5.1 Spending too much time on history taking

History taking has been for many therapists the essential focal point of their work. It is often difficult, especially in the first session, to avoid a good deal of fact gathering about the partners' individual histories, or at the very least listening empathically to what they wish to say on this subject. We would, however, advocate as far as possible that therapists should avoid history taking in sessions, especially where, as in our setting, some history has already been obtained by postal questionnaire.

In place of history taking the therapist should concentrate on the couple's present relationship and how things have been in the past few weeks.

Example: 4A

THERAPIST
Can you please begin by telling me what the main problems have been in the past week or so?

> BEN
> Well you see five years ago Anna had this affair when she was working at the local pub, and I had absolutely no idea that she was actually seeing this bloke almost every evening after the pub closed and I actually believed her that she was staying extra time at the pub to wash up the glasses . . .

THERAPIST (*interrupting*)
Ben, can you say in what way that has affected how you relate to Anna now, and what you would like to change about that?

> BEN
> Well, I don't trust her any more, after all those months of her lying to me, every time she came home, and saying she was working late . . .

THERAPIST (*interrupting*)
Anna, your husband says that he doesn't trust you now. Is that what you see as the problem in your relationship now?

> ANNA
> No, not really.

the video camera, and sits down with his or her back to the screen. The setting is then introduced in such terms as:

> 'I'd just like to explain the way we work. As you can see this is a one-way screen, and some of my colleagues are sitting on the other side of the screen where they can see and hear us. We find it helps the therapy to have this sort of supervision for the therapist. I'll be going next door for a consultation with them after some time with you, and if they want to contact me during the session they can buzz me on this telephone'.

Usually the couple will have recieved the appointment letter described in Section 4.2.3 which makes this explanation much easier, but it helps to explain the situation anyway as it breaks the ice and helps the therapist to grasp the initiative. A small number of individuals have difficulty with the one-way screen. They can sometimes be reconciled to it by being taken behind the screen to meet the team, and in this way the majority of initially reluctant clients can accept the setting. There are, however, occasional clients who cannot accept observation of their therapy, and reluctantly we have at times had to agree to carry out some or all of the therapy without the advantage of the one-way screen observation.

Apart from the great advantage of live supervision which is lost in these cases, the teaching aspects of therapy are also lost for those observers who are undergoing training.

In many cases we also record the therapeutic sessions on video tape and the same considerations apply here as for one-way-screen observation, although with recording the issues are sharper and the procedure perhaps more threatening. The proportion of clients declining to be recorded is somewhat greater than those who cannot accept team observation and may approach 30%. The same kind of introduction is used as for screen observation, and may go as follows:

> 'We also find it helpful to record sessions of therapy on videotape. This helps me to look back on the session and see what went well and what went badly. It is also helpful to students of this kind of therapy to see how it is done. The recording will be shown only for these purposes and only within the hospital here and the Institute of Psychiatry. We are asking you now to agree to being recorded and at the end we will ask you to sign consent for us to keep the recording.
>
> If you change your minds at the end of the session we can agree to erase the recording.'

Again we have to understand that some couples may not wish to be recorded and we can usually cope with this by simply not turning on the recorder or turning it off if it has already started. As already indicated, therapists who work alone or who have no access, as we have, to a one-way screen and a supervision group, may be helped by using audiotape recorders or a colleague who sits in the session as an observer. In such a case the therapists will need to be imaginative and supportive when helping the clients to accept the situation. We find that being direct and confident usually gains acceptance.

4.6.2 Creating rapport with both partners

Much has been written in family therapy texts (see Minuchin 1974 and Glick and Kessler 1980) about 'touching down' with each family member at the outset of therapy. This is sometimes quite difficult in families with a large number of children and a self-appointed spokesman, but if done successfully it establishes the role of the therapist as being in control, and at the same time makes each member feel part of the therapy and appreciated as an individual. In couple work the task is much easier, in that there are only two partners present, but at times it is still too easy to listen without interrupting while one partner describes the problems and the relationship and the other says nothing.

At this stage in therapy, when the therapeutic alliance is being formed, it is very important to make sure that both partners feel they are each given a hearing, that neither of them feels any hostility towards the therapist and that their problems are understood at an emotional as well as a practical level. The therapist may have to interrupt quite frequently to clarify what has been said, to check whether the second partner agrees with the first partner's view of the situation and at times simply to stop the flow of information from one side and ensure that the other partner contributes. An essential part of the exercise is that the therapist should show empathy with both partners.

Some types of relationship can cause great difficulties with this process. For example, there are some couples who present a kind of courtroom conflict while attempting to describe their problems. The implication is that the therapist is being asked to judge who is right and if s/he empathises with one partner they may both immediately assume that s/he is against the other partner. A very difficult balancing act may then be needed on the part of the therapist to show empathy without appearing to take sides.

Example 4B

JOHN (*to the therapist*)
You see, she always over reacts to these situations. Last Sunday I was quietly getting on with the gardening and she rushed out saying that it was time for me to take Debbie back to boarding school. I just had two rows to finish, so I kept on until I had done them and walked over to the garage. By that time she had got out the car and was in a foul temper, reviving up the engine and swearing at me. Debbie was crying . . .

JANET (*interrupts*)
But this was the fourth time I had reminded you. He never thinks about other people. Debbie would have got into a lot of trouble if she'd been late . . .

JOHN (*interrupts*)
She wouldn't have been late. I had all the time in the world . . .

JANET (*interrupts*)
He always says that. But I know you can't get there in less than half an hour without risking an accident.

This was explicitly shown in the study reported by Crowe (1978) in which the target problems changed more quickly in the first three sessions than the subsequent seven. It is also not uncommon for couples to default from therapy after one or two sessions, so it would be unwise to assume as a therapist that one can make a leisured assessment of the couple before drawing up a therapeutic plan (see also Section 8.5.4).

Probably, however, the main consideration in trying to keep up the momentum is that if changes begin to happen at the beginning of therapy the couple will have become adjusted from the outset to the idea that they can take action to change their behaviour. This should facilitate a greater expectation that change is possible, and result in a more rapid and effective therapeutic experience.

There are many ways in which the behaviour of participants in couple therapy may slow down the momentum and the opportunities for change. These difficulties in therapy and the therapeutic moves necessary to counteract them and keep up the momentum will be dealt with in Chapters 5 to 10, but it would be helpful at this stage simply to name some of the difficulties which can arise. Some of these have already been described under the heading 'Difficulties and pitfalls' in Section 4.5 of this chapter, and it will suffice to list them at this point.

4.6.5 Obstacles to therapeutic momentum

(1) Spending too much time on history.
(2) Listening too long to one partner (who speaks in monologues).
(3) Being too passive, i.e. relying on warmth and empathy and doing nothing else.
(4) Intractable arguments involving repetitive statements and adversarial attitudes.
(5) Looking for solutions in either the medical or the individual dynamics sphere, e.g. focussing on one partner's depression, lying or temper tantrums.

In general, if a therapist finds him/herself having a conversation with the couple which feels like a social one, then he or she should try another tack, because it is almost certain that very little change will result from this form of interaction. As explained in Section 4.5.2, the therapist risks becoming part of the homeostatic process.

Similarly, when the couple are either arguing directly with each other in a repetitive way or are 'triangling in' the therapist as a judge of who is right or who is wrong, then again another tack is required to get over the block to the momentum in the session.

A good session is rather like mining a rich seam of coal: the therapist gets a sense that there is good material being discussed and that continuing on the same track is going to be fruitful. Some examples of good and bad sequences within a session may help to clarify this idea. It doesn't matter whether the couple are negotiating a more rewarding form of exchange (reciprocity negotiation), learning about new patterns of communication (communication training), having an unaccustomed argument (structural therapy) or answering the therapist's circular questions about a recent problem in the relationship (stragetic therapy). In all these cases the therapist can feel confident that change is either occurring there and then or that some appropriate homework task can be framed which will lead to change eventually.

If, however, none of these things is happening, if there is a sense of loss of momentum, a feeling of slowness about the discussion or if the therapist feels stuck or lost, he or she should seek for a way out of the impasse. Here the observation team can often help, both to alert the therapist to the fact that momentum is being lost and to suggest ways of overcoming this. The therapist should trust the team's judgement at this point, because they have a much broader overall view of what is happening and are not inhibited by the anxiety of being face to face with a couple and of failing in their responsibility for helping them.

The therapist may also be hampered by the couple's subtle forms of control of the session, by which he or she can be trapped into inactivity and powerlessness without even realising that it is happening. Such a situation is probably more likely to occur with intelligent, middle-class couples who can speak to the therapist on equal terms in his or her own vernacular, and who can present very plausible reasons why previous attempts to solve the problem have been useless and why the therapist's wish to look at the relationship as the focus for change is mistaken.

The remedies for this state of powerlessness, whether it is brought on by too much history taking, too many monologues, too much listening, too many repetitive arguments or too much individual focus, are spelled out in the following sections. Any of these tactics may be used, and reasons for choosing a particular one will be one or more of the following: the level of problems presented by the couple (the ALI hierarchy as presented in Chapter 3), the advice of the observation team, the intuition of the therapist and a simple judgment of what seems useful at the time.

Some useful ways of speeding up the session are described in Sections 4.6.7 to 4.6.11, for example decentring, interrupting monologues, limiting the duration of comments, bringing out the silent partner, changing the subject to one of practical relevance or asking circular questions. In all these ways the therapist will be able to convert a rather slow, unproductive session into one in which there is at least the promise of change. As a result of some of these interventions the change should occur in the session itself, while from others the message at the end will lead to a task which may produce change in the interval between sessions.

Whichever intervention is used the couple should find the session more meaningful and memorable than if they carry on in the previous

THERAPIST
No, I think we should leave it to him; in any case he could always go to a different off-licence. But what about the whisky already in the house?

HUSBAND
She can lock it up and keep the key.

WIFE
All right.

There are a number of instances here of steering the session towards interaction. At the beginning the therapist asked the couple to talk to each other about the problem, rather than simply relay it to him. This in itself focusses on interaction and shows the therapist in an immediate way how they communicate.

They got into a poor pattern however just before (1) where Terry was planning for Peggy without really consulting her and Peggy was mind-reading that Terry wanted to 'unload' her. The therapist, in asking her to check with him, attempted to overcome the mind-reading and got them to answer each other directly rather than making two separate points in competition.

The therapist both at (1) and (2) made his point without interrupting the husband and wife interaction, by putting the onus on Peggy to ask Terry a question at (1) and getting Terry to answer her question at (2).

The couple were getting off track again just before (3), where they were getting into the pattern of mind-reading and planning for each other, and the therapist had to bring them back to the interactional task. This might have been handled better, for instance in asking the couple to deal with a more specific interactional issue, but in the event they chose a good area, the effects of drinking on his behaviour towards her, and Terry came up with a very constructive solution. Towards the end of the excerpt the therapist took a more organising role in sorting out the details of the compromise to be put into practice. One good feature of this plan is the way in which both partners seemed quite enthusiastic about putting it into effect. It is also noteworthy at this point that the couple are using shorter sentences and more rapid replies than at the beginning. If this doesn't happen with simple decentring it may be necessary for the therapist to insist on it as a technical move, so as to speed up the interaction and help the partners to take notice of each other's ideas and suggestions.

At (4) the wife nearly undermined the compromise by putting the blame on her husband's addiction to alcohol. This is a very individually-orientated account of the problem, and the therapist could have had them argue it out in detail, encouraging the husband to prove that it was only whisky which brought on the prolonged outbursts. However, the momentum of the session was moving towards compromise with the husband's suggestion of giving up whisky, and it seemed better at the time to encourage the compromise rather than challenge the individual focus.

4.6.7 Bringing out a silent partner

Sometimes, especially when depression is present, one partner may sit silently in the session and allow the other to do all the talking. This fits very well with the traditional psychiatric model in which there is a patient and an 'informant', but is not conducive to effective couple therapy. (See Chapter 10 for greater detail of working with couples where one partner is depressed.)

A similar situation can arise when one partner cries for much of the time, leaving the other one to explain what has been happening. This causes great difficulty for the therapist, who does not want to appear critical towards either partner, but who equally does not want to deal exclusively with the partner who is talking. Several approaches can be used, none of which are guaranteed to be effective, but all of which have been effective at least once in practice.

One way to tackle the situation is to ask the competent partner *to encourage the other one to talk* (i.e. *to ask the question in a way that will not be threatening*). This is preferable to the more obvious approaches of the therapist talking to the silent or tearful partner and trying to bring them out; the latter approach might be effective but puts the therapist too much in the individual counsellor position in relation to the disturbed partner and could bias the therapy against conjoint work. The therapist should try to remain in touch with the relationship rather than with either partner individually.

Another useful approach is to seek for the competence of the tearful partner. This could be done by asking the tearful one to bring out some aspect of the competent partner, for example *to help that partner to show feelings that seem to be suppressed and which the tearful partner is so good at showing*. Needless to say, this approach needs a good deal of experience and finesse to be successful, and should not be pursued if it does not seem to produce effects quite quickly.

A more reliable way is to ask *circular questions* (see Section 4.6.11). In this approach the competent partner is being asked about the depressed partner, and the depressed partner about the competent one; people who are silent or tearful are much more likely to answer questions about someone else than about themselves. Such questions should, if possible, not touch on feeling, since feeling questions are less likely to be answered by a depressed partner than factual or behavioural questions, especially at this stage in treatment.

In using circular questions the therapist needs a ready supply of simple questions in reserve so that when one question is answered another can follow before the partners can retreat into their accustomed roles of tearful or silent patient and competent informant.

All these approaches may fail, especially with a silent partner, and a fall-back position, fairly reliable but less satisfactory than the above approaches, is to ask the competent partner to *speak for the other partner*. It is more likely to be successful because the competent partner is likely to comply with the suggestion. It is less satisfactory because it leaves the

to co-operate and find new solutions to problems. The decentred position has since been advocated for communication training (Crowe 1985) as an improvement on the more traditional approach in which the therapist acts as an intermediary or interpreter (Jacobson and Martin, 1976).

The technique is easy to describe but often difficult for trainees to put into practice. The main problem is the tendency for the couple to wish to triangle in the therapist, despite strong efforts by the latter to avoid it.

In order to initiate the process, the therapist should give the couple a task, for example to discuss a disagreement or negotiate an exchange of positive behaviour. It will be rather strange for many couples to talk to each other in front of a third person (even a therapist) and it may be necessary to explain the reasons for asking them to do so. A good introduction might be:

'I feel it would be useful for you to discuss this together without referring to me. This is so that I can get an idea of how you deal with each other directly. It will also help me to see how misunderstandings arise, and will give me some ideas as to how you could clear them up.'

This would then lead to an attempt at problem solving.

Alternatively, in order to help the couple to have an unaccustomed argument:

'You seem to have quite a difference of opinion on this, and I wonder if you could try and explore these differences between yourselves without referring to me.'

Sometimes couples are quite compliant, and indeed with some it is unnecessary to give the suggestion because they already refer to each other directly a good deal of the time. With others, however, there is quite a strong resistance, and if one wants to use the technique a fair degree of pressure may have to be put on them. If there is any doubt about their collaboration, it is a good idea to get up and ask them to stand also while they move their chairs to face each other directly. Even then it can be difficult to stop them turning to the therapist to address him/her, and several reminders may be needed for them to continue to address each other, leaving the therapist decentred.

If either of them asks the therapist a question at this stage it is better not to reply directly. A comment such as

'I don't know, I wonder if you could ask your wife what she feels about it . . .'

or

'Could you check that with your husband first?'

will restore the pattern of the couple talking to each other.

If conversation ceases in this setting, the therapist will have to prompt the couple to continue, unless at this stage he/she chooses to feed back on their communication. Prompts for their continuing might be any of the following:

- Could you explain to your husband how that affects your feelings towards him?
- I don't think she really understands how you feel about it. Could you put it a bit more strongly?
- Could you try to think of a suggestion to put to your wife?
- Could you check whether that's acceptable to her?
- Can you try to help him to talk about his feelings?

The variety of such interventions is almost infinite, but they all have the characteristic of asking the couple to continue addressing each other without including the therapist.

Having achieved a decentred position it is then possible to make use of it to alter the interaction in a favourable direction. The details of this will be described in Chapters 6 and 8, under the headings of communication training and structural intervention strategies. What should be emphasised here is the importance of balancing two aspects of the decentred approach: (a) allowing the couple to generate their own solutions and (b) using the exercise to help them to alter their interaction.

If they are producing constructive suggestions, communicating more positively than usual, having an unaccustomed argument or learning how the other partner feels it may be sensible for the therapist to sit back and allow them to continue. If, however, either the arguments become repetitive, the criticisms are destructive, one partner is talking at length while the other remains passive or there seems to be no empathy or understanding, the therapist should intervene to put them back on track without losing the decentred position (see above).

We are not advocating the decentred approach as the remedy for all 'stuck' situations in couple therapy. Indeed, much can be achieved in more conventional ways by the therapist who acts as a switchboard operator between the partners, or reacts purely empathically to both. Circular questioning (see Section 4.6.11) can be a very useful approach, even where decentring does not produce an increase in flexibility. However, decentring can be of great help in many cases, especially when a session is proving rather slow or unproductive, or when one wishes to encourage negotiation, communication or argument. For a more detailed discussion of the implications of decentring see Section 6.4.1.

4.6.10 Open communication of feelings and mutual empathy

Communication is a word which tends to be over-used by both therapists and clients. 'We have a problem of communication' can mean many things, from the couple who live in complete silence to the couple who talk a lot but have many misunderstandings or mis-read each other's feelings. The techniques of communication training will be dealt with in

same direction' after circular questioning. It may also reflect some of the non-verbal features discussed by Schaap, and those described in the Munich Marital Study as the 'emotionally-affective quality of the relationship' (see Section 1.2.2); perhaps too this begins to parallel the concept described as 'shared mental state' (Winnicott 1965, 1971).

The expression of feelings and the achievement of mutual empathy is a central issue in communication training, which is dealt with in more detail in Chapter 6. At this point we hope to have alerted the reader to the importance of the area, and to have pointed out some of the techniques for exploring and changing the expression and understanding of feelings.

4.6.11 Circular questioning

In the first interview it may be necessary to resort to circular questioning. This is a particular technique developed by the Milan group (Selvini *et al.* 1980) as part of their systemic approach to family therapy. It is not clear which aspect of the questioning gave rise to the epithet 'circular' (see Chapter 9 for a fuller discussion) but the three main circular features are (a) asking questions of each family member in turn, (b) asking one person about other people rather than him/herself and (c) implying a circular rather than a linear causality in the content of the questions.

Questions should be simple, closed-ended and, if possible, address a difference in a relationship or define a relationship more specifically. They should ideally be based on exploration of a particular hypothesis about the family's functioning, although it is in fact possible to carry on quite extensive circular questioning without a pre-discussed hypothesis.

This use of circular questioning in relation to the current family interaction we find very useful, although we recognise that in its original use by the Milan group it had a wider application, including the gathering of information about the extended family and its history.

It is an approach which, if followed rigorously, puts the therapist firmly in control of the session, since each response should be followed by another closed-ended question from the therapist exploring a further aspect of the interaction. The other advantages of the technique as we use it are its emphasis on looking at the relationship rather than at an individual's problems and its ability to involve the couple's attention on the content of the questioning so that they are both psychologically 'facing in the same direction'. This in turn prepares them to receive fairly uncritically whatever message or task is given to them at the end of the session.

In practice, most therapists who adopt the circular questioning approach are not as rigorous as the Milan group, and may simply ask a few circular questions to unstick the discussion in the course of a more conventional session.

Example 4D

THERAPIST
I'd like to ask a bit more about that incident last week. Joy, what was the first thing that Alan did when he came in?

JOY
He came through the door with a frown on his face and accused me of messing up the arrangements for the theatre trip.

(1) THERAPIST
Alan, how did Joy respond? Was she apologetic or defensive?

ALAN
No, very defensive. She said it was my fault.

THERAPIST
Joy, what did Alan say when you said it was his fault?

JOY
He exploded and said I was always blaming him.

THERAPIST
Alan, how did Joy take that? Was she continuing to blame you?

(2) ALAN
Yes, it's typical of her. If she's in the wrong she swings the blame on to someone else.

THERAPIST
I really want to know more about this incident. How did Alan follow up his complaint about you blaming him?

JOY
Well, he went out of the room and began to sulk. He didn't speak to me until we were sitting down to the meal.

(3) THERAPIST
Alan, how does Joy respond when you go silent?

ALAN
Well, she usually goes silent too, but she sometimes tries to make peace by smiling or doing something nice for me.

THERAPIST
Joy, who's the first to start speaking again when this happens, you or Alan?

JOY
Usually me. I can't take the aggravation for long.

THERAPIST
Alan, do you agree with that?

ALAN
No, I think we both give a little. I don't hold grudges for long.

In this excerpt the couple were quite co-operative with the technique, although at **(2)**. Alan was giving a more general answer than the

can be given in that knowledge and not be subject to revision because of a changed timescale.

The message itself may be of many different types, ranging from a straightforward behavioural task through various strategic tasks or time-tables to a 'no change' message or a split-team message. Sometimes there may be no task at all, but simply an expression of empathy with the feelings of both partners and the difficulty of achieving change. Sometimes, rather than giving a task, the therapist will return after the break to continue an exercise in communication in the session and then simply give an appointment at the end. For further examples of the various types of message which may be given see Sections 9.2 to 9.5.

In giving any kind of message it is best to ensure that it is the last thing to be done in the session. If the task is behavioural, some negotiation is often needed to finalise the arrangements, so it is better to do the necessary negotiation and repeat the final version of the task at the end. If the message is strategic, and especially if it is paradoxical or split, it is better not to allow any reply or comment after the task is given, but in the event of questions to say something like:

'Perhaps we can discuss that next time; I'm afraid we have to finish now.'

In many cases it is helpful to write a letter to the couple immediately after the session, to include the message, with the positive connotations of their own efforts, the task and the reasons for carrying it out (including alternative reasons in the case of a split message). This is especially helpful in strategic and paradoxical messages, while in the case of behavioural tasks the couple may prefer to make their own notes at the end of the session (Section 9.5.3).

4.7 Working alone

The ways of working summarised here, including team discussions, tasks and messages, apply of course to those settings where live supervision is available. Where the therapist is working alone or where only post-session supervision is available the basic process, including the giving of tasks and messages, will be very similar, but without the benefit of the team's extra capacity for observation and hypothesising. When working alone it is a good idea to experiment with a break in the session, in order to formulate a message. To make this as simple as possible for all concerned the therapist can explain to the couple at the beginning of the session that s/he will be taking a break after perhaps 30–35 minutes, and then returning to make any suggestions which seem useful regarding their relationship. This will allow the therapist to go out of the room to think about the case before framing the task to be given. For those therapists who are wedded to the 50 minute session, this will no doubt seem somewhat unusual. Our experience is that the couple seem reassured when the therapist takes time to consider their relationship seriously, and are not in the slightest put off by the therapist leaving and returning with a well considered message. For the inexperienced worker this break, in order to formulate 'what next', may take a little longer than usual; however, with experience the total session does not need to exceed 50 minutes. The benefits are likely to be that the message has been well considered. Therapists are not miracle workers and should be confident enough to share with clients that they need time to think about each particular couple.

Where post-session supervision is available, it is useful to have the session recorded on audiotape or videotape in order to have a more accurate record of it to discuss with the supervisor. It is perhaps more essential if the therapist is working entirely alone.

Working as we do, with the assistance of an observation team, we are constantly reminded just how involved the therapist becomes in the couple's perception of their own difficulties, no matter how experienced, and consequently just how difficult it is to be impartial. We do therefore recommend that wherever possible therapists find ways of monitoring their interventions and of getting support and supervision from colleagues. (We make some suggestions in Chapter 12 as to how this might be achieved.)

4.8 Ending therapy

The question of when and how to end a series of therapy sessions is not always an easy one to answer. Behavioural-systems couple therapy aims to be short-term, perhaps lasting for up to ten sessions over a period of six months or so. It also has, like many other forms of psychotherapy, the goal of helping the clients to be more independent and manage without further therapeutic input in the future. The difficulty is for the participants, whether couple, therapist or supervising team, to know when is the best moment to stop therapy.

We have found by experience that there is a kind of 'window of opportunity' in this kind of therapy of about ten sessions, and if changes occur it is most likely that they will occur within that window. Unlike those who advocate some longer-term therapies, we believe that worthwhile changes can and do occur in this shorter timescale, and that such changes may be lasting. Carrying on beyond the tenth session is quite an attractive proposition for the therapist with enthusiasm and optimism, but in our experience the therapy develops into a kind of supportive exercise rather than producing change, and the therapist and the couple can both become in some way dependent on the meetings without producing much in the way of benefit (see Sections 4.8.4 and 4.8.5).

Ideally, the end of therapy is a planned event, with agreement between the couple and therapist that the goals have been reached, the problems solved and that the couple feel quite confident to continue

4.8.3 Couples who decide to drop out of therapy

As the couples who drop out of therapy are often also reluctant to communicate with the therapist afterwards, we do not know in many cases why they dropped out or whether they have gained anything from the experience of therapy. In some cases where they have dropped out and then returned at a later stage for further sessions they have given various explanations for leaving, from family commitments and holidays to ambivalence towards the treatment, but it is not always clear whether such explanations are really valid.

With some couples, however, it is reasonably clear that the two or three sessions they have had with us have made a worthwhile difference to their relationship. The couple described in Section 9.6, for example, attended for only one session and obtained considerable benefit from the suggestion for twice-weekly talk sessions which they were given together with some positive connotations of their behaviour.

Other couples have clearly not made a good commitment to therapy and their defaulting is probably an indication that they have not benefited and that couple therapy, especially of the type we offer, is unlikely to help them. If they have a problem such as depression in one partner which is labelled as an individual illness, they will presumably seek help for the depressed partner elsewhere. They may, in other cases where the problem is accepted as one of interaction, feel that they need a different kind of approach, based on the more detailed elucidation of feeling, and seek help from an appropriate agency.

However the dropping out occurs, it usually leaves a sense of disappointment in the therapeutic team, as we tend to put the responsibility for it on ourselves and the therapy rather than blaming resistance or other factors in the couple.

4.8.4 Couples who are unwilling to terminate therapy

There are couples at the other end of the spectrum who begin to be dependent on the therapy and who presumably come to therapy for their own needs which are different from those for which we aim to provide. For example there are some couples who tell us that the clinic is the only place where they ever talk to each other and, in spite of instructions to talk at home, perhaps on a timetabled basis, do not seem to develop independent skills in communication. Since we neither aim, nor have the resources, to provide long-term supportive counselling, therapists will be asked to find ways of ending therapy with these couples.

Couples who have been used to supportive sessions together in other settings, as in the couple who were referred by our day hospital for marital work 'because the nurse who had supported them for three years had left', face us with similar problems. In this case (Example 9E) we were able to help them to be much more independent and discharged them after about a year of therapy.

One very difficult couple had begun their contact with us with moderately successful sexual therapy at another of our clinics, which reduced the wife's sexual reluctance. However, they then developed a strong and ambivalent dependence (especially from the wife to the male co-therapist) and insisted on ongoing marital therapy, in which they spent much of the time saying how useless the therapists and their therapy were. When after some years of monthly sessions they were discharged, their marital problems remained unresolved and they spent the subsequent years attending various other agencies for these problems, with mixed results.

Quite often in such cases the supervision team has to intervene to help the therapist to be strong enough to move the couple towards discharge. It may also be useful, in cases where the therapist senses that dependence is building up, to make it clear early in therapy that it usually only lasts for about eight to ten sessions. This is not something that we usually spell out, although we always tell couples at the outset that therapy is short-term, because we prefer to remain somewhat flexible and not tie ourselves down to a pre-arranged number of sessions. In this situation, however, it is wise to be a little more specific.

4.8.5 Therapists who are reluctant to terminate therapy

Sometimes it is the therapist who is reluctant to terminate the therapy. This is not uncommon, especially in trainees in this kind of work, and it requires some experience to know when either the couple's goals have been reached or they have reached a plateau in which more improvement is unlikely to occur.

Sometimes the problem is that the therapist has learned (either in psychodynamic or Rogerian therapy) to wait for the couple to suggest that therapy should end. It can also arise when therapists are very enthusiastic to help the couple and formulate new goals just as the couple are thinking of termination. It may sometimes occur because the therapist finds the couple charming and rewarding to talk to, or because both the therapist and couple have been through some very intense and intimate experiences together and the therapist does not want to let them go.

However it may arise, the supervision team should help the therapist to think it through and to accept the valid reasons for continuing therapy while rejecting those that are less valid. Where therapists are working alone the question of ending short-term intensive therapy can be quite difficult. Both therapist and supervisor may need to keep this question under constant review.

As mentioned above, there seems to be a noticeable loss of therapeutic efficacy after about the tenth session, and if changes have not occurred by that time it is then rather unlikely that they will occur thereafter.

(3) An assessment of the usefulness of these particular skills for this particular couple.

By asking the couple to negotiate in the session for a small immediate change in their relationship the therapist can observe how the couple interact and can make an initial assessment of the couple's current negotiating skills, and whether they can begin to make changes in their relationship.

Not all couples are ready to negotiate with each other for a change in their relationship. If it seems that they are unready, the therapist can then choose (after due perseverence) to use a different form of intervention. Put in a more systemic way, the flexibility or rigidity of their present pattern of interaction can be tested out, and where the present interaction seems too fixed or rigid the therapist can change to working systemically (see Chapters 3, 7, 8 and 9).

5.2 Stage one – simplifying requests

Reciprocity negotiation is based upon 'social exchange theories' developed initially by Thibault and Kelley (1959) and built upon by a succession of therapists (Stuart 1969; Liberman 1970; Azrin *et al.* 1973, Gottman *et al.* 1977, Birchler *et al.* 1975; Crowe 1982, 1985; MacKay 1985). For a review of exchange theory see Chadwick and Jones (1976).

The theoretical basis of reciprocity negotiation is that a high level of satisfaction in marriage is said to depend upon each partner receiving from the other positive reactions to their behaviour, that is 'maximum rewards for minimum cost'. A corollary to this is that each partner, in a satisfactorily functioning marriage, is prepared to exchange positive behaviours with the partner and at the same time accept positive reactions, hence the ability of couples and families to negotiate mutually satisfying activities.

It is thought that, where couples run into difficulties, this is because they no longer give each other sufficient positive reactions to each other's behaviour. In effect each partner is saying 'if you do what I want I will stop complaining, and if you don't do what I want I will go on complaining.' They also seem to assume that by explaining what is wrong with the partner's behaviour they can influence the partner to change for the better. Research suggests that both these negative approaches to influencing each other's behaviour are ineffective, especially in distressed couples (Weiss 1978).

Schindler and Vollmer (1984) describe the characteristics of distressed couples as having

(1) a low rate of mutual positive reinforcement,
(2) a high rate of aversive reaction,
(3) inadequate problem-solving behaviour.

There is usually evidence, however, that the partners do indeed have the skills of communicating and giving positive responses, but they have ceased to use them with each other (Birchler 1972; Vincent 1972).

It is assumed that most couples 'expect a fairly equal sharing of rewards and costs (or duties) between the partners. In unsuccessful or problematic marriages this sharing has either reached a very low level or is unequal' (Crowe 1982). Mackay (1985) lists behaviours he describes as communication skills deficits and looks in detail at the lack of reciprocity in the communication. In particular, he suggests that the lack of reciprocity in perceiving, transmitting and receiving emotional messages will significantly reduce the level of mutual satisfaction within the relationship. Here we see a direct overlap between what we are describing as reciprocity negotiation and communication training. For the sake of clarity, however, we shall deal with the perceiving, transmitting and receiving of emotional messages in Chapter 6 under the heading of communication training, while acknowledging the considerable overlap with the process of reciprocity negotiation.

Many couples enter therapy in a state of emotional turmoil, and share a common sense of despair that they are in a mess. In such a situation, encouraging empathy alone may add to their despondency, because they may each feel more acutely the despair of the other partner. A constructive approach, such as reciprocity negotiation, which offers small but achievable steps towards changing their relationship, is likely to give them some hope.

Reciprocity negotiation attempts to change these features of distressed or dysfunctional couples and aims to establish a pattern of interaction which is more mutually rewarding. This change can be either on a 'give to get' basis, in which each partner agrees to do something which pleases the other in direct exchange for a reciprocal piece of positive behaviour or, as Gottman suggests, it can be 'unlatched' from the partner's contribution and is on a 'bank account basis' in which each partner offers to do something positive, but is not dependent on the other's response (Gottman *et al*. 1976).

While mindful of this alternative, we feel that it makes sense for the therapist to model first the ideal of reciprocity in which each partner compromises in order to gain some desired change in the other partner.

Other approaches which use methods very similar to those of reciprocity negotiation are variously described as 'quid pro quo'; 'contracting'; or 'problem-solving' (Baucom & Mehlman 1984). Baucom describes 'quid pro quo' as a situation in which the couple are asked to reach solutions on two problem areas such that the solution to one problem involves behaviour change on the wife's part, and the second involves behaviour change from the husband. These are then interwoven so that one depends upon the other.

would like' from therapy, he or she should move gently but firmly into reciprocity negotiation (see Section 4.6.5). Each couple and therapist will vary in their pace and willingness to engage with the work, but the therapist will need to take the initiative in making this move.

This shift from listening to the difficulties experienced in the relationship to intervening actively to assist the couple to change their interaction is sometimes experienced by therapists as premature. This seems to be an issue for the therapist rather than the couple, and should be discussed with the supervisor or supervision group (see also Chapter 12). So long as the therapist is able to be empathic, supportive and understanding of the couple's situation, then the move to active work within the session should be experienced by both the therapist and the couple as a lively engagement with the couple and their expressed wish to improve their relationship (see Example 5A).

It is also helpful, as part of the framework for reciprocity negotiation, for the therapist to become decentred while the negotiation goes on (Sections 4.6.8. and 6.4.1). Although in most behavioural texts the therapist seems to take an intermediary role and pass proposals from one partner to the other, we have found that the process moves more quickly if the partners talk to each other directly and the therapist comes in only to comment on the negotiation and suggest alternatives.

5.4 Stage one of reciprocity negotiation: simplifying requests

The task for the therapist is to intervene and focus the work on simple specific requests from each partner for small changes in behaviour, which each partner is asking of the other. Usually one or two pieces of behaviour are quite sufficient as a starting point.

As the therapist introduces the task, a partner will often respond by saying 'I want him to be more open towards me', or 'more loving', or 'I would like to feel safe'. Such global requests need to be simplified until they become achievable and observable.

In describing examples we are aware that we may be giving the impression that with skill and tenacity these steps are easily achieved. It is in fact very easy to be deflected from apparently simple objectives and the therapist will need all his/her patience and good humour in helping couples to focus and to simplify requests.

Example 5A
Caroline has just suggested that she 'would like Douglas to be more open with me'.

THERAPIST (*to husband*)
Do you know what Caroline means when she says she would like you to be more open with her?

DOUGLAS
Yes, I suppose so, she means she wishes I would talk to her more.

THERAPIST (*to Douglas*)
Can you check with Caroline if that is what she means?

DOUGLAS
Is that what you mean, you want me to talk to you more?

CAROLINE
Yes you never talk, you've always got your head under the bonnet of the car, or out with your mates, or watching . . .
(Caroline is digressing and being negative.)

THERAPIST (*interrupting*)
OK, let's hold it there for the moment. One of the things that Caroline would like is for Douglas to talk more to her. Now let us see if, as a couple, you can think of a time which you could set aside when that can happen? Perhaps, since you are both such busy people, you could think of three or four half-hours each week, which you could set aside for talking to each other.

In such a way the therapist works patiently helping the couple find small discrete behaviours that are observable and achievable, as a first step towards change. Here the request came from Caroline. It has been turned into a joint task in which they will spend time together. This task could be amended so that, for example, they each have 15 minutes to talk about themselves; or alternatively, Caroline could be asked to allow Douglas to talk all of the time. (See also Chapter 9 for discussion of timetabled tasks.)

So far we have worked at honing down a global statement into a more discrete request for a change of behaviour in the other.

5.4.1 Reciprocity

With the above example the task was a request from Caroline to Douglas. In order to work within the guidelines of reciprocity, the therapist should then go on to ask Douglas what request he would like to make of Caroline for a positive change. His request might be something equally global and negative such as 'I wish she would stop nagging me all the time'. This would need to be simplified and made more concrete and achievable before the next session. One option might be to add something to the above joint task so that, for example, Caroline might be asked to use 15 minutes of the half-hour to talk to him without nagging him and Douglas could be asked to use 15 minutes to talk to Caroline about himself. Thus the task would take on a more reciprocal aspect. Each partner would be giving something to gain something.

It is important to check with the couple that the task is acceptable to both partners. If it is their first attempt at making a positive request of their partner within therapy, there may be a fair degree of cynicism in the couple that it is not achievable. Comments such as 'It won't work', or 'I can't see him doing this', or even 'I've tried it before, she didn't notice' are quite common.

The therapist would be wise to acknowledge this cynicism but light-heartedly ask if the couple can have a go and see how they get on between the sessions.

These are the kinds of situation in which the therapist will use his or her own particular skill in helping the couple feel comfortable enough to be prepared to 'risk it' and see what happens between sessions. The therapist may want to acknowledge some doubts as to whether the chosen task will be attempted. If the task is not attempted in any way 'What got in the way?' can be a topic for the next session.

5.5 *Stage two: complaints become wishes*

The couple may not express any clear wishes but continue to complain about the behaviour of the other partner regardless of the therapist. As soon as the therapist is clear in his/her own mind that the couple are continuing a pattern of complaint/complaint (this does not usually take very long to notice), these complaints need to be good-humouredly noted.

Example 5B
THERAPIST
I'm wondering if you have noticed how you each continue to complain about the other instead of making a positive request.

HANNAH AND HARRY (*in unison*)
Oh God yes, we're always at each other.

After noting the pattern of continuous complaining the therapist should spend time with the couple helping them find ways of restating at least one of the complaints as a request for positive change in behaviour. For example, to change 'I hate him coming in late from work' to 'I would like you to be home by 7.30 on Mondays, Wednesdays and Fridays'.

Again the therapist is expected to be active and to ask for a change in the way the couple are relating to each other. This can become an empathic experience for all concerned. Such couples have often struggled themselves to understand why they have developed this stressful and unhappy way of relating. They have probably tried in various ways to make things better and have failed. The fact that the therapist is able to identify quickly a pattern of interaction which is contributing to much of the discontent is likely to give the couple a sense of some hope that change might be possible.

Some therapists find it difficult, at first, to draw attention to behaviour patterns such as the complaint/complaint behaviour of this couple and to ask them to change complaints into positive requests. They may worry that this is a criticism of the couple and, in an effort to be non-judgmental, may be reluctant to intervene. However, without some direct intervention from the therapist the couple will be unlikely to change this behaviour on their own. They have already demonstrated this in the session. The therapist's task is to be supportive, to help the couple understand what is being asked of them, and to feel safe enough to encourage them to experiment – in this case to make a specific positive request rather than a complaint.

5.5.1 Turning complaints into requests

Example 5C
(see also Sections 6.4.8.1 and 6.4.8.2)

EMMA
Frank is always cold and distant to me these days, he never cuddles me, or even gives me a kiss, he can only snap at me and tell me that the house is untidy. The only time he is ever kind to me is when he is drunk and then he brings me chocolates and wants to make love to me when he's drunk. I can't stand him when he is drunk . . .

THERAPIST (*interrupting*)
Emma can you turn one of those things that you complain about into a request to Frank to change?

EMMA
Like what, he'll never change.

THERAPIST
Like . . . would you want to ask him perhaps to cuddle you more often?

FRANK
That'd be a laugh, she just pushes me off.

EMMA
No I don't. When do I get the chance?

THERAPIST (*interrupting*)
Emma is that one of the things that you might want to ask Frank to do? To cuddle you more often?

EMMA
Well, yes, if I thought he would.

If the therapist is making a suggestion, as in the above example, it should be clear and specific. It does not matter whether the couple pick up the therapist's particular suggestion; indeed it is probably better that they reject an idea of the therapist (Jacobson 1984) and choose reciprocal behaviours which they themselves initiate.

The key aim of the intervention is to model a change from complaining to a specific request for change. The therapist may have to spend some time with the couple helping to make the move from the complaint/complaint behaviour to making positive requests. Having found positive requests, the work needs to continue until both partners feel relatively sure that the requests are achievable, or at least are prepared to try it out between sessions.

Since, however, research shows that this is a basic behaviour pattern of distressed couples, it is well worth the therapist's persistent effort. The couple may have lost a fair amount of hope that change is possible. These are all good reasons why the therapist, while being empathic with their difficulties, can persist with some degree of optimism.

The couple's sense of hopelessness is an important element in the search for small behaviour changes. The therapist should bear this in mind and try to ensure that the requests are clear, small and achievable before the next session. A cup of coffee made by the man and a hug in return from the woman may be the most that can be attempted at first.

5.6 Stage three: working together on the tasks

If tasks do begin to emerge in the session they should be worked at together, until they are the following:

(1) specific,
(2) reciprocal,
(3) repeatable,
(4) positive,
(5) attainable and realistic in the time available and
(6) acceptable to both partners.

5.6.1 Specific

Couples usually find it difficult to be specific enough and the therapist must take responsibility for ensuring that requests are not left vague and unwieldy. What specific behaviour is being considered, where, for how long and at what time of day? How can the behaviour be recognised by the partner? These questions need a clear answer.

Example 5D
Henrietta has asked if George can 'be more friendly' when he returns home from work. After discussion as to what exactly Henrietta means by this, it appears that when George returns from work he goes straight down the garden to feed his show rabbits and spends his first 20 minutes back home attending to them. Henrietta feels very unhappy about this. George, on the other hand, complains that he does this because Henrietta is very punctual with mealtimes and he feels he has to rush to attend to the show rabbits. He knows Henrietta doesn't like his rabbits and complains that they smell too much. He tries to be helpful by keeping them very clean. Henrietta is very fastidious about the house and George is constantly being criticised for being too sloppy. (This takes some time to unravel.)

The tasks which were finally negotiated were:

(1) That George on returning home from work, will spend the first 20 minutes with his wife talking with her.
(2) That the supper will be put back another 20 minutes so that George can keep his rabbits clean.
(3) Because they both feel that supper would then be a bit late, they would have a cup of tea together during his 20 minutes time with Henrietta.

So the general request that George be more friendly becomes a three-step task clearly spelled out in terms of time and content. It has also become reciprocal in that Henrietta has had to 'give' by moving her time of supper, in order to 'get' her time with George.

5.6.2 Reciprocal

It is quite usual for one partner to be more willing than the other to change particular behaviours. However, the therapist's role is to help the couple negotiate a task which carries an offer of behaviour change from both partners, as in the above example of Henrietta and George.

Some therapists may prefer to use their discretion regarding reciprocity. As already noted, Gottman prefers to use a 'bank account' system. Our experience suggests, however, that reciprocity should be taught and can usually be achieved. A practical check can be made by asking the couple if they feel they have each given reasonably equally.

5.6.3 Repeatable

The behaviour chosen should not be a 'once off' behaviour, such as buying a washing machine or organising a holiday. It should be something that can continue over time as behaviour that pleases the other partner, such as keeping a room tidy or helping with the washing up.

5.6.4 Positive

This has been touched on in stage two above. As already mentioned, negative perceptions of partner's behaviour are usually part of the distressed couple's way of interacting. Not only do distressed partners perceive each other as being more negative towards each other than is intended, but they will usually also reciprocate negative behaviour with negative behaviour (Jacobson 1984; Schaap and Jansen-Nawas 1987). Tasks must therefore clearly be sought which demonstrate that the couple are making small but positive efforts to change behaviours which have been seen by the spouse as negative. The therapist needs to check with each partner that the behaviour being discussed falls into this category.

5.6.5 Attainable and realistic in the time available

Couples can be very unrealistic about what is possible. Bearing in mind that the couple's motivation is likely to be affected by the success or failure of the tasks set, the therapist should take trouble to ensure that the couple actually think that the task chosen could be achieved in the timespan available. This means looking with the couple as to when, where and how the task will be performed. None of these areas should be left to chance, particularly when setting tasks in the engagement phase of working with the couple. Later the couple may need to notice for themselves if they are setting each other impossible tasks.

Example 5E
If the request of the couple is to spend two quiet evenings at home, together, during the next week, on Tuesday and Thursday, but the wife's mother is coming to stay, then they have probably set themselves an impossible task. Unless the therapist helps them to decide what to do with the mother on those two evenings the task will probably fail.

5.6.6 Acceptable to both partners

The therapist should check with each spouse that the tasks being discussed are indeed acceptable both to the person carrying them out and to the person requesting them. For example, if a husband is asked to give up watching football altogether, he might feel resentful that he is being asked to give up too much. Similarly, a wife who has become preoccupied with quilt-making may equally find it unacceptable to be asked to give this up completely. Checking this out with both partners may seem tedious but is important.

5.6.7 Teaching the model of reciprocity

While working with the couple in this particular way it is important that the therapist remembers the modelling aspect of what s/he is doing. The therapist should endeavour to seek for a balance between the couple so that one partner is not giving a great deal more than the other. Even if the couple find this exercise difficult, the teaching of the concept that each partner can contribute to the changes which are being sought may encourage the couple to think about their own part in their relationship difficulties. It is also helpful for the therapist to model being non-critical when dealing with the couple in this way. Such an approach may be able to influence the couple to be less critical, and any criticism on the part of the therapist will probably undermine what s/he and the couple are building up together.

5.7 Stage four: monitoring the tasks

Whatever reciprocal tasks have been set within the session, it should be made clear to the couple that these tasks will be reviewed in the following session. This reviewing or monitoring of tasks performed should happen at the beginning of the next session and should include what was attempted, what was left out, who did and who did not achieve their tasks. Again the review is undertaken to help the couple look at the minutiae of their relationship, but also to understand what gets in the way of their actually achieving the tasks.

While reviewing, the therapist keeps in mind the reciprocal nature of the tasks and is careful to ensure that both spouses are asked to speak for themselves about how each managed his/her own task. The reviewing should be done thoroughly but with a light touch, as reviewing tends to throw up in rather stark detail all kinds of situation which the couple find difficult. It is easy to become side-tracked into following one of these difficulties at too early a stage. We would suggest that the therapist is attentive and empathic regarding these other difficulties, but not too easily side-tracked from a reasonably thorough review of the tasks. The difficulties described or the resentments encountered can be stored by the therapist as issues which may need to be attended to later. A thorough review will probably allow a more complete picture of their relationship to emerge. Couples often find it difficult to speak together about what went wrong, or the things that bother them about their relationship. This is a chance offered to them to talk together, in a safe place, about one small area in which things went wrong.

Where only part of the task has been attempted or only one partner was successful, then the work of the session might become that of trying to work out a better reciprocal task. The main purpose of the review is to monitor sympathetically how the couple got on, and what were the difficulties and/or pleasures of the attempted task. This gives the couple an experience of reviewing without blaming and also enables them, with the therapist's assistance, to make choices about what can next be attempted.

5.8 The basic process

The basic process for the therapist is quite simple. It requires close attention to detail and a patient and supportive attitude while assisting the couple to choose and practise simple steps toward a more positive relationship. These steps in summary are:

(1) Complaints become wishes.
(2) Wishes become tasks.
(3) Tasks are reciprocal.
(4) The tasks are monitored.

The concepts are transformed so that:

(1) Past becomes future.
(2) Negative becomes positive.
(3) General becomes specific.
(4) Destructive becomes constructive.

5.9 Keeping the exercise interactive

Throughout this process of working to develop reciprocal tasks which the couple can take home and practise between sessions, the therapist should be helping the couple in the session, from the decentred position, to interact with each other to discuss, refine and amend their tasks. In this way the couple are being assisted to be their own therapists and develop their own way of changing under the guidance of the therapist.

The therapist is on his/her part demonstrating the need for the tasks to be reciprocal, to be considered in the sort of detail that will make them simple, positive and achievable. The therapist is not prepared to put up with complaints or woolly alternatives but is patiently supportive and tenacious in pursuit of positive goals.

5.10 Notes for the therapist

There are some simple guidelines for the therapist of things to avoid as much as possible (see also Chapter 4 for more detail). The therapist should avoid

- history taking,
- rationalisation or explanations by the couple of why things went wrong,
- long tautological statements of any sort,
- vagueness or generalisations,
- becoming caught up in the content of the session.

These are all more difficult to achieve than to state here. We have all had experiences of becoming engrossed in the fascinating detail of what happened 16 years ago. What is important is the impact of past experiences on the present relationship, and it is the present relationship which should be kept in constant focus.

5.11 Assessment

As the therapist works with each couple there is a constant need to stay open to the question as to whether the current intervention is the most effective for this particular couple at this particular moment in their relationship. There is never a definitive answer to this impossible question. However, it is the therapist's responsibility to be constantly alert to alternative effective interventions.

We have found that it is often helpful to begin therapy with reciprocity negotiation, to move as appropriate into communication training and, as one learns more about the rigidity of the system, to decide that it is more appropriate to be working systemically, thus moving up the ALI hierarchy (see Chapter 3). Equally, as will be seen in later chapters, where couples have been treated systemically and are becoming more flexible, then they may be helped to use reciprocity negotiation skills in later stages of therapy (i.e. move down the ALI hierarchy, Chapter 3).

This process of intervention followed by observation and assessment of the impact of the intervention is an essential ingredient of the behavioural-systems approach. In a crude and simplistic sense, the intervention strategies can be seen as assessment tools which assist the therapist to choose which interventions may be most effective.

When it becomes clear that a particular form of intervention is not facilitating change in the couple's relationship, the therapist should consider using an alternative strategy.

5.12 *Choosing an alternative strategy*

Where it is clear that the couple are not ready to engage in reciprocity negotiation, alternative strategies might be considered in the session: session:

(1) If 'mind-reading' is very evident try discouraging it (see Section 6.4.6).
(2) If they constantly speak for each other try asking them to use 'I' messages (see Section 6.4.5).

(In general, keep the structural and strategic interventions until you have tested out the couple's ability to effect changes in their communication pattern.)

(3) Where one partner is symptomatic try putting the symptomatic partner in the 'caring' position (Section 10.7.3).
(4) If at the end of the session you think the couple will have great difficulty changing, you may wish to consider a paradoxical message (Section 9.12).
(5) Do not give up, there will probably be a strategy to help – it is just a question of being flexible enough to find it.

As therapy continues and some changes occur in the relationship of the couple, one may find that couples who were unable to use reciprocity negotiation at an earlier point in their therapy are now able to do so. Within the behavioural-systems approach the therapist changes the style of intervention as the couple themselves change. The therapist must therefore be constantly alert to any modifications in the couple's relationship and be flexible enough to vary interventions accordingly.

Chapter 6

Communication training

6.1 Introduction

Ruesch (1957) described communication as 'knowledge in action' and made the 'bio-social function of communication' the centre of his investigations. He credited the sixteenth century Florentine Niccolo Machiavelli as the first person to chronicle the role of communication in human relationships and formulate techniques for gaining and keeping political control.

Current students of communication might well consider that Ruesch himself, together with Bateson, fathered the detailed study of the ways in which human beings relate to each other. An early contribution to communication theory was Bateson's notion of the double bind (1956). Grinker (1967) described the importance of communication patterns in maintaining behaviour while Virginia Satir (1964) was instrumental in shifting the emphasis from the individual patient to the interaction between couples or family members. Satir, in emphasising the centrality of communication as a focus for treatment, moved towards seeing the family as a system. She underlined what has become increasingly obvious, that communication of necessity requires two persons and their interaction. Satir, like Ruesch, emphasised the minutiae of the interaction as between the sender and the receiver, the message sent and the message received. She developed coherent therapeutic programmes based on her concept of the centrality of communication difficulties within distressed families.

Watzlawick *et al.* (1967) emphasised that one cannot 'not communicate', while Haley (1980) suggested that communication patterns develop a system of rules over time. These rules, according to Haley, are both explicit and implicit and govern how couples relate. Berne (1964) developed transactional analysis as a conceptual framework in which individuals are said to communicate with each other from the adult, child or parental position. For most of these practitioners, according to L'Abate and McHenry (1983)

> 'the treatment focus for the communication approach becomes one of correcting communication which will lead to self correction in the interactional system'.

Behaviourists such as Weiss (1978) and O'Leary and Turkewitz (1978) have incorporated communication training into the mainstream of their therapeutic efforts, developing painstaking steps towards greater clarity between couples or family members.

Communication programmes have also been developed in self-help manual form so that couples who are not necessarily distressed can develop their ability to relate to each other more effectively; for example the *Minnesota Couples' Communication Program* (Miller 1975) and the *Marital Enrichment Programmes* (Gurman and Kniskern 1977).

Many forms of therapy would now include within their therapeutic repertoire that of communication training when judged to be appropriate (see for example Gottman 1976; Jacobson 1978; Beavers 1985; McKay 1985).

6.2 The use of communication training within the framework of a behavioural-systems approach

6.2.1 To assist the couple to develop their ability to communicate

According to Crowe (1982), communication training

> 'shares with reciprocity negotiation the rather naive idea that both partners wish to have a good and peaceful relationship, with logical and matter of fact communication.'

However, although couples may wish to have a good and peaceful relationship, it is clear that many distressed couples find it extremely difficult to communicate simply and directly with each other. The aim therefore is to provide the couple with an experience, within the therapy session, of more effective ways of communicating. In this sense the therapist becomes an educationalist: hence the term training.

6.2.2 To assess which approach may be most effective

In this sense, as with reciprocity negotiation (see Section 5.11) the therapist is using the responses of the couple to communication training as a way of assessing the rigidity or adaptability of the couple's interaction.

Olson *et al.* (1983) write

> 'Positive communication skills (i.e. empathy, reflective listening, supportive comments) enable couples and families to share with each other their changing needs and preferences as they relate to cohesion and adaptability. Negative communication skills (i.e. double binds, criticisms) minimise the ability of a couple or family members to share their feelings and thereby restrict their movement on these dimensions.'

The therapist continuously notes the particular pattern of communication that each couple has developed. It may be that for the moment the couple are too entrenched in their present pattern of communicating to give any evidence within the session that they are willing to change it. However, the therapist should be quietly persistent and proceed on the basis that communication patterns can be changed. The therapist has several alternative interventions which can be used. The couple can be asked to experiment, to pretend, to act as if things were different, or to role-play being the other partner. The aim is to find an intervention which will help free the couple so that they can practise or try out alternative ways of communicating with each other. The therapist's sense of humour and quiet confidence that it is possible to experiment with different ways of interacting may assist even the rigid couple to soften and experiment (see also Section 4.4.1). However, where a therapist has attempted to help a couple to change a way of communicating with each other and this has not been effective, another intervention style may have to be considered. Using the ALI hierarchy described in Chapter 3 the therapist can choose to move up the hierarchy and use an alternative, usually systemic, intervention. In this way, communication training can be seen as a way of assessing the rigidity or flexibility of the present interaction of the couple.

6.3 What then are the communication skills which facilitate good relationships within couples?

According to Olson *et al.* (1983)

> 'Positive communication skills include the following: sending clear and congruent messages, empathy, supportive statements and effective problem-solving skills. Conversely, negative communication skills include the following: sending incongruent and disqualifying messages, lack of empathy, non supportive (negative) statements, poor problem-solving skills, and paradoxical and double bind messages.'

Others might simply state the need for open and clear communication. Indeed, L'Abate and McHenry (1983) suggest that one of the common approaches amongst diverse methods of marital therapy is that of helping couples develop open and clear communication. However, Stuart (1980) takes issue with this goal for couple therapy and writes

> 'Evidence suggests that discretion rather than overexuberance is a better goal for relationship enhancing communication patterns.'

He quotes Fritz Perls as having said

> 'Blunt or brutal honesty is seldom a disclosure of intimacy . . . the blunt truth is, in fact, more often an exaggeration.'

He suggests that communication is about 'well chosen messages and judicious self expression.' The Munich Study (Hahlweg *et al.* 1984) breaks down communication into speaker and listener skills, rather as Virginia Satir had done in 1964.

The behavioural-systems approach described here deliberately draws from a wide range of therapeutic styles. While drawing interventions from the field of communication training, we also try to use them in an inventive and flexible way in order to fit in with the wishes and the uniqueness of each couple. We also bear in mind the tendency of couples to respond negatively to each other (see Chapter 5) and therefore aim to help the couple to develop more positive ways of communicating with their partner. Positive communication carries the possibility of more options for the next step, and may remind the couple of forgotten aspects of their relationship.

Within these guidelines the couple are the final arbiters of their own requirements, which means that communication training focusses on issues which the couple bring to the session which they feel need to be discussed between them. From the therapist's point of view the couple's communication needs to contain three parts:

(1) A simple statement.
(2) Feedback to ensure that the statement has been understood.
(3) An empathic element.

Communication training in its simplest form, as described by Satir (1964), assumes that a person who communicates in a functional way can

(1) firmly state his or her own views,
(2) yet at the same time clarify and qualify what he/she says,
(3) and be receptive to feedback when he/she gets it.

or stated again:

(1) I [the sender]   (1) I [the receiver]
(2) am saying something   (2) am receiving the following
     [the message].   the message
(3) to you [the receiver]   (3) from you [the sender]
(4) in this situation.   (4) in this situation.

6.4 Guidelines for the therapist who wishes to encourage good communication

In discussing guidelines for the therapist, examples are given throughout the text and are broken down into separate skills for the sake of clarity and discussion. It cannot be stressed too frequently that the therapist, when working, needs to relate accurately and empathically to the immediate issues which arise within the session, to the specific language and to the particular phrases, intonations and non-verbal responses of each particular couple.

At the same time, it is important not to become engrossed in the detail of the couple's own life history but to observe the current pattern of their communication. This is difficult and therapists can sometimes lose the focus of the interaction; when this happens the therapist can simply take a couple back to a topic which has been lost.

For the purpose of clarity we have presented these guidelines as simply as possible, and as a consequence they may appear clinical. Our expectation is that each therapist will adapt them to his/her own individual style and be able to use these skills without losing contact with the specific difficulties faced by each couple.

Communication training at its best requires an active involved and empathic relationship with the couple. Many couples come to therapy feeling completely overwhelmed with their inability to relate to each other sensitively and effectively. 'I really don't know what has gone wrong, we are constantly bickering, constantly upset with each other. We don't know if anything can be done,' is a theme that is often presented by couples where communication difficulties are paramount.

With such couples it seems appropriate that the therapist is able to carry the hope that things can change and is able to share this hopefulness with the couple. This enables the therapist to join with them in the search for the dysfunctional communication patterns that can be changed. It may be this knowledge that patterns can be changed which contributes to making communication training rewarding for the therapist.

6.4.1 The therapist chooses to decentre

An appropriate early intervention, in order to focus on the couple's communication, is to decentre. This simply means that the therapist stays out of the discussion for some time so that the couple can experience using the session to talk to each other (Section 4.6.9).

It will probably be necessary for the therapist to be kind but repetitive. Thus from the onset of treatment the aim is to ensure that the couple use the session to communicate directly with each other. The therapist sits silently, often turned away from the couple, and avoids being pulled into the communication between them. This small act of turning the couple towards each other and persevering until they are able to use the session to talk directly may be a hopeful sign that some change is possible.

We usually find that therapists new to this way of working find this intervention quite powerful and couples may initially be hesitant about talking directly to each other in-session, even though they may have said 'we have come because we want to communicate more openly with each other'.

We speculate that there may be a variety of reasons why in spite of its usefulness decentring may initially be somewhat anxiety-provoking for both couple and therapist. The couple may feel that they will give themselves away and expose aspects of their relationship which they would prefer to keep hidden. They may have hoped that the therapist would be able to offer a solution (rather as a doctor might prescibe medicine) which would not involve them in being active.

From a behavioural perspective the intervention allows the therapist to observe more accurately how the couple interact, and passes some of the responsibility for change back to the couple, both of which may leave the couple feeling more exposed and the therapist less in control. It may also have something in common with past experiences of teacher/pupil interaction and being asked to perform in front of the class, which again may have negative connotations.

From a systems perspective, decentring can be said to draw a boundary around the couple and give them permission and support to work together as a couple, decider sub-system or parental alliance (Section 7.3.6). At the same time, it could represent a challenge to the couple's current process of distance regulation (Section 1.2.5) drawing them uncomfortably close together in trying to solve the problem.

From a psychoanalytic point of view, the process may highlight issues around the mutual transference between the couple and therapist and therapists may regret losing the opportunity to demonstrate to each partner that they are now understood by this therapist (see Pincus 1960; Pincus and Bannister 1965; Dicks 1967; Guthrie and Mattinson 1971; Segraves 1982). When used effectively one could say that it is a little like a parent who holds a child who is facing a dreaded experience (see also Section 11.6.4).

It may be that all of these alternatives have some validity and that theoretical concepts based on the behavioural-systems approach do not always have to be at variance with analytical concepts. Experience teaches us that this is a useful intervention which should come as early as possible in therapy and can be used by therapists as a basic intervention in most sessions.

6.4.1.1 *Avoiding non-verbal contact while being decentred*
The therapist should be careful to avoid non-verbal contact between him/herself and one partner while being decentred, except when choosing to intervene deliberately to alter the communication pattern. This means that the therapist may need to sit in such a way that there is little possibility of direct eye contact between him/herself and the couple. Some authors suggest that the therapist should always look at the non-speaking partner; our recommendation is that the therapist should be aware of the possibility of being pulled in by one partner non-verbally and attend to this in whatever way is most comfortable for the individual therapist.

6.4.1.2 *Decentring in the first interview*
(*see Section 4.6.9*)
Decentring may very appropriately be used within the first interview as a technique for gathering information from the couple about why they

have come for therapy, particularly if one partner describes the other partner as being the problem.

Example 6A
THERAPIST
Would one of you like to tell me why you have come for marital therapy?

IAN
I've just come to accompany my wife, and she's here because she wants somebody to sort out her depression. She's been depressed so badly.

THERAPIST
Can you ask Julie if she will explain why she is here?

HUSBAND
Well I've talked to her often and I know why she's here.

THERAPIST (*gently persisting*)
I would like you to ask her now what she hopes to get out of coming for marital therapy with you? Can you turn your chair towards her and ask her now?

The therapist should not give up easily and should bear in mind his/her own ambivalence about not being central to each partner, as well as the couple's fears in facing each other.

6.4.2 The therapist observes

The therapist is attempting to do many things simultaneously. One of these is constantly observing the detail of how the couple are communicating with each other, now, in the session. An assumption is made that the couple communicate with each other in the session in the way that they usually do at home. The therapist is therefore concerned to observe the manner in which the couple communicate with each other, rather than what is actually said, in order to notice whether the couple's way of communicating might be improved.

6.4.2.1 *Observing verbal and non-verbal interaction*
Therapists should constantly search for clues to indicate whether couples have difficulties in their communication pattern. The non-verbal interaction is a fertile source of information, although frustratingly ambiguous.

How do they enter the room, who sits where, how do they sit, how are they dressed, who speaks first, who speaks for whom? Do they look at each other? If asked to turn their chairs towards each other do they both turn their chairs, or does only one partner move? What level of voice tone do they use with each other? If one is angry what is the other's response? If one cries does the other touch, turn away or what? What messages are they giving to each other with their faces and their body language? Is he sexually provocative to either the therapist or his wife? Does she respond to his sexual overtures, and in what way? The list is very long.

If a team is observing, they can obviously help a great deal; a single observer sitting in the session is also valuable. Where these options are not available it is useful to video a single session occasionally to help spot non-verbal interaction which can easily be missed when working.

6.4.2.2 What does the therapist do with these observations?

A word of caution regarding the therapist's use of observations of non-verbal interaction. Perceptions of non-verbal behaviour are unreliable. The therapist's perceptions are therefore best seen as tentative clues to potential areas of concern. The therapist's task, in many ways, is to model to the couple that it is unreliable to take for granted their individual perceptions of each other without first checking it out with each other. In order to encourage couples to take nothing for granted in their communicating with each other, each one should be asked to check constantly with their partner.

It is helpful to consider what relevant research findings are available to assist the clinicians with this uncertain area. Mehrabian (1972) believes that 7% of the total feeling conveyed by the spoken message is verbal feeling, 38% is vocal feeling and 55% is facial feeling. This suggests that the actual verbal content is given much less priority than the facial expression or the voice tone, in understanding the message sent. Stuart (1980) makes quite an issue of the power of non-verbal communications. He suggests that

'When the content and relationship qualifying dimension of communication are inconsistent, the non-verbal layer always has the greatest effect.'

Gottman *et al.* (1976) conducted two studies which persuaded them that distressed couples recorded the partner's messages as far less positive than was intended. Jacobson (1984) also describes how distressed couples reinforce each other's negative behaviour by responding to negative comments with negative comments and being hypersensitive in this area. Schaap and Jansen-Nawas (1987) compared the non-verbal interaction of distressed and non-distressed couples in some detail. An important finding was that distressed couples are less likely to look into each other's eyes (called by Schaap 'not tracking') than non-distressed couples. Distressed couples are also much more likely to judge their spouse's behaviour more negatively than do non-distressed couples. This is particularly true for eye contact, facial expression and gestures (see also Section 1.2.2).

These research findings are not necessarily conclusive nor well understood, but it is unwise for therapists to assume that their perceptions of verbal and non-verbal interaction are an accurate representation of how the partners perceive each other. The therapist therefore needs to model greater clarity and humility in this area, by constantly asking the couple to check with the other the meaning of their verbal and non-verbal messages. From the therapist's point of view this is a vital source of potential for change in the couple. Spouses are frequently astonished that areas which they had taken for granted (sometimes for many years) are not always as they had assumed, when they are encouraged to check it out with each other.

6.4.2.3 Interactional feedback
Feedback is a very straightforward use of information gained within the session, which is fed back, or described, to the couple for further discussion. It can be used to focus on a particular aspect of their relationship, which the therapist may choose to emphasise.

Example 6B
(1)   Feedback of areas of agreement

THERAPIST
You seem to agree that you are both upset by your son. Can you discuss together what exactly upsets you about him.

(2)   Feedback of non-verbal interaction

THERAPIST
Paul, when you talked about always being late home from work Olive pulled a face. Can you ask her why?

(3)   Feedback of voice tone

THERAPIST
Mary, when you were disagreeing with Peter, as soon as you raised your voice he stopped talking. Can you now ask him what it was about your raised voice that made him stop talking?

6.4.2.4 Feedback and checking
Therapists often become experts at observing discrepancies between the words spoken and the non-verbal interaction. This expertise can be used in many different ways, to interpret to the client a feeling, an unspoken response, a reason, links to the past, etc.

Within communication training the therapist is being asked simply to *select* an observation which suggests some inconsistency in the interaction and ask one partner to *check* with the other what was intended. It can lead to new and useful communication.

Example 6C
THERAPIST
Ian, I noticed that when you said 'We both want to move out of the area', Jenny sighed loudly and turned away from you. Will you check with Jenny what she meant by her sigh?

IAN
OK Jenny. Why did you sigh when I said we both want to leave Brixton. You know we both badly want to get out into a better class area.

JENNY (*hesitating*)
Did I sigh? (*defensively*)

IAN
You know we want to move, don't you?

JENNY
Still, most of my friends live here, and my mum.

THERAPIST
Ian, can you ask Jenny a little more? Perhaps you need to ask her if she does want to leave Brixton?

IAN
Well do you, do you want to leave Brixton or not?

JENNY (*rather tearfully*)
I don't know. I'm not sure if I could manage without my mum and my friends all around me.

IAN (*puzzled*)
But you're always complaining that Brixton isn't what it used to be.

JENNY
I know, but that doesn't mean that I want to leave.

IAN (*angrily*)
What do you mean? I'm looking for another job so that we can move out. I thought that was what you wanted.

JENNY
I know, I'm so miserable about it all.

THERAPIST
This seems an important area for you both. I wonder if you can spend some time now discussing just that. Do you both want to leave Brixton?

> Then followed, with some help from the therapist to stay with the topic, the first real discussion that this couple had had about whether they should actually leave Brixton and what that would also mean for their two children.

Of course not all non-verbal responses lead the therapist to such extensive disparity of understanding and verbal communication. However, as we have said, well selected observations of this nature are often fruitful clues to difficulties in communicating more directly. (Notice also that in this example Ian was also speaking for Jenny; we will come to that in a moment.)

6.4.2.5 Use of positive and negative feedback
(*see Section 5.5*)
As already described, couples in distress tend to respond to a negative statement with a negative statement. Therapists should therefore be on the lookout for this pattern, which is relatively common. Once recognised, the therapist can use the observation to help the couple change. The therapist can, with an uncritical and supportive statement, draw the couple's attention to this pattern and suggest a positive way to alter it.

Example 6D

THERAPIST
Ken and Louise, I notice how good you both are at describing each other's irritating habits. Can you now each tell your partner what pleases you about them?

If the couple are very stuck in their complaint/complaint behaviour, the therapist will probably have to work quite hard to help the couple switch to being able to make any comments about what pleases them. This might be made into something of a game by the therapist; humour or light-hearted comments can be very supportive to couples, particularly perhaps when both partners are caught in the act of continuously criticising. It may take away a sense of being blamed by the therapist, who is after all the person who has spotted their ritual dance of criticism/criticism. Each therapist will choose the appropriateness of such interventions. Those therapists who find it easy to use humour have a natural leavening skill which others can slowly develop.

Consider Example 7A (Tony and Jane M) which is an example of a couple locked into a criticise/criticise relationship but unable to see this for themselves. There are many points in the interchange where a therapist might intervene. It is also a powerful interchange which the couple have probably experienced many times before with minor variations, rather as jazz players improvise around a familiar tune. A therapist will need to be tenacious and persistent to interrupt this familiar sequence. The therapist is unlikely to succeed the first time. (See also Chapter 12, training.) The key points are that the therapist should find a way of developing the positive aspects of their relationship while drawing attention to their ritualised repetitive sequences. One simple intervention is for the therapist to ask the couple to say what pleases them about the other, being careful to keep them to the task by gently or teasingly pointing out that they find it easier to complain than to say positive things. Again this may be a small, but significant, shift in the way they communicate with each other and it is to be hoped should occur, in some small way, in the first session.

6.4.3 Keeping the couple to the topic

Example 6E

Ken and Louise above (Example 6D) are hesitating to respond to the therapist's suggestions.

THERAPIST (*being more specific*)
Ken, perhaps you could start by telling Louise two things about her that you like.

KEN
Yes (*pause*) well I've always liked the way Louise looks after the house, she's always been very tidy and meticulous; but oh my God Louise, what a mess

you've got us into with the telephone bills I'd no idea that you'd never paid . . .

THERAPIST (*interrupting*)
Ken, you started well and made a clear positive statement about Louise. That was good, but then you switched back into your complaint ritual. Can you try again and tell Louise a second thing that pleases you about her?

6.4.3.1 *Keeping the couple to the topic interactionally*
In the above example the therapist interrupts and speaks directly to one partner. Wherever possible within couple work, unless deliberately allying with one partner in order to unbalance the relationship (Section 8.3.2), it is useful to keep putting the work to be done back to the couple. Thus instead of the therapist reminding the couple to stick to the topic, one of them can be asked to remind the partner of the topic and the need to stay with it for the moment.

Example 6F
THERAPIST
Mary, we haven't heard an answer to your question yet. Can you ask Peter again?

This puts the responsibility for getting an answer back on to Mary and, at the same time, reminds both of them of the task in hand.

6.4.4 Being impartial and keeping a balance between the partners
(see also Section 4.6.2)

Unless making choices to ally deliberately with one partner in order to unbalance a situation or escalate an argument, the therapist should stay impartial. Being impartial means not taking sides with one partner against the other, not making value judgments regarding choices made by the couple together, and in general not being pulled in on one side. It also means taking account of which partner is being asked to take initiatives in communicating, whether it be to ask questions, to rephrase things positively or to check out non-verbal behaviour, etc. As far as possible, the therapist should model reciprocal interaction within the couple. In this way a question that has been addressed to one partner is generally also addressed to the other partner. If the therapist asked the husband to make a positive statement to the wife, then the therapist should ensure that the wife is encouraged to do likewise.

It is worth remembering that it is remarkably difficult for the therapist not to be pulled in on one side or the other and to be constantly attentive to the need to model a balanced interaction. In our experience it is one of the hardest skills for trainees to learn (Section 12.3).

6.4.4.1 If the therapist does get pulled in, what can be done?
As soon as the therapist is aware that s/he has been allowing one spouse to take charge of the session s/he can:

(1) Interrupt a monologue to ask the other partner what s/he thinks of the subject matter of the monologue.
(2) Cut across the talkative partner to ask him/her to find ways of helping the less talkative partner to talk.
(3) Ask the less talkative partner what the difficulties are in talking about the subject.
(4) Reflect back to the couple the opinion that the interaction is unbalanced and ask the less involved partner to judge whether that is a common experience in their relationship.

The key issue is the balance of interaction and reciprocity within the couple and between the couple and the therapist. The therapist's aim is to model reasonably equal interaction between the partners and to model an experience for the couple where they are asked to work together on their communication and not rely upon the therapist to do all the work (bearing in mind that the ideal is rarely attainable).

6.4.5 'I' messages

Many couples who seek therapy seem to have developed a chronic inability to speak only for themselves. A rather typical example would be one in which one spouse speaks continuously for them both. For example, 'We hate going out to a pub. We've always really disliked her brother,' and the other partner makes no contrary comments.

Another variation is where one partner speaks for the other as though the other partner is not in the room. For example, 'Mary feels fed up with her boss at work; he's always picking on her and finding fault'. 'Peter feels that it is all his fault that our son Tim didn't pass his A-levels. He thinks that he should have been at home more.' Usually no attempt is made either to ask the partner to speak for himself or to check with the partner if those indeed are the feelings.

This is in many ways such a common aspect of general communication that it is often not noticed by therapists as an area requiring change. This particular phenomenon of communication is best described as 'mind-reading'. It is considered in detail in Section 6.4.6. Within communication training there is a basic requirement that eventually the individual partners will be able to speak for themselves and at the same time allow their partner the same freedom and respect (see Section 6.3). Depending upon what is happening between the partners, a variety of alternatives are available.

Example 6G
(1) I notice that you, Timothy, have got into the habit of always speaking for Suzanne. Do you think that you can speak just for yourself? Could you use

'I' instead of 'we', then Suzanne can be asked to speak for herself also.
(2) Suzanne, I wonder if you can help Timothy by speaking for yourself and see if you can find ways of helping Timothy to do the same. Try to help Timothy to use 'I' instead of 'we'.
(3) Timothy, can you ask Suzanne if she wants you always to speak for her instead of letting her speak for herself.
(4) I would like you to develop a new rule when you talk to each other. Please use 'I' each time you are talking about yourself, do not use 'we' for the moment.

As always, it is probably better to be able to find a phrase which places the request interactionally within the couple. However, since we are talking about communication training it is also perfectly acceptable to make a direct request to the individual. If such a request is made, remember not to get trapped back into a one-way conversation with one partner unless, of course, purposely allying with one partner.

As the couple work towards changing their style of communication and become more able to speak from the 'I' position, the therapist should feel free to encourage or congratulate them. Development of empathy between the couple and the therapist encourages the couple to take more risks, and each therapist will want to develop his/her own personal style. One therapist might say 'Whoops! you just slipped back into speaking for Suzanne; not to worry, you're being much more careful about letting her speak for herself'. Another might be able to say more directly 'No, try again, you have just spoken for Suzanne, now say it again but this time using 'I'. Keep at it, you're doing fine'. Each therapist should work at finding his or her own style, while paying attention to the requirements of teaching clear communication and being positive and encouraging about any changes observed.

6.4.6 Discourage mind-reading

Mind-reading is a pervasive and dysfunctional form of communication in which many couples indulge. It simply means one partner speaking for the feelings, motives or experiences of the other, without first checking whether they speak with accuracy or not. It is this lack of checking with the spouse which is of central concern, and which leads to distortion of understanding and perception.

There may be a confusion in the minds of both therapists and couples about the value of mind-reading. This may arise from a misunderstanding of the distinction between empathic understanding, in which partners do check with each other that they understand the other's feelings, experiences or motivations, and mind-reading, where little or no checking is done and where erroneous assumptions are often made (Gottman *et al.* 1976; Jacobson and Margolin 1979). From our perspective it is wisest to establish that partners do not speak for each other and that mind-reading is questioned by the therapist as it appears within the sessions. Experience suggests that mind-reading is rarely empathic in couples who seek marital therapy.

There is a sense that mind-reading is an interaction which enables one spouse to control the relationship and disables the other partner from disagreement. This control of the relationship can be just as much from the down position as from the up position.

Example 6H

Pat and Theresa K came to the marital therapy clinic after 15 years of marriage. They were extremely concerned that their marriage might be at an end, and wanted desperately to see if there was any way it could be saved for the sake of the children. Pat stated that he was anxious to continue in the relationship, his wife Theresa was not sure as their difficulties were longstanding. A typical interaction was:

PAT
My wife has given up on me. She doesn't even want me in the same room with her.

THERAPIST
How do you know that Theresa doesn't want you in the same room with her?

PAT (*irritably*)
It's clear to me that she doesn't.

THERAPIST (*pressing the same point again*)
How do you know? What does Theresa do that makes you think that she doesn't want to be in the same room with you?

PAT
I just know.

THERAPIST (*again*)
What exactly makes you so sure?

PAT
I know, because every time I go into a room she always leaves it.

THERAPIST
Have you ever asked your wife if that is correct that she leaves the room because you have gone in?

PAT (*by now visibly somewhat angry*)
I know, I don't need to ask.

THERAPIST
Well, let's see, why don't you ask her now?

PAT (*rather flustered*)
Well, Theresa; isn't that what happens, every time I come into the room, you leave the room.

THERESA
I have to admit I haven't noticed that happening. I don't think that I do that on purpose.

PAT (*disbelieving*)
Come on Theresa you know you can't stand to be in the same room with me.
Isn't that true now?

THERESA
No, it's not true. At least not all of the time. Sometimes I quite like being in the
same room with you and sometimes I can't stand it.

THERAPIST (*to Pat*)
Did you understand what Theresa has said?

PAT (*rather astonished*)
Yes, but I don't know if I should believe it.

The couple then go on to discuss times when Theresa enjoys being in
the same room with him and times when she wants to be on her own.
This leads to a reframing of the problem which is much more about
Theresa needing time and space for herself within the house, which so
far her husband had not understood. Rather than checking with his
wife, whether he understood or not, his mind-reading had prevented
them both from looking at this issue. Mind-reading can be thought of as
performing a function for both partners of controlling the interaction. In
this particular relationship the assumption that his wife can't stand
being in the same room with him controls their interaction and prevents
them making any changes.

Once this couple were able to set aside mind-reading they began to
move from fixed and intractable positions to a more open discussion of
their current relationship. They had first of all to learn that their fixed
perceptions of the other partner were by no means exact. When this
happens in therapy (and it usually doesn't happen without a lot of hard
work by all concerned) it is stimulating. It is as though the couple
suddenly wonder if they have ever really known their partner. One has
a sense of a rather fragile and tender relationship emerging from behind
a gnarled and intractable exterior. At this stage the therapist needs to be
particularly empathic with this fragility and help the couple to recognise
this sense of naive newness. A good therapist will ensure that they
receive positive strokes from him/herself and the team (if there is one)
for their hard work in getting to this point. Some reassurance that they
can be of most help to each other by being gentle, as they renew
acquaintance with each other in those areas where previously they have
been mind-reading, is usually received and acted upon.

Example 61

Billy and Brenda O had been referred by the general practitioner because of
constant arguments and because Brenda was complaining of depressive
symptoms. This is Brenda's second marriage. In the second session the therapist
enquires about their sexual relationship.

BILLY
We have a great sex life. Brenda can't get enough, she wants it every evening.

THERAPIST (*to Billy*)
It seems that you enjoy your sex life, but I wonder if you could just ask Brenda if she agrees with you?

BILLY
You do, don't you? We have great sex every evening, near enough.

Brenda does not reply.

BILLY (*enthusiastically*)
We really enjoy each other's company. We go . . .

THERAPIST (*gently interrupting*)
Can you persevere and see if you can help Brenda reply to your question.

BILLY
We do enjoy sex a lot, don't we Brenda?

BRENDA (*turning to look out of the window*)
Yes. It's all right. I suppose.

THERAPIST
Can you check what your wife means by 'It's all right'?

BILLY (*now looking rather concerned*)
Come on Brenda? What do you mean. Do you mean you don't actually enjoy sex? I can't believe that!

BRENDA (*squirming a little with embarrassment*)
Well let's say I could do with a bit more quality and less quantity.

The therapist then asks then to continue this discussion about the quality of their sex life in the session.

As they explored this in more detail it became clear that Billy's mind-reading and Brenda's inability to challenge it had made their sex life rather a strain. He had been having sex each evening to satisfy her and she had assumed that he was doing it for his own needs. They were both relieved to discover that they could allow themselves to enjoy each other's company without always having to have sexual intercourse.

Discouraging mind-reading is a powerful intervention which allows couples to open up discussions about difficulties which have somehow got locked away by the impact of mind-reading on their relationship.

6.4.7 Discouraging sting in the tail interaction

The sting in the tail can easily be missed by very competent therapists as it usually follows a positive statement.

Example 6J
WIFE
You are trying now, but why couldn't you have done so five years ago?

Therapists have to listen carefully for the sting. It is so easy to get caught up in any positives that are emerging, that therapists may prefer not to notice the sting which follows. In the above example it would be simple to hear only 'you are trying now'. However, within communication training the work for the therapist is to find a way to help the wife to rephrase this along the lines of:

WIFE
I've had a long time to wait, but you are trying now.

In a sense we are simply advising that the couple should stay with the positives and not spoil it by adding an undermining statement. Couples often seem very reassured to let go of these habitual patterns once they have been pointed out. The sting in the tail often raises a wry smile from both partners, who may be equally skilled in both using, and being abused by, such a painful but familiar tactic.

A useful alternative for the therapist is to ask the couple to remind each other in some way that they are using stings. This can be done by the couple choosing a codeword or raising a forefinger to indicate that stings are being used. A couple can often come up with a creative and lighthearted way of reminding each other, which can help to soften their interaction. They can be asked to practise in the session with the therapist. One couple chose to use a child's Union Jack as a sign. They would sit down after supper by the fire and discuss together for 30 minutes (as prescribed, see Chapter 8). The Union Jack would be raised whenever stings were used. They were rather a bright older couple who had had many battles about the children and finances, which they kept wanting to re-enact in the present. The Union Jack seemed to be some kind of symbol of their mutual aggressiveness and seemed to help them convert this behaviour into a more peaceful relationship.

Such patterns of communication are often full of resentment and recrimination. The renewal of more empathic ways of communication can be thought of as helping a couple get back in touch with their lighter and more youthful selves. The therapist is encouraged to get in touch with his or her creative self in assisting the couple to find playful alternatives. The notion of learning to play again is itself a vital ingredient in couple work and particularly appropriate in rather stuck interactions.

6.4.8 Encouraging an increase in positive interaction

Research tends to suggest that positive interaction does not necessarily increase as a result of a diminution of negative interactions of the kind we have been describing above (Orden and Bradburn 1968; Wills *et al.* 1974; Weiss 1978). This means that the therapist should also find ways to increase the level of positive interaction between such couples, such as in the following example.

6.4.8.1 *Changing destructive criticism to constructive requests* (*see Section 5.5*)

Example 6K

THERAPIST
Jennifer, you have just criticised Sam for groping you at the kitchen sink, when the kids are around. Can you turn that into a request as to how you would like Sam to approach you?

JENNIFER
Well certainly not at the kitchen sink!

THERAPIST
Good; let's start with how you would like him to approach you if you are in the kitchen.

JENNIFER
When I'm at the sink I'd prefer it if he didn't touch me at all.

THERAPIST
Can you now put that as positively as you can to your husband. Try and suggest an alternative to Sam.

JENNIFER (*turning to face her husband and taking a big breath*)
Sam, could you please not grope me at the kitchen sink? Could you possibly just kiss me on the cheek instead?

In this way a destructive criticism gets translated into a specific request for a change in behaviour.

6.4.8.2 *Complaints can be changed into requests* (*see Section 5.5.1*)

Example 6L

HORACE
My wife never notices me when I come in from work; it is just as if I was invisible the amount of notice she takes of me.

THERAPIST (*to wife*)
Bertha can you tell Horace how he can help you notice him more when he comes in from work?

BERTHA
I suppose he could come and find me and tell me that he is home. He often sneaks into the sitting room and I find him fast asleep, and I'd no idea that he was already home . . .

THERAPIST (*interrupting*)
Bertha, can you now ask Horace if he can help you in this way?

After Bertha has made this request it is Horace's turn to be asked by the therapist.

THERAPIST
Horace can you now tell Bertha in what way you would like her to greet you when you tell her that you are home?

HORACE
Well it would be great if she could be a bit warmer towards me.

THERAPIST
That is still rather too vague a request; can you be more precise about what you would like her to do?

HORACE
Well perhaps Bertha could at least smile and say, 'Hello, what sort of a day have you had?'

In this way, slow and sometimes very small steps are made along the path to increase the number of positive interactions between partners. This central aim of increasing the level of positive interactions within the couple can best be achieved by first actively rehearsing with the couple in the session the ability to change criticisms and complaints into simple, concrete requests for alternative positive behaviour (Chapter 5).

Research suggests that once such behaviour has been learned, it tends to transfer into the environment back home and becomes part of the standard repertoire of the couple. For some this may seem too slow and painstaking work. However, therapists should be encouraged by the enhanced capacity that this gives the couple to cope more effectively with their daily interaction. Research also demonstrates that where couples are able to increase their level of positive interaction their satisfaction with the marriage is seen to increase (Jacobson and Margolin 1979). Equally, most couples who report a high level of marital satisfaction also report a high level of positive interactions (Birchler *et al.* 1975).

(See Chapter 9 for tasks and timetables which focus on ways to increase positive interactions.)

6.4.9 Encouraging rapid interaction
(see Section 4.6.4)

When we come, in Chapter 7, to consider a couple's interaction from a systems perspective, we begin to think about the pace of the interaction as being part of the homeostasis of the system as a whole; so that changing the pace, length, or intensity of an interaction becomes one of the objectives of intervention, as a way of changing the homeostasis of the system.

Within communication training there is a similar requirement to observe and intervene in the pace and timing of interactions, but the reasons are different. They are to encourage more spontaneous, clear and reciprocal communication. If one refers back to Virginia Satir's description of functional communication between the sender and the receiver, one can see a requirement for reciprocal interaction between two people. In dysfunctional communication there is often little reciprocity of interaction. There are several useful interventions.

6.4.9.1 *Interrupting a monologue*
A monologue is where one partner monopolises the conversation and interaction is minimal. The other partner may well have become so accustomed to one-way conversations that s/he may have developed a habit of 'switching off' during monologues. The content for the moment is immaterial. It is the length and the deadening impact on the communication between the partners that is important.

The therapist will be able to recognise couples where one partner talks in monologues within minutes of meeting. Having spotted this pattern, which is all too frequent (particularly in older marriages, or where one partner is symptomatic or submissive) the therapist should find ways to interrupt the monologue and to alter the pace and frequency of interaction within the couple. Done with confidence, the impact can be to change a rather tedious and tiring session into a lively and more profitable one. Some alternatives are

- Ask the partner to comment on the point just made.
- Ask the non-speaker to intervene and stop the other from using up all the space.
- Ask the silent partner what it is like having to wait so long for a space to respond.
- Ask the partner why s/he allows the other to talk so much.

Where monologues seem to interfere in a rather chronic way with a couple's interaction it may be necessary to ask the couple to

- Make short statements and then wait for a reply from the spouse.
- Make a rule that nobody should talk for more than 15 seconds at a time.
- Suggest to the couple that after 15 seconds the partner should hold up a hand to indicate that it is his/her turn to speak.

From experience, such practical suggestions are often seized upon with enthusiasm.

6.4.9.2 *Preventing the couple reliving, reviewing or going over the past*
The focus for the therapist is how the couple are communicating in the present. This means that any time the couple return to how they used to be reduces their concentration on their present relationship. The therapist should therefore stop this happening.

Many therapists have been trained to take detailed social histories and find it difficult to work without knowing the full history of the couple and the two individuals. We advocate that they should be discouraged from going over the past, in order to increase the effectiveness of the couple's present communication. It is not that we find the history of the couple irrelevant, simply that on these occasions it adds little to their present ability to re-establish effective current communication. If, for example, a couple seem to have a great need to go over the past, and this makes therapeutic sense, then they could be encouraged to use their 'talking timetable' for this at home (Chapter 9). The aim is to give the couple the experience of increasing their ability to communicate effectively and reciprocally with each other in the session.

Example 6M
The couple have been remembering how they enjoyed bathing the children together in the house they lived in 15 years ago when the children were small. The children are now 19, 18 and 16. Some possible interventions are

- Can I bring you up to the present, can you talk together about what is happening for you as a couple now your children are much older?
- I understand what you are saying about how things used to be. Can you talk together about what is different in your relationship now?
- When the children were small you obviously did have times when you enjoyed each other's company with the children. What we need to know is how you see yourselves relating to each other now.

Each individual therapist will find his/her own way of facilitating this transition.

The past is obviously of tremendous significance to some couples and needs to be recognised as such by the therapist but, having respected this, the task is to use one's therapeutic skills to bring the couple back to current interaction. It can be very fascinating to allow oneself to become engrossed in the intricacies of life histories. However, within communication training it is nevertheless a diversion from the task in hand.

6.4.9.3 Stopping one partner from focussing on individual pathology
This is a difficult area and one which is dealt with in some detail in Chapter 10 in relation to specific problems. Couples will expect the therapist to be sympathetic with whatever pathology they present, and the therapist should be empathic with their perceptions but at the same time not become trapped into accepting the individual pathology as the complete answer (see Section 4.4.1).

Many of the interventions described in Section 6.4.9.1 can be used to take the emphasis away from the individual focus. The therapist may well have to intervene to say:

I understand what you are saying about Mary's depression and the impact you see that having on your marriage, but can we now look at what else is happening in your lives as a couple?

The therapist may have to be a little directive in order to help the couple find other aspects of their relationship to describe. They may have become so overwhelmed by the nature of the individual pathology that they need help to think about other parts of their lives together, such as

- Their daily routine: who does what, when do they meet together as a couple?
- What do they do together, or separately?

When the therapist takes the focus off the pathology, it is important to ensure that the couple carry on a discussion in the session on a simple, different topic. Where couples have a fixed notion that the individual pathology is the complete explanation for their marital difficulties the therapist may find that they are not yet ready for communication training. However, it is usually helpful to test out whether the couple are flexible enough to respond to communication training before deciding to change to another form of intervention such as structural or strategic interventions (see Chapters 8, 9 and 10).

6.5 *Encouraging mutual exchange of emotional messages*

It is, perhaps, in this area of communication of feelings and mutual empathy that the couples we see have the highest hopes, fears, disappointments and struggles. It is, perhaps, also not too surprising. The concept of falling in love itself (where mutual) implies a relationship of intense and intuitively shared feelings for the other person, a sense that this particular person knows and cares for me alone and a relationship in which nothing needs to be explained or communicated because one is simply in a state of being in love (see Section 1.2). It is perhaps not surprising that a sense of disillusionment is often part of the current relationship. Somehow the fantasy has not materialised.

Some of the patterns which seem to develop between couples in their wish to relate to each other at this more intuitive and sensitive level of feelings are described elsewhere in the book (Sections 1.2.1, 2.3 and 3.2). We are here trying to consider what alternatives the therapist can offer to such couples. A note of caution needs to be sounded. Because of this disparity between the ideal and the reality, the fantasy and the familiar relationship, we feel that a delicate path should be trodden by the therapist when working with a couple's emotional interactions. Each therapist no doubt carries some model of his/her own ideal relationship, some concept of what a shared state of intimacy might be, some sense of the best level of emotional interaction.

Chapter 1 examines some of the questions raised regarding a couple's search for intimacy, closeness and distance. These issues will not be rehearsed again here. However, the concept that each couple may well be trying to negotiate a degree of emotional distance or closeness which each spouse can tolerate is a valuable metaphor and a useful backdrop to our work. What we seek to do in therapy is to assist the couple to develop a level of emotional interaction which meets their joint needs and fulfils, as closely as possible, their requirements for an emotionally satisfying relationship. However, one must bear in mind that they may have quite dissimilar desires and may seek very different levels of emotional intimacy.

Equally, the therapist's own ideals may well be quite different. In order to achieve more mutual satisfaction in their relationship we offer to the couple interventions designed to give them greater flexibility in how they relate to each other at an emotional and empathic level. In order to avoid the therapist imposing his/her own values, although he/she may be very active in assisting the couple towards sharing emotional issues, he/she tries to ensure that each partner's own needs and wishes are respected by both the other partner and the therapist.

A rule of thumb, therefore, is to ensure that as far as possible individuals are asked to speak for their own emotions. The therapist may ask a spouse to guess what he thinks the partner is feeling, but this should be checked with the spouse as soon as possible (see Chapter 4).

Alternative interventions are discussed in the following sections.

6.5.1 Asking the expressive partner to encourage the spouse to speak about his/her feelings

Example 6N

Pat and Theresa K (*see also Example 6H*) had been married 15 years and came to the clinic worried that their relationship had severely deteriorated, but desperate to see whether their marriage could be saved for the sake of the children. Pat expressed more hopefulness about their marriage than did his wife. However she cried a great deal in the session and was expressive about their difficulties while Pat spoke in a stony monotone and sat stiffly erect, remaining apparently unresponsive to his wife's tears. The therapist, seeing how easy it was for Theresa to communicate her feelings openly and how apparently difficult it was for Pat, intervened to ask Theresa if she could ask Pat to tell her what feelings he had about their present, very deteriorated relationship.

THERAPIST
Can you see if you can find a way to help your husband to tell you how he feels about your present relationship?

THERESA
He won't talk about it.

THERAPIST
I realise that it may be difficult for you both but I'd like you to try and see if you can ask him now.

THERESA (*turning to her husband*)
OK. How do you feel about the way our relationship is at present?

PAT
Dreadful!

This was followed by a pause in which Theresa looked at the therapist and shrugged her shoulders.

THERAPIST
Great you've made a start. Carry on gently, see if you can help your husband say what he means by dreadful.

THERESA (*this time in a slightly softer voice*)
Paddy, what do you mean it's dreadful?

PAT
You surely know what I mean, there's no affection, no comfort around for any of us.

THERAPIST (*pressing gently*)
Theresa can you find out what that is like for him, to feel there is no affection around?

THERESA
So, what's that like for you?

PAT (*slowly with obvious feeling*)
Completely devastating, I feel depressed most of the time, I feel life's hardly worth living, and wonder what in God's name is going to happen to us all.

THERESA (*looking quite concerned*)
But Paddy you've never said that it upset you before now.

PAT
I suppose I've never been asked before.

With the therapist's help they carry on to explore further together how Pat has been; moving on later to consider how Theresa felt to hear her husband talk about these feelings for the first time.

In such a way the therapist was able to add a degree of flexibility into their communication about feelings, and help them share more equally the difficulties they both faced, but did not express, thus increasing their awareness of their personal and shared emotional experiences.

With such couples this seems to make it more possible for the expressive partner to develop some of the more rational attributes of the relationship which had been expressed previously by the other partner, and for each to be a little more empathic with the other.

6.5.2 Where a couple express a limited range of feelings, encourage them to explore together other feelings

The therapist may wish to use one of the following alternatives:

- Feed back to the couple that they are skilled at showing their anger to each other and ask them to see if they can talk to each other quietly about a particular topic which can be chosen in the session. The therapist should feel free to join in and help them to find a suitable topic, but couples are usually quite good at suggesting one. It should be made a light and playful experience.
- If a couple usually treat each other very gently the therapist may choose to suggest they talk about their irritation with each other.

- If sadness is their familiar emotion the therapist can help them to talk about some exciting or dangerous feelings.
- Whatever feelings seem to be being withheld, the therapist can try to help them to increase their repertoire of shared emotional experiences.

6.5.3 The committee meeting

Where current issues are being presented factually, and difficult feelings are not being stated, ask one partner to see if s/he can explore with the other, the feelings involved.

Example 6O
Billy and Brenda O (see Example 6I) were negotiating to sell their separate houses and to buy a third house in a new area, in the country, into which they would move together with Brenda's two children by her first marriage. This was being described in a very matter of fact voice by Billy while Brenda sat fidgeting in her chair, but joining in with the same unemotional manner . . .

THERAPIST
Billy can you ask your wife Brenda how all of these changes make her feel?

Brenda began by being very unemotional and then burst into tears. After some time she was able to say how impossible it all was for her and the children.
This couple were trying to build a new marriage together and had been very practical about the selling of their previous homes, the new mortgage arrangements, plans to move house, etc. They had not felt safe enough to discuss the impact of all of these changes on each other. They were able to go on and discuss very tenderly the pros and cons and difficulties they shared in building a new life together.

Once the therapist has learned to focus on the couple's own ability to share or withold their emotions, s/he can adapt the intervention to suit the special needs of each couple. Giving the couple a secure experience, in the session, of expressing other emotions is an effective way to increase their flexibility. It also increases their ability to relate to each other at an emotional level while respecting each other's separateness.

6.6 Choosing alternative interventions if communication training is too difficult

Within the behavioural-systems approach the therapist has a wide spectrum of alternative interventions to use, depending upon what is being presented by the couple. If the therapist finds that the couple are not responding to communication training then an alternative form of therapy should be considered, and the therapist can move up the ALI hierarchy into a structural or strategic approach (see Chapter 3). Communication training may be reintroduced later in therapy, when they have become more flexible. Alternatively, where the couple have learned more communication skills then the therapist may wish to move down the hierarchy and reintroduce some reciprocity negotiation. In this way (as with other interventions) the therapist uses the introduction of communication training as part of ongoing assessment.

Where communication training is having little effect alternative suggestions might be

(1) Try a structural approach (Chapter 8).
(2) Keep a paradoxical message in mind. But do not use simply because you are feeling frustrated.
(3) Do they have a specific issue as a couple? Is one partner depressed or jealous, or is the woman reluctant to have sex? If so try special strategies (Chapter 10).
(4) Don't give up; there will probably be a strategy, it is just a question of being flexible enough to find it.

Where communication has improved try moving down the ALI hierarchy to reciprocity negotiation.

Chapter 7

Systems thinking

7.1 Introduction

At this point in the book and in the hierarchy of alternative levels of intervention (ALI), we change gear from the more behavioural approach to therapy and describe how within the behavioural-systems approach we select from the body of systems theory those concepts which we find most useful.

In Chapter 8 we go on to describe structural interventions which can be used in-session to facilitate changes in a couple's interaction. The systems approach is developed further in Chapter 9, where the focus is on how messages, timetables and tasks can be used to take further the work begun in-session. These messages often contain tasks which have been started in-session and are to be continued by the couple at home between sessions. Chapters 8 and 9 are therefore somewhat arbitrarily divided between in-session work and messages, with some obvious overlap between the two chapters.

The behavioural approach has been well tested and can be said to be a reliable treatment method for many couples, particularly those who are mildly to moderately distressed (Gurman 1973; Jacobson and Weiss 1978; Gurman and Kniskern 1981). Systems approaches, on the other hand, have been inadequately researched, but are increasingly used by experienced therapists who find that they offer a new and imaginative perspective to working with families and couples, being perhaps most useful where negotiation between the partners is unproductive. They bring flexibility and purpose into many situations which therapists might have found intractable.

We use the phrase systems theory in a general sense to indicate that body of knowledge, derived from general systems theory and the physical sciences, which has provided therapists with a useful metaphor to describe family interaction since the 1960s (see Hoffman 1981).

Since the purpose of this book is to describe the behavioural-systems approach of the Maudsley marital therapy clinic, in as practical terms as possible, we will not be devoting much space to the debate about the various aspects of systems theory, except to note that there are some unresolved issues about which healthy disagreement continues (see Section 7.4).

In introducing a systems approach we wish to be cautious about claims that it is anything other than an innovative extension to the inventory of alternative strategies so far available to therapists. To Salvador Minuchin, systems theory is a revolution or paradigm shift in thinking that has occurred in psychotherapy over the last 40 years (Minuchin *et al.* 1978). We, on the other hand, feel that systems theory provides us with a helpful, but incomplete, conceptualisation of human relationships which allows us to develop useful hunches about the dynamics of couples' interactions. Research is needed to determine whether systems theory has produced a real increase in the effectiveness of therapy. However, we feel confident at a clinical level that systemic interventions can succeed with couples who are unresponsive to the more straightforward behavioural techniques.

7.1.1 Reformulation

As we move within this book, and within our way of working, from reciprocity negotiation and communication training to a systems approach, we are accepting that a shift is necessary. This shift requires a reformulation of conceptual thinking and a restructuring of the way of working with the couple. To quote Minuchin

> 'Identical observations yield radically different working formulations when they are organised according to different conceptual frameworks.'

The systems approach provides a useful way of reformulating the data observed and of working with the couple. It is like looking at a three-dimensional scene from a different position. By taking a different viewpoint it is possible to extend one's repertoire of skills and facilitate some modifications in the couple's interaction, where other methods have failed.

This shift from observed data to hypothesised patterns is innovative and problematic for the worker: innovative because it offers a reformulation of the way of working and an extension to one's skills, and problematic because it is neither a complete answer nor conceptually clear. However, familiarity with this perspective and competence in using a systems approach is a desirable extension to one's knowledge and skills. Systems thinking makes it easier to facilitate changes in couples who previously have seemed too rigid, or where one partner is seen by the other partner to be the problem or is ill in some way (see Chapter 10).

7.1.2 Phraseology

While acknowledging an indebtedness to systems theorists and practitioners, we are concerned that the terminology used is too mechanistic: for example, positive and negative feedback loops. Where possible we prefer to use phraseology which reflects more nearly the observed interactions of the couple in therapy, for example circularity, alliances and boundaries (Sections 7.3.1 and 7.3.6).

7.1.3 Wider focus

When using reciprocity negotiation or communication training the therapist focusses on the detail and content of the interaction, both stated and unstated, and intervenes actively to change some small parts of this interaction (for example how not to add a sting in the tail of a positive statement, Section 6.4.7). Within a systems framework the therapist is asked to widen the focus from observing small details of the interaction, to observing the total context in which the participating individuals find themselves. This means noticing the process and pattern of the interaction, rather than the content and specific details of how the couple communicate with each other.

7.1.4 Alternative transactions

When intervening, the therapist endeavours to give the couple an experience in the session of alternative transactional patterns rather than to become more efficient at using current transactions. According to Minuchin *et al.* (1978)

> 'The systems model which focuses on the individual, the context, and the feedback loops that connect them, leads to the contextual methods of therapy.'

7.1.5 Simplification

Sluzki (1978) states that a systems model also requires an ability to simplify by

> 'focusing on certain behaviours and interpersonal processes at the expense of others – selectively observing events, filtering in those observables that are relevant to the model.'

This simplification makes systems work attractive, but also raises doubts regarding the arbitrary exclusion of data which do not fit the hypotheses being considered.

7.1.6 Gains for the therapist

While acknowledging these uncertainties there are some definite gains for both the therapist and the couple. Once the therapist has practised moving backwards and forwards across this boundary, it is expected that s/he will experience an increase in confidence, a growth in flexibility and creativity and a greater ability to respond to the individuality of each couple. Perhaps the therapist is learning to model an adaptability which the couples may themselves be seeking from therapy (see Olson *et al.* 1983). The benefit to the therapist is then a greater flexibility and sense of freedom, an increased repertoire of skills, as well as perhaps an acknowledgement that one does not need to cling dogmatically to one coherent set of skills and defensively attack others.

7.1.7 Gains for the couple

The benefits to the couple are an enhanced opportunity to break out of painful and rigid interactive patterns, or to make modifications to relationships where a symptom has become lodged in one partner or where an 'illness' which can be seen as illness behaviour is damaging a couple's relationship (see Chapters 3 and 10).

7.2 When to choose a systems approach to therapy
(see Chapter 3)

(1) When the therapist has worked with the couple in a session to negotiate reciprocal changes in behaviour, but the old pattern has remained intact.
(2) When the therapist has attempted to improve the couple's communication and, for the moment, nothing changes.
(3) When the couple both agree that one partner is the only cause for concern, e.g. where both agree that the problem is his drinking/her affair/his gambling.
(4) When one partner's symptoms are stated as the problem. For example, 'we are here because of my husband's depression', or 'the problem is my partner is agoraphobic'.

If, after assessment, any of the above four patterns are prevalent the therapist may choose to work systemically with the couple.

7.3 Concepts forming the basis of our systems thinking
(see Sections 2.2.4 and 12.12 for an exercise in thinking about a relationship systemically)

The behavioural-systems approach uses some systems concepts but finds others less helpful. In this section we describe the key concepts which we find useful. Interventions such as challenging, reframing or intensifying are explained through the use of case presentations in later chapters.

The key theoretical concepts which we find helpful are circularity (Section 7.3.1); rules which appear to govern repetitive sequences of behaviour between couples (Section 7.3.3); the notion of consistency of the interaction (homeostasis) (Section 7.3.4); and the concept that the observed interaction may be serving a function for the present system which can be hypothesised, though not tested (Section 7.3.5). Alliances, boundaries and hierarchies and the concept of overt or covert alliances are also valuable; in particular the quality of the alliance within the parental pair or the decider sub-system is central to couple therapy (Section 7.3.6). Finally, the concept of closeness and distance regulation, though still inexact, provides a useful way of thinking about many aspects of couple relationships (Section 7.3.7).

As already stated, we wish to avoid much theoretical discussion of the systems approach as our aim is to present material which is practical and usable. We have, therefore, set aside any debate regarding whether a systems model is static, as Haley (1980) believes:

> 'The chief demerit of systems theory is that it is not a theory of change but a theory of stability'

or whether it has some inherent ability to change: morphogenesis (Maruyama 1968).

We prefer to assume that a systems model which is useful for clinical purposes must be compatible with the developmental model. We therefore assume that healthy systems have a capacity to change over time as the life cycle progresses (Dell 1982; Skynner 1982). Equally, we assume that a healthy family system will have the ability to encourage a degree of autonomy in its individual members enabling a maturational process to occur, as a result of which children will eventually leave the confines of the family and thus spell the end of the nuclear family as it was in their period of growing up. Hence enmeshment and autonomy are concepts which we find useful (Section 2.2.4). We also find useful the concept that systems may develop various sequences over different time dimensions (Cooklin 1982), and that family legends and intergenerational patterns may be a powerful influence upon the present system (Byng-Hall 1982).

Since we are selective in our use of a systems model, the phrase 'systems thinking' describes most aptly our approach, in that we use key concepts to help us think about the couple's interaction and to make choices about which intervention style may be most effective with each couple, rather than carry out purely systemic therapy.

7.3.1 Circularity

According to Hoffman (1981)

> 'The central concept of the new epistemology – both the homeostatic and the evolutionary paradigm – is the idea of circularity.'

In the following verbatim extract from a couple's first interview, we can see that the couple are searching for causes of their difficult relationship and blaming each other. From a systems perspective such notions as cause and effect, allocation of blame and responsibility are considered to be inappropriate. Rather it is assumed that, in a relationship, things happen not because one person is sick, wicked or irresponsible, but as a result of a complex cycle of interaction in which both partners participate.

Example 7A
Tony and Jane M have been married for 18 years and the marriage has become a burden over the last two years. They have the following conversation in a session following a silence.

JANE
Your ideas politically are over the top.

TONY
You always say that I am rigid and you can't agree with my political views.

JANE
I don't bother to point things out any more, or respond. You really are no good at communicating interesting ideas.

TONY
You aren't interested in political things.

JANE
You always have to read moral rules, everything for you is either a wrong position or a right position. You are all over the place and exaggerate everything. You're full of anxiety.

TONY
You panic over a 15 year old being alone on a continental holiday.

JANE
I know more about children than you do.

TONY
I don't think the way you do.

JANE
I've closed off. I've stopped listening to you.

This was followed by silence.

Considering this interaction systemically, by simplifying and abstracting, one can describe the interaction as being one in which criticism is followed by criticism. Within this interaction it could be assumed that if wife criticises – husband cirticises. It could also be assumed that the problem could be stated as if husband criticises – wife criticises. The two statements are seen systemically as arbitrary ways of punctuating the interaction, neither of which has any more validity than the other.

One might hypothesise either that Jane would criticise less if Tony criticised less or vice versa. In either case, the interdependence of action and reaction can be said to be circular and neither partner can be seen as the cause of the argument. This notion of circularity is one of the central concepts of systems thinking.

Working within a communication training framework one would be observing the detail of this interaction as one in which there are many negative statements, mind-reading and speaking for the other person (see Chapter 6). However, from within the systems framework one is looking at the totality of the interaction.

Circularity can be summarised as follows:

(1) The individual is not considered to exist as an isolate, but is viewed as both an initiator and responder to a process (see Example 7A).
(2) This process is patterned by the participants in such a way that each participant is both constrained and supported by the other's behaviour.

Circularity is then a central concept in which there is no beginning point nor a linear causal sequence. Instead, each interaction is perceived to have both an antecedent and a response which moves in an 'infinite dance of interacting parts' in a circular fashion (Bateson 1979). It is circular because one cannot define a beginning point, even though sequences of behaviour can be observed.

7.3.2 Exclusions implied by circularity

Some of the more releasing aspects of a systems approach are the consequences of non-linear thinking. Because we are no longer being asked to define cause and effect we can set aside some of the potentially damaging linear constructs regarding interpersonal dynamics. The following are some of the major ideas that are now excluded from systems thinking.

(1) Blame, fault and responsibility are generally excluded from consideration, i.e. therapists are not engaged in searching for who is to blame for any particular interaction.
(2) Behaviour such as gambling, drinking or excessive involvement with computers, work, the children, his mother, her affair, etc., is excluded from being the sole responsibility of one partner.
(3) Symptoms such as depression, anorexia or panic attacks are no longer seen to rest solely in one person but become part of the observed interaction. Many aspects of illness are ignored (see Chapter 10 for special issues).

The concept of circularity seems to us a very useful one. Particularly useful is the concept that any labelling of a person as sick or bad is now seen as a process arising from the context of the total relationship, rather than as a purely individual illness or behaviour pattern.

We realise that in formulating individual behaviour in systems terms, and thereby excluding concepts of individual blame or responsibility, we are going against what we have already said in Chapter 5. In reciprocity negotiation, each individual is asked to take responsibility for his/her own actions; whereas in systemic work circular causation excludes the idea of individual responsibility. Neither of these formulations should be accepted as a complete explanation of the behaviour, but should rather be seen as alternative views of it from different perspectives. We use the concepts empirically and work within the different paradigms according to their effectiveness in altering the problematic behaviour. Obviously the therapist has to live with this conflict of theoretical perspectives and is expected to move from one to the other without losing sight of the ultimate goal of improving the relationship.

7.3.3 The rules which appear to govern repetitive sequences

From observations of Jane and Tony M's interaction (Example 7A), various rules can be described in a way which suggests that they operate to control the interaction, particular attention being paid to the length and intensity of the exchanges.

Jackson (1965) spent some time trying to understand the nature of these rules and concluded that they are best understood as descriptions of the interaction. He preferred to use the phrase 'as if'; that is, for the purpose of conceptualization, it is useful to describe the system as functioning 'as if' there were such and such a rule. This is a helpful clarification. Thus in Example 7A one can describe the relationship 'as if' a rule can be formulated which controls the repetitive sequence of interactions, in which the couple move from silence, through a series of communications complaining about the other's behaviour, back to silence. The interaction can be seen, in the session, to take the same form regardless of whether the husband or wife initiates or closes the repetitive sequence.

The concepts of positive and negative feedback loops can be used to explain these repetitive sequences, although these are limited and mechanistic concepts which do not necessarily help the therapist understand the repetitive behaviour. From the therapist's viewpoint, what is most helpful is to learn to recognise repetitive sequences and to find ways of intervening, for example either to intensify the interaction or to change the time dimension of the sequences, and so facilitate a required change (Hoffman 1971; Feldman 1976).

The repetitive sequences are sometimes conceptualised as symmetrical, complementary or a balanced mix of the two (Jackson 1968). Bateson (1958 and 1971) suggested that in symmetrical relationships 'the behaviour of A and B would be essentially similar, as in cases of rivalry or competition'. In the complementary relationship 'the self generating actions would be different, as in cycles of dominance–submission or succoring–dependence'. The interaction of Tony and Jane would be described as symmetrical, whereas the interaction between Samuel and Diana S (Example 8C) can be seen as complementary.

These rules seem to act 'as if' they are a regulatory mechanism governing the repetitive sequences of interaction, keeping the interaction within an accustomed level of functioning. Each system is said to be on a spectrum between, at one end, a very closed and internally self-regulating system with fixed and rigid boundaries and, at the other end, a system which is very open, has few if any clear boundaries, has few if any internal rules and is sometimes described as chaotic (Beavers 1983; Olson *et al.* 1983).

7.3.4 Consistency of the interaction (homeostasis)

A further assumption taken from systems theory and based on observation of couples and families is that any interaction tends to have an internal consistency, such that one can often predict the reaction of either partner within a given situation. The concept of homeostasis, with positive and negative feedback loops which together perform the function of keeping the system stable, is a theoretical framework which seems to fit this observed phenomenon. The usual example given by family therapists is that of the central heating system with its thermostatic control which turns off the heating as it reaches the temperature on the thermostat and turns it on again as the heat drops, thus keeping the house in a stable and controlled environment (Skynner 1982).

While accepting that the concept of homeostasis is helpful in understanding this phenomenon, we prefer to think in terms of consistency of action and interaction over time. This is similar to what Dell (1982) describes as coherence. Dell is worried about what he calls 'paradigm protecting patchwork' in which he sees systems thinkers adding to and patching systems theory in order to accommodate the question as to whether systems change, and if so what mechanisms are used. He prefers the concept of coherence which, he suggests, embodies within it both the notion of stability and change:

> 'Coherence simply implies a congruent interdependence in functioning whereby all aspects of the system fit together'

He uses the saying of Heraclitus 'You can never step into the same river twice' to underline what in his view is the inevitability of change in any system. He suggests that any system has an inherent ability to adapt over time, as for example

> 'If a woman continues to jog, both her physique and her physiology will become coherent with her behaviour. In addition even her social behaviour and daily life will become coherent with her jogging.'

In this example one can see both consistency of action and interaction over time and the ability to change.

Whether we use terms which are somewhat mechanistic and limited, such as homeostasis and feedback loops, or whether we can describe exactly the mechanism involved, consistency is observed in many couples' interaction. As therapists we are also constantly surprised by the ingenuity and responsiveness of couples and their ability to develop alternative and unexpected reactions; this may happen spontaneously or as a result of therapeutic input.

7.3.5 Hypothesising and the function of the current repetitive sequences

The three concepts, circularity, rules which appear to govern repetitive sequences and the concept that there is a consistency of interaction over time, when taken together form the basis on which hypotheses are developed.

A variety of alternative hypotheses are considered, first to think about what function the repetitive sequences of interaction might perform in maintaining the system as a whole, and second as a basis upon which to choose which intervention is most likely to be effective in changing the system.

Example 7B
Bill B, 36 years old and Mary, 38 years old, had been married for six years. For five years they had been trying to have a baby and had had many infertility tests. When Mary eventually did become pregnant, she was excited and Bill was horrified. He did not think that he could cope with 'being a dad'. After childbirth Mary suffered from postnatal depression and Bill could not understand why she was depressed. Over the past few months Mary had become preoccupied with the care of the baby and Bill had become more and more involved with his work, working late hours at the office or at home. They rarely talked to each other any more. Both would say that the baby kept them in the marriage.

So, what was causing the problem? Was it the mother's excitement or the father's horror at discovering that Mary was pregnant? Was it the mother's postnatal depression or was it the father's lack of understanding regarding his wife's depression? Was it the mother's preoccupation with the baby or the father's preoccupation with his work? Thinking systemically the problem is none of these things; the problem lies in the system as a whole and the rules and the repetitive sequences that govern the totality of their interaction. For example, a variety of hypotheses might be developed containing the following elements:

- that Bill's horror and anxiety about 'being a Dad' is maintained by Mary's expectations and excitement;
- that her depression is maintained by the husband's lack of understanding of her situation following the birth of the baby;
- that the husband's preoccupation with his work and Mary's preoccupation with the baby are maintaining each other;
- that their inability to talk to each other is maintained by Mary's initial excitement and Bill's initial horror at the thought of being a dad, and so on.

One has the experience of 'here we go around the mulberry bush!' which is a characteristic of circularity. The above statements might be considered to be hypothesised rules governing the functioning of the system as a whole.

Hypotheses which seem to fit many couples who attend the clinic are that the couple's interaction may be said to perform in one or more of the following ways:

- Avoidance of conflict (see Section 8.2.1).
- As a distance regulator keeping the couple at an acceptable emotional distance by, for example:
  (a) avoidance of sexual intimacy
  (b) avoidance of physical or non-verbal closeness
  (c) avoidance of emotional empathy
  (d) avoidance of operational closeness (see Section 1.2.5).
- Depression (or other symptoms) in one partner may be a way of protecting the other partner from showing his/her depression (or other painful feelings) (see Sections 9.7 and 10.7).
- triangles, in which a third person is involved in the couple relationship, may be a way of:
  avoiding intimacy between the partners (Section 1.3)
  bringing excitement into the couple relationship
  avoiding separation from the family of origin (see Section 10.13)
- Difficulties experienced in the older marriage may function
  to keep adolescent children tied to the home
  to avoid boredom in an older marriage (see Section 10.14)
- The reciprocal elements of jealousy from one partner and pleas of faithfulness from the other partner may serve to remind couples who have a low self-esteem of their attaction to and need for the other person (see Section 10.5.5).
- Sexual refusal by one partner may be part of a power struggle in which one partner dominates in their non-sexual interaction and the other dominates in their sexual relationship (see Section 10.10).

Some elements of the above hypotheses are common to many interactions, but equally each couple will present with its own unique interaction. Part of the skill and creativity in developing hypotheses is to ensure that the individuality of each couple is reflected in the content and wording of each hypothesis.

In presenting the above material, we admit to experiencing some difficulty in fully accepting this level of simplification, as there are likely to be many other factors affecting the behaviour of each spouse. However, within systems thinking one is asked to conceptualise in this simple and selective manner in order to hypothesise about possible key circular interactions which can be considered to maintain the status quo of the system (Feldman 1976). Within this approach hypotheses are thought of as tools for the use of the therapist, rather than truths which can be tested. Used in this manner hypothesising is a flexible and innovative way of thinking about the couple in order to find alternative effective interventions.

7.3.6 Alliances, boundaries and hierarchies
(see also Section 2.2.4)

The concepts of appropriate alliances, boundaries and hierarchies are said to be essential to a healthy functioning family system (Minuchin 1974, 1981). Conceptually at the top of the hierarchy is the parental alliance or couple who share the positions of authority and have responsibility for each other and for their children (in extended families there may be several overlapping hierarchies). How the parental alliance exercises authority and takes responsibility, whether jointly by considered agreement, jointly in resentful acquiescence or in total disagreement, becomes material for the systems therapist. The parental authority and control influences the whole family constellation (Haley and Minuchin use the term decider sub-system, see Section 7.3.6.3).

Alliances are also said to form between different members of the family. How these alliances function within the family system is observed and used in developing working hypotheses. An assumption made by systems thinking is that a firm boundary needs to be maintained around the parental couple so that there is a sound parental alliance and a workable distance kept between the children and the parents. According to Minuchin (1981)

'One of the spouse sub-system's most vital tasks is the development of boundaries that protect the spouses, giving them an area for the satisfaction of their own psychological needs without the intrusion of in-laws, children, and others. The adequacy of these boundaries is one of the most important aspects to the viability of the family structure.'

In the next example (7C) there was little, if any, firm boundary being maintained around the parental pair, and the children were therefore at risk.

Example 7C
The family consisted of father Tim aged 37 years, mother Tina aged 36 years, three daughters Merryl 18 years, Sandra 16 years and Samantha aged 14 years and Billy, a 10-year-old son. This is a family in which the father had sexually abused the daughter Merryl, for two years from 15–17 years of age. During that time Sandra and her father had also had some contact of an intimate sexual nature. The two younger children were not said to be at risk from the father's attentions. Tina had also been sexually abused as a child by several different people.

The husband was sent to prison for one year for his offence. After he had served his time, the question arose as to whether this family could be reunited. We were asked to help in the assessment of the couple's relationship by the hospital unit which had been helping the children and carrying out family therapy.

As they allowed us to get to know their situation more thoroughly a complex pattern of interaction emerged. Tina had always spent most of her time with the children, with whom she felt she had a warm relationship but of which Tim said 'she's got no control of the kids'. It seemed that she was more often 'one of the kids' than the parent. She found it hard to discipline the family, especially her daughters.

A typical interaction would occur when Tim came home in the evening and Tina would recount to him how the children had misbehaved. However, if Tim tried to intervene with the children he would be prevented by Tina who would defend them. Tim would easily become moody, 'blow his top' and refuse to talk to his wife. He became increasingly taciturn and his most effective way of helping Tina with the family was by shouting at them. This would upset Tina who complained 'I wish he would talk rather than shouting at them'. His response was 'someone's got to keep them in line and stop them abusing their mother'.

The husband increasingly found himself isolated from all affection, both emotional and physical, and from any practical involvement in the daytime activities of the family. He was volatile and somewhat punitive towards the children, except towards the eldest daughter who often intervened between the couple as a peacemaker and seemed to be trying to placate both parents by being helpful to both.

Tina for her part had always found sexual intercourse difficult, and for several years prior to the sexual abuse she had been regularly refusing to have intercourse. She found it difficult to allow her husband to touch her or to enjoy physical closeness. If he did approach her for sexual intercourse they would usually have a violent row, with a certain amount of physical fighting.

The aim of therapy was initially to explore the couple's relationship and to see whether there was any possibility of building a better relationship between the couple. At the beginning of treatment Tim's concern was to help his wife accept him sexually. He wanted to persuade her to see herself as sexy and be more prepared to dress up to look young and attractive. He was upset that she did not seem to want to try to have sex with him. Tina was prepared to try to overcome these difficulties but was most concerned that the family should be reunited. It seemed that she was prepared to do anything to enable this to happen, and felt that her refusal to have sex with her husband might have contributed to Tim's incestuous relationship with their daughter.

Initially neither parent seemed particularly concerned that the eldest daughter had been sexually abused by the husband. Their wish, at that time, was to persuade the authorities that it was acceptable to allow Tim to return home permanently. Both of the elder daughters had, however, insisted that if he were allowed to return they would certainly leave home.

The next two sections are commentary on this case, while discussion continues also in Section 10.12 and Example 10H.

7.3.6.1 *Overt alliances*
We can see in this family that the overt alliance between the parents was both fragile and shifting and was easily disrupted. These disruptions

occurred either around their own sexual relationship or regarding the control of the children. Tina sometimes sided with the children against the husband whom she wished was 'more understanding with the children'. The hierarchy of responsibility and control was diffused and boundaries had become blurred.

In this family the boundaries around the overt parental alliance had become so blurred that the eldest daughter had been used by the husband to satisfy his sexual needs: a very severe and damaging crossing of boundaries. Equally one might suggest that the wife was uncertain about her parental role, preferring to ally with the children as part of the sibling group, rather than exert her authority as part of the parental alliance.

Neither parent, at this stage in therapy, seemed to understand the need to keep the children out of the parents' bedroom, either literally or metaphorically, nor to understand the responsibility of parents regarding the sexual development of their children. In this sense there was no overt parental alliance and their joint executive functions in relation to respecting the sexual boundary between parent and offspring did not exist.

Although they did struggle to communicate with each other about the general disciplining of their family, one could also say that there was little overt executive alliance in this area either.

7.3.6.2 Covert alliances
We also know that other alliances in the family had been covert and had crossed the sexual boundaries usually seen as the sole province of the parents. These covert alliances had been between the eldest daughter Merryl and the father, and possibly a more tentative alliance between the father and Sandra. These alliances can be said to contain an unequal power relationship with the daughters submitting to a powerful father who had set aside the taboo against a sexual relationship between father and daughter. The taboo defines a boundary which carries with it heavy penalties both at a personal and legal level, yet within the family this boundary was not well kept.

The parental alliance became so weakened that this covert alliance between father and daughter was allowed to develop, both partners playing some part in allowing this to happen. When this occurs everyone is disadvantaged.

7.3.6.3 The parental alliance: the parental pair (Minuchin 1974) or the decider sub-system of Haley (1976)
(see also Section 2.2.4)
Systems thinking considers that for a parental alliance to function optimally there should be an overt, agreed and consistent approach to the children carried out by both parents (or partners). At the same time, there should be a clear boundary around the parents, so that children do not intrude into the parental alliance.

The parental alliance is most easily understood when considering the need to keep the parental sexual alliance intimate and separate from involvement of the children, whatever their age. There are, however, many other aspects of family life that are most appropriately dealt with by the parental pair without the involvement of any of the children. Examples might be choices about major items such as work and management of the family budget, general disciplining of the children and choices about schooling and religious education. These may all be dealt with by the parents without the involvement of the children. As children grow up so their opinion may well be sought about some of the matters which affect them. However, a separate agreement between the parental alliance about how such matters are best handled is also needed.

Equally, there are significant times in the life cycle of a family when the parental alliance becomes of necessity temporarily blurred. When a baby is born into a family it intrudes into the parental alliance by the very nature of its dependence upon the mother. When children are ill and sleep in the parental bed, for the comfort of both child and parent, then boundaries are temporarily blurred. When the whole family spends a holiday in a tent, sharing the same space for eating and sleeping, one could say that the alliances are opened up, the hierarchies flattened and the boundaries temporarily set aside. Such examples are accepted as part of the flexibility of healthy family life, that is the ability of the family to adjust its patterns of interaction to accommodate the immediate family situation (Beavers 1985). They can also become areas of difficulty for couples who continuously have to share overcrowded accommodation with in-laws, children or non-family members.

It is also clear that standards vary from community to community and that there are cultural variations about such issues. Sharing the same room or the same bedspace as the parents, and at what age it is seen as appropriate and possible to have separate sleeping accommodation, must depend somewhat on circumstance and culture.

Prolonged or acute illness in the family affects the management of boundaries and may have a disastrous impact upon the parental alliance. There are many examples of one parent being deeply and necessarily involved with children during illness, but being unable to reinstate these boundaries after the illness. This leads to structural distortions which affect the whole family (see Example 8A).

The anorexic girl may also have developed an over-involved or enmeshed relationship with one parent whilst the relationship with the other parent may be cold and distant, again intervening in the parental alliance (Minuchin 1978). The impact of emotional over-involvement of one parent with a family member who has been diagnosed as schizophrenic can be seen as evidence of similar inappropriate alliances and an intrusion into the parental alliance (Leff 1976, 1982).

In adolescence the boundaries become more difficult either to describe or to manage. For, in this period, the growing child is sometimes co-equal with the parent and almost part of the parental alliance, and sometimes the dependent child. This is in some way re-experienced by middle-aged couples who care for their aging parents and find the relationship oscillating between a parent/child/parent relationship as their parents grow more frail and become more dependent upon them.

7.3.7 The concept of closeness and distance
(see also Section 1.2.5)

Closely related to the concept of boundaries and alliances is the concept of closeness and distance. We have already discussed this in Section 1.2.5 and pointed out that closeness or intimacy can have at least four facets: sexual closeness, physical and non-verbal closeness, emotional empathy and operational closeness. In much of the literature on family therapy these aspects are combined in the concept of closeness and distance. Byng-Hall (1980) refers to the way in which a symptomatic child can help the parental pair to cope with their fears of intimacy by acting as a distance regulator. Other family members or friends can be triangled in to the relationship in a similar way, with the effect of diluting the exclusiveness of the couple relationship (for discussion see triangles, Section 10.13). Couples can also be said to be maintaining distance by generating arguments whenever they become too close and affectionate for comfort.

At opposite ends of the distance/closeness spectrum are the concepts of enmeshment (Minuchin 1974) and disengagement (see also Section 2.2.4). These are used by Olson *et al.* (1983) as criteria for their cohesion scale in the assessment of family function, and they suggest that well functioning families are somewhere in the middle of the scale, showing a balance between connectedness (a milder form of enmeshment) and separateness (a milder form of disengagement). Allied to this is the flexibility shown by well functioning families in their ability to move from one end of the scale to the other in response to circumstances without remaining rigidly separated or connected. A more specific form of enmeshment is described by Leff and Vaughn (1985) as emotional over-involvement by close relatives of schizophrenic patients which is associated with a high rate of recurrence of the illness.

In couples, such enmeshment can be seen as contributing to problems presenting as illness behaviour: two examples in other chapters are those of jealousy (Example 10C) and depression (Example 10F). Excessive disengagement can also be seen in other couples, for example when they are leading very separate lives and never have time for each other (Example 9C).

A further difficulty which can arise in the area of distance and closeness is when one partner desires more intimacy (whether emotional or sexual) than the other. A kind of chase can then ensue in which the partner desiring more involvement actually drives the other partner into more disengagement by his/her demands, which can become strident and aversive in response to the other partner's lack of involvement.

7.4 Areas of uncertainty in the systems approach

We have described the key concepts which we take from systems theory to use in the behavioural-systems approach as an aid to thinking about alternative intervention strategies. As already stated, systems theory brings a refreshing new perspective to old problems.

However, sufficient uncertainties regarding the validity of systems theory exist to make it necessary for the therapist using it to retain a degree of scepticism. The major uncertainties revolve around how systems theory encompasses questions such as physical and mental illness, change and developmental factors such as the emergence into adulthood of the child, environmental factors such as poverty or bad housing and the part played by the individual dynamics or personal history. Although different theorists have provided alternative solutions to these uncertain areas, we do not feel that any one theory has yet been able satisfactorily to take account of them.

7.4.1 Illness

In most of systems theory the place of physical and psychiatric illness is glossed over or else not written about. Systems theory allows for the possibility of hypothesising about the function of the illness in the couple or family system, and encourages therapists to take a fresh approach to the search for helpful strategies, but seems to ignore the demonstrable facts of genuine illness (see Sections 4.6.7 and 6.4.9.3).

This simplification, however creative, must be questioned as evidence from many fields of study suggests that illnesses must have multi-dimensional explanations. In thinking about the cause of a particular illness, the following factors might be considered:

(1) Infections caused by bacteria and viruses.
(2) A new formation of tissue in some part of the body (tumour).
(3) Illnesses due to age and degeneration of the body.
(4) Genetic make-up and individual vulnerability.
(5) Family environment.
(6) Stress from life events such as loss of job, status, physical well being, a close relationship or a familiar environment.
(7) Social and cultural factors such as physical environment, diet, ritual and custom.
(8) Drugs and alcohol.
(9) Environmental hazards such as traffic- or work-related accidents.

Any of these elements may play a part in the eventual emergence of an illness.

Some of the illnesses experienced in couples who attend the clinic include severe depression, manic depressive psychosis, schizophrenia, dementia, phobias and obsessions, epilepsy, multiple sclerosis, diabetes, AIDS and many other psychiatric and medical conditions which have a central core of symptoms or behavioural problems which cannot be argued away by taking a systems perspective (Clare 1976; Wing 1978).

We would also wish to take issue with the traditional medical concept of illness as an inevitable and physically determined event, which is too rigid. It may well be that illness could be conceptualised on a sliding scale, with the individual having varying degrees of control over the symptom. Or again, perhaps it could be better described as a spectrum of illnesses over which different individuals have varying abilities to control the symptoms.

We do not feel that the systems approach, any more than other approaches, is an adequate or complete explanation of the concept of illness. It does, however, bring a welcome flexibility into this complex area.

7.4.2 The developmental cycle

A second uncertainty is whether systems theory adequately accounts for the developmental cycle of the individual within the family. We find a high degree of complexity in considering the position of adolescents in relation to boundaries, hierarchies and alliances within the family (Haley 1980). Although little discussed, there are likely to be similar difficulties in conceptualising the changing status of aging parents in relation to their adult children. Rather than enter this discussion, we have stated our view that for most practical purposes it is helpful to assume that developmental theory and systems theory are compatible, and acknowledge that Dell's concept of coherence goes some way towards resolving this difficulty. Skynner (1982) presents a useful framework for viewing the family throughout the life cycle (see also Sections 1.6, 4.3.1.1 and 7.5).

7.4.3 Environment

In order to take into account the influence of circumstances such as poor housing, poverty or wealth, cultural and social pressures, the concept of the wider system is used. Again there seem to be contradictions within the theory which at one time describes the couple as having executive authority, but also assumes a wider system over which the couple may have little or no control.

7.4.4 The individual

Perhaps the most complex omission is that of the individual's contribution to the system. Neither the internal world of each participant nor the personal history of the individual is given any separate validity within the systems perspective. Feldman (1979) makes an eloquent plea for an integration of psychodynamic, behavioural and systems theory, as he sees the internal world of the individual as a powerful factor determining the quality of relationships. He suggests that

> 'the integrated combination of behavioural and psychodynamic interventions offers, in my opinion, far greater therapeutic leverage than either approach by itself.'

Dell (1982), who has produced some thoughtful work on systems theory, suggests that the individual determines the system

> 'in other words, the interactional system is a consequence of the nature (i.e. the behavioural coherence) of the individuals who compose it.'

or again

> 'it is the way it is because that is the way those individuals fit together.'

7.4.5 Summary

In using systems interventions the therapist has therefore to develop the ability to use these alternative approaches and to believe sufficiently in the conceptual framework of systems theory in order to be effective. This means being able to accept that an individual can be diagnosed as schizophrenic, but at the same time to work towards improving the relationship between the patient and his/her partner by focussing on the relationship rather than on the illness; or in a case of depression to acknowledge that a partner is currently depressed but intervene to put the depressed partner into the caring position (Section 10.7.3) and focus away from the illness.

The therapist who wishes to work within the behavioural-systems model is being asked to work from a rather complex theoretical position, sometimes working within a behavioural model and sometimes making a conceptual shift into a systems framework.It is recommended as the position from which the therapist can be of greatest service to the clients and to the interaction observed, thus retaining the option to change his/her way of working to fit the requirements of each couple. This openness, creativity and flexibility are also recommended as useful modelling for very stuck or rigid families.

7.5 *Why use a systems approach in therapy with couples?*

How can a systems approach, which was developed by therapists working with families, be applied to working with the couple? The answer to this question lies in the special significance of the couple within the family, as the couple have a very powerful influence over the healthy functioning of the total family system (see Chapters 1 and 2 and Section 7.3.6).

The couple has a central position in the human life cycle. For those couples who have, or hope to continue in, a long-term relationship, the relationship has to weather many changes in their family system: pregnancies, wanted, unwanted or aborted; babies, healthy or handicapped, being born, going to school, leaving home; illnesses of family members, loss of relatives and parents through illness or accident; the growth of the family through marriage and grandchildren, the shrinking of the family through separation, emigration, or death; increase or loss of status, through work opportunities or unemployment; failure and achievement, success or difficulties. Throughout these life situations, there is a common expectation that the couple can find ways to survive together. It is of some significance that, although divorce is now an acceptable and viable alternative to long-term relationships, by and large two-thirds of marriages survive until the death of one partner.

To work with the couple, separate from the rest of the family, acknowledges the central significance of the couple in the life cycle of an extended family. The couple who desire to improve their relationship are likely to be aware, at some level, that they are a central point of stability which, when functioning reasonably well, can enable the family to survive and to make many of the adaptations which are required of it during its life cycle.

To work with the couple separately from the family may already be creating a structural change in the current functioning of the family system. Many marriage guidance workers and social workers will be familiar with the situation where a wife is concerned about her relationship with her husband, but apparently cannot persuade him to attend with her. She may have little difficulty in persuading her father, mother-in-law or other significant family members to ally with her and come to seek help; however, persuading her husband to accompany her may be difficult (Mattinson and Sinclair 1979). Should the spouse change his mind and accompany her that might indeed be a significant structural change in the couple and family relationship.

These two issues, that of the survival of the couple through many life cycle changes and the centrality of the creative power of the parental alliance in the development of family health, form the basis of our belief that therapy with couples is of the utmost importance to the family.

Within family therapy, where families find themselves in difficulties, the focus of therapy is often to assist the couple to redraw boundaries around themselves as a couple and establish appropriate joint parenting (Minuchin & Fishman 1978; Haley 1980; Hoffman 1981). Indeed Selvini Palazzoli, having spent much of her life working with families, is increasingly suggesting that much important work can be achieved by working with the couple rather than the family (Selviri Palazzoli 1989).

When working with couples where children are causing concern, again the therapy may necessarily focus on their joint parenting skills. Indeed the management of the children is often an area of discord and dysfunction in couples attending the clinic (see Examples 9A and 9B).

It is our experience that problems of parenting and relationships with the extended family members are effectively influenced by working with the couple. As the relationship within the couple improves, so they are more able to share together and resolve difficulties with family members. Although primarily working with couples, we do allow ourselves the flexibility to bring other family members into therapy if it seems sensible. In such situations, family members might attend for a few sessions, after which work would continue with the couple. Finally, although the couple is the unit present in the room for therapy, the couple carry their relationships with their families with them into the sessions.

Having dealt with those aspects of systems theory which we find most helpful, we now move on in Chapters 8, 9 and 10 to show how we apply systems thinking to our clinical work. In these chapters we describe in detail some therapy done within the Maudsley marital therapy clinic, emphasising how the therapist intervened and explaining the thinking behind these interventions. In this way we hope that our readers will find that they can understand not only the theoretical approach but also the manner in which we conduct therapy.

Chapter 8

Structural interventions in-session

8.1 Introduction

Structural interventions (Minuchin 1974; Sluzki 1987) are part of the systems approach in that they derive not from what the couple say they need, but from hypotheses which the therapist or the team has made about their relationship and what is necessary to change it. Thus the task suggested will usually be directed to a different area of interaction from the couple's initial complaint, as the examples of therapy sessions in the chapter will show.

Typical of the interventions we use in the session are those encouraging the couple to communicate more openly, and one way to do this is to induce a heated discussion or argument. We have found that many couples who are rather inhibited about emotional expression can be much more open when they are aroused in argument, and that this can facilitate other changes such as sexual openness and assertiveness. In addition, we use such interventions as asking them to change their positions in the chair, their tone of voice and their hand or arm movements. We may also at times use 'sculpting' as a way of giving them a new experience of interaction (see Section 8.6.3).

The aim of a structural intervention is for the therapist to intervene in such a manner as to enable the couple to experience a different way of relating to each other within the session. In systems language, the therapist is attempting to push the system beyond the accustomed boundaries of interaction. We usually follow this up by setting a task or timetable to be continued at home, which will encourage the couple to build on this experience by practising these new ways of relating to each other on a regular basis. These are described in detail in Chapter 9.

8.2 Encouraging arguments over trivial issues

A structural intervention which we find very helpful for many couples is to encourage arguments over trivial issues in the session. The aim is to give the couple a safe and contained experience of having an argument which has successfully gone beyond their habitual non-productive pattern of interaction.

Many couples seem to have developed a fear of expressing open disagreement with each other and may have developed a sophisticated ability to detour around arguments (see Section 1.2.5). Because of this fear it is important that the topic is chosen by the couple and is seen by them as a trivial disagreement which has not been resolved. Examples of such trivial issues might be the question of who puts or doesn't put the top on the toothpaste tube, who washes up the pots and pans, who locks the door at night, who feeds the cat, or any similiar topic.

Our experience is that such trivial issues, which are nevertheless constant irritants to couples, tend to be meaningful and often symbolic of their relationship as a whole. Resentments and struggles which are felt in the relationship seem to find expression within these trivial issues. However, since the issue is trivial to the couple, they are much more likely to feel safe enough to allow themselves to explore it in therapy.

The therapist may have to be quite active in order to support either or both partners to begin and to continue this argument and should not be tempted to interrupt once it has begun, unless perhaps to tell the couple that they are doing well and could perhaps risk being a bit more forceful. Certainly defusing such an argument (a temptation that most therapists might feel quite strongly) would be counterproductive and should be avoided.

Encouraging arguments over small issues is a useful intervention which helps to increase the mutual exchange of emotional messages. We have included it as a structural intervention within the systems framework because the repetitive sequences which it addresses are not those that the couple seem to be aware of and are therefore not asking to be changed; however, it could also be said to be another form of communication training.

We have described three examples in some detail to show how such in-session arguments might be used with different couples. We find increasingly that encouraging arguments in couples where the husband is reluctant to have intercourse and where he needs to become more assertive seems to facilitate a renewed interest in sex, and such a case has been included. This approach is also quite useful where one partner is depressed to a moderate degree or has low self-esteem accompanied by a lack of assertion.

Several other examples of encouraging arguments over trivial issues can be found in Chapters 9 and 10 (see Sections 9.7 and 9.10). They are described there in order to show how the in-session argument is followed up in the message, in which the setting of tasks and timetables asks the couple to continue at home with the work which has been practised in the session.

8.2.1 Good couples do not argue

Many couples seem to have developed an unstated rule that 'good couples do not argue'. In our experience this often occurs when the presenting issue is a complaint that one partner is depressed, or where the therapist is able to observe a pattern of helplessness in one partner and overprotectiveness in the other. Another familiar pattern is where one can observe sulky silences or sense unspoken resentments in one partner. Similarly, as stated above, in a couple with sexual reluctance, there may be many an unspoken resentment from the man who feels that he should not argue but is finding it difficult to assert himself adequately in the relationship.

In such couples we would try to alter this unspoken rule ('good couples do not argue') by enabling them to have an argument in the session, thus interacting in a way they have so far not allowed themselves to experience (Bach and Wyden 1969, Gordon 1975).

We can help them vary their interaction in several ways. They can be helped to extend the length of the argument. The intensity with which they discuss can be heightened. The pattern of interaction can be changed so that the partner who feels s/he 'usually loses' can be helped to be more assertive and state some request more clearly (see Example 8A). They can be encouraged to continue beyond the particular moment when they would previously have stopped. In all these ways the therapist joins with the couple to assist them to change the rules of the interaction.

Since such couples are usually anxious about arguments, the therapist will need to be confident and persistent in his/her interventions. Also it does not come amiss to enjoy the session, and to encourage the couple to experiment with voice tone, gesture, body position and language. If for example, as often happens, one partner has a loud voice, the therapist can ask that partner to 'teach your partner how to speak in a louder voice'. This in its small way is a structural move to change their accustomed pattern of interaction. The therapist should feel free to encourage the couple to enjoy experimenting.

Example 8A

Edith and Robert S had attempted in the past to argue but had developed a modification of the rule 'good couples do not argue': theirs had become 'it's no good arguing because he always wins, and she always ends up in tears'.

The therapist's plan was to see if he could help them to have a different experience in which Edith might eventually ask for something and Robert might agree to give a little instead of always winning. In order to achieve this with this particular couple the male therapist allied heavily with the wife who was quite depressed (see also Section 10.8).

The couple, both aged 35 years, had met as boss and secretary and married within nine months. They had conceived their first child on the honeymoon and were expecting their second child 11 months later. He was a blunt northern businessman and on referral she was a tearful and truculently silent spouse. Robert's immediate response, in the session, to any effort she made to describe her difficulties was 'Oh for goodness sake, stop whining!', at which Edith would burst into tears and retire behind a soggy handkerchief.

On their second visit, Robert started by complaining that his wife 'doesn't know what a woman ought to know'. She would not initiate sex and this made Robert angry. Edith, through her sobs, said everything is 'terrible'.

THERAPIST (*interrupting and addressing both partners*)
Can you talk about your relationship and what needs to change?

ROBERT
Things are not right, we need to make some real effort to get it sorted out. But my wife doesn't want to try. She doesn't want to make any effort.

(1)   THERAPIST
Robert, I wonder if you would check that out with your wife.

ROBERT (*aggressively*)
What?

(2)   THERAPIST
Whether you are correct that your wife doesn't want to put any effort into getting your relationship sorted out.

ROBERT
Oh I know her, she's not prepared to put any effort into changing things.

THERAPIST (*quietly persisting*)
Well use this opportunity to ask Edith if she is prepared to.

(3)   ROBERT (*rather angrily*)
Well are you? I don't see any evidence of you making any effort.

EDITH (*somewhat roused*)
Why do you think I am here? Anyway what about you? You're the one who should be making some effort especially at the moment.

(4)   THERAPIST (*allying with Mrs S*)
What do you mean when you say Robert could be making more effort. What sort of thing would you want him to do?

EDITH
He's looking for a new job at the moment, I think he shouldn't be looking for a job at the moment. The baby is to be born in June. Surely he should be providing us with more stability rather than looking to change his job just as the baby is born.

ROBERT
What difference does it make to you whether I change my job or not?

With encouragement from the therapist Edith is able to tell her husband what other things she would like to change. She has quite a long list. She'd like him to trust her more with the housekeeping instead of checking on her all the time; she wishes she could have a separate account for herself, as she did before marriage. She begins to say that he has misused her car.

(5)   ROBERT (*aggressively and angrily shouts*)
There you go again, 'my' car, 'my' money, 'my' house. Can't you ever think of anything but 'my'?

EDITH (*now on the edge of tears*)
I wish you wouldn't shout.

(6) THERAPIST (*interrupting to Mrs S.*)
What is it that is happening that is difficult for you.

EDITH
I wish he wouldn't shout. He never seems to consider that I am pregnant and feeling more on edge.

(7) THERAPIST
See if you can find something that you could now ask your husband to do at home. Something small that would show you that he understands that you are pregnant and that he is making an effort to help you.

EDITH (*suddenly seeming to be more perky*)
Yes, I'd like to ask him to get up on Sunday morning to look after Philippa so that I could have a lie in.

ROBERT (*somewhat quieter*)
Yes I could easily do that.

EDITH (*with a wry smile*)
Do you think that you could not shout at me.

ROBERT (*edgily*)
Well I'm not so sure about that.

EDITH
You know how it upsets me.

(8) THERAPIST
I think you had better ask him that directly. Say 'do you know that you upset me when you speak so loudly?'

ROBERT (*irritably, his voice rising as he says it*)
No I don't. How can I? You knew me at work, you saw how I was with the other men. What did you expect?

EDITH (*sniffling quietly*)
That's true, but see I'm pregnant. I feel different. I am so easily upset now.

After this they had a quieter discussion about the effect of the second pregnancy on their marriage. They both agreed it had been a shock that Edith became pregnant so soon with both babies, and that it was going to be harder for them both than they had ever realised. This they had not admitted to one another before now.

The process of helping the couple to have an argument in which each spouse was able to state his/her wishes continued throughout therapy. This meant often allying with Edith to encourage her to be more assertive. By the fourth session Mrs S was more able to speak without dissolving into tears and Mr S was able both to show a tender side of himself to his wife and acknowledge some of his fears of being too soft and therefore not manly enough. He was much reassured to discover that his wife preferred a gentle man. (This case is written up further in Section 10.8 as an example of work with a depressed spouse.)

8.3   The therapist's interventions in the above case

Many of the therapist's interventions, within a systems framework, are designed to find ways of challenging the rules which seem to govern the repetitive sequences of behaviour.

8.3.1   Challenge the assumptions being made
(see point (1))

(In communication training this example could be described as intervention to stop mind-reading.)

If we review the interventions of the therapist we can see at point **(1)** that the therapist challenges the husband's assumption that he understands what his wife wants, by asking him to check it out with his wife.

This is, in systems thinking, a direct challenge to the system; it is therefore not surprising that the therapist experiences some unwillingness on the part of Robert to do so. The therapist should be aware that each time s/he challenges the rules previously adhered to by the couple that there is likely to be some initial unwillingness to do so. This may take many forms, for example the couple may not understand the therapist's request, (this was Robert's first reaction), or may resist it by questioning the need to do so (at point **(2)**), or may show some anger at being asked to do so (at point **(3)**) or make some other equally daunting response for the inexperienced therapist.

It does seem that the therapist has to risk all of these reactions and persist. This could be seen to be modelling for the other partner that it is possible to be assertive rather than be helpless.

8.3.2   Challenge the status quo, or unbalance the system by allying with one partner

Until Edith says 'you're the one who should be making some effort especially at the moment', we were being asked to believe that Edith is not putting any effort into their relationship, and that Robert is doing everything that he can.

At point **(4)** the therapist challenges this by asking Edith to say what effort Robert could be making. At **(5)** we can see that the status quo or homeostasis is almost reinstated with husband angry and wife in tears. At **(6)** the therapist makes another effort to ally with Edith in order to prevent the status quo reasserting itself, and to tip the balance of the interaction in favour of a different experience.

At **(7)** the therapist asks Edith to make a request of her husband, which she does. At this point the purpose of the interventions has been achieved. The couple have succeeded, with the assistance of the therapist, in having a new experience in the session. That is, they have gone past the point where Mrs S would give in and collapse into tears with Mr

S feeling frustrated and shouting at his wife, to a situation where she can make a request of her husband and he can respond positively to this.

8.3.3 Challenge the patterns which are developing within the session

At **(8)** the therapist has so far been allying fairly heavily with Edith; however at this stage in the session the therapist switches to challenge one of her assumptions about her husband. In doing so the therapist reasserts the neutral therapeutic position by asking the same question of the wife which was previously asked of the husband. At the same time, the therapist changes the pattern that was developing within the session of always being allied with the wife.

This ability to escape from repetitive patterns that develop and become triangled in is difficult, and is greatly enhanced by having an observer in the session, if a one-way screen is not available. Needless to say, there is little point in having overcome one pattern just to be trapped by another. When allying with one partner it is essential that the other partner is not alienated into feeling that his position is totally misunderstood by the therapist. This is always difficult to judge, but is perhaps facilitated by the therapist allying first with the partner in the down position. This ability to ally successfully with one partner without alienating the other is a powerful intervention which makes it more possible to facilitate change in the system.

(See Chapter 10 for other examples in a depressed partner.)

8.3.4 Keeping the issues small and trivial

With this particular couple the concerns which emerge are complex and emotive and the therapist judges that the couple are not yet ready to discuss these in any depth in this the second session of therapy, and that it is sufficient that they have been spoken about. They are discussed in detail in a later session (see Section 10.8).

If, as in this example, the aim of the therapist is to enable an argument to continue and escalate, we recommend that the issues chosen should be small and apparently inconsequential, rather than those which seem central to the couple's difficulties.

8.3.5 Gaining experience of arguing successfully over small issues

Example 8B

Mary and Bill B (*see also Example 7B*) had been having very serious difficulties in their marriage following the birth of their child. They had had infertility tests for five years and had nearly given up hope of ever having a child. The baby was now 1½ years old. Since the baby's birth they had grown apart, Mary being anxiously absorbed with the baby and Bill spending more and more time at work. They rarely talked together. They still felt attracted to each other sexually although they had little if any physical contact at present and their sexual life had ceased.

From the small amount of evidence the team had available it was hypothesised that during the five years of struggle to see if Mary could become pregnant they had become quite clinical about their sexual intercourse. They took temperatures, and 'had sex' on the correct evenings in order to 'get pregnant'. Mary had stopped asking herself if intercourse was tender or enjoyable, and Bill seemed to have grown to think of himself as a 'fertilising machine' rather than a sensual husband. This seemed a very central and painful area for each of them, and we would expect that the couple could be helped to discuss this gently together either in the session or at home at some point in therapy. Although this issue is touched upon in the session described here, the therapist chose not to focus on it, but encouraged them to argue about the more trivial question of bedtime, which had been raised several times but not resolved.

> MARY
> In any case, we rarely go to bed at the same time. I'm usually asleep by the time Bill comes to bed.
>
> BILL
> You're always so tired these days. I don't know why you have to be in bed at 9.30.
>
> MARY
> You never understand that it is hard work bringing a baby up. Particularly on your own.

(1) THERAPIST (*interrupting*)
I would like you to stay with the issue of bedtime. Can you talk to each other now about finding an evening when you could go to bed at the same time and at what time that would be.

> BILL (*after a silence, to the therapist*)
> That'd be the day. Mary's never going to find time.

(2) THERAPIST
Can you turn your chairs to face each other and see if you can have this discussion about finding time to go to bed at the same time.

> Bill and Mary turn their chairs part way towards each other. The therapist stands up, walks across and helps them turn their chairs further around so that they are facing each other.

(3) THERAPIST
OK. Imagine that I'm not here. Go ahead and see if you can agree on a time and an evening when you can go to bed at the same time.

> BILL
> You'd never agree to going to bed later would you?
>
> MARY
> Well, what about you, you're the one who stays up late into the night playing with your damned computer. Anyway why can't you understand that I am actually very tired? Brian is a real handful these days. But of course you wouldn't begin to understand that.

BILL
That's not fair. You know I'm very pressurised at work. I can't both do my job and look after Brian. After all you wanted the baby.

MARY
You always come back to that, as if you didn't!

(4) THERAPIST
That is a very important issue for you both, but for the moment try to stick to the question of bedtime. See if you can come to a decision about a time when you could go to bed together.

BILL (*exasperatedly*)
Damn you Mary why are you always going to bed so early. You never give me a chance. You're asleep by the time I get to bed. It's as if you just don't want to spend any time at all with me, let alone have sex.

MARY
But I do! I do! I'd like nothing better than us actually going to bed at the same time. We always used to before Brian was born.

BILL
OK then. Can't you ever stay awake until I come to bed?

MARY
Huh that's a good one. I do try, I often lie awake waiting for you to come to bed. What do you do? You go up into the attic room and spend hours working on your computer. You must know that I am waiting for you to come to bed.

BILL (*showing some surprise and resentment*)
How should I know? You always avoid me, if I try to touch you, when I come home from work.

MARY (*heatedly*)
There you go again. When you come in I'm usually bathing Brian or changing him or feeding him. You expect me to want to have sex with you then?

Angry and aroused silence. Each partner is now sitting up facing each other directly.

(5) THERAPIST
You're doing well but try to stick to the topic of going to bed at the same time. I'm aware that there are many things you need to talk about, but let's see how you get on with this one.

MARY(*in a softer voice*)
Look Bill, I know that you are pressurised at work but say on a Friday night, surely you've no need to work at home that night, couldn't you come to bed a bit earlier on Fridays say?

BILL (*shouting in a rather hurt tone of voice*)
I could but what difference would that make. You'd be asleep as usual, and I'd be lying awake wondering why I bothered.

MARY (*to the therapist*)
You see it's no good. This is what always happens. We try but then Bill starts shouting and that's the end of the discussion.

(6) THERAPIST

Good, so you're aware of what happens and when things start to go wrong. Let's see if this time we can help you get it right. You've each asked each other to make a small concession. See if you can talk about those a bit more.

BILL (*to the therapist*)

Mary won't. I really think that Mary has gone off me entirely, and just doesn't want to have anything to do with me any more.

(7) THERAPIST (*keeping the couple to the topic of bedtime*)

Lets take it step by step, Mary see if you can persuade Bill to come to bed earlier on a Friday night. You had already asked him if he could come to bed earlier and Bill had said that he could. Bill seems to need you to reassure him that you will stay awake.

MARY

Bill have you said that you would come to bed earlier on a Friday night?

BILL

I would if I thought it would make any difference. But it seems to me that you are always asleep by 10.00 pm.

MARY

Suppose I made an effort. What would you do.

BILL

I don't know why you have to ask, you know I'd make the effort too. I always have in the past.

(8) THERAPIST

You seem to be coming to some sort of compromise; can you just say what the compromise seems to be?

BILL

It's a bit hard to believe but we seem to be agreeing that on Fridays we could go to bed at the same time.

MARY

We haven't decided what time yet. But I've said I'd be sure to stay awake if Bill comes to bed a bit earlier.

The therapist works with the couple until they have made a choice about time.

The couple manage the rest of the discussion in good humour, a feeling of warmth and empathy emerges and they seem to be more sensual towards each other in the session. In the message at the end of this session, the team prescribe a ban on sexual intercourse on Fridays, when they would go to bed at the same time. (We learned at the next session that they had made their own choice about this and had had enjoyable sexual intercourse for the first time since the child was born.)

In following sessions the couple were encouraged to have more arguments. Many of the issues raised in this session were brought up for discussion. They also learned to use a 'talking timetable' in which the discussions are continued at home (see Section 9.10.6).

Our experience suggests it is helpful if the couple can gain experience of heated discussion on small issues. In this way their confidence grows as they learn that it is possible to stay with one subject and successfully follow it through. These arguments over small issues set the scene for later discussions of more complex and emotional material.

Later discussions may happen at home rather than in the sessions. They may happen spontaneously as with Penny and Paul S (Example 9A) who shared their concerns about Penny's earlier suicidal feelings and Paul's consequent response of both anger and fear in one session. The therapist may choose to reintroduce a more emotive topic as the couple become less fearful. In this way the couple learn through experiences in-session to trust each other more and overcome some of their fears of intimacy (see Sections 1.2.5 and 1.3).

8.3.6 Challenging the rules that govern the system
(in Example 8B above)

Notice in Example 8B the therapist has to work very hard to encourage Mary and Bill to relate differently. Interventions **(1)** to **(5)** are all aimed at helping the couple to work on a simple issue which they have so far failed to solve. It is not surprising that it is hard work for the therapist. Systems thinking assumes that at this point one is trying to push the system, or challenge the rules, so it is bound to be difficult. Interventions **(6)** and **(7)** are aimed at helping the couple notice that they are beginning to achieve their objective of a joint solution to bedtime. Intervention **(8)** asks the couple to affirm their achievement in the session. Notice too that after the breakthrough in a small area the couple relate to each other more empathically and go on to make further progress in later sessions.

8.3.7 Focussing in order to intensify the interaction

An aim of systems intervention is to change either the length or the intensity of the interaction. Choosing simple issues and ensuring that the couple stick to the selected subject parallels the interventions of Minuchin relating to focussing and intensifying. We are not necessarily recommending that therapists should be as persistent as to take up three hours of interview with 75 repetitions of the same question from the therapist to the couple (Minuchin & Fishman 1981). However, focussing on one issue as Minuchin describes has the double impact of intensifying the interaction and lengthening the time during which the couple work on the issue. Both of these are changed experiences for the couple and as such are ways of changing the structure of the repetitive sequences.

8.4 Encourage arguments over small issues where the husband is currently reluctant to have sexual intercourse

In couples where the man has ceased to have any interest in sexual intercourse with his partner (although previously having enjoyed sexual intercourse with her, and usually quite capable of achieving erections) we recommend that therapists consider encouraging arguments over trivial issues.

In such couples one might additionally expect to find a pattern of interaction in which the woman has become the verbal and critical partner and the man has become passive, reluctant to enter into an open argument and generally submissive to the woman. Where these two phenomena occur together, arguments over small issues may be a useful intervention.

Example 8C

Samuel and Diana S had been married 24 years when they started this therapy. Their central complaint was that Sam experienced recurring bouts of impotence. The couple had already been treated (at weekly intervals for about nine months) at another centre where the treatment had focussed on Masters and Johnson techniques, with no improvement.

Mr S had had neither any desire nor any erection, except in the early morning, during the three previous months. During the previous six years they had had intercourse, but infrequently, and for the earlier seven years it had been only marginally better. Their own description of their difficulties focussed entirely upon their sex life which was described as 'very pleasurable when it happens'. Diana said that she missed sex a great deal, and as time passed without intercourse she became first tearful, then angry and resentful and would find herself being hostile and aggressive towards her husband.

Samuel reported that he actually did not seem to miss sex too much, but felt very 'got at' when his wife became upset. When Diana criticised or attacked him he would withdraw into a haughty silence; he would avoid confrontation and refused to communicate at these times. For the past two months they had had separate bedrooms.

When exploring their social life it seemed that Sam saw himself as a loner and something of a workaholic. Diana felt ignored and isolated as they had few friends locally, having only come to live in the area in the last two years. She had experienced a bout of severe depression several years ago and felt quite upset and unattractive at present. They had teenage children, one of whom was already away at college and the other due to follow in eight months' time. In general they considered that they enjoyed each other's company, particularly when on holiday, and shared many interests in common. They were an intelligent and verbal couple.

The aim of therapy was to change the rules governing the repetitive sequences in their relationship, but giving them some new structures with which to work. An hypothesis might be that Diana had become the aggressive outspoken partner and Sam the submissive and compliant partner in their social life, but in their sexual life Sam was able to dominate by his withdrawal of sex from his wife. Hence an attempt was made to see if he could become more assertive in their social interaction, with a possible impact upon their sexual life. There was thought to be a circular connection between these different elements in the relationship.

Throughout the sessions the aim was therefore to focus on their social interaction and see if Sam could assert himself in small but progressively significant ways. Arguments must therefore be about small issues. The therapist must be patient and persistent. The couple were seen for a total of ten sessions over a period of 12 months.

The sessions took a similar structure and each session is therefore presented, in abbreviated form, under these headings:

(a) The therapist joins with the couple, and either discusses what they want from therapy (as in session 1) or reviews their homework assignment (as in all other sessions).
(b) The therapist focusses on small current issues and encourages arguments over these issues in the sessions.
(c) Homework is set for the period between sessions.

Session 1

(a) The therapist joined with the couple.
(b) Focussed on current relationship difficulties interactionally.
(c) Homework: relaxation exercises are set and a ban is placed on sexual intercourse for the moment.

Session 2

(a) Reviewing the homework:
The relaxation exercises had not been helpful.
They had had a 'monumental argument' at home
(b) The monumental argument was re-enacted in the session in order to clarify how they interacted. It became clear that Diana usually set the agenda for the quarrels. Sam described her as verbally adept, and as a consequence he felt that he 'usually loses arguments' and then withdraws into silence as he 'hates being dragged into scenes'.
Encouraging arguments:
In the session they were encouraged to argue about Diana's complaint that Samuel 'leaves the toilet seat up after urinating.' Sam was supported by the therapist to 'hold his own in the argument and to tell his wife when he thought she was wrong' (i.e. be more assertive). With a certain amount of reassurance and cajoling by the therapist, Sam was able to tell Diana that he thought she should not be so fussy over such a simple issue and allow him to leave the toilet seat up.
(c) Their homework task was to spend a half-hour each evening (9.30–10.00 pm) holding conversations in which they should negotiate an acceptable compromise for each partner about similar small conten-

tious issues. The time was to be divided equally so that each partner had 15 minutes of the time for his/her own issues.

Session 3

(a) They reported that they had had sexual intercourse in the husband's bedroom which had been particularly good.
(b) Discussion in-session regarding their back home timetable for negotiation, in which Diana did not like Sam shutting off; he did not like her pressurising him. Diana was 'too quick with words,' and Sam was 'too sensitive'. Sam wanted them to sleep in the same bed again, Diana declined. They suggested an alteration to the time-table: they would like to hold their arguments in his bedroom (his territory!).
(c) Homework was set to move the place of their arguments into his bedroom and to continue with the half-hour discussion of trivial arguments.

Session 4

(a) They reported that they had sexual intercourse three times during five weeks.
(b) In-session the therapist encouraged them to focus on their inter-action:
   Samuel expressed the fear that he may lose his temper, get irritable, or even shake with rage.
   Diana was worried that he dismissed everything she said as trivial.
   They both felt that they were more relaxed with each other and less upset by the other's responses.
(c) Their improvement was noted but they were told not to be com-placent and to continue with their timetable for arguments in the bedroom.

Sessions 5 and 6

• Similar progress continued; the husband had become more spon-taneous and able to speak about small issues that bothered him, the wife had become less irritable, strident and critical.
• They had moved back into the marital bed. Sexual intercourse happened about once a week and was usually very enjoyable.
• Samuel talked about his difficult feelings of 'soliciting his wife' if he initiated sex.
• Diana admitted she would prefer her husband to be more assertive with her both sexually and in arguments.
• They were to continue to discuss and argue over small issues for 30 minutes each evening.

At this stage both the couple and the therapist felt that the improvement was sufficient for them to be discharged, with the clear knowledge that they could refer themselves back if they felt it necessary. Four months later they requested further therapy.

Session 7

(a) Their main source of concern was that they had been on holiday and had had some unpleasant occasions. Diana had become sexually frustrated and Sam had seemed disinterested in helping.
(b) In-session they were asked to discuss their sexual difficulties as experienced on holiday. Each spoke about finding it difficult to solicit the other. Each had guilty feelings about asking for sexual gratification. Each also felt selfish or unloving if they sought to gratify their sexual desires.

   They agreed after discussion to find a code word which Diana would use to indicate to Samuel that she would welcome a sexual advance from him. Samuel wanted more opportunity to talk frankly together about their sex life.

Session 8

(a) The intervening month had been a bit uncertain. Last week Sam had 'flipped his lid' at work. He was however surprised at himself and delighted that he had been able to 'say a few things that had to be said' to colleagues. Their sex life was somewhat interrupted, they had had good sex twice but Diana had been feeling rather depressed. She complimented him on how much more assertive he had become. He still felt that she was too quick to comment with a criticism.
(b) In-session discussion of what alternatives he had in order to interrupt her critical comments. (During intercourse he had occasionally lost his erection.)
(c) Timetable for discussion and argument to be continued.

Session 9

(a) The previous four weeks had been difficult. They had had some violent arguments and periods of depression which they had both shared. Sam was under stress at work. Diana was considering getting a job and using her degree. She had become a housewife immediately after college.
(b) They raised the issue, in the session, of the possibility of separation; the therapist encouraged them to consider the pros and cons of such an arrangement.
(c) They were to use their timetable for discussion to make a 'rock bottom' agreement about their marriage; both were to stop trying so hard.

Session 10

(a) They had had a crisis three weeks ago in which they decided that it was necessary to separate. They had discussed this together and had agreed that things were too impossible and separation was necessary. During the separation she had felt very sorry for her 'inadequate' husband and assumed that he would be totally unable to manage without her. In fact, he reported on her return that he had had quite a peaceful time and had managed very well. She had been rather shocked by this, but her respect for him had gone up a great deal.

After this crisis, things had improved enormously, Diana described Sam as much cheekier, and Sam felt that Diana was no longer badgering him. They both felt that they had relaxed, sex had improved and become more spontaneous and frequent. Sam no longer felt afraid of his wife.

They both felt more open and free.

Final review

In reviewing what would make things go wrong Sam said 'I'd have to go back into withdrawing rather than being more assertive' and Diana that she'd 'have to become demanding and unreasonable again'.

The therapy was ended at this point by mutual agreement with an understanding that they could refer themselves back if needed in the future. After four years they reported that their sexual life was still good.

8.4.1 Discussion of the interventions used with Sam and Diana S

By arguing over small issues in the session and continuing this with regular, time limited, practice of similar arguments at home it was hoped that the couple could learn to relate to each other more openly: Sam could gain the experience of being more assertive with Diana and she in her turn might allow herself to enjoy his greater assertiveness in their social interaction.

8.4.2 Hypothesis

We hypothesised that this change in the power structure of their daytime relationship might enable them to alter their relationship with each other at the more intimate level of their sexual life.

8.4.3 Regular review of tasks

We also assumed that, since the difficulties were longstanding, it would be important to work consistently to help the couple to practise these newly acquired skills of arguing or discussing difficult issues together. Hence the regular setting of tasks and reviewing these in detail in the following session.

8.4.4 The difficulty in finding a subject for argument

As a team we call this couple affectionately 'the toilet seat couple', perhaps because we think they helped us to understand some of the details which make up successful arguments over small issues.

The male therapist felt that Sam was much too prone to give in to his wife and sought to discover a topic about which Sam felt his wife was too fastidious. It took some time in the session to find such an issue, as Sam protested that his wife was very nearly perfect. However, eventually he did suggest that there was perhaps just this one issue over which he might disagree with her. The therapist had however to taunt 'Surely there must be one thing your wife does which you find at least a little irritating' before he described his irritation at her criticising him, for leaving the toilet seat up after urinating. We also felt that the couple began to change as soon as Samuel found that it was possible to stand up to Diana in a small way and not be overwhelmed by her powerfulness.

We have learned from experience that similar couples usually have at least one issue which is a constant irritant, to which the man has so far submitted, but is aware of his resentment. Other examples are the woman who constantly nagged her partner because he 'flops around in sloppy slippers'; or the wife who insisted that 'the toilet roll should always hang down with the paper next to the wall'.

8.4.5 Developing confidence

It seems to us that focussing on these small niggling issues gives the couple, and particularly the husband, a safe and boundaried experience which enhances the husband's confidence and helps them to face together other issues which are getting in the way of a tender and passionate relationship.

Notice how Sam and Diana were able to review the possibility of separation on their own at home (session 10), after they had discussed the same question in the previous session (9) with the therapist's help. This question had not been discussed between the couple in any way until this point. They seem to have learned that it is possible to face difficulties which previously they have avoided through hostility and withdrawal.

8.4.6 Separation or a second chance?

It is also interesting to note that, as this couple were finding ways to be more independent within their marriage and their relationship was improving, so they considered the possibility of separation.

This phenomenon is one which we feel inexperienced therapists should learn to expect: at a point in therapy when the couple's relationship seems to be improving, some couples may wish to talk together about the real possibility of separation. Each partner may wish to demonstrate that they have discovered a greater sense of their own value and independence which means acknowledging that it would be possible to live without the other partner. It may be that in order to come together in a quite different relationship there is a need to admit that the old relationship is finished.

It seems important that therapists should learn to recognise this development as part of the couple's search for a different relationship together, and not rush to the conclusion that the couple will therefore act upon their new discussions and actually separate. The therapist may need to wait for some time before it becomes clear in which direction the couple will actually proceed. Sometimes of course this does lead to eventual separation. However, as with the above couple Diana and Sam S, our experience also teaches us that it may lead to a more satisfying relationship (session 10).

8.4.7　Circularity of the system
(see also Section 12.12)

From a systems perspective the rules were changed and the husband was enabled to become more assertive, while the wife became more flexible and less hostile.

Perhaps the notion of circularity was of central significance in being able to hypothesise that a change in one aspect of their relationship might have a significant impact on another aspect of their relationship, in this case their sexual difficulties.

8.5　*Problems for the therapist when encouraging arguments over trivial issues*

These couples, Robert and Edith S, Mary and Bill B and Sam and Diana S, were treated at the marital therapy clinic by encouraging them to engage in arguments about trivial issues. Although simple to describe, this method presents some difficulties to the therapist. Amongst those difficulties may be the following:

8.5.1　The couple may suggest that the issues are too trivial

Many couples do face very severe and complex difficulties in their relationship and the therapist must acknowledge the depth of their concern. As part of the engagement process the therapist will have worked to create rapport with both partners (see Section 4.6.2), and in doing so will already have shown empathy with the couple and the intensity of their difficulties.

Where the couple reiterate their concern about the totality of the relationship, the therapist will need to restate to the couple that s/he is aware of, and shares, this concern, but suggest firmly that it may be best tackled by taking small simple steps towards a solution. The couple may need to be helped to be patient. The therapist should not be rushed into trying to refocus back on to the total relationship, but should feel comfortable in allowing the couple to talk about their uncertainties in working in this way.

8.5.2 The couple may take exception to being treated 'like children'

From experience we suggest that if the couple express these or similar anxieties the therapist is most facilitative if s/he can accept in a relaxed and supportive way that what the couple say is reasonably accurate. They are being asked to practise in the session, to do exercises and also to take tasks home as homework and it is all a little reminiscent of school days. (The therapist should also consider whether his/her manner and voice tone are rather schoolmarmish; this may be what the couple are indirectly indicating.) A confident and empathic therapist can use such a conversation to turn the session into a more playful situation where the couple can enjoy learning and experimenting with different ways of relating to each other. The therapist's own ability to be relaxed is usually communicated to the couple. It may be helpful to keep in mind the concept of experimenting together, and the need for adults to rediscover the fun of playing together.

8.5.3 'You make us feel that we never talk to each other at home'

This is rather more difficult, as although the couple may talk to each other at home, the negative repetitive patterns make it difficult for them to resolve their relationship difficulties. The therapist will want to be supportive of such a couple and acknowledge what they say.

It may be helpful to say 'Perhaps you could use this opportunity to let me see how you talk together, since I have not seen you do so'. Each therapist will find their own suitable words. It is important not to become paralysed. Couples rarely refuse, indeed sessions often become much more alive and worthwhile after this particular hurdle is passed.

8.5.4 One partner complains s/he is being ignored by the therapist

Occasionally even though the therapist feels s/he has been totally neutral, one partner may complain that his or her particular wishes are being ignored.

Example 8D
As an example, Tom says to the therapist 'You always seem to be picking topics that Elizabeth wants to sort out and you never seem to concentrate on any of my problems'.

This is a difficult situation, particularly for the inexperienced therapist who has been working very hard to stay neutral. However, there will be a way forward. Whatever happens do not get into an argument with Tom! Instead, ask Tom what he particularly wants to discuss in the session. Give him time to make suggestions and then ask him to select one for discussion (help him to make it small and simple enough if necessary). Then encourage him to persuade Elizabeth that this should be discussed. Once he has made his complaint he may be reluctant to follow it through. However, he should be helped gently and firmly to focus on the subject he has chosen and see if he can engage his wife in the discussion. Be patient and supportive. Remember this is a new situation for the couple which they so far have been unable to handle on their own, and they need the therapist's help to get started. Remember too that if these small topics represent, in a symbolic form, their general relationship difficulties, what is being asked of them now is enormously difficult.

8.5.5 The therapist worries that the issues are too trivial

If the therapist shares some of the above concerns and feels that major issues should be faced first, we would ask the therapist to resist the temptation to work on the major difficulties but rather to see what occurs by working in the above way. Discussion of such questions should also be taken to and explored in supervision.

8.6 Alternative structural interventions in-session

So far we have described how in-session arguments can be used. We now go on to suggest other alternatives for in-session structural changes in the couple's interaction. (These in-session strategies can be developed further and used as timetabled homework tasks, see Chapter 9.)

8.6.1 Where couples continually bring the children into discussions
(See also Section 10.13 on triangles)

One aim of in-session work is to redraw the boundary around the couple and focus on discussion of their joint relationship and, where necessary, to help them develop appropriate executive functions as parents. This will be facilitated if the couple can work together as a coherent and consistent parental alliance, making shared decisions which they can both actively support. Some couples will need to learn that they rarely relate to each other directly, without bringing the children into the conversation. The therapist might have to be quite interventionist in-session to remind the couple of this and to enable them to discuss their relationship rather than their children.

We seem to have developed into such a child-focussed society that some couples feel quite guilty if they actually spend time looking after the relationship with their life partner. With these couples the therapist should actively encourage them to feel it is important that they find time for each other; an in-session discussion with such a couple might be one in which the therapist decentres and asks the couple to discuss, in detail, where, when and how they are going to find time just for themselves at home. Such a couple may be helped if the task they are sent home with is something such as 'go out together, at least once, without the children, and enjoy yourselves!'. It may be useful to tell other busy couples to 'plan some time when you can be together and do nothing' (see Section 9.8.1).

8.6.2 Alternatives: where the couple's non-verbal behaviour is static

This is difficult to describe accurately; however, sometimes couples stay in very fixed physical positions throughout a session. The wife might be very upright and stiff with her legs twisted tightly together and arms crossed; the husband might be lying back in his chair looking vague and passive. Both of their responses may lack spontaneity and the session has an air of boredom.

In such a session the therapist may be wise to choose to focus on their non-verbal positions using one or more of the following alternatives.

(1) Suggest that each partner observes how the other is sitting; then ask them to change chairs and imagine themselves to be their partner while continuing with the discussion for about five minutes. Pause. Review together what it felt like being the partner, what they learned about their partner and about themselves.
(2) Suggest that they change their positions in some way, for example, to sit on the edge of their chairs, to look directly into each other's eyes and continue to talk. Pause and review how that felt.
(3) Ask one partner what it feels like to have the other partner sit in this way, and vice versa.
(4) Suggest to each partner that they try to help the other partner to change their posture in some way.
(5) Ask the couple to stand up, suggest that they walk towards each other, one at a time, and decide at what distance they each find it comfortable to stand facing the other.

Suggest that they sit down and talk about this experience.

The above are structural interventions in the session and are designed to intervene directly into the non-verbal communication which is rather fixed and feels as though it is controlling their spontaneity. Experience suggests that such interventions can be helpful in freeing a rather tedious and non-productive session. Systemically they are designed to interfere with the timing and structure of the couple's rather rigid interaction. They do also seem to give a couple a feeling of release of tension and a greater ease in interacting with each other.

(See also role reversal, Section 10.5.2.)

8.6.3 'Sculpting' for couples who desire a more intimate relationship

Some couples express a wish to develop a more intimate relationship and complain that their present way of relating is too cold, distant and impersonal, and yet have been unable to change.

A useful non-verbal intervention is to use 'sculpting' as a way of breaking through some of the reserve that inhibits greater intimacy. Sculpting means that the couple use their own and each other's bodies to demonstrate non-verbally some of the things they wish to convey about their relationship, by making a living sculpture. This living sculpture or sculpt can sometimes help the couple to express feelings which have been difficult to put into words.

One wife who had spent some time trying to tell her husband how she felt about their present relationship was asked to show him through a sculpt. She was a little hesitant at first, then without a word took hold of her husband's hand, clenched his fist and raised the arm in a threatening gesture while making him lean forward. She then crouched down on the floor beneath him, raising her arms above her head as though to protect herself from him. The husband was surprised and alarmed by this as he was totally unaware of any feelings from his wife that she felt threatened by him. In this way the sculpt can often demonstrate feelings, attitudes or desires which some couples may have difficulty communicating to each other.

Sculpting should be conducted with as little verbal interaction as possible between the couple. They should be asked to touch and mould the other into the position which represents what they wish to show and to feel free to experiment with different postures until they are satisfied with the sculpt.

Sculpting can also be used in the following ways:

(1) Suggest that in turn they make a sculpt which represents the kind of relationship they would prefer to have with each other. No words should be used. (In order to do this one partner will therefore be touching and moving the other partner into various physical positions until s/he is satisfied that the sculpt represents visually his/her hoped for relationship.)

An example of this was one in which the woman stood side by side with the man who had his arm gently placed across her shoulder and they were looking into each other's eyes.

Once each has had their turn, ask them to sit down and discuss together what they learned from that exercise. Try to make it relaxed and help the couple play with this idea.

(2) The above can be done in two stages. Stage one would be a sculpt of their present relationship as they each see it. (An example might be a sculpt in which they stand some distance apart with their bodies partly turned towards each other but their heads turned away and eyes looking out or downwards.) Stage two would be a sculpt of how they would like their relationship to be.

Try to ensure that as each partner places the other into the sculpt they use few words. In this way the couple are encouraged to touch and move each other into different positions, which again may be a change in their current behaviour.

(3) Use a variation of the above sculpt to match the couple's difficulties. In Example 8E below the therapist chooses to ask Derek and Sylvia B to move into a position chosen by the therapist, and not yet part of the repertoire of the couple. In systems language the therapist was helping the couple to experience a different interaction.

Couples are usually a little shy at the beginning of such exercises but often warm to them enthusiastically. It would seem as though the non-verbal messages given and received are powerful and unique to the couple, and as such not able to be shared with the therapist (see Section 1.2.2).

Perhaps the touching and moving of the partner into a more desired position is enabling changes at other levels of interaction. Such interventions are often very helpful when a therapist feels that the momentum has gone out of the session and the system is powerfully stuck.

Example 8E
Derek and Sylvia B, both aged 28, had been married for seven years with a four year old son. They were referred by the GP from whom the husband had sought advice. He was increasingly anxious about his intense need to masturbate, his heightened enjoyment of masturbation and his diminishing interest in having sexual intercourse with his wife. He was alarmed by these experiences and concerned at the impact on his marriage, which he was determined to save if at all possible. Four months previously he had had a brief affair about which his wife knew and found upsetting. She did not know about his need to masturbate and Derek was concerned that she should not find out. The GP who knew and cared about both partners promptly made an appropriate marital referral.

It was agreed that Derek would be seen on his own at the commencement of therapy as he was quite desperate to talk to the therapist in confidence. He was seen on his own for one session. He presented as a very neat, well dressed young man with a rather conservative respectful attitude. He was an only child and now worked in his father's business selling books and stationery. Although he claimed to run the business, his father did not yet pay him a regular wage. He described his wife Sylvia, as 'kind, intelligent, more assertive than himself, rather extrovert but also with low self confidence'.

They had met at college. She had taught until their child was born. Derek felt that Sylvia had been more interested in him than he in her. From his viewpoint their sex life had been better before marriage when it was rather 'illicit and exciting'. He had enjoyed sex on Sunday afternoons when they had been to the pub and he was feeling relaxed; otherwise sex was a strain. More recently, perhaps once a month, he would 'think of England' and somehow manage to have sex with his wife. Otherwise he preferred masturbating. He was now very concerned to 'get myself straightened out, as the marriage is worth it'. He was also extremely concerned that his wife should not know about his enjoyment of masturbation.

It was agreed that they would be seen together for conjoint therapy and that during therapy his masturbating would not be mentioned, and Derek would refrain from masturbating throughout therapy.

When seen as a couple they appeared to be quite polite and kind with each other, and not at all vindictive. Sylvia felt that their relationship had deteriorated since the birth of their child; she was puzzled at this and was upset and jealous that he had had an affair.

They were started on relaxation and sensate focus exercises, and were asked to talk to each other during these exercises about their emotions. By the fourth session the pattern of their relationship seemed to be that Derek was somewhat overwhelmed by Sylvia who was more dominant in discussion, took the initiative sexually and felt rejected that he was unresponsive. He felt embarrassed that Sylvia was so prepared to take sexual initiatives and felt turned off after a time. The focus of discussion, when left to take its own course, was that of Derek and Derek's problems. They had been practising sensate focus exercises which they had both found relaxing but had not helped Derek to feel 'turned on'.

8.6.3.1 Non-verbal sculpt in-session

In order to break through this pattern, which seemed quite rigid and difficult to modify, the couple were asked to notice their physical positions in the session. Sylvia was sitting with clenched hands in a powerful upright posture looking down at Derek who was sunk low in his chair apparently relaxed. However he said he felt stupid.

The therapist suggested that having noticed their positions Sylvia should sit on the floor at Derek's feet. Derek should encourage her to talk about herself and not to get drawn in to talk about his problems. Sylvia readily took up this position, resting her arm against Derek's knee and leaning her body gently towards him.

At this point the therapist felt the mood of the session change dramatically, the couple became quite sensual towards each other. Sylvia who had been stiff and dictatorial seemed to soften and become more open. The tempo and focus of the discussion changed with Sylvia revealing that she had great difficulties with her own mother, whom she felt had always dominated her, and would not allow her to be an independent adult. Derek became animated as he listened.

For their homework they were asked to continue with relaxation and foreplay, but to choose to have sexual intercourse only if it felt right. At the next session they reported that they were feeling much more relaxed with each other, they had had sexual intercourse a few times; Derek felt much less tense about their physical relationship. He had also negotiated with his own family and the help of a solicitor for a separate income, which had been agreed.

The therapy continued for four more sessions during which Derek became more assertive and occasionally more aggressive. Sylvia was able to ask for sympathy from Derek and to receive his physical support. They were able to look together at their involvement with their families and to make some further changes. Their sex life became more spontaneous and adventurous, Derek looked forward with eager anticipation to intercourse and together they were exploring Comfort's book *The Joy of Sex* and experimenting with oral sex.

It seemed to us that the non-verbal sculpt in the fourth session was a turning point in this therapy, when their interaction began to change significantly. Until this point their relationship was static. Such interventions, which are a little unconventional, may make a major contribution when other more conventional approaches seem inadequate. Perhaps one indication for the possible use of non-verbal exercises is where the couple themselves sit continuously throughout the interview in a position which is constrained and static. One can hypothesise that the therapist, in using such interventions, joins sufficiently with the system to feel his/her own discomfort at the way the couple are sitting or behaving. The alternative interaction suggested may help both the couple and the therapist to feel more comfortable at several levels simultaneously.

8.7 Summary of structural interventions and when they can be used

Case examples have been described in some detail in order to show how structural interventions might be used in-session. Structural interventions are based upon hypotheses developed by the therapist which consider the circularity of the system and are designed to give the couple an experience in-session of a different way of relating to each other. In summary, the structural interventions which can be used fall into two categories: verbal and non-verbal interaction.

Where the focus is on verbal interaction the therapist works from a decentred position and can:

- Challenge the assumptions which are being made about the couple's immediate interaction by varying the length, intensity or outcome of interactions (Section 8.3.1).
- Unbalance the interaction by allying with one partner (Section 8.3.2)
- Move in and out of the interaction and maintain an overall neutral position as therapist by changing alliances which develop within the session (Section 8.3.3).
- Encourage heated discussions over issues, ensuring that the topics chosen are small and trivial (Section 8.4).

- Set tasks which enable the couple to continue restructuring their relationship at home by timetabling the discussions (Section 8.4.3).
- Focus on the couple relationship and exclude discussion about others who are triangled in to the relationship (Section 8.6.1).
- Set tasks which also focus on the couple relationship.

Where the structural interventions centre on non-verbal interaction the therapist can:

- Ask the couple to experiment themselves with different non-verbal positions in the session (Section 8.6.2).
- Suggest specific changes in how the couple relate to each other non-verbally within the session (Section 8.6.2).
- Use non-verbal sculpts in-session (Section 8.6.3).

In general the therapist uses the session as a place in which the couple can have a different experience of how they relate to each other and designs messages, timetables and tasks which will take this work further at home.

Structural interventions are particularly useful for the following relationship difficulties:

- Couples who seem to feel that 'good couples never argue' or 'its no good arguing because . . .' (Section 8.2.1).
- Where couples can discuss some issues but not others.
- Couples who are excessively polite to each other (Section 11.4.1).
- Where modesty or inhibitions hold the relationship static (Example 8E).
- Where one partner is submissive or depressed (Section 10.9.1; Example 10E).
- Where the woman presents with vaginismus (Section 11.6.2).
- Where one partner is reluctant to have intercourse (Example 8C).
- Where a relationship has developed a too rigid or too fragile structure.

In Chapter 9 we go on to describe the formulation of messages, tasks and timetables as part of a systems approach to therapy.

Chapter 9

Systems approach: messages, formulations, tasks and timetables

9.1 Introduction

As part of the systems approach, we now describe the use of messages. Our main aim is to show how messages can be used to continue what has been begun in the session by asking the couple to work on some aspect of their relationship at home. In this way we hope to stimulate further changes in their relationship between sessions.

Many of the tasks used are also carefully designed to be reciprocal and to improve the couple's communication, so there is a constant cross-fertilisation between the behavioural and systems approach. This is most in evidence in the formulation of messages. The uses and limitations of the paradoxical message are also considered.

Messages, formulations, tasks and timetables are designed to change the current interaction of the couple. They must therefore accurately reflect the detail of information gleaned from the couple in the immediate session, and use the language and idiom of the couple.

Within the marital therapy clinic we break during each session to discuss with the team or a colleague what formulation, timetable or task we should give to each couple as they leave the session (see Section 4.6.12). Many therapists who work in more isolated situations find it difficult to allow themselves a break in the session. However, in order to develop skills in the use of messages, it is helpful if therapists can learn to move out and sit alone in order to think about the couple, and to formulate a message (see Chapters 4 and 11).

The word message is used to describe the total package of considered thoughts and interventions given to the couple at the end of the session. The total message can vary; it may be a simple formulation of our concern for their present difficulties; a detailed response to, or formulation of, the intricacies of their relationship; or a paradoxical or a split team message. Timetables and tasks as appropriate are included as part of the message.

9.2 The message

A message usually begins with a positive statement about the good aspects of the relationship or the good qualities of the individuals. It then collects up and reflects back to the couple significant work done in the session and includes some aspects of the team's understanding or formulation of their current relationship. This can be a very simple statement about the difficulties faced by the couple. It might also involve some statements about the future of their relationship.

We may then go on to add a variety of alternatives to the message, depending on what we hope to achieve between sessions. Timetables or tasks may be included, and these may be straight or paradoxical.

Any task included must be small, achievable and acceptable to the couple. If there is a timetable this can vary from a tightly designed and highly structured agreement to an open-ended suggestion of events which might occur before the next therapy session.

These three elements can be used in any combination to continue the work of the session and to stimulate further work on the relationship in the period between sessions. Thinking systemically, each element of the message is designed in such a way as to challenge the rules governing the repetitive sequences (see Chapter 7).

Included within the text are several examples taken from our clinical practice. They are presented in order to demonstrate the variety and flexibility available for the worker. We do not wish to give the impression, however, that messages must be complex. Simplicity, clarity and empathy are the most important ingredients.

Where much work has been done in a session, or where a message seems to be inappropriate, the couple can simply be given their next appointment. No message needs to be given. If it feels helpful to say something, a straightforward supportive statement about the couple's current difficulties may be all that is necessary. Do not be over-sophisticated in formulating a message. A statement such as 'We can see that you are both finding life very wearing at the moment' may be sufficient.

The use of messages has been developed from the work of Erickson (1967), Haley (1973), Minuchin (1974), Sluzki (1978) and Selvini Palazzoli *et al.* (1978). It builds directly on the work of many behaviourists, notably Stuart (1969), Azrin *et al.* (1973), Gottman *et al.* (1977) and Crowe (1982) (see also Chapters 5 and 6).

Although the messages we give are not all paradoxical we acknowledge a debt to Selvini Palazzoli for a useful framework in designing messages. She uses the term 'prescriptions' and suggests a prescription can have various goals, which might be:

(1) To mark the context as therapeutic.
(2) To provoke within the family a feedback which indicates compliance and motivation for treatment.
(3) To limit the field of observation.
(4) To give structure to the following session.

9.2.1 The time element in messages

Sluzki adds an emphasis on the awareness and use of the time dimension when designing prescriptions. He writes

'The way in which a sequence of events is punctuated and reality is organised results from (arbitrary) agreements by the participants: this principle has clear consequences in planning therapeutic interventions; a change in punctuation breaks stereotypes and may radically alter interactional rules and family myths.'

We suggest that the time dimension should be considered and varied for couples where this might either:

(a) bring an out-of-control behaviour under control, e.g. a timetable for jealousy (see Chapter 10) or
(b) bring some flexibility into a stuck or rigid system; e.g. where couples report that they 'always argue over supper' encourage them to 'make sure to have an even more heated argument every morning over breakfast'.

Cooklin (1982) draws attention to the differing patterns of interaction over short, medium and long periods of time, and suggests that interventions should be designed to take specific account of these variations over time.

Byng-Hall thinks that therapists make a common mistake of leaving the extended family out of therapy and gives coherent reasons for suggesting that, for some couples and families, patterns may repeat themselves over several generations. Consequently cross-generational coalitions may need to be considered within therapy. Such aspects of the time dimension should be born in mind when framing messages.

9.2.2 Symptoms and labels

When formulating messages for a couple where one partner is symptomatic or carries a label, a goal might be to frame a message which:

(1) labels the problem as belonging to the relationship (see Chapter 4),
(2) describes the non-symptomatic partner as carrying the same or another symptom or
(3) reframes the symptom as of value to the couple.

Symptoms and labels are usually experienced as being beyond the control of the couple. With such couples this perception can be interrupted by recommending that the couple change the time of day, the duration or intensity of the occurrence of a symptom; for example, by suggesting to a man who usually wakes up depressed but is better by tea time, to 'be depressed between four and six in the afternoon'. Notions of pretending to experience a symptom at times when symptoms do not usually occur, or asking that the symptom be intensified when it does occur, begin to change the perception of control over the symptom. Sluzki writes

'One of the key interactional attributes of symptoms, by the participants, is drastically questioned by a well-placed symptom prescription.'

9.2.3 Metaphors in messages

An area of increasing interest in formulating messages is that of the use of metaphor. It seems that suitable metaphors may add intensity to messages and give to a couple a depth of understanding which may not be conveyed by more direct approaches. We often find that the use of characters or situations derived from fairy tales, common legends or familiar couple relationships adds lightness and empathy to a message which is helpful to couples. Familiar concepts such as 'saint and sinner' might be used to describe one couple while 'the judge and the accused' may portray a couple where one partner is very critical of the other. Words from songs such as 'It takes two to tango' can be used to underline the involvement of both partners; or putting an issue 'on ice' or 'on the back burner' can quickly help a couple set aside a question for the moment.

These are mundane examples, but simplicity and appropriateness are key elements in the use of metaphor. Their discriminate use can be helpful in adding colour and meaning to a formulation. It is, however, essential, when using metaphors, to be attuned to the couple's own language and to derive any metaphor from issues, words or idiom from within the couple's own interaction. (See Example 9.C where the metaphor of 'changing the union rules' is used).

9.2.4 Summary

In summary, messages can range from a simple sentence to a detailed formulation, timetable and task, each element of which is designed to challenge or interrupt the rules which govern the system. For therapists new to the use of messages it makes sense to begin with modest goals and slowly develop a wider repertoire of alternatives.

9.3 Tasks

Minuchin (1974) thought of tasks as being part of the 'restructuring of the family'. He wrote

'Tasks create a framework within which the family members must function. The therapist can use tasks to pinpoint and actualise an area of exploration that may not have developed naturally in the flow of family transactions. Or he can highlight an area in which the family needs to work.'

Minuchin clarifies further how he saw the purpose of tasks.

'At the same time, the task, like many other therapeutic interventions, is no more than a probe into a family system. The therapist assigning a task does not know how the family members will cope with it. Since he is not committed to the fulfilment of the task, he cannot be disappointed. Giving a task provides a new framework for transactions. The therapist observes the results with a view toward unearthing alternative transactional patterns.'

Whilst agreeing with Minuchin that the therapist does not know how the family members will cope with the task, and is not committed to the fulfilment of the task, we aim to design tasks which are sufficiently realistic for the couple to engage with, and either achieve some measure of success or find it useful to understand what got in the way of completing the task.

The task uses the therapeutic framework to encourage the couple to work together to facilitate some small immediate changes and, as such, should not be used lightly. Clients are often balanced on a fragile edge between helplessness and hopefulness. The ability to engage successfully in even minute changes can help tip the balance in the direction of greater optimism that change is possible.

9.4 Timetables

Timetables, as already noted, can be used in reciprocity negotiation and communication training and in work focussing on sexual dysfunction (see Masters and Johnsons 1970; Belliveau and Richter 1971; Brown and Faulder 1977; Kaplan 1979; Crowe 1982).

Within the clinic we are becoming increasingly aware that by providing a time-limited framework for interaction, one is providing an essential element of greater security to relationships which may have got out of control, are feared or are difficult to contain (Crowe and Ridley 1986).

Bion (1970) presented the notion of the container and the need to be contained. He extended this concept to the analytical hour, the needs of both analyst and analysand and how each could best use this highly structured time in exploring the unstructured fantasy life of the patient. The notion of the container/contained may have additional implications beyond the boundaries of the analytical hour. One can speculate that within a timetabled situation, where work is being done which is anxiety-provoking, then clearly identified time, place, structure and ending may help provide a secure base for the gradual development of a more intimate relationship (see Bowlby 1969, Ainsworth and Bell 1970; Rajeki *et al.* 1978). It is also possible that the notion of a play space, as described by Winnicott (1971), has some relevance to the usefulness of safely timetabled spaces set aside for specific interpersonal issues.

Rosenblatt (1980) sees the child as progressing from a situation in which play as a child

'is essentially social in nature, the child learns about the world through his social interactions with caregivers and he will progress inevitably towards using this knowledge in more mature forms of interchange in play with his equals.'

A corollary to this might be that if a couple have not developed mutually satisfactory ways of interacting then there may be a need to rework this process by having a playtime together, or a timetable in which the issues they need to work at have a chance to be played with. The homework exercises of Masters and Johnson (1970) such as non-genital sensate focus also have the element of timetabled playtime, in this case in the sexual sphere (see Section 11.6). Piaget (1929 and 1951) too saw the relevance of play and step-by-step learning as being the cornerstone of later social and intellectual development.

Timetables can also be considered from a systemic point of view (see chapter 7). Asking a couple to use a timetable can provide boundaries to behaviour which has been experienced as out of control. It also legitimises pathological behaviour by encouraging its expression at certain times but not at others (see Section 10.4) and goes some way towards removing the pathological label in the process. For unpredictable behaviour the timetable can be used to develop structure, and for rigid behaviour to encourage flexibility. It may create a structure which enables couples to maintain a safe emotional distance and thus perform a distance regulatory function (Section 1.2.5 and Byng Hall 1982). At the simplest level it may provide a better chance that tasks will be performed by the couple. Through the use of timetables, for a variety of outside social activities, the couple may be helped to develop a more flexible relationship or to rediscover the ability to enjoy their interaction at other levels.

Hence we speculate that the modest timetable may contain within it many of the conditions necessary for the secure development of more pliant relationships in which sensitivity, intimacy, assertiveness, disagreements, intense emotion, playfulness and vulnerability can be experienced by couples as they develop greater security and expressiveness within these structures.

The efficacy of timetables has attracted little research interest. It is our hope that the nature and efficacy of timetables can be researched more adequately in the future. Experience tells us that they are of therapeutic value.

9.5 Messages should be simple

9.5.1 A word of caution

Formulations, tasks and timetables can be used separately or together in many ways. A word of caution and encouragement: therapists can become over-involved in the intricacies of the formulation and the metaphor used. This is a trap which should be avoided as the final formulation needs to be simple and understandable. (See Spiegel 1957; Rapoport 1965; Caplan 1964 and Lask 1982)

9.5.2 A rather complicated split-team message
(See Section 9.18).

Example 9A
Penny and Paul S were referred by the GP who wrote:

> 'In summary Penny S is prone to episodes of depression and has had a long history of psychiatric therapy of one sort or another. Her husband has been married in the past and there is a son of 9 years of age called Roger who spends time with the couple at the weekends. Mr S is quite happy to insist that all the problems are on Penny's side, but in fact it seems that the interaction of all three of them is the main reason for her low self esteem, lack of assertion and general lack of ability to cope with situations such as arguments within the family.'

The GP had assessed this couple very accurately. During the first interview their difficulties as a couple centred around an interaction in which Paul would tease or joke about Penny and would rarely listen attentively to what she said. Penny's response was to give up or to chide Paul about his relationship with his son Roger about which she was envious, feeling that he had only married her to enable him to have access to his son. Penny's relationship with Roger was very tenuous.

If we examine the formulation given to Paul and Penny S, with hind-sight it may be too complicated. Perhaps there could have been more emphasis in this first formulation of the couple's strengths and their courage in coming for marital therapy.

The message given to them at the end of the first session was as follows:

The team are concerned about you, as a couple, because they think you are both in a very complex situation.

(1) The team are divided, half being quite optimistic about you both, and half being rather pessimistic.
(2) Because part of the team felt optimistic about your future relationship, they suggested that you be asked to do some simple tasks between now and when we meet in two weeks' time. One task is to spend 30 minutes each day talking to each other. During this 30 minutes you are to take each other seriously. Alternate the topics each day and also alternate who chooses the topic. If Penny chooses the topic on day one, then Paul is to choose the topic on day two. They suggest that you talk about topics such as the dogs, what you are going to do at Christmas, whether you want to work together, Paul's son Roger, and so on. Be strict with the time.

The therapist then negotiated with the couple what exact time of the day they will carry out the task.

(3) Another task is to do one small thing to please each other: we suggest that Penny take the dogs for a walk at the weekend with Roger, and that Paul should go shopping twice with Penny. For the rest of the time you do not need to take each other seriously. Finally,

about Roger, if you behave as a united couple we think that Roger will feel more secure.Part of the team feel that you can manage these tasks.
(4) Part of the team feel, however, that you are not yet ready to do any of these tasks as you are not yet sufficiently committed to this marriage. They feel that you need Roger to misbehave in order to remind you of Paul's previous marriage and to keep you distant and uncommitted to each other at present. So this part of the team think you are not yet ready to behave as a united couple in relation to Roger, or to carry out the discussion task.
(5) They think that you should continue as you are for the moment, since greater commitment to each other is quite hazardous for you both.

The message contains four main elements:

- At (1) an introduction to the split-team formulation.
- At (2) a task for the couple.
- At (3) a task to include the step-child.
- At (4) a continuation of the split-team formulation which addresses some of the possible dynamics of the couple's relationship.
- At (5) a prescription to continue the behaviour.

The team thought that the couple were sufficiently verbal and intelligent to be able to understand and work with this message. On reflection, although the couple understood, and did in fact perform the tasks successfully, the message could perhaps have been simpler.

9.5.3 Writing a letter containing the message

Because it was somewhat complicated, and in order to give the message additional significance, it was written as a letter and sent to the couple. This is useful when the message is deliberately complex, or if the therapist wishes to reinforce either the message or the concern of the team for the couple. We hope that by receiving a letter the couple are encouraged to work at their relationship at home between sessions.

Our constant aim throughout therapy is to encourage couples to work at their relationship at home rather than wait for a 'magical' therapist to work miracles in the session.

9.6 Violent arguments about the children

The following is an example of work done with one couple whose central difficulty centred around disagreements over the children.

Example 9B
Tom aged 42 and Evie aged 39 had been married for 20 years and had five children, ranging in age from 5 to 19 years old. The reason for referral was angry

outbursts and physical violence; they were referred by their GP. Tom had recently been made redundant. This couple were known to the social services, whom they had seen at intervals throughout their marriage but not during the last five years.

Tom had become severely depressed and hospitalised at the age of 20; since then bouts of depression or anxiety had twice led to brief spells in hospital. From their social history sheets it was learned that they were continually having rows, his temper being described as uncontrollable. He had been physically violent towards his wife in the last six months and she was worried in case this would recur.

In the first session Tom's concern about the marriage was that 'my depression and anxiety holds me back' from being an effective husband and father. Evie described the problem as being one in which there was 'no confidence, trust or security within the family'.

Both Tom and Evie expressed warm and loving feelings for each other. They seemed genuinely puzzled why, in spite of their deep affection for each other, they had such a difficult relationship. 'We rarely laugh together, we argue a lot, we cry a lot, we fight a lot. We rarely have fun together. There's no reason for such dreadful things to happen!'

By exploring the detail of their interaction at home it became clear that the children were the focus for most of the disagreement. Rows over the children escalated into violent squabbles. They had also received reports from school that the youngest son was occasionally absent. Tom had tried to sort this out without consulting Evie, who had become upset. Evie usually made all the decisions about the children and saw herself as the authoritative competent parent; although she spoke highly of Tom she excluded him from family decisions. When asked by the therapist 'How do you decide as a couple what to do about the children?' they replied 'We don't decide together. We let things go'.

They had recently moved to a new house where they had hoped to start afresh with no family or marital problems. Tom had worn himself out by working long hours to redecorate the house.

9.6.1 The message

The following message was given at the end of the first session of therapy.

9.6.2 Formulation

(1) The team feel that as a couple you are both trying very hard to be good parents. Evie has been working hard to keep the family together and bring up five children successfully.
(2) Tom has put tremendous energy into the home of late, to the extent that he seems to have put the house and family before himself and is now somewhat weary.

(3) Tom has also been taking responsibility as the father to look after your youngest son in his difficulties in adjusting to his new school.

(4) You both seem to be making it difficult for yourselves by setting yourselves too many tasks. There is a need to slow down, and take settling in to the new home step by step.

9.6.3 Task

We would like you to find time twice each week to sit down together, without the children, for 30 minutes, and discuss an issue about the children about which you disagree. We want you to continue to discuss the subject until you agree about it. If you need to carry the issue over into another talking session, do so. Make sure you keep strictly to the time, i.e. 30 minutes. Wait until your next talking session to continue the discussion.

9.6.4 Timetable

The couple chose Mondays and Thursdays from 8.30 pm to 9.00 pm each week for these sessions.

9.6.5 Letter

The above message was sent to the couple as a letter with a reminder of their next appointment.

9.6.6 Framing the above message

The message in total was trying to focus on the following issues.

At (1) The violent outbursts, arguments and disagreements were given a positive connotation by stressing that as a couple they have been trying very hard to be good parents. This marks the context as therapeutic. They were both included specifically as we felt that there was a sense in which the father was being denied his parenting role.

At (2) the message gives a positive reframe to the anxious activities of Tom, and characterises him as a particularly concerned and hard-working father by including his concern to provide a suitably attractive home for the fresh start for his wife and family. The team sensed that Evie saw herself as the competent parent and Tom as the inadequate parent. The message was addressing this imbalance by describing Tom as a competent father.

At (3) the message focusses on the complaint of Evie that Tom had acted separately in relation to the youngest son, and gives this a positive reframe by complimenting him on his independence and his responsible attitude. Again this is attempting to address the imbalance in their relationship to the children.

At (4) the message describes the anxiety and pressure as something they both experience, rather than just experienced by Tom. Anxiety is reframed as trying to get too many things done at once.

The task addresses in a simple straightforward way the central problem described in the session, that of their arguments over the children. These arguments also seem to contain within them the difficulties this couple have, first of sharing their parenting and second in the complementary relationship in which Evie does not acknowledge the competence of Tom and Tom submits to this (see Minuchin & Fishman 1981).

The timetabling of these discussions gives a structure which this couple admit they need in the session by saying 'We let things go'.

9.6.7 Single-session therapy

Tom and Evie came for one visit only. As far as we know through GP contact, they have since settled down to a more harmonious relationship.

Many couples are not highly motivated to continue to come to therapy and therefore it is important to be able to give them a sense that work begins in the first session and can continue at home. It may also be that, in one such session, the therapy can address the central questions which are making the relationship dysfunctional and provide sufficient appropriate interventions to make further visits unecessary. Additionally, the above couple had sought the help of other agencies over the years and had perhaps already developed the pattern of brief consultations in crisis situations.

We were not aware at the time that they would not return for their next appointment or that the work done would suffice from their viewpoint. From our perspective, if sufficient work can be achieved in the first session there should not always be an expectation that couples will engage in a long series of sessions.

9.7 Depression in an older marriage or the empty nest phase

Example 9C
Frank aged 51 and Felicity aged 49 had been married for 25 years. The reason for referral was his depression, difficulties at work and in the marriage. Both Mr and Mrs C had had individual therapy.

Frank, a management consultant to a large institution, had sought help because he was depressed and having personal difficulties at work. These were loss of confidence, feeling overstressed and uncertain and finding it increasingly difficult to carry his senior management role as well as his consultancy to the institution and to a large trade union organisation. At home he was having more frequent arguments with his wife and children, his wife telling him that the 'union had become his mistress'. He wondered if he could any longer tolerate his marriage, and felt he was being asked to make impossible choices between competing demands for his time. He was feeling thoroughly depressed.

During the first session it emerged that not only were the couple having violent and repeated arguments but these arguments were affecting their sex life. Felicity was becoming increasingly demanding of sex, feeling more attracted to him by the arguments; at the same time Frank found his sexual desire reducing, particularly as arguments tended to occur when he was ready for sex but 'turned him off badly'. Felicity felt miserably neglected and certain that Frank must choose between her or his work.

They had four children, the youngest being 18 years old, and had moved many times because of Frank's work. The most recent move occurred 18 months ago. As a result they now saw little of their children who had stayed in the previous locality. Bill, the youngest, had lost his job and was temporarily at home again and a source of disagreement.

Both Frank and Felicity felt that they were at a critical time in their marriage. They could no longer agree about the children, their home, their sex life or his work. Frank felt burdened and depressed. Felicity had given up a good job to make their recent move and was now bitterly regretting this. They described their earlier marriage as good. They agreed that the deterioration began with their recent move.

During the first session they both said that they desperately wanted to work out a solution to their dilemma. Since they were a highly intelligent couple they were asked to think about alternative solutions to their difficulties in the session. They eagerly worked out three possible alternatives which they call scenarios. It worried them both that they felt making choices between these scenarios would be enormously difficult. The message was designed to make it easier for them to discuss the alternative scenarios at home.

9.7.1 The message

The following message was given to the couple after the first session of therapy.

9.7.2 Formulation

(1) The team noticed just how very depressed you both are and how much you are both sacrificing in the present situation.
(2) Felicity, you have changed your job several times to move with Frank, and several homes have been left behind; your sex life together is being sacrificed and your relationship with the children is very stressed at present. Frank, you too are sacrificing your home life in order to continue your work with the union, as well as the institution.
(3) We feel you are both depressed because you are both at a natural life stage with children no longer at home. Also because you have done so much sacrificing of yourselves you have become isolated from each other.
(4) However we don't think you should move too quickly to 'deinstitutionalise' yourselves. We feel you will need to do this little by little,

maybe by changing some of your 'union rules', and we think you both know how difficult it is to change union rules.

9.7.3 Task, timetable and ground rules for the task

We want you to find half an hour each evening when you can sit down and talk to each other.
(5) (Felicity interrupts the giving of the task to say 'I have tried that and it doesn't work'.) The therapist continues giving the task and adds that it is not Mrs C but the marital therapy clinic which is asking that they both find this time together. They suggest 6.30 each evening.
(6) The ground rules for the task are as follows:
  (a) They are to talk about the future and not the past.
  (b) They are to consider the three scenarios already suggested today.
  (c) In doing so they are to consider each other's feelings and discuss together the pros and cons of each scenario.

9.7.4 Framing the message

The therapist worked with the couple's high levels of anxiety in the session about the future of their relationship by giving them the immediate opportunity to discuss alternatives for their future. The team felt pressure from this couple to sort out their problems. This was experienced in the volume of information that had come out of the first session, the difficulty of slowing down the interaction and the urgency with which the couple faced their dilemma. The team experienced some indecision (perhaps reflecting the indecision of the couple, see Berkowitz 1984). The team were anxious not to ignore the sexual aspect of their marriage which was so obviously stressful for them both; but also wanted to pay attention to the presenting difficulty which was described as the husband's depression. This too seemed to have got lost in the mêlée of the session. Being aware of the team's responses helps to understand what quality of message may be most helpful. With this couple it seemed essential to take hold of the confusion and anxiety and bring some simplicity and order into a fluid and panicky situation.

9.7.5 Commentary on the above message

At (1) the presenting symptom was described as being present in both spouses. The evidence for this is taken from the session and restated to the couple with the positive connotation that they have both made personal sacrifices which have contributed to their present situation.

At (2) these sacrifices are listed as clearly as possible and are taken directly from the material presented by the couple. This step is particularly important where one partner has been labelled as ill or bad and is designed to reduce the labelling and at the same time challenge the system (see Sections 4.6.7, 10.5 and 10.7).

At (3) the concept of a natural life stage is introduced to the couple. The empty nest phase in a family life cycle when the family leave home with the consequent readjustments often brings sadness to both spouses and recognition of this as a natural adjustment normalises the experience for the couple.Often too the couple find themselves isolated from each other and there is the need to renegotiate their relationship at this time. In this message it was felt sufficient to state this simply and come back to the readjustments necessary in later sessions.

At (4) this message is in danger of becoming too sophisticated. The aim here was to use the language of the couple's interaction and incorporate their concepts into the message. Felicity had said that 'the union had become Frank's mistress'. It was hoped that the couple could understand and enjoy the play on words (or metaphor). The setting of their relationship into the institution was meant to empathise with both the age of their marriage, the union involvement and the pace at which change was possible. As we have already indicated, it can become fascinating for the therapist to be creative in this way and often is valuable to the couple. But there is always a danger in being too clever. We think that we judged this couple accurately and that they too enjoyed the *double entendre*; if in doubt whether the client will understand the subtleties do not use them. It is essential not to be patronising or too sophisticated.

At (4) we were also introducing a paradoxical element into the message by telling them not to change too quickly.

At (5) the task is challenged by Felicity, but the therapist simply continues with giving the message, whilst at the same time taking responsibility for the framing of the task.

Therapists will wish to handle such reactions from the couple in their own way, but it seems wise not to be easily deflected from the task. Although this therapist's response was somewhat peremptory, it seemed to give the couple confidence that the therapist expected them to be able to complete the task.

At (6) the therapist sets clear and specific guidelines for the task. This was felt necessary for this particular couple who were full of anxiety and felt very pressurised to find a solution.

9.7.6 Changing the tasks as therapy proceeds

Frank and Felicity C attended the clinic for six sessions over a six-month period. At a later stage in therapy the tasks were changed. They were asked to counsel each other on one evening a week, then deliberately have an argument on the next evening, and to continue alternating between counselling each other and arguing with each other as their timetabled tasks.

At discharge they had made many significant life choices together to simplify their life style. They were increasingly able to talk together, share their feelings more freely and to have good sex together (at least once a week instead of once a month or less.) They enjoyed each other's company more but also were taking days away from each other. Interaction with their grown-up children had stabilised to a more comfortable relationship.

9.8 Alternative uses of messages, formulations, tasks and timetables

Once a therapist has become familiar with the use of messages, timetables and tasks, there are a wide range of alternatives available which can be tailored to each couple and to the specific relationship difficulties they face. They can also be varied as the couple's relationship alters to keep pace with any changes which may occur.

Some examples of messages are given in the next section.

9.8.1 Messages including timetables for enjoyment together (or 'married couples should not have fun together')

Many couples who come for therapy are preoccupied and worried about their relationship. In their intense search for solutions they become quite miserable. Life seems to be grey, solemn and wretched. Often such couples have many responsibilities for family, mortgages, work and friends, all of which are carried out with dedication, but little joy. It is as though they carry an idea that 'married couples should not have fun together'.

Teisman (1979) discusses this quality of many couples, particularly where jealousy is a feature, and comments

> 'Couples who enter therapy, are dead serious, lack a sense of hopefulness and are usually unimaginative in the face of their problems. Their attempts to solve problems are painfully difficult work bearing little fruit.'

(See also Section 10.2.) He goes on to say what seems to be missing is a sense of play. It is this sense of play, fun or pleasurable activity which we wish to introduce to couples through a timetable for an enjoyable activity together.

A simple and often highly effective formulation and timetable is as follows.

(1) Positively connote the behaviour of the couple by for example telling them that their dedication, sense of responsibility and seriousness is very impressive (see Section 9.13), remembering always to be specific to each couple's own lifestyle and activities.
(2) Suggest that they do something as a couple which is just for enjoyment.

(3) Work together with the couple to select a day of the week when they can do this and set the basic guidelines which ensure that they do allocate time together.

Presenting such a message often opens up a whole area of strain and tension which the couple have been feeling but not expressing. It allows them to acknowledge that, indeed, they have done little to look after themselves for some time. Such couples may respond that there are baby-sitting problems, money problems, etc., which will make it impossible. However the therapist can often help them think through these difficulties and usually they can be overcome. It seems as though such couples may need the encouragement and permission of the therapist to go out and enjoy themselves together. For the therapist this can be a rewarding and releasing experience too. As therapists we often are too preoccupied with grave issues to consider relaxing and enjoyable activities.

In presenting such a message to the couple, the therapist should therefore allow time, in the session, for discussion of alternatives and practical problems. For the first such relaxing activity the therapist may well have to be supportive of the difficulties faced by the couple, at the same time ensuring as far as possible that they are overcome. Couples who have so far been unable to find time to enjoy themselves together are unlikely to do so without the therapist's active encouragement.

9.8.2 Finding an enjoyable activity

The following is an example of work done with a young couple during the giving of a message to help them decide upon an enjoyable joint activity:

Example 9D
(Christopher and Mabel J also described in Example 10 F)
Christopher aged 23 and Mabel aged 22 had been married for five years and had no children. They were referred by the emergency clinic at the Maudsley Hospital, which they had attended constantly, requesting help following several overdose attempts by Mabel. One aspect of their relationship was that they were each over-involved with the other's problems.

Christopher was a very anxious, poorly paid research worker who worried about his work, and Mabel had given up her job to stay at home and look after him. Their married life was without any outside stimulation, they had neither family nor friends in the neighbourhood. They lived in an expensive but tiny dismal flat which Mabel found difficult to make into a home. Their preoccupation with Mabel's depression seemed the only excitement in their lives.

9.8.2.1 Presenting the message
During the giving of the message the therapist helped the couple to use five minutes of brainstorming to find alternative inexpensive and enjoyable joint activities.

9.8.2.2 Formulation

(1) The team think you are a very dedicated couple, with a very intense and loving relationship. You care deeply about each other and find it quite hard to be separate.

(2) By Mabel giving up her job to stay at home and look after Christopher in a difficult flat she is showing her determination to be a 'perfect' wife for Christopher no matter what the losses are for her.

(3) Christopher equally worries about his work and being a good provider for you both. He also worries a great deal about Mabel in order to show Mabel that she is central to his existence. This is a very intense and powerful relationship.

9.8.2.3 Setting the task

(4) What we would like you to do is the following. On one evening a week we would like you to go out together and do something which would be enjoyable for you both.

The above statement was greeted with loud exhalation of breath from both partners, accompanied by some laughter and relaxation in their postures. Mabel instantly touched Christopher on the shoulder and coquettishly said 'Take me to Hard Rock'. Christopher grinned boyishly but then looking sad said 'God, that'd cost us my week's wage'. They both became still and glum.

THERAPIST
OK. Hard Rock isn't a possibility because it is too expensive. But what would you enjoy doing that isn't expensive. There are quite a number of concerts, places to visit, interesting walks which are free.

(5) The therapist spent about five minutes with them brainstorming inexpensive alternatives which would be relaxing and enjoyable.

They came up with a list which included

- Going to the Battersea Festival.
- Buying Mabel a new dress together.
- Christopher having a radically different haircut (they would go together to the hairdresser).
- Going for a long walk along the Thames (something they used to do when courting but have not done since marrying.)
- Visiting Grandma (Grandma had never been mentioned till this point. It transpired that Grandma is somewhat senile but Mabel felt very close to her and always found her fun to be with).
- Ringing up a couple who were best man and bridesmaid at their wedding and meeting them in town for a drink.

The above list might sound mundane and ordinary; however this couple were excited and animated as they contemplated these alternatives. It is essential to stay with whatever their perception of enjoyment would be. The couple chose to go for a walk along the banks of the Thames.

(6) They were left to finalise the day, time and place of this walk as the therapist felt it was intrusive to enter into what was now becoming for the couple a private affair.
(7) At the next session they reported that they had added in a stop at a pizza place and some cheap red wine. It seems that sexual intercourse together had been more vivid and sensual that evening.

Such couples seem to need the authority of the clinic (or therapist) to allow them to go out and enjoy themselves together. It is as though they carry the concept 'married couples should not have fun'.

9.8.2.4 *Framing the message*
This couple presented the therapist with a very enmeshed and dependent relationship. They seemed to be typical 'babes in the wood', with Mabel being labelled depressed and accepting this. The formulation is deliberately framed to avoid accepting the couple's definition of the problem, at the same time accepting many of their anxieties and preoccupations.

9.8.2.5 *Commentary on the above message*
At (1) the message tries to empathise with the intensity of their relationship but give this a positive connotation. The phrase 'find it quite hard to separate' was used to emphasise their over-involvement, but again to connote this positively.

As already stated, where one partner has been labelled as ill or bad, the contribution of each spouse to the interaction should be described in a balanced fashion so as to dilute the effect of the labelling (see Section 10.7.2).

At (2) and (3) the individual contribution of Mabel and Christopher to their joint interaction is clearly stated. This is an important systemic step and is often difficult for therapists trained in individual work, or in linear causal thinking, to conceptualise. It is, however, central to the delabelling process.

At (4) the therapist had to work quite hard with the couple to stay with the hopefulness that fun was possible and within their reach. Here the skills of each individual therapist are used empathically to help the couple look at the practical difficulties and to moderate their wishes to the reality of their circumstances. This part of the process should not be rushed as the couple are breaking new ground together.

At (5) the therapist uses a brainstorming five minutes to help the couple feel free enough to explore a range of ideas without feeling burdened by committing themselves to any of them. This simple technique has much to commend it (see also Section 9.10.1).

At (6) the therapist uses his/her discretion and leaves the detailing of the task to the couple, sensing intuitively that the couple were entering into an intimate experience into which the therapist chose not to intrude.

9.8.2.6 Timetables for enjoyment

There are difficulties about using the term 'timetable for enjoyment', as it is in some ways impossible to instruct couples to enjoy themselves. For those who feel weighed down by the daily demands of their lifestyle, a suggestion that they go out and enjoy themselves could be experienced as just another burden. For Mabel and Christopher there was the added difficulty of financial worries (at **(4)**). Some partners have very different interests and finding an activity to share together may be quite problematic. Some are so busy that there is little room for yet another activity. For these couples a possibility might be to find ways of allowing themselves time to do nothing together, choosing specific times and days when this could occur.

In all of these situations the therapist works together with the couple to distil from their life pattern something that might be enjoyable and relaxing for them. It is preferable if the couple are encouraged to make their own suggestions, but the therapist should feel free to feed back to the couple any aspects of their lifestyle, pattern and mood which might be helpful.

The timetable is thus used to challenge the assumptions that have previously been made about being unable to find time to enjoy themselves and relax together. Some examples from the clinic are:

- Doing nothing together.
- The wife being treated by her husband for a whole day as a baby, and having everything done for her.
- Going to a Swedish massage parlour together.
- Playing table tennis together.
- Spending a day in bed together.
- The woman surprising her partner by arranging an event of her choice.
- The man being allowed to cook his favourite meal of Polish sausage, potato salad and rye bread for his partner, while his partner listens to Fats Waller and reads.
- Having Sunday lunch without the children.
- Locking the doors and having a shower together.
- Using body paints to explore each other sensually.

None of these may strike the reader as necessarily their own particular brand of enjoyment; the skill of the therapist is to ensure that each couple choose activities about which they can say 'this is relaxing and enjoyable for us'.

9.9 Timetables for joint activities

Many couples are so preoccupied with the practicalities of life that they rarely have any time together as a couple. One partner may complain bitterly that the other 'never finds time to be with me', but it is often found that both partners are equally busy. The first task for the therapist may then be to use a session to help the couple to discuss what activity they would like to do together and second, how they are going to make time for this.

Joint activities may include or exclude the children, depending upon the current relationship of the parental pair with their children. If one partner is in alliance with the children and the other is excluded, then an activity in which both parents go out together without the children reinforces the boundary between the parents and the children. On the other hand, where a couple usually disagree about how to handle the children, if the parents can agree how they will relate to the children then a family outing with both parents and the children might be planned. Again each activity should be tailored to the current needs of the couple (see Section 7.3.6).

Occasionally a couple will be so overwhelmed by their extended family that an activity together which is kept secret from the extended family helps the couple to see themselves as a separate unit within the wider family. If one or both partners are engaged in a relationship outside the marriage, then an activity which the couple keep secret from the 'affair' may help bring excitement back into the couple's relationship (see also Section 10.13).

From our recent experience, some examples are

- Where the husband had always seen the decorating as his priority and the wife had always wanted to join in they agreed to ask a friend to take the children for the weekend so that they could both do the decorating together.
- Where the husband had always gone to a tennis club without his wife because she hated tennis, they agreed both to join a different club where yoga was available and attend an evening class once a week together.
- Where the wife had always seen the front garden as her responsibility and the back garden as his, they agreed to garden together once a week.
- She cancelled her night out with the girls and he cancelled his night out with his friends to go to a dancing class together.
- Where they rarely watched television together they agreed to sit together, hold hands and watch television.

It is interesting to note that many couples chose quite simple joint activities. The difficulty seems to be in acknowledging the need to arrange something and negotiate it together. We find that after the couple have achieved one simple joint activity together they may then go on to explore other things they can do together.

9.9.1 Activity tasks

There are two other areas of activities for couples which should be mentioned. These are

(1) Separate activities designed for each spouse.
(2) Activities designed to include one spouse more fully.

9.9.2 Separate activities for each spouse

These activities are designed to assist couples to participate in and enjoy separate interests. Some couples are like 'babes in the wood' and are dependent upon each other for almost all of their nurturing and interests and may do everything together (see Section 7.3.7). For instance, in Example 9C Mabel and Christopher J found it difficult to have separate interests or to seek friends outside their relationship. Many couples naturally go through this intense preoccupation with each other in the beginning of their relationship. Where it becomes prolonged difficulties may arise (see Section 1.2.3 and example 9F).

In our experience women, more often than men, feel that they have given up a great deal for the relationship. For example, a woman who has given up work to be a 'good wife' may become resentful at the partner's apparent greater freedom since he is unlikely to have given up a job for their relationship. Unspoken resentments coupled with an inability to change their over-involved relationship may present therapists with a painful impasse situation in a couple who otherwise seem well adjusted and loving.

For such couples timetables for separate activities can be fruitful. The first essential step is likely to be discussions held in-session about alternative activities for each partner. It is helpful if the couple can encourage each other to find outside interests. Brainstorming, listing of alternatives, prioritising and thinking through the pros and cons for each activity, with the therapist present, may all help give the partners greater confidence. Consideration of the practical, financial and emotional difficulties may be too risky for the couple to undertake initially on their own.

Experience suggests that such couples may cling to each other partly because of difficulties they each have in socialising with others. The encouragement they give to each other may therefore be essential to the success of such separate ventures.

The simpler the activity, the more likely it is to be achieved. Examples might be

- He goes to the pub with a male friend, while she goes late-night shopping with a female friend.
- She goes to an exercise class and he goes to visit his parents.
- He goes to a football match and she goes to a matinée show.

Again, each activity should be arrived at from the couple's own life style, wishes and interests. Activities which might seem over-simple to the therapist may well be quite challenging to such couples. The therapist must appreciate the difficulties couples face and where appropriate tailor the time span and activity accordingly. One such example is the couple who always cut each other's hair. For them it was an achievement to go separately to the same hairdresser and to be patient enough to wait to see the other's hair style. Another example is the couple who married in their early forties and found that they had given up all of their friends, did everything together and would not let the other out of their sight. It took this couple some discussion before she would allow him one evening to visit the friend with whom he previously shared a flat and he reciprocated by allowing her to visit her previous place of work.

Once achieved, these activities can be built upon steadily to interrupt the pattern of interaction which has become stultifying and can bring a greater flexibility and interest into the relationship.

9.9.3 Activities designed to assist one partner to participate more equally as a parent

Within this section, one is thinking specifically of family interaction. In Chapter 7 we describe the need to strengthen the parental alliance, at the same time paying attention to the nature of alliances between different parts of the system. With some couples, one member of the parental alliance has become detached from the family and the other spouse has taken over parts of his/her responsibilities. In many cases the husband has become peripheral to the lives of the children; this was so with both Mary and Bill B (Example 7B) and Tina and Tim (Example 7C). For such families, activities can be designed so that the spouse who is peripheral is enabled to take more responsibility as a parent.

For Penny and Paul S (Example 9A) this was a second marriage for the husband in which the relationship between the stepmother and stepson was uneasy and distant, so part of the first message was designed to begin work on changing this relationship. At (3) the message was

We would like you to do one small thing each to please the other. We suggest that Penny should take the dogs for a walk at the weekend with Roger, and that Paul should go shopping with Penny twice.

These particular activities derive from this couple's own lifestyle, in which Penny's dogs were difficult for her husband to integrate into their new relationship and Paul's son by his first marriage had not yet been fully accepted by Penny. Activities are woven together in this way to try to help the couple to overcome these difficulties.

When Mary and Bill B (Example 7B) came into therapy they had an 18-month-old child Theresa, from whom Bill was isolated to the extent that he had rarely held, played with or talked to her. One of the early activities, which falls into this category, was to find ways for Mary to support Bill to become more involved with his daughter. Mary was by now very possessive of Theresa and was also becoming afraid to leave her or allow anyone else to look after her. She felt there were hazards everywhere from which her daughter must be protected, and which she was finding increasingly anxiety-provoking.

In the session the therapist encouraged the couple to discuss the question of hazards in the home environment from which they as parents could find ways of protecting their daughter. During these discussions Mary expressed some relief at being able to share these anxieties with her husband, and surprise at just how practical Bill was when thinking about the inevitable risks. They were set homework to continue these discussions and to see if they could prioritise the risks that were avoidable and those that were in some ways beyond their control. This step was achieved successfully and Mary again expressed both relief and surprise that her husband, whom she had thought disinterested, was in fact full of good practical suggestions. The next step was to give them the opportunity to discuss, in a session, simple ways in which Bill could spend time with Theresa, and reassure Mary that Theresa would be secure in his care.

This step proved much less difficult than was anticipated from the previous attitudes of both partners. For the first two weeks, between sessions, Bill looked after Theresa in one room while Mary ironed in another. In the next two weeks Bill took over two evenings of bathing Theresa while Mary cooked the evening meal. By the fifth week Mary was able to go out shopping and leave Bill for a whole afternoon with Theresa. Bill, for his part, was enjoying learning about being a father and was greatly encouraged to discover that Mary did not resent his involvement but found it supportive. Mary was relieved that she had been able to share her anxieties about bringing up Theresa. She also admitted that she had the occasional twinge of interest in returning to part-time work and wondered if they might use a childminder in order to make this possible. She was a highly qualified computer programmer who had given up her work to have a child.

The setting of simple tasks designed to give a greater balance to the parental alliance and to the involvement with their daughter allowed this couple to make some major adjustments to what was becoming an intense and potentially damaging triangle of interaction.

One might conjecture that the simplicity and non-threatening nature of such tasks make it more possible for adjustments to be made to current interactions. Many of the anxieties and interpersonal difficulties are discussed by the couple in the context of the simple task set; this may provide a sufficiently secure framework for difficulties to be expressed without becoming overwhelming.

9.10 Timetables for discussions, building on in-session work

In Chapters 5 and 6 we describe in-session work on reciprocity nego-tiation and communication training which the therapist can use to help the couple develop a more effective relationship. Chapter 8 discusses some in-session structural interventions which focus on encouraging arguments or discussions (Section 8.2). We now offer further sugges-tions showing how such in-session work can be developed as home-work tasks and included in the message. (See also Example 8C for an example of in-session arguments which were set as homework tasks, first as conversations (session 2) and later as arguments (session 3).)

9.10.1 Problem solving and time-limited discussion in a 'psychiatric' couple

The following example is one in which the husband was diagnosed as schizophrenic and the wife as having bouts of depression: a problem-solving approach is used.

Example 9E
David aged 38 and Marcia aged 39 had been married for five years. The reason for referral was concern about the ability of the couple to care for the baby due in five months.

David and Marcia were referred when Marcia became pregnant. They had been married for five years, and throughout this time had been given support together by the psychiatric services for his schizophrenia. David had been receiving medication and support for about 15 years since he was diagnosed schizophrenic. Marcia presented as a powerfully built and competent woman who held down a good job as a secretary, while David presented as light-weight, shy, sensitive and intelligent. Although it was clear that Marcia easily became depressed and relied heavily upon David for emotional and practical support, it was David who was labelled by the couple and the psychiatric services as the patient. As a couple they had become very dependent upon these services.

The couple were both extremely anxious as to how they would manage after the baby was born and each had heavy anxieties about the impact of David's illness on the baby. Initial work in the session was to delabel David and help the couple to work together, rather than focus all their concern on David's illness (see Chapter 10). At the same time, the aim was to help them to learn a problem-solving approach to tasks which they could use in the future to solve difficulties as they arose, including how to look after the baby.

There is a growing body of knowledge regarding factors affecting the relapse rate of people diagnosed as schizophrenic which indicates ways of working with such individuals. We are mindful of this research in presenting this couple and were following the general guidelines set down by Falloon *et al.* (1984) regarding a problem-solving approach, and by Leff and Vaughn (1985) in working at a low level of expressed emotion and critical comment. Evidence seems to be growing which suggests that people diagnosed as depressed may also have a low tolerance of critical comment, which would indicate that this approach was as essential for the wife as for the husband in this couple (Vaughn & Leff 1976; Kuipers & Bebbington 1985). In addition we used our usual method of focussing on the relationship rather than on the illness.

9.10.2 In-session practice

During the third session David and Marcia agreed that they had many unresolved difficulties which niggled them and needed to be sorted out.
(About 10 minutes into the session.)

(1) The therapist suggested that this might be a good homework task in which they could use 30 minutes, twice a week, to talk to each other about one thing each which 'niggled' them about the other's behaviour. David, dropping his head and lowering his voice, said almost inaudibly 'I don't think that I could do that'.

(2) The therapist, decentring herself, asked them to turn their chairs towards each other and discuss in-session what the difficulties might be for both of them with such a task. It emerged that if Marcia described something which 'niggled' her, David instantly felt very criticised and responsible for putting it right. He hated this so much that he avoided discussions with Marcia. Marcia, on her part, spent her time following him around trying to engage his interest and finally 'blowing up' in an angry outburst, resulting in Marcia in tears and David upset.

(3) THERAPIST
That sounds a very unhappy situation but helps me to understand why practical discussions are difficult for you both. Let's see if we can find a way together to help you overcome these situations by doing some practising now. Can you each choose one small 'niggle' you have with the other, and let us try working for five minutes, no more, now in the session, on one issue each. Let us see if we can find a way for you to have this discussion without David feeling overly criticised and without Marcia 'blowing up'.
(4) David how about you going first?

David, now more animated, began to tell Marcia how embarrassed he felt when they went to the vet together with their two squalling cats, one in a cat basket, one in an old laundry basket tied up with string and cardboard, and various additional assorted bags. David described an 'eccentric scene' (his words) which they both found hilarious and dissolved into laughter in the session. Marcia admitted that she had never thought about it but agreed that David would find this embarrassing. David acknowledged that over the years as a 'patient' he had become very sensitive about how he appeared in public. They were able to go on to decide that they could solve this by buying another cat basket.

(5) The therapist stopped them here, announcing that they had used their five minutes. Marcia was then encouraged to speak about her 'niggle'.

> MARCIA (*her voice becoming strident and attacking*)
> For me it's the mess in the garden. (*Turning to the therapist*) You see we have this large garden and the weeds are knee high and I just wish David would get out there and do something about it!

David, by now sunk low in his chair, does not want to reply.

(6) THERAPIST (*to David*)
Are you feeling criticised now?

> DAVID (*shyly*)
> Yes, I am, but . . . I don't see how I can find time to do the garden . . . , I mean I am keeping the house going and . . . I am trying to look after Marcia, now she is pregnant, I do more of the chores . . .

(7) THERAPIST (*interrupting*)
We know already that if a matter has been raised by Marcia then David thinks he must find a solution on his own. Let's see if you can face this rather differently. See if you can talk together about the mess in the garden, and see if together you can come up with some solutions. Try to treat it as a problem you both share.

> MARCIA (*to the therapist*)
> I wish, if he can't do it himself, he would let us pay someone to tidy it up for us.

(8) THERAPIST
Try asking David now if that is something he can consider.

> MARCIA (*hesitantly*)
> Well would you? We could just about afford it.

> DAVID
> I would find that a bit difficult because I suppose I think I should be able to do it. (*Turning to the therapist*) You see Marcia used to do the bit of the garden which has got overgrown but now she is six months' pregnant she can't do it any more.

(9) THERAPIST (*to Marcia*)
This used to be your responsibility?

> MARCIA (*looking embarrassed to admit this*)
> Well yes, but now I'm pregnant I don't feel I should.

(10) THERAPIST
That makes sense, so can you continue together to think of alternatives to help you both get this job done?

The following discussion is lighter; alternatives emerge, such as:

- Paying some neighbouring boys.
- Asking Marcia's father.
- David gardening if Marcia sits near him at the weekend.

(11) The therapist stops them as they have used their five minutes.

(12) After congratulating them for developing such a sensible list of alternatives, the therapist asks them to say what the experience of discussing together had been like.

> DAVID
> I actually enjoyed the bit about the cats, and when we started to see it as our problem, and not just mine, I felt good about the garden discussion.

> MARCIA
> Yes I felt good too, and a bit surprised that we actually managed to have the discussion. I was very pleased that we did manage to have the discussion.

9.10.3 Setting the homework

(13) THERAPIST
You did very well to carry through that discussion here, since you had both expressed considerable concern about this. I am aware that you were being asked to do something that was difficult for you both and yet you persevered. This shows just how determined you are to sort things out as a couple, and also that you can be successful when you take time to work on small concerns one at a time. It is also satisfying that you could let each other know what was good about it.

As homework we would like you to use this session as a model, and do as follows. Find some separate 30-minute periods when you can discuss one topic together. In this session we attempted to discuss two topics: this was too hurried, so at home you should use the 30 minutes to concentrate on one small difficulty at a time.

The therapist went on to ask them if this was possible for them and, if so, how often in any one week they felt they could find time. After discussion they chose Tuesdays and Thursdays after supper from 7.30–8.00 pm. They were also given guidelines for discussion and in particular the concept of brainstorming was explained so that they were clear about its usefulness.

9.10.4 A follow-up letter

These guidelines were sent to them in a letter as follows.

(14) Dear David and Marcia
As promised, here is the letter reminding you of the guidelines for your homework task.
(1) It was agreed that on Tuesdays and Thursdays between 7.30 pm and 8.00 pm you would set aside 30 minutes for discussion.

(2) You agreed to discuss one topic only in the following manner.
- Brainstorm as many alternative solutions as possible.
- Prioritise these alternatives by listing the best three options in order of preference.

(3) Be clear about ending the discussion promptly, and leaving any loose ends until your next session. Use a kitchen timer or alarm to help you to time your discussions.

(4) Give yourselves 5 minutes at the end to say what was good about your discussions.

In general be supportive to each other during these sessions, give yourselves time to reflect.

Looking forward to finding out how this goes when we meet at our next session.

Yours sincerely,

(Therapist)

9.10.5 Discussion of the interventions used with Marcia and David T

The above work is described in some detail as an example of work with a couple where both partners were vulnerable and had been treated for a psychiatric illness. In this couple the husband had become quite severely labelled as a chronic psychiatric patient rather than a competent person, whilst the wife's depression and dependency upon her husband seemed to have been de-emphasised. The first task within therapy was therefore to work with the couple in such a way that they became prepared to acknowledge relationship difficulties which could be tackled within the marriage. In the above session the couple were beginning to accept this.

The session is used to give the couple the opportunity to explore their fears about working on relationship issues, at **(1)** and **(2)**. Having understood what repetitive sequences occurred at **(2)**, the therapist helps the couple to practise in the session at **(3)**. The therapist is respectful of their fears and suggests they practise for five minutes only and strictly keeps the time herself (at **(5)** and **(11)**).

At **(4)** the therapist joins with David to give him confidence to use the session. By insisting on David going first, the therapist was challenging the rules that governed their interaction as Marcia invariably took the initiative in discussions.

At **(6)** the therapist again joins David to ask him to speak about his feelings of being criticised; and again at **(7)** the therapist joins David to think about alternative ways of solving the problem. The therapist reframes the problem as a joint one and asks the couple to see if they can solve it by working together. At **(4)**, **(6)** and **(7)** the therapist is trying to unbalance the system so that Marcia acknowledges her contribution to the problem.

This seemed to be successful; however joining with one partner can alienate the other one and the therapist should try to be supportive of both of them. The risks are great at this point, either to alienate one partner or to be ineffective by not allying sufficiently with the other partner (in this case David) to unbalance the system and so facilitate change (see Section 8.3.3).

The therapist who wishes to work with couples who are fixed in a rigid system which maintains one member as 'ill' learns to be sensitive to this powerful interplay and to tread lightly, firmly and empathically, but not to be intimidated by the risks. In order to counterbalance the risks the therapist at **(9)** and **(10)** joins with Marcia.

At **(12)** the couple were both congratulated and encouraged to discuss together the experience. At **(12)** and **(13)** the therapist was mindful to be empathic and complimentary to the couple for the work they had done in-session, and ensured that the couple were given the freedom to choose whether they would do the homework, when, how often, etc. She was also at pains to give clear guidelines for the homework task and to follow this up by letter. (Some therapists find this tedious but the detail is necessary.)

It is useful to rehearse in-session the homework which will be set. The couple can then understand clearly what is being suggested and can be helped to relax and enjoy the task. The therapist's own sense of freedom to experiment, to make mistakes and persevere, to interrupt light-heartedly and remind the couple of the task in hand will all help the couple work towards a change in their own interaction. The notion of play and playtimes can be kept in mind as such homework is introduced (Section 9.4).

Even with careful preparation, such a couple may not manage to do homework at the first attempt and may need more practice in-session before they can tackle what is a 'scary' experience on their own. The therapist can then start the next session with 'what got in the way' of doing the homework. In Minuchin's terms this is both 'limiting the field of observation' and 'giving structure to the following session'. It is also allowing the couple to return to the session for further in-session practice. If we think of the couple experiencing in the session an alternative way of interaction which changes the pattern of their relationship it is not surprising that couples may prefer the safety of the session before practising at home.

There is no correct intervention style: each therapist works towards greater refinement of knowledge, skill and intervention. In the above description, as with all the examples in this book, one can think of alternative and possibly better interventions. We do not claim to have discovered the right way, but offer these in-session interventions and take-home timetables and tasks as a modest step along the path towards greater confidence and competence for couples who seek help with relationship difficulties.

9.10.6 When to include timetables for discussion in the message

Timetabled discussions can be used for a wide variety of relationship difficulties, and therapists will slowly build up their own repertoire of how and when they are useful. We have already seen how these can be used for couples where one partner is diagnosed as schizophrenic, and in Chapter 10 we describe how homework timetables can be used for discussion of one partner's jealousy.

For clinical purposes, one could also consider using structured and timetabled discussions in the following situations.

9.10.6.1 Where couples are highly sensitive about arguments
(see Mary and Bill B, Example 7B and 8B)
Such couples may be best helped by starting gently with structured discussions in-session with no homework task. When homework is eventually set it may be helpful to add a slightly paradoxical element to the message by suggesting that any discussion may be rather difficult 'for the moment', and predicting that they may fail to discuss at home in the way that they have done in-session.

9.10.6.2 Where there are intractable arguments
For these couples (see Examples 7A and 9B), arguing had become part of the repetitive sequences maintaining a dysfunctional system. Or more simply, arguments resolved nothing and were experienced as a series of unhappy events.

For such couples timetables for discussion might be prescribed with additional ground rules. For example, it might be prescribed that they 'must not go over old topics', even if this means that they sit in silence for some time. This is particularly effective with some older relationships which are characterised by ritualistic arguments (repetitive sequences) of safe, stale, old ground. Other additional rules might be:

- Each to speak one sentence and wait for a reply.
- To divide the time into talking and listening sessions, for example A talks for five minutes and B listens, then the order is reversed.
- For a code word to be used by one partner to stop the other 'monologuing'.
- For the couple to choose an object to hold, rather like the mace in the House of Commons, which was used earlier to allow one Member only to speak at a time.

These new rules should be lighthearted but clear, possibly followed up in a letter.

For these couples such guidelines help to establish a greater security in which to develop a fresh and more vital relationship. Setting a timetable for discussion with, for example, old ground forbidden provides a forum for exploration to take place without too many risks.

9.10.6.3 *Where the pattern of discussion is quite fixed*
Examples of common patterns are:

(1) Where one usually speaks and the other is usually silent.
(2) Where both speak and neither listens.

(See Chapters 5 and 6 for additional examples of fixed patterns dealt with as communication difficulties.)

For (1) above, an additional rule might be that the non-speaker should talk while the other is asked to listen. For (2) the time might be structured so that both partners have equal time either talking or listening. Additional rules could be, for example, that the listening partner must attempt to find ways to show that he/she was attending carefully to what was being said.

9.10.6.4 *Where a couple continually avoid finding time to discuss significant issues*
Couples often avoid discussion of areas of controversy, but meanwhile anxiety and tension increase. For such couples it may be helpful to encourage the couple to work out an agenda in the session and to help them to start with the simpler questions first.

9.10.6.5 *Where separation has become an issue for the couple (see Section 10.16)*
Many couples who feel that their relationship is facing severe strain, and one or both partners have suggested separation or divorce, may generally avoid facing this issue squarely. Such suggestions may have been tossed out in a heated exchange or as a parting shot from one partner who leaves the scene, and each partner is uncertain of the exact meaning of these statements. A threat? A question? A decision made? An angry statement which is readily withdrawn when tempers cool? It is easy to undertand why such couples rarely find time to consider the difficulties quietly. Meanwhile fears mount and fantasies can run wild.

By the time such couples come to therapy they have usually built up a hidden reservoir of uncertainty and misery. They may also be extremely anxious about uncovering their fears to each other. (One cannot help wondering how many relationships could be enhanced and enriched and even separation avoided, if the couples had sought early assistance in facing joint difficulties rather than leaving anxieties unsaid and unresolved.)

These rather tortured relationships need to be delicately attended to, as beginning to talk to each other will be surrounded by many unspoken fears. The couples will usually need the support of the therapist in making choices about where to start. They will almost certainly be helped by experiencing in the session, with the therapist as facilitator, that it is possible to begin to talk to each other.

It is also likely that there will be pressure from the couple for an immediate answer to the dilemma 'are we going to stay together?'. This question can be reframed as a positive and purposive aim for therapy in which the answer can be discovered gradually, and the pressure from the couple can then be channelled into a slower step-by-step enquiry into the areas of their relationship which have become painful or difficult, preferably with the therapist in the decentred position.

The therapist should on no account try him/herself to answer this question; responses which underline the seriousness of their difficulties and the solemnity of such decisions is all that can be offered by the therapist (see Section 2.4.3.5). An alternative positive reframe might be to describe their seeking therapy as a determination on their part to help each other find a way through the very painful period they are now experiencing. In this way they are being very caring of each other.

By setting the couple structured timetables for discussion, with a possible agenda worked out in-session, the therapist is offering them a way of attending to the questions they are raising about the permanence of their relationship. The in-session work may require many of the skills described in Chapters 5 and 6 in order to ensure that the couples are equipped with the communication skills necessary to develop their discussions.

Again, the therapist should encourage the couple to start with simple and manageable discussions, and leave the mountains to be climbed later. (It is surprising how often the mountains become more manageable if approached in a step-by-step process rather than a massive assault.)

9.10.7 When to include timetabled arguments in the message

In Chapter 8 we described examples where encouraging arguments might be a useful strategy in-session. We suggested that arguments over trivial issues might be used, for example, with couples who seem to have developed a rule 'good couples do not argue' or some variation of this (see Section 8.2.1). Samuel and Diana S (Example 8C) are an example in which arguments are encouraged where the husband is reluctant to have sexual intercourse.

The pace at which both the couples and therapist can move depends a great deal on the therapist's confidence to work actively with heightened levels of emotion, the therapist's accurate empathy with the couple's difficulties and a shared sense of confidence, both in-session and at home, that change is possible, that difficulties can be aired, emotions roused and communicated and the relationship enhanced by a more empathic and intimate level of understanding between the partners.

It occasionally seems that therapists prefer to keep the peace rather than encourage sufficient freedom to help couples develop confidence in their ability to relate at this more empathic and emotionally open level.

(See Chapter 12.11 for further discussion of the therapist's role when increasing awareness of emotions. See also Section 1.3.)

Examples where timetables prescribing arguments might be included in the message are:

- Couples who never argue.
- Where one partner seems to dominate the other.
- Where the man is reluctant to have sexual intercourse and appears to be somewhat powerless in the relationship.
- Where there are issues about which the couple have hidden resentments.

When prescribing timetables for arguments the same guidelines apply as those for discussions.Some North American therapists will also prescribe books to read or give handouts about 'fair fighting' (see Weeks 1989). In our setting, where couples may be somewhat inarticulate or have low literacy levels as well as language difficulties, these may be inappropriate. It is, however, necessary to spend time with the couple setting guidelines for the arguments, and possibly following this up by a letter. This all takes time but is good modelling for the couple and also enables timetables and tasks to be individually crafted for each couple. Guidelines should include time, place, duration and any don'ts the couple wish to include. Keep in mind the element of play, fun and experimentation when setting these guidelines.

9.10.8 Choosing how timetabled discussions or arguments should end

Where couples have found discussions or arguments upsetting in the past, then it is helpful to decide together how the session for arguments should end. According to the couple's past experience they may feel that a 'kiss and make up ending' would be helpful. Other couples suggest having a cup of tea together or a walk in the fresh air. Yet others may want to have a few minutes apart from each other. David and Marcia T were surprised to discover that they each wanted different things. Marcia wanted some time alone and David was surprised to learn this since he himself felt he would want a kiss and make up session. It came as a relief to both of them that they could acknowledge and accept their different needs.

Discussing and planning how such timetabled arguments or discussions should end lends a sense of security and normality to the occasion, as well as encouraging the couple to be aware of each other's feelings and be supportive. This small intervention is also a positive experience for many couples who have usually experienced the ending of discussions or arguments as angry, hostile and isolating occasions. Therefore to choose to end by looking after their own and each other's needs is a significant change in their interaction.

9.11 *Summary of messages, timetables and tasks*

We have described a wide selection of alternative messages, timetables and tasks and have included several case illustrations; in doing so we are aware that we are in danger of confusing the reader. However, we offer this material so that the therapist can be selective and choose from amongst these alternatives in order to design messages, timetables and tasks specifically for couples with whom they are themselves working. We hope to have shown that the message, formulation, timetable and task can be used to add specificity, flexibility and resourcefulness to therapy.

9.12 *The paradox and its uses*

9.12.1 When to use a paradoxical message

So far in this chapter we have considered a variety of messages, for couples who demonstrate a willingness and an ability to engage with these interventions both in-session and at home between sessions. In Chapters 4, 5, 6, 7 and 8 we have, by and large, been describing therapeutic interventions which are built upon the observed interaction and stated desires of the couple for changes in their relationship. The couple and therapist have entered into a joint contract to work together to facilitate these desired changes, whether from a behavioural or a systemic point of view.

We now look at an alternative strategic approach to therapy for some couples, that of the paradoxical message (Example 9A).

9.12.2 When all else fails

Therapists will have experience of couples who seem to defy all efforts to enable them to alter their interaction and engender in the therapist a sense of being 'up against it'.

It may become obvious in the first session or it may take a series of sessions for the therapist to be clear that the couple are stuck or rigid, or in some way curiously wedded to their current interaction so that there seems little hope of change occurring by using any of the straightforward interventions. At this point one has available the paradoxical intervention.

Examples where the therapist has tried and failed might be:

- Where one partner is very dependent and the other is overprotective (complementary relationship).
- Where there are inequalities of power in the relationship, for example she manages all the finances and decisions because he is too 'irresponsible'.

- Where there is a power struggle: 'I won't give in until he/she gives in'.
- Where 'history' is treasured: 'You've hurt me so much I'm going to punish you for ever'.

9.12.3 Where the problem is presented as one partner's problem

Many couples seek help for one partner while apparently immune to any sense that their relationship might be involved in the difficulties encountered, even though others, including the referring agent, may find this self-evident.

Examples might be:

- Where one partner is excessively jealous of the other.
- Where one partner is severely depressed.
- Where symptoms are experienced by one partner such as panic attacks, inability to go out alone, recurring headaches.
- Where one partner indulges to excess in drinking, gambling or drug taking.

Such couples, whatever their specific 'symptomatology', are likely to feel poorly motivated to change and have a general sense of helplessness. They may have been to many other caring agencies, doctors or hospitals to no avail. According to Crowe (1982)

> 'This "clinging" to the symptom may lead to prolonged ineffective attempts by the therapist (e.g. in behavioural marital therapy or structural marital therapy) to change the relationship and/or remove the symptom'.

9.12.4 Where couples rapidly become dependent on therapy sessions

In our experience there are some couples who perhaps fall between the two general categories above, and who could rapidly become quite dependent upon regular therapy sessions. These couples are very responsible about coming to therapy and work well with the therapist, but do not make any change in their relationship. They are usually engaging couples who seem to find therapy an interesting event in their monthly calendar, but do not make any progress towards changing their interaction.

For these three groups of couples the paradox offers a somewhat unconventional, strategic, alternative which may effect changes for couples who are very stuck or rigid. This is to be found in the use of the paradoxical message.

9.13 The paradox as a therapeutic tool

The paradox, as a therapeutic tool, has been developed by a succession of therapists, notably Mara Selvini Palazzoli who, with her Milan team, used the paradox with families containing an anorexic family member (Selvini Palazzoli *et al.* 1978). The team further developed the concept of the paradoxical injunction by working with families containing a schizophrenic family member. The Milan team were influenced by systemic thinkers such as Bateson, Haley, Watzlawick and Shands.Such workers had examined verbal and non-verbal transactions perceived by them to form the labyrinth of communications in families in 'schizophrenic transactions'. This quest for an understanding of schizophrenia led them to delve deeply into how human beings communicate. They became fascinated with the nature of language, which was said to be linear and therefore severely limited thinking into a causal, linear mode. Communication and metacommunication, double bind and schizophrenic transaction became part of their enthusiasm and therapeutic repertoire (see Whitehead and Russell 1910; Bateson 1955; Wynne 1958; Watzlawick *et al.* 1967, 1974). Bateson writes

'We suggest that paradoxes (similar to the paradox of play) are a necessary ingredient in the process of change which we call psychotherapy.'

In the foreword to *Paradox and Counterparadox* (Selvini Palazzoli *et al.* 1978), Helm Stierlin states that the paradox is a

'potent therapeutic instrument that utilizes two main elements:

(1) The therapist establishes a positive relationship with all family members. To do so, they accept and "connote positively" anything the family offers, avoiding even the faintest hint which might be construed as a moralising stance or accusation, or which might otherwise induce anxiety, shame or guilt.

(2) The therapist aims at a radical reshuffling of the relational forces operating in these families; they shake the family out of its destructive clinch, as it were, and try to give all members a new chance to pursue their own individuation and separation. Like any other potent instrument, such injunctions can harm as well as help.'

Like many family and couple therapists we have been curious about the value of the paradoxical message. What was the nature of this paradox and in what way could it give all members a new chance to pursue their own individuation and separation? Was this a powerful claim for a new form of wizardry or a creative solution to damaging long-term illnesses?

To do justice to the growing debate regarding the paradox is both impossible and unnecessary here; it is perhaps helpful to point the reader towards the literature. (See Weeks 1978 for a bibliography and Cronin *et al.* 1982, Dell 1981 and 1986 and Cecchin 1987 for useful criticisms and suggested modifications.)

When faced with claims of wizardry we feel that therapists are wise to be sceptical, yet at the same time when faced with clients seeking amelioration of their chronic condition one must consider all potential alternatives. From experience, the paradox can have a beneficial impact in couples and families which respond to nothing else.

9.13.1 Formulating the paradox

The key concept in strategic work is the consistency of the interaction or homeostasis (see Section 7.3.4). This concept indicates the way in which in a relationship each partner uses various communications or pieces of behaviour to ensure that there is no overall change in the 'distance' or power structure between them.

In formulating an hypothesis about a marital problem, the therapist (with or without an observation team) tries to construe the symptom of one partner and the reciprocal behaviour of the other as both serving a homeostatic function and keeping the relationsip intact and unchanged. Such an hypothesis would also suggest that, if the symptom and the reciprocal behaviour were to disappear, some consequence would occur which is greatly feared by both partners. A deduction from this formulation would be that both partners would resist strongly any move by the therapist to initiate changes which would be likely to remove the symptom (Crowe 1985). Crowe describes three crucial aspects:

(1) The symptomatic behaviour.
(2) The reciprocal behaviour, i.e. the behaviour which can be said to be maintaining the symptom.
(3) The feared consequence of removing the symptom and the reciprocal behaviour.

This is easily understood where a symptom is present (see Section 9.12.3), but perhaps not so easily seen in a situation where there is no clear symptom but a plethora of interactive behaviours, as in the following example.

Example 9F
Timothy (31 years old) and Rosanna C (30 years old) had been married for five years and had no children. The immediate problem was presented by Rosanna as 'him'. She described his lying and his irresponsible behaviour: joining a telephone group 'talk in' and consequently running up excessive bills, as well as non-payment of mortgage. Rosanna earned a living for them both and as the bills mounted so she worked longer hours to pay for them. They were now threatened with the bailiffs for non-payment of mortgage, a fact which Timothy had lied about to Rosanna. Rosanna was distraught and worried, Timothy was outwardly disinterested.

On examining their interaction it seemed that Timothy had always been a 'bit of a tearaway', which attracted Rosanna to him; and Rosanna had always been responsible, anxious and a good manager, which was attractive to Tim. For two years their marriage had been 'bliss'; they did everything together and they seemed to friends to be a 'perfect couple'.

They then experienced a slow drift into a situation where Rosanna continuously worried, nagged about money, managed their finances exclusively and constantly questioned his honesty. Timothy became increasingly rash, spending money and hiding the bills. Timothy generally drove Rosanna into a frenzy of anxiety by his irresponsibility, so she constantly nagged, questioned and distrusted him and Timothy responded by telling lies or withdrawing to the telephone. This cycle had become chronic, their marriage and livelihood were threatened. Rosanna saw the problem as being all Timothy's fault and Timothy acquiesced.

Using Crowe's three-point plan, and simplifying for the sake of the methodology:

(1) The symptom can be described as Timothy's lying and irresponsible behaviour.
(2) The reciprocal behaviour can be described as Rosanna's assuming all responsibility for finances, her nagging, questioning and lack of trust in Timothy.
(3) The feared consequence of removal of the symptom in this couple was a little difficult to understand at first. After some exploration of alternative hypotheses, the following emerged as the central possibility.

Both Timothy and Rosanna had imagined themselves as a couple who were ideal together, only needing each other. After two years Rosanna began to feel that their togetherness meant they were now mature enough and ready to have a baby. Timothy agreed overtly to this plan, but privately felt that to have a child would threaten their ideal relationship, and that they were not yet responsible enough to be parents. Up to this moment in their relationship there had been no occasion on which they had disagreed. Their relationship deteriorated as described.

The feared consequence of the loss of their present behaviour could be hypothesised as the fear of the emergence of open conflict about the meaning of having a baby to them as a couple; this would threaten their togetherness in which each was central to the other. The permanence of their relationship might also be questioned if it became clear that Timothy did not want a relationship interrupted by a baby, and Rosanna only wanted to continue in a permanent relationship if they had a baby. It could be further hypothesised that Timothy's lying and irresponsible behaviour was designed to remind Rosanna of their lack of maturity as a couple; and by Rosanna's assuming responsibility for finances and nagging she was reminding Timothy of their need to prepare for parenthood.

The above description is a simplification of a complex relationship and all that having a child might mean to such a couple. In order to formulate a message it is important to be able to simplify and abstract out key issues to form the basis of hypotheses.

Simply then, the feared consequence might be the loss of their togetherness, each being central to the other, and their shared anxiety about the emergence of conflict regarding whether they were as a couple responsible and capable enough now to have a child. The symptoms and the reciprocal behaviour can then be seen as ways in which each partner is attempting to bring back togetherness and to reinstate the status quo.

9.13.2 The elements of a paradoxical message

A paradoxical message may contain the four elements listed below. These are all necessary when hypothesising about a message, although when framing and delivering a message it may not always be necessary to include every element. Each message should include (1), positive connotation, and end with (4), some 'don't change' statement.

Where a couple are particularly rigid or where the message needs additional bite it might then be useful to include (2), some statement about the function of the present behaviour pattern and (3), the feared consequences of changing. Often the various elements are woven together (see Chapter 10).

(1) Positive connotation of the symptom and the reciprocal behaviour.
Positive connotation of the behaviour was developed by the Milan school who felt that it would be illogical to prescribe the continuation of a symptom which they had just criticised (Selvini Palazzoli *et al.* 1978):

> 'It thus became clear that access to the systemic model was possible only if we were to make a positive connotation of both the symptoms of the identified patient and the symptomatic behaviours of the others, saying, for example that all of the observable behaviours of the group as a whole appeared to be inspired by the common goal of preserving the cohesion of the family group.'

The Milan school suggested that it was necessary to connote positively all aspects of the interaction. We feel that it is preferable to concentrate on some of the significant behaviours. Otherwise messages can become very long and tautological.

(2) Reasons why these are useful behaviours for the couple.
In looking for positive reasons why the behaviour is useful or is needed by the couple, one is attempting to hypothesise about the function of the rules governing the current repetitive sequences (see Section 7.3.5). The reasons should be of a sufficiently challenging quality, with a certain amount of bite, so that the couple are made to think seriously about what has been said.

(3) A statement about the feared consequences (see Section 9.13.2.3).
Again the feared consequences can only be an hypothesis based upon the pattern of interaction, and as such can only be presented to a couple as a tentative thought about what might be feared if the couple were to lose the symptom or the present behaviour pattern.

(4) Prescribing the symptom.
This means a statement that it is wisest for the couple to continue with the described behaviour as any alternative is, for the moment, too difficult, painful or uncertain. The words chosen must fit as closely as possible to the therapist's perceptions of the couple's fears.

The kind of paradoxical message which might be given to Timothy and Rosanna could be as follows:

Positive connotation of the symptom and reciprocal behaviour
You are obviously very close to each other, as you were in the first two years of marriage when you thought of yourselves as the 'perfect couple'. You are still trying to do the best for each other, but have had to find more extreme ways of showing how much you mean to each other. Timothy has given up work, run up bills and relies entirely on Rosanna financially. Rosanna continues to support his extravagances, by spending more time working.

Reasons why these are useful behaviours for the couple
You are both upset by this situation, but Timothy in his own way is being as caring as Rosanna, since Timothy's dependence gives Rosanna the experience of having a sort of baby in the family in place of the real one which you can't decide whether to have.

Statement of the feared consequence
If you stopped behaving like this to each other, you might be worried about the possible break-up of your relationship and feel that the potential ideal marriage was being thrown away.

Prescribing the symptom
So for the present you should continue as before, Timothy spending all the money and not working while Rosanna works extra hours to pay for the bills.

9.13.3 Escalating the behaviour (an additional option)

When using the paradox, if the therapist feels that the couple are particularly rigid or stuck in their present interaction, it is possible to suggest to the couple, not only that they should make no attempt to change, but they should escalate and intensify the behaviour which is causing concern. Using Rosanna and Timothy as an example this would have meant giving a message such as:

During the next two weeks see if you can each find yet more extreme ways of testing each other out; you Rosanna by nagging and questioning Timothy and you Timothy by telling lies and being irresponsible. This way you will each feel safe that you mean everything to each other.

9.13.4 Other paradoxical messages

There are an increasing number of useful examples of paradoxical interventions described in the literature. One which we are fond of is the message described in Crowe (1985):

'For example, in the case of a wife who continually expresses depressive ideas and who is labelled as the "problem" by her husband (who persists in speaking for her) the therapist might remain bland and non-committal during the session, asking many questions about the couple's interactional behaviour, cutting short the wife's depressive complaints but instead asking her how the husband reacts to her depression. The exact form of prescription at the end of the session would vary according to the fine details of the case, but would probably include the following elements.

(a) It is important for the wife to remain depressed for the present because she believes that in this way she can protect her husband . . . (the symptom)
(b) It is important for the husband to continue speaking for his wife because rightly or wrongly he feels that she needs looking after . . . (the reciprocal behaviour)
(c) Try not to change the status quo because you would both be very upset and anxious at the furious arguments you might have if the wife's depression and the husband's protection ceased . . . (the feared consequences and prescribing the symptom)'

(See also Chapter 10 for additional examples of the use of the paradox.)

9.14 *The therapist's attitude while using a paradox*

The paradox as an intervention may be abused, particularly when the therapist is feeling frustrated or fed up with the progress of therapy, as the paradox may then be experienced by the couple as rejecting or punishing.

A first rule should be never to use the paradox in a crude way simply because the therapist is frustrated and has temporarily run out of ideas. It is better for the therapist to recognise the feeling of being 'up against it' and to go through the process of thinking systemically about the couple's interaction, looking for the function of the symptom, the repetitive patterns and the value of these to the couple's relationship. In this way the therapist converts a feeling of frustration into a resource.

In presenting the message to the couple the therapist should be careful to use supportive and kind words to reframe and positively connote the behaviour patterns. Do not 'send up' or belittle the couple. When suggesting reasons why the behaviour is useful to the couple the therapist should feel some empathy with their predicament.

As therapists become familiar with the paradox they may begin to feel that such an intervention is no longer paradoxical (Dell 1986). If the therapist feels that the paradox may come across to the couple as far-fetched or outrageous it is helpful to introduce the paradox with a phrase such as 'You probably think this is a crazy idea but . . .'

In summary, in presenting the paradox much care must be taken with the formulation, use of words and presentation to the couple so that the maximum impact is possible and it is not rejected out of hand by the couple. From experience it is important to make messages simple and brief, and with hindsight we would probably have shortened some of the messages quoted in this book: indeed as therapists we are constantly learning and modifying our interventions.

9.15 The impact of the paradox on the couple

Our experience is that when the paradox is useful the couple are likely to react immediately in the session. They may try to engage the therapist in discussion of the message, they may disqualify the message or in some situations tell the therapist that s/he must be mad. Occasionally a couple may understand and comment that the message is a paradox (oddly enough this does not mean that the paradox will be ineffective) and others may enter into a reflective silence.

It is best to find ways of avoiding any dialogue with the couple about the message as any discussion of it dissipates its impact. Comments such as 'bring any questions to the next session' may help you to end the session. Do not be abrupt and rejecting; enjoy the couple's reaction but try not to comment except to accept in a non-defensive way that you could indeed be 'mad'. The phrase 'chuck it and run' describes in a rather crude but effective way how paradoxical messages are best de-livered. Inexperienced therapists usually find both the giving of para-doxes and the impact on the couple quite difficult to manage. However, a good message will usually stimulate some immediate questioning. If the couple seem totally disinterested then perhaps the message was not well chosen.

9.15.1 What to do if the therapist gets entangled in the message

If the therapist does find him/herself drawn into discussion with the couple, he/she should simply go back to the beginning of the message and repeat it slowly and carefully, ending with some statement about having the opportunity to discuss it in the next session. The therapist should then stand up and show clearly that the session is over.

9.16 Why does the paradox work?

Any answer to this question can only be conjectural, and outside un-connected events may have been involved in initiating change. Where the paradox was effective the reasons may be among the following:

(a) The impact of positively connoting the symptomatic or distressing behaviour patterns and describing their positive function in the rela-tionship may take much of the guilt and anxiety out of a fraught and emotionally draining situation. As Selvini Palazzoli (1978) suggests, the positive connotation prepares the way for the following paradox

> 'Why should the cohesion of the group (or couple) which the therapist describes as being so good and desirable, be gained at the price of needing a "patient"?'

(b) Where couples are accustomed to defying instructions from therapists or those in positions of authority, then by changing their behaviour they have simply been true to their own pattern of defying instructions.
(c) The couple may find the therapist's explanation ridiculous and respond to this by refusing to accept it and therefore change.
(d) The couple may become angry with the therapist for suggesting that they should not change and take responsibility for themselves rather than waiting for the 'crazy' therapist to help them change.
(e) It may be (as some systemic workers believe) that there is an ability to speak or metacommunicate with the system as a whole which liberates the system to respond differently.
(f) The couple may have felt understood by the therapist at a deeper more subconscious level which helps them to feel accepted and therefore less alienated and therefore freer to choose their interaction rather than being purely reactive.
(g) Unquestioned assumptions the couple have made about their behaviour are challenged so that some new perceptions may be stimulated at different levels of the dysfunctional system.

There are many alternative explanations, each having some validity.

In commending the paradox as a useful addition to the range of interventions available, we are mindful of examples where the paradox seems to have been ignored, or experienced as rejecting or was effective for only a brief period of time. We therefore prefer to use the paradox sparingly after due consideration, giving the therapist time to formulate the message and to choose the wording with the utmost care. Our aim would be that the therapist is sufficiently 'empathic' with the plight of the couple to ensure that such a paradox is not punitive.

Additionally, we often use positive connotation in messages which are otherwise non-paradoxical (see Example 9D and Section 1.2.3) and may also use a slight paradoxical statement such as 'don't change too quickly' in otherwise straightforward messages.

9.17 Limitations of the paradox

Although the paradox is now accepted as a useful intervention, it carries with it some major disadvantages, particularly in relation to research. Since the therapist is uncertain as to whether the couple or family will change as a response to the paradox, and is unable to predict how it will be received or acted upon, the paradox cannot be a measure for assessing change. *It is essentially an unpredictable tool.*

Since the paradox prescribes the symptom, it is impractical to use it in relation to some of the more dangerous symptoms found in couple's interactions. It would be unwise to suggest that a husband should go on beating his wife, or that an addict should continue with his/her addiction or go ahead and commit suicide. It would be unacceptable for therapists to instruct clients to continue stealing or embezzling, or even to continue with divorce proceedings.

Some couples seem to use the paradox to complain to the referring agency about the treatment being offered. This may be misunderstood by (for example) the referring general practitioner and where possible the therapist should keep agencies who are involved with the couple informed when paradoxical work is being done (see Example 10F).

The paradox is then a useful and complex intervention which must be treated with respect and used selectively.

9.18 The split-team message
(see also Example 9A)

Where there is some uncertainty as to whether the paradox may be experienced as rejecting or unhelpful, but the couple are very stuck, the split-team message can be used. This means that the couple are presented with two alternatives, one of which is a direct task or timetable which would be useful for the couple and the other is paradoxical. The choice as to which part is presented first will depend on the therapist's perceptions of the couple. If the paradoxical part is presented first this will be introduced with a statement such as:

The team are divided in opinion as to what you now wish to do. Half of the team think that you are not yet ready to make any changes. For the following reasons they feel you should not change for the moment.

This can then include the four elements of the paradox (see Section 9.13.2).

The non-paradoxical part of the message is then presented with a statement such as:

However half of the team (or one of the therapists) feel that you are now flexible enough to make some progress towards modifying your relationship and so would like to suggest the following task (timetable or activity).

As with all of the formulations, timetables and tasks described in this chapter, a split-team message should be designed with care and be relevant to the work done in the session using the information, language, idiom and uniqueness of each couple.

9.19 Indications for alternative treatment – beyond the paradox
(see Section 3.4.14)

Therapists should be aware that an alternative treatment may either be necessary or be chosen by the couple themselves. Examples of some of these situations are listed below.

(1) Where one or both partner(s) has made a final decision that the relationship is over.
(2) Where a couple themselves decide that they wish to seek alternative treatment.
(3) Where a physical illness needs to be attended to first (see Section 3.3.3).
(4) Where the couple are unable to change but may need ongoing supportive work (Section 3.4.14).
(5) Where individual therapy is chosen by the couple as most useful or is seen by the therapist as necessary (Section 3.4.15).

Where a couple are separating, the therapist may seek either to work with the couple in order to facilitate a creative separation which enables the couple to continue as 'good enough parents', or facilitate a referral to another agency (Chapter 10). Where a referral is being made it is important to ensure that a useful link is made so that the couple do in fact transfer.

Alternatively, when a couple's relationship is improving within the behavioural-systems approach, the therapist can change the intervention by moving down the hierarchy of alternative levels of intervention (ALI), leaving behind paradoxical interventions and focussing on in-session work and take-home tasks or timetables as appropriate.

Chapter 10

Couple therapy in jealousy, depression, sexual conflicts and other specific problems

10.1 Introduction

Having described in some detail the behavioural and systemic interventions we use in therapy (the ALI hierarchy, Section 3.4) we now go on to discuss the more flexible use of interventions for couples with a range of specific problems. The problems are not linked by any intrinsic similarities, but all present the therapist with the challenge of working on a problem which is unusually difficult to treat, and which is often located by the couple and by other professionals in one partner, despite being quite legitimately defined alternatively as a relationship problem. The three areas are also ones in which we believe we have developed in our clinic some useful and original interventions.

Three specific patterns are considered in detail:

(1) Where one partner is seen as unreasonably jealous and the other may show a variety of behaviour such as angry denial, reassuring or provocative responses (Sections 10.2 to 10.5).
(2) Where one partner has been diagnosed as depressed and the other may be 'caretaking', rejecting or disqualifying (Sections 10.7 to 10.9).
(3) Where the male partner is enthusiastic and demanding and the female partner reluctant for sex (Section 10.10).

Seven couples are described from referral to completion of treatment in order to show the work done in-session, the messages which built on the work of these sessions and the progress of therapy.

We deal more briefly with couples where sexual abuse has occurred within the family or where a child has been physically abused (Section 10.12). These are particularly difficult and emotional areas of work, and deserve more attention than we are able to give here. Because of their importance, however, we felt that we should include some basic guidelines.

Triangular situations such as an affair (Section 10.13) or over-involvement with work or family, which disrupt the couple's relationship, are discussed and interventions suggested. Ways of working with the older marriage (Section 10.14), couples with an alcohol or drug-abuse problem (Section 10.15), the separating or divorcing couple (Section 10.16) and the 'reconstituted' family (Section 10.16.3) are touched upon and interventions proposed.

10.1.1 Why couple therapy for these problems?

Jealousy, depression and frigidity have traditionally been treated by offering medication, support or individual counselling. While accepting that medication and other individual approaches can be part of the treatment plan, we also feel that couple therapy has an added advantage. Couple therapy reduces the labelling of one partner as sick and we feel that this is a goal whose benefits are self-evident. We would also suggest that an improvement which results from changed behaviour in both partners is likely to be more stable and long-lasting (Section 2.4) than if just one partner changes. Another benefit is that if medication is used it may be able to be discontinued earlier if combined with couple therapy. Lastly, whether the problem is seen as arising from the relationship or not, the relationship is almost always adversely affected by it and needs attention apart from the problem itself.

10.1.2 What strategies are used?

The strategies used are taken from various levels of the ALI hierarchy, ranging from encouraging positive interaction (Section 10.7.6) through timetables (Section 10.3.1) and reversed roles (Section 10.5.2) to paradox (Sections 10.4.2 and 10.5.5).

These specific strategies are offered in the hope that therapists will feel encouraged to use some of them in their work with couples where previously they may have thought there were few appropriate interventions.

We describe case material to show how these specific interventions might be used. We have not included the general process of therapy and ask the reader to bear in mind the approach to therapy as described in Chapter 4, with the focus being upon interaction, the momentum of therapy and the contribution of the non-symptomatic partner to the relationship problems.

Jealousy

10.2 Couples in which one partner is excessively jealous

Shepherd (1961) wrote in a scholarly article

'Jealousy is more than a psychiatric symptom. Its language is universal: the conduct and feelings of the jealous man and woman have repeatedly drawn the attention of the great observers of human nature, the moralists and the philosophers as well as the poets and novelists.'

He draws attention to the gradual debasement of the word in its transmission from the Greek into other European languages. 'In transmission the word has ceased to denote "zeal" or "ardour", the "noble passion" which stood opposed to envy for the Greeks, and has acquired a pejorative quality.' Writing as he did in 1961 he was able to state 'the standard textbooks devote little space' to the issue of jealousy. This statement accurately reflects the current picture.

Teisman (1979) and Im *et al.* (1983) are among the few who have developed some useful alternative interventions focussing on the interaction of the couple and building on a systems approach to couples.

Within the marital therapy clinic we have been treating couples presenting with jealous behaviour with some success using three approaches: the jealousy timetable, role reversal and paradoxical injunctions.

10.2.1 Description of jealous behaviour in traditional terms

Where couples complain of jealousy within the marriage, the relationship will usually contain the following features. One spouse may complain that the other is having one or several illicit relationships. This spouse, often the man, may express firm convictions that his partner is deceiving him; as evidence he may quote examples such as her late arrival after work by a few minutes, phones being replaced as he arrives in a room, a casual smile cast at a man when together in a public place. These convictions may be of delusional intensity, or he may sometimes have doubts as to whether he is right in this understanding of the situation.

The jealous spouse may have developed the habit of interrogating the partner about all of her daily movements, obsessionally repeating questions and accusations as to her whereabouts and companions. The jealous spouse is usually inconsolable. He may have started to examine her diary, her handbag and her underwear for signs that she is indeed having an illicit relationship with another man. He may feel he knows who the other person is, or he may feel that it could be one of several potential lovers.

The partner, on the other hand, is usually aghast at such accusations. She has probably spent long hours trying to persuade her partner that none of the fears are logical or realistic. She may have become angry or overwhelmed and anxious about his attitude, feeling that somehow she should be able to prove that she is faithful to him. Her tears and pleadings have been to no avail. It is this pattern of accusations from one spouse and denial and reasoning from the other, together with the assumption by the non-jealous spouse and the referrers that the jealousy is caused by some sort of illness, which seems to characterise these couples and which we attempt to reframe and challenge.

10.2.2 Jealousy in systemic terms

The above description of jealous behaviour, which is individually orientated and assumes that the problem is all on the jealous partner's side, is the traditional way of formulating the problem, and individual treatment would be given. However, in systemic terms one has to look at the contribution of both partners, especially in those couples whose jealousy is not seen as delusional or psychotic.

Perhaps the non-jealous partner is socially more confident than her partner, and may be less committed to the relationship as an exclusive one. She may seem to pay more attention to friends or acquaintances than to her jealous partner when they are together. She may indeed not be as possessive as one might have expected and may not seem to take him seriously in other aspects of the relationship. She may be prone to take the advice of others in preference to her partner, and seem to feed his lack of self-esteem by putting others first, whether family or friends.

In addition, the jealousy can be construed as being a positive influence on the relationship itself, increasing excitement, reassuring the woman that she is attractive and providing the man with a reason for constantly seeking reassurance from his partner that he is her favourite and that she is faithful to him alone (though he of course does not usually believe the reassurance) (see Sections 10.4.2.2 and 10.5.8).

10.3 Examples of couples in which one partner is jealous

We now give examples of the work done with three couples who presented with excessive jealousy. These three cases have been chosen to present couples where jealousy is affecting their relationship with increasing degrees of complexity, and to show the reader how different interventions may need to be used depending upon the intensity and rigidity of the jealousy. Nelson and Abigail G (Example 10A) were quickly able to alter their relationship, Alan and Jemima P. (Example 10B) had rather more problems to face, whilst Susan and Roger B's relationship (Example 10C) seemed to be a complex and rigid web of interaction which was most difficult to change or modify.

The paradox was used least with Nelson and Abigail G, but was used consistently for the first three sessions with Alan and Jemima P. After several unsuccessful attempts at using the timetable for discussion of the jealousy with Roger and Susan, and an unhelpful attempt to use role reversal, the paradox was eventually used (see Section 10.5.5). In spite of considerable improvement, this couple continued to have difficulties which seemed to recur at times of stress.

The alternative interventions which are described in detail can be used with other couples who show similarly rigid patterns of interaction and where symptoms other than excessive jealousy are prevalent. Examples might be where one partner indulges in excessive gambling, compulsive lying, general irresponsibility or other more clearly psychiatric problems.

10.3.1 Example in which the jealousy was reframed and a timetable for discussion established

Example 10A

Nelson aged 38, born in Jamaica, and Abigail aged 40, born in Liverpool, had been married for 18 years. They had two children: a boy aged 15 and a girl aged 17. This black couple were referred by the GP with complaints that they were always quarrelling because Nelson continually accused Abigail of having an affair. Abigail denied having an affair and could not persuade Nelson to accept this. She worried secretly that he wanted to leave her for someone from Jamaica, but needed to have an excuse to do so.

Abigail had had an operation six years ago for a cancer on her jaw which had terrified her. At that time she had felt very alone; she had not told Nelson about the cancer and the doctors had rarely discussed its implications with her.

They now quarrelled constantly, his accusations wearing her down and her moodiness being very unsettling for him. Their sex life was unsatisfactory; Abigail complained that it was too mechanical and too rough; she wanted to feel more that she was 'being made love to' rather than just 'having sex'. Nelson felt that her 'affair' was what was interfering with their lovemaking.

During the first session their interaction was characterised by lack of trust in the detail of their daily life. Nelson made all the decisions about finances. If Abigail made a tentative suggestion that they should share these decisions Nelson either did not hear or ignored her suggestion by changing the subject. When on the other hand he expressed a concern about the children she laughed at him and ignored his comments. Whatever subject was touched upon by one partner, the other partner either seemed disinterested, changed the subject or joked about the issue. They each accused the other of not sharing decisions, yet each seemed unprepared to share. There was an undercurrent of distrust regarding their different backgrounds, his being Jamaican and hers being English. They each expressed concern that the other would have preferred to marry someone from identical cultural backgrounds and neither was satisfied by the other's reassurances.

10.3.2 Positive reframe of jealousy

Although the jealousy was presented by the couple as the most important problem, the interventions during the first session and the messages at the conclusion of the first session were deliberately focussed away from the jealousy and concentrated on the emerging issues of trust and sharing between the partners.

10.3.3 Message (formulation)

(1) We think you have a very interesting and lively relationship. One of the important issues for you as a couple seems to be whether you can trust each other enough to share some of the things you both want to share, but do not feel confident enough to do so.

(2) Nelson does not trust Abigail and feels she must be unfaithful to him; while Abigail for her part does not expect to be believed or even heard when she tells the truth.

(3) Neither of you takes the other seriously: Nelson mistrusts Abigail and Abigail laughs at Nelson.

(4) In a sense we see you as complementing each other, Nelson being passionate and in touch with his Jamaican beginnings and Abigail being cooler and in touch with her Englishness. Thus you both manage to keep alive the things that attracted you to each other in the beginning of your relationship.

You seem to be confused as to when you can take each other seriously and when you can have fun together. Because of this confusion what we would like you to do is the following task.

10.3.4 Tasks focussing on seriousness and fun

Each day we would like you to have a serious discussion about how much you should share together. We would like you to include some of the issues you have raised here such as whether you should have a joint account, how you would like to pay for the road tax, how as parents to manage your teenage children.

(5) Use half an hour each day and during that time take each other seriously. Hold these discussions for six days a week, that is 'six days of labour' and on the seventh day we would like you to take the day off and 'make fun' of each other.

We feel you both need to learn to take each other seriously and also to find time to laugh and make fun of each other, thus possibly combining the fun of Jamaica with the seriousness of England.

10.3.5 Discussion of the message

At (1) the message was designed to encourage them to think more highly of themselves, as we felt that they each had a very low sense of self-esteem.

The difference between their English and Jamaican origins was an obvious irritant between them, but it also seemed likely that trust was an issue not only between them as a couple but also between them and the white English therapist and team. The cultural significance of place of birth and cultural heritage seemed very divisive and outweighed the fact that they were both black.

At (2) and (3) the message reframes the jealousy as a question of lack of trust and confidence between them. We were careful to share these concerns equally between the two partners, as we do in most cases (see Section 9.2.2) where one partner carries a label or is symptomatic.

At (4) the message is again giving a reframe or a positive connotation to their concerns about their different origins and reminds them of the attractiveness of these differences.

At (5) attention is drawn to the couple's wish to have more fun together and this positive task links cultural differences which were rarely spoken about. They are also reminded that they could undermine each other by not taking each other seriously. While impossible to be certain that such a message makes a difference, after this message Abigail and Nelson were able to use the timetable for discussion, their relationship improved and the jealousy abated.

10.4 *Example in which the paradox was used followed by a timetable for jealousy*

In the following example the paradox is introduced from the beginning of treatment because of the crisis in which the couple presented themselves. They were already very distressed and had little hope that any change could occur. In such entrenched and painful situations paradox may be the only type of intervention likely to make any difference. Even so, it may take several sessions before any improvement occurs. Meanwhile the therapist has the difficult task of being empathic with the severity of the couple's difficulties whilst holding firmly to the possibility that the paradox might be the most helpful intervention currently available.

Example 10B

Alan, aged 27, was a carpenter and Jemima P, aged 25, a housewife and mother. They had been married for eight years and had two children. During the 18 months prior to therapy Alan had accused Jemima of having affairs, of not being a virgin when they first made love, of fancying his friends and of hiding facts about previous boyfriends. One of his most frequent approaches was to say the names of the various boyfriends he suspected and watch Jemima intensely to see which name caused her to blush. Jemima insisted 'I have never been with, done anything with, or ever thought of having sex with anyone else. Alan asks me questions all day long, on buses, in shops, and he doesn't seem to listen to my answers'.

Both partners were feeling overwrought and in despair. Jemima cried a great deal each day and Alan was very fearful that Jemima would leave him at any moment. They were in a state of crisis and under severe strain. They were deeply attached to each other but also feeling helpless in the face of Alan's powerful jealousy.

10.4.1 Summary of therapy

This couple were seen for ten sessions over a period of four and a half months. Intervals between sessions varied from two to four weeks. During the first three sessions the therapist worked using two main thrusts of therapy.

The first was to allow the couple to use part of the session, with the therapist decentred, to rehearse their current concerns regarding Alan's jealousy. Alan would be asked to tell Jemima how he felt and Jemima would try to persuade him of her fidelity.

The second was to understand what else might be happening in their current life situation which might form the basis of an hypothesis as to why the jealousy was so necessary for this couple at present, i.e. the search for the 'function' of the symptom.

After the third session some improvements occurred which made it possible to start asking the couple to use a timetable for jealousy, which in turn led to further improvements.

The following picture emerged during the first three sessions. Jemima was the eldest child and only daughter of an East End family where there were three sons and the father was a dominant and despotic man who ruled his sons and the neighbourhood rather like a mafia boss. Jemima was something of a local beauty and 'the apple of her father's eye'. Alan, on the other hand, came from a small family, his parents were now divorced, and he did not feel close to his family. As a teenager he had been on probation for a minor offence and was seen by Jemima's family as unsuitable for their daughter. Jemima's father and brother were noted locally for occasional bouts of physical violence, and they had once beaten up Alan when they heard about his association with Jemima.

After their marriage, Alan and Jemima lived for two and a half years with Jemima's parents. Her parents had slowly taken over the running of Alan and Jemima's family to such an extent that when Jemima went into hospital to have the second child, 18 months before therapy, Jemima's mother had taken the eldest child to stay with her without consulting Alan. Alan was extremely upset at this and was now refusing to see Jemima's parents. However, Jemima still spent much of her time with the children at her parents' house while Alan was at work. Their main area of agreement as a couple was that they had lovely children whom they both loved deeply.

10.4.2 Paradoxical message

Because the couple were in a crisis situation with the jealousy affecting their lives so powerfully, it was felt that they should be given a paradoxical message from the onset of treatment (see Section 9.13).

10.4.2.1 *The first paradoxical message*
The first paradoxical message contained the following elements.

Positive connotation
We are impressed because although you have major problems, you have a good basic relationship. It is clear that you are also good parents as so far you have not allowed your difficulties to affect your relationship with the children.

Don't change
For the time being Alan should continue to interrogate Jemima and Jemima should continue to be in the middle between her own family and Alan.

Function of the symptom
For the moment we think that this is helpful for both of you. It helps Alan as it makes him fight to become head of his own family and helps Jemima as it enables her to become a real woman and not simply a little daughter to her parents.

At the next session, three weeks later, the picture had changed little, except that Alan was angry with the team and complained bitterly that he is by no means 'head of his own household'. They had an angry and hostile discussion in the session in which Alan said either Jemima had had various affairs or he was 'mad'. The team felt that they both were quite depressed, but were also pleased that Alan had understood and accepted the part of the previous message which referred to his fight to become head of his own family.

10.4.2.2 *The second paradoxical message*
The second paradoxical message which followed this session therefore attended to his concern about his 'madness' and their depression as follows.

Positive connotation and the function of the symptom
Nobody in the team thinks that Alan is mad. We do feel, however, that you are both depressed, and that Alan feels helpless because he feels he cannot fulfil Jemima's unsatisfied needs for support and that Jemima feels helpless because she is looking for support and is not satisfied. We also think that Alan's accusations are a way of expressing his positive feelings for Jemima and of getting a passionate reaction from her in the way that she denies them.

Feared consequence
Until you both realise how depressed the other person is feeling, the arguments you engage in will continue.

The next session, two weeks later, was again one in which they spent much of the session in a very painful interchange of attacking and defensive behaviour, with Alan still saying 'if she isn't having various relationships I must be mad'.

10.4.2.3 *The third paradox*
In this paradox we addressed the question of 'madness' by suggesting that the team might be mad, thus hoping to 'normalise' the idea of madness in the following manner.

Positive connotation
We feel that your torturing each other and yourselves shows just how strongly you need each other and gives your relationship a real intensity. At the same time you seem to try to keep at a distance from each other.

Don't change
You might think that we are mad! But we would like you to carry on exactly the same way.

Timetable for jealousy; escalating the symptom
Also we would like you to try particularly hard to torture each other for one hour every evening: you should start at 8 pm and stop at 9 pm. We would like you to do this every day except Saturday evenings, when you need to do something different but also exciting. Alan will need to choose what to do on this occasion.

Two weeks later some changes were occurring. Alan was speaking with concern about himself and why he should be so jealous. Jemima was speaking with more assurance about herself. They were more relaxed with each other and held a discussion about their children which revealed that Alan was rather isolated from his children, with Jemima making decisions without consulting him. He felt resentful about this. The session was not so pressurised and they were both listening to each other more attentively.

10.4.2.4 *Message including a timetable for expression of jealousy*
This message is less paradoxical as their situation is now improving.

Positive connotation
We realise how painful and difficult the situation is for you and we are very impressed at how hard you both try to make things better. We feel that you have in fact made some progress, in that Alan seems to understand Jemima's feelings better and Jemima seems to be a little more assertive. Now we would like you to do a slightly different task. We would now like you to stop arguing, except for two hours each day from 10 to 11 in the morning and from 9 to 10 in the evening. Alan is to be responsible for starting and ending the sessions and Jemima should make sure that both of you do not get involved in arguments at other times. If Alan wants to talk about his jealousy at other times Jemima

should say 'Yes, I understand. Can we talk about that at the next one-hour session?'.

Putting the symptom bearer in the caring position, see Section 10.7.3
While asking you to do this we are at the same time worried about how stressful it will be for both of you not to argue and we would like Alan to watch Jemima carefully to see what effect it has on her.

Alan was also asked to take the children shopping on Saturdays for an hour or so while Jemima did something for herself.

At the next session, two weeks later, the couple had again improved. They had been able to confine discussions about his jealousy to the pre-scribed times. These improvements continued and allowed the sessions to be used to help the couple look together at their relationship with each other and with the extended family. Their joint parenting was also explored and Jemima was able to allow Alan to take more responsibility for the care of his children, and the household in general.

Continue prescribing the symptom
After a further two sessions Alan requested that the timetables for expression of his jealousy be stopped, because of the impact on Jemima, who he decided could no longer stand being questioned in this way; he had already on one occasion given up a session as Jemima had had a severe headache. It was agreed that the timetable could be dropped down to half an hour per day, but that he should not let go of it entirely.

On discharge they were a happily united couple who were becoming more able to work together in relation to both parents and children. Even though the jealousy seemed to have abated they were reminded to continue with the half-hour expression of his jealousy.

10.4.2.5 The concluding message
Positive connotation
We would like you to know that we think you have done extremely well and have worked very hard. We also feel that you have been very courageous in facing up to the many difficulties you have had, and we are pleased that you have managed to do this together.

Prescribe the symptom
We feel, however, that it is necessary to carry on with the half-hour in the evening of the timetable for jealousy. We noticed this time that you were a little more irritated with each other, and we would like you to be irritated with each other in the half-hour sessions too. At the end of these sessions we would like you to thank each other. Because things have been rather serious we would also like you to find things to do for the other which you know they will enjoy.

They were offered the opportunity to come back for further sessions in the future should they both feel that this was necessary. Three years have gone by without a return of the extreme jealousy and they seem to be satisfied with the state of their marriage.

10.4.2.6 Discussion of the treatment

The treatment has been summarised rather briefly because of space. However, the key elements were that of persevering with the use of the paradox for three sessions and concurrently spending some time, in the session, working on their immediate relationship. Notice, too, that we persevered with the timetable for expression of jealousy beyond the time when Alan had requested that it stop. Additionally, the couple were asked to continue with the discussion timetable after termination of therapy. It was anticipated that as time passed these sessions might become a focus for discussion of their irritability, rather than his jealousy, thus leading to a deepening of their ability to share daily events and perhaps the development of greater intimacy. We also felt that important changes had occurred outside the marital relationship, in that Alan was genuinely more involved with the children and Jemima was beginning to spend less time with her mother. Both these changes were felt to have a stabilising effect on the marriage and to render the symptom less necessary.

10.5 Example in which a timetable and role reversal were used, and when these failed the paradox was used

The next couple are described because they presented with heavily symptomatic, at times almost psychotic, behaviour and although the jealousy eventually subsided it also continued to re-emerge over several months, coinciding with times of great stress in their lives.

Example 10C

Roger B, aged 44, was married to Susan, aged 39. This was the first marriage for Susan and the second for Roger, who had two children from his first marriage, now aged 20 and 24. There were no children in this marriage and Roger had undergone a vasectomy after the break-up of his first marriage.

The reasons for referral were complex. Roger had become intensely jealous and over several months had accused his wife of having relationships with other men, including the window cleaner and a man who called to collect the rent. Susan was both appalled and angry and was determined to 'give as good as she got'. Heated rows ensued, each being physically violent against the other. Roger would then become moody and Susan would try to placate him in many different ways, showering attention and affection on him. Occasionally he would have attacks of diarrhoea, or wakeful periods during the night when he would wake Susan and accuse her of infidelity. Susan's response was to deny the infidelity, to reason, cajole or swear she would take the truth drug, but Roger was never reassured. On referral they were both upset, tired and generally overwhelmed by the impact on their lives of these events, which had started 15 to 18 months ago.

Therapy with this couple was slow and difficult. Over a period of eight months they were seen eight times; at first the gaps between sessions were two weeks, reduced after the paradoxical message to one week and then lengthened to a month over the summer break. Changes began to occur after the fourth session when a paradoxical message was used. The jealousy became more manageable but remained as a factor in their relationship.

10.5.1 Summary of sessions

During the first four sessions one major stress factor which emerged for Roger was the fact that he might be made redundant after being promoted to an instructor's position within the firm and finding the increased responsibility and the speed at which he was being asked to work very worrying. He was both upset at the possibility of being made redundant and worried as to whether he would get any redundancy payments or pension. Susan was much admired by Roger for being a very competent and successful manager. She had become redundant after many years with the same firm and now worked in a small part-time job. She, however, enjoyed her greater freedom and did not seem to share Roger's intense anxiety about their future financial position.

A second stress factor was the impact of the first marriage on this relationship. Susan felt that Roger constantly put her into the position of the first wife who had indeed had an affair and left him for another man. This made Susan angry and rather hostile to Roger whom she felt was being unfair to her. There were also children from the first marriage whom Roger never saw and about whom he would rarely talk.

The therapist worked throughout these sessions to be supportive of the couple's great difficulties, to give a positive reframe to the jealousy, to put the symptom bearer in the caring position and to help the couple extend their repertoire beyond the jealousy interaction, both in the session and at home between sessions. The timetable for expression of jealousy was used together with suggestions about how to end the sessions and how to manage the jealousy when it was expressed at other times. For example, at the end of the session one part of the task was:

If Roger wakes in the night and wishes to talk about his jealousy, Susan is to go and have a hot drink somewhere away from him. If he talks about his job worries, Susan should respond by giving him a hug and comforting him.

By session 4 both partners felt that their condition was very serious and that something must be done.

10.5.2 Role reversal

The team were concerned both at the lack of any improvement and at Susan's apparent detachment from Roger's intense worry about his Work and future financial position and her inability to enter into his distress about her. It seemed appropriate to see if they could be helped to understand how the other felt by practising role reversal in-session (see de Silva 1987).

Role reversal means that Susan would be asked to pretend in-session to be like Roger and to be very jealous of him by accusing him of having close relationships with friends or acquaintances. Roger would be asked to pretend to be like Susan and try to deny, plead or explain away the behaviour and plead innocence. (Role reversal can be used in many different ways, but it is often helpful to couples who have got very stuck in their attitude to each other. It can break through fixed ways of seeing each other and enable the 'normal' partner to understand how their own behaviour might be adding to the problems.)

With this couple, unexpectedly, Susan was extremely reluctant to do this. The therapist tried showing her in-session how to 'pretend' to be jealous. While the therapist was accusing Roger of indiscretions with other women Roger was delighted and seemed to enjoy the accusations to the full. His usually despairing face lit up, he smiled and joked with the therapist as though it made him feel good to be accused of being a 'womaniser'. Susan, however, constantly insisted that she could on no account be jealous of him and was thoroughly confident that he would never find another woman interesting. She therefore adamantly refused to pretend.

10.5.3 Team discussion and concern at slow progress

The team were by now concerned that little progress had been made with this couple; indeed any changes could be described as deterioration in each spouse. Roger was increasingly experiencing other symptoms such as diarrhoea, wakeful nights and inability to face going back to work, and Susan was looking increasingly depressed and physically low as a result of the demands on her. The team now felt that a well designed and powerful paradoxical message should be used.

10.5.4 Framing the paradoxical message

In order to frame the message the team reviewed the couple's relationship, seeking for systemic ideas, to understand the circularity of the system, to tease out the rules governing the repetitive sequences and to develop an hypothesis which might explain the function of the symptoms (see Sections 7.3.1 to 7.3.5). As described in Chapter 7, this requires the therapist to simplify and abstract data which adds to the hypothesis and builds a coherent picture of mutually interacting parts, each maintaining the other in a fixed pattern.

Hypothesis
The team felt that a powerful factor in their relationship had been the circumstances in which they met. Roger's first marriage had broken up four years before they met but he was still despondent, particularly about his children. Susan had described his anguish at having to give up

his two children. He had then decided to have a vasectomy and have no more children.

For Susan, who was marrying for the first time, having children within the marriage was therefore impossible. Could this have formed the basis for their relationship, in the sense that Roger would provide Susan with the baby she had never had by himself becoming the baby, and would Susan provide the parenting for him which he had needed so badly when his first marriage broke up?

10.5.5 Paradoxical message

Positive connotation
We feel that you have a very stable marriage and a very deeply intimate relationship. We think that what has happened is that Susan is attempting to be for Roger the perfect mother who took him in, and rescued him when he was 'orphaned' after the losses of his first marriage. Roger, for his part, is acting like a needy baby that Susan can nurture and cherish. If Roger has diarrhoea Susan helps him with this. If Roger wakes in the night Susan feeds him by looking after him and attending to his worries. Roger now gets looked after more because Susan works fewer hours. If Roger is jealous it is a little like a baby crying and seeking reassurance that he is loved and does not want to share her with any one else. Susan responds by reassuring him, no matter how long it takes. In a way you can say that Roger is providing an ideal baby for Susan to look after and is testing her mothering skills to the limit, and Susan is responding very well.

The function of the symptom
We think that this is something that you both need for the moment. It is helpful to Susan as it provides a purpose and appeals to her motherly instincts. It is helpful for Roger as his confidence was shattered after his first marriage broke up, so that for the moment he seeks constant reassurance and comforting.

Don't change
We feel that it would be dangerous to give this pattern up as Roger would lose a very reassuring mum and Susan would lose a very demanding baby.

Feared consequences
In addition, if you gave this up you would probably fight with each other, and since you don't want that, you would have to find another way to negotiate rather than fighting. We feel it would therefore be very risky for you both to change.

10.5.6 How the message was received

Susan responded 'I don't think I rescued him', Roger said 'So you think we would quarrel, do you?'. The couple seemed to accept this message in a contemplative mood and left discussing whether she had really rescued him from being an 'orphan'.

10.5.7 Summary of further treatment

Roger began the next session by suggesting that he had probably become very jealous because he was actually very worried at work. He felt that if he worried about his wife he did not need to worry about work. Susan was very supportive and suggested, to his surprise, that she would like him to seek early retirement rather than be so upset about work. These anxieties about Roger's retirement on medical grounds, their future financial position, where they would live as a couple and how they would occupy their time together continued as central to the work done in-session and the jealousy became secondary to these questions. The fact that Susan encouraged Roger to retire seemed to give him greater confidence in their relationship.

Therapy continued for altogether 15 months and the jealousy returned at times of stress and with varying intensity, but when these difficulties became more manageable the jealousy seemed to moderate. Over this time, the frequency of jealous periods reduced very considerably, from more than once a day at the beginning to less than once a month at the end.

The timetable for expression for jealousy has continued to be used by this couple and may have helped to contain some of the more damaging aspects of his jealousy. What seems to have happened is that although the jealousy has not disappeared, it has to an extent been normalised and incorporated into their relationship as some of the anxiety-provoking aspects of their life together have become more acceptable.

10.5.8 Incorporating the jealousy into the relationship

In considering the three cases of jealousy and their treatment, the main new form of intervention used is to incorporate the jealousy in the couple's general relationship, and to examine and use the contribution of the non-jealous partner. All three interventions, whether paradoxical message, timetable or reversed roles, have the effect of normalising the jealousy by either prescribing it or by suggesting that it should be used in a different way by the jealous or the non-jealous partner.

We do not claim to cure the jealousy, and indeed the systemic approach would not see such a cure as desirable, as it would label one partner too strongly as the symptom-bearer or sick member. Instead, as with most other symptoms, we would hope to see the emphasis changed so that it becomes just another legitimate way in which the couple communicate with each other. In those cases where such interventions are not successful in making the problem bearable and helping the couple to live with it, there is often a psychotic aspect to the jealousy, and it is quite reasonable to combine couple therapy with the use of medication. This may be prescribed by the team itself or perhaps preferably by the general practitioner or psychiatrist seeing the 'patient' in parallel with couple therapy. The therapy is still a useful adjunct in such cases, helping the couple to adjust to the illness and to improve their general communication.

10.6 Summary of the interventions for unreasonable jealousy in one partner within the behavioural-systems approach

We have presented these cases of jealousy in some detail, both because of the interest that the individual cases present and because it is perhaps easiest to understand the interactional treatment for a problem like jealousy by commenting on the specific details.

It is, however, also timely to summarise at this point the types of intervention that can be used in jealousy within behavioural-systems couple therapy. We will list the interventions in accordance with the ALI hierarchy first presented in Chapter 3.

(1) Negotiation to help the couple to improve their general everyday interaction (Chapter 5).
(2) Communication training to improve general communication and empathy (Chapter 6).
(3) To increase the jealous partner's self-esteem by encouraging arguments and thereby redress the balance within the relationship (Chapter 8).
(4) To suggest role reversal, in which the non-jealous partner is asked to express jealousy and possessiveness. (Section 10.5.2).
(5) To suggest specific tasks for the non-jealous partner, for example leaving messages for the jealous partner when going out (Chapter 9).
(6) To impose a timetable for the discussion of jealousy. (Section 10.3.1).
(7) To relabel the jealousy as helpful and the partner as being in need of assistance, (e.g. to control flirtatiousness) (Section 10.3.2).
(8) To connote positively and prescribe both the jealous behaviour and the partner's response (paradoxical message, Sections 9.13 and 10.5.5).

Depression

10.7 Working interactionally with couples where one partner is depre ised

Depression and its predecessor, melancholia, have been written about for over 2500 years, from Hippocratic times to the modern era (Jackson

1986). The characteristic symptoms of depression include sleeplessness, loss of appetite, loss of weight, constipation, loss of sexual interest, restlessness, irritability, anxiety, self-derogatory concerns, suicidal inclinations and delusions. These symptoms are not present in every case, but most psychiatrists would be unhappy to diagnose depression unless at least two or three of them are present. The main distinction between different forms of depression is the question whether the depression seems to be 'understandable' in the light of recent experience, or whether it appears to have arisen for no obvious reason.

There has been a debate which need not concern us here as to whether there is a clear distinction between 'reactive' depression, which is the understandable form, and 'endogenous' depression, which comes 'out of the blue', or whether the two types of depression are essentially the same, one being a milder degree of depression and therefore less likely to lead to admission to hospital.

What is agreed by all who see patients with depression, however, is that the biological symptoms (loss of sleep, loss of weight, loss of appetite and constipation, for example) are more likely to respond to physical treatments such as antidepressants than to talking treatments. Perhaps the most significant single contribution to the treatment of depression has been the discriminate use of antidepressant drugs, whose efficacy in reducing the depressive symptoms, especially the biological ones, is well established.

Where, on the other hand, there are clear reasons to be seen for an episode of depression, it seems that the treatments involving understanding of these reasons and working through them in therapy are more appropriate. Paykel *et al.* (1969), Weissman *et al.* (1972) and other researchers have established the correlation between the experience of a significant life event and the onset of depression, and there is no doubt of the effectiveness of, for instance, bereavement counselling in cases where depression has followed the loss of a close relative (Kubler-Ross 1970; Parkes 1972). Cognitive therapy has more recently demonstrated that it, too, has a major contribution to make in the treatment of depression (Beck 1979).

In some people the main factor in the initiation or maintenance of their depression may be the poor quality of the relationship with a partner or close family member, and it is with the ways of helping depression through modifying close relationships that this section will be mostly concerned (see discussion in Section 1.1.9).

Within the behavioural-systems approach we aim to help both depressed patients and their partners to ameliorate this distressing condition. We retain an eclectic approach, and would not withhold either medication or individual counselling from a depressed patient. What we have attempted to develop in addition is an approach to making progress by altering the relationship of couples where one partner is depressed. We are aware that, in contrast to the rather well developed research into individual factors in depression, our work is still quite poorly researched. However, we have found that, particularly in some resistant cases, we can help a depressed patient by altering his/her relationship with a protective partner in a way in which conventional treatment does not seem able.

10.7.1 In-session intervention techniques

Working interactionally within a behavioural-systems approach the following techniques should be considered for in-session work with couples where one partner is depressed.

(1) Reframing the depression as interactional, by
  - putting the depressed partner in the caring position,
  - asking the depressed partner to help the spouse to express feelings.
(2) Increasing the assertiveness of the depressed partner.
(3) Helping both partners to interrupt the negative self-denigratory cycle by encouraging positive interaction.
(4) Encouraging interaction in which the couple increase their understanding of each other by taking each other seriously.
(5) Giving the couple the opportunity to use structured timetables to develop their abilities in areas such as:
  - speaking about resentments,
  - problem solving,
  - developing enjoyable activities which give both pleasure.

10.7.2 Reframing the problem as interactional

Until the studies by Brown *et al.* (1976) there had been little interest in the interactional aspect of depression within marriage. It is partly as a result of Brown's work that we have developed the approach of treating a depressed spouse within the dyadic interaction of the couple relationship. Brown and Harris (1978) developed the thesis that a confiding relationship with a spouse was protective against depression, even in the presence of other precipitating factors. Although this research has been difficult to replicate, the findings are relevant to marital work.

Weissman *et al.* (1972) demonstrated the devastating effect that depression in a mother could have on her relationships with her children and her spouse and heightened the search for therapeutic management of the depressed mother. However, in spite of the knowledge about the impact of depression on social role performance, little had been done to find ways of intervening to change the social role performance of the depressed spouse.

Friedman (1975) looked at the interaction of drug therapy with marital therapy in depressed patients and summarised as follows:

> 'Both drug and marital therapy showed substantial beneficial advantages over their control conditions, but drug therapy was faster and generally superior

in symptom relief and clinical improvement. Marital therapy was superior in family role task performance and perception of marital relationship. For reducing hostility and enhancing the perception of the marital relationship, drug therapy had a better early effect, but marital therapy had superior effects by the end of treatment.'

This research, though not definitive, lends credence to the possibility that by working with the couple's interaction an impact can be made on the depressive symptoms and the social role performance of the depressed spouse.

Thinking systemically about depression, one is not looking for causation or to allocate blame (see Section 7.3.2) but searching out interactive behaviour which may be initiating or maintaining the symptom (see Section 7.3.3). The couple are likely to present with a very fixed idea that the depression resides firmly in one partner and that the other is helpless in moderating or ameliorating the depressive symptoms. A common feature of couples presenting at the clinic where depression is present in one partner is that the 'well' spouse is reluctant to attend together with the depressed spouse, feeling that s/he can contribute nothing (see Section 10.9.3).

The partner's reluctance should be acknowledged directly and without defensiveness by the therapist; perhaps a statement such as 'we understand how you feel and thank you for coming as we find it is usually most helpful if the partner can join in and work together with us'.

In setting out to reframe the depression as interactive within the couple, the therapist, as described in Section 4.4.1, must tread a delicate path between accommodating the couple's point of view and encouraging an interactional perspective. The therapist must empathise with their point of view, but at the same time begin to find ways to elicit from the non-depressed spouse how s/he responds during depressive episodes. This may mean interrupting a monologue about the depression and the history of treatment to ask of the depressed spouse 'Josie: when you are finding it difficult to get up in the morning, what is Thomas doing?'.

10.7.3 Putting the depressed partner into the caring position

If a situation emerges where, for example, the depressed wife rarely sees her husband because he is extremely pressurised at work, the therapist can intervene to put the depressed spouse into the caring position, by asking her to 'find out from her husband how his high work load affects him'.

This strategy is part of the reframing process, which is useful when working with couples where one partner is symptomatic. The therapist deliberately intervenes to shift the focus from descriptions of the 'illness and its history' *by* the non-symptomatic partner to the concerns *of* the non-symptomatic partner. This structural intervention puts the depressed spouse in the position of carer and the non-symptomatic partner into the position of being cared for.

This intervention also challenges the system at several different levels. At the observable behavioural level the symptomatic spouse is changing a behaviour pattern of being the partner who is seen as needing support and is asked instead to be supportive to the spouse. At the systemic level the interactive pattern is being unbalanced and tipped in the opposite direction. At a symbolic level the depressed spouse is being told that s/he has the ability to be a carer and a competent partner. At perhaps a deeper level of communication the non-symptomatic partner's concerns and vulnerabilities are being acknowledged. This harmonises with the intervention already described which 'reframes the depression as interactional'. (Section 10.7.2).

10.7.4 Supporting the depressed partner to help the other to express feelings

Part of the picture presented by couples where one partner is depressed is that the non-symptomatic partner is super-rational and may rarely express his/her feelings. It is as though the depressed partner has taken on the role for both partners of carrying and expressing feelings. (One sometimes feels that the non-symptomatic partner's inability to express emotions is sufficiently chronic to be also thought of as a symptom which might be best described as 'alexithymia'.)

We use the word feelings in this context to describe the whole gamut of feelings from ecstatic pleasure to suicidal negativism, not simply depressive feelings.

We are not suggesting that these interventions can be achieved immediately or effortlessly. The pattern of interaction within the couple is usually quite rigid and may have been supported by medical, psychiatric and social work interventions over the years; such fixed patterns take time to change. With gentle perserverence, however, it is possible in many cases. When the non-symptomatic partner is finally helped to speak about any daily concerns, it often becomes apparent with surprising consistency that both spouses do indeed have similar worries, disappointments, anxieties and sadnesses.

When this happens within therapy there is usually a very intimate sense that both partners have revealed their vulnerabilities to the therapist, and to each other, and that this has been a unique experience for the couple. As with all such therapeutic experience the therapist must be aware that such experiences are to be nurtured and affirmed. It may be that fear of exposing vulnerability in the non-symptomatic partner is the complementary element to the symptomatic behaviour in the depressive interaction.

10.7.5 Increasing the assertiveness of the depressed spouse

Friedman (1975) hypothesised that

'individuals who may be predisposed to depression may not be typical of the general population'

in that they express less verbal hostility when depressed, and conjectured that the inability to express verbal hostility may predispose individuals to depression.

Friedman did not himself make a connection between his hypothesis regarding the inability to express hostility and the concept raised frequently in analytical literature that depression is 'anger turned in towards the self'. To quote Freud from *Mourning and Melancholia* (1917)

'So we find the key to the clinical picture: we perceive that the self reproaches are reproaches against a loved object which have been shifted away from it on to the patient's own ego.'

It has seemed to us that these different approaches to depression have a common core (which meshes with our experience of the depressed person), involving some inability or fear of expressing hostility or anger towards the spouse. Hence we have developed some interventions designed to facilitate over time a greater freedom to be more expressive and assertive.

Our aim is to convert the negativity of the depressed partner into greater assertiveness, rather than a direct expression of hostility. Our experience is that the non-depressed spouse may find it easier to accept a greater degree of assertiveness in their partner rather than to accept hostility. Equally, the depressed partner may find it easier to learn to be assertive and make requests for him/herself rather than express open hostility.

In addition the results of the expressed emotion studies (Leff & Vaughn 1985) and the impact of the expression of hostility on either a person diagnosed as schizophrenic or depressed suggests that both types of patient may be very sensitive to expressions of hostility, which is perhaps best avoided in their spouses if possible.

The therapist may have to be active and assertive while assisting in this reframing process.

10.7.6 Encouraging positive interaction

Another aspect of the depressive picture is that of the low self-esteem of the individual which can often seem immovable and self-destructive and in some leads to suicidal attempts.

Aaron Beck has developed an approach to depressed individuals through the use of cognitive therapy. Cognitive therapy tackles directly the low self-regard of the depressed person by assuming that it may be maintained by 'automatic thoughts' experienced by the depressed individual which are self-denigratory, self-blaming or punishing. These automatic thoughts are identified in detail and alternative positive thoughts are designed for each individual. The individual is taught to substitute these more positive thoughts for the negative automatic thoughts, and a slow process of self re-education begins which seems to have a beneficial effect upon the individual (Beck 1976).

Within a couple's relationship it seems likely that some couples develop an interaction which encourages and maintains the self-denigration and negativity of the depressed individual. From experience it would appear that some non-depressed spouses are able to precipitate an automatic thought in the partner by suggesting for example 'You find it difficult to cook meals for the children, don't you, dear? You think you are a thoroughly bad cook'. As we have seen, negativity from one spouse tends to breed a negative response from the other (see also Section 6.4.8) (McLean 1976; Paterson and Hops 1982).

Less formally than within cognitive therapy we work towards spouses supporting the development of positive interaction and thus decreasing the level of negativity. From a systemic perspective, by intervening to ask the couple to relate more positively to each other one is challenging the rules which may have led to the self-denigratory spiral.

In Chapter 4 we introduced several interventions which are particularly useful when attempting to interrupt negative interaction: these are to keep up the momentum for change (Section 4.6.4), to keep the focus on the interaction (Section 4.6.6), interventions designed to bring out a silent partner (Section 4.6.7), as well as suggestions as to how to reduce the labelling of one partner as sick or bad (Section 4.6.8). These interventions should be considered when working with couples where one partner is depressed.

In our experience such couples have often lost the art of negotiating together. Usually one partner has taken over the decision-making for both of them and may well have taken over the responsibilities of the depressed spouse. If the situation has been long-standing, the non-symptomatic partner may have ceased to ask the partner for his/her opinion on almost anything. Hence the need to re-establish the ability to negotiate effectively and relearn many communication skills. The therapist will therefore need to have available the interventions described in Chapters 5 and 6 and to use them as necessary to help the couple get back in touch with each other's resources. Another way to state this is that it is important for both partners to take each other seriously, and we often incorporate this task into the timetables we give them for regular discussion at home.

10.7.7 Attitude of the therapist

These interventions are all available to the therapist and should be borne in mind while working towards interrupting and changing negative interaction into more positive patterns. In our experience, where one partner has become accustomed to the role of depressed partner, initial sessions may seem slow and pedantic because of the difficulty of bringing the depressed partner out.

The therapist who enjoys working quickly, or who has difficulty imagining that change is possible in such couples, will need to learn to be patient and to observe the minutiae of interaction. Changes that do occur initially will be small interaction patterns, slight shifts of mood, slight indications that the non-symptomatic partner can begin to show outward displays of feeling. These should be noted as hopeful signs, but the therapist should not necessarily express any hopefulness to the couple. It is better to tell the couple that changes may be slow and hard won. The therapist should be able to project a sense of confidence that the couple have the ability to develop positive ways of supporting each other in their present difficulties.

10.8 Examples of work done with couples where one partner is depressed

Couples initially presenting with one partner who is depressed often reveal a complicated series of interactional difficulties which seem to underpin or accompany the depression. This raises a question whether depression may be a convenient umbrella term, or a container covering a confusing mass of difficulties facing such couples.

We describe work done with three couples to show the different levels of complexity which can be presented within the ambit of depression in one spouse.

Example 10D
Robert and Edith S (already described in Example 8A) are among the more straightforward couples. Robert, aged 35, and Edith, aged 35, had been married 18 months, with one child aged eight months. This was Robert's second marriage and Edith's first. Robert had two children by his first marriage with whom he had lost touch. They were referred by their local GP to the community psychiatric nurse because of Edith's severely depressed state, and because she was already four months pregnant with their second child. The psychiatric nurse astutely arranged to see her and her husband together, as their marriage appeared to be under considerable stress. She then made a skilled assessment of their marital situation and consequently referred them to the marital therapy clinic, sending a useful summary in the referral letter. To quote:

> 'Mrs S. is an only child whose father died 12 years ago and whose mother died last July of cancer at the age of 64. She is still grieving over this loss, and this appears to be a significant factor regarding her present depression. Apart from this stress, Mrs S. became pregnant on her honeymoon and has a daughter Philippa aged six months. She has also discovered recently that she is pregnant (about 15 weeks). Finally in May this year she moved house. I feel the adjustment from being a single working woman to being a housewife and mother has been considerable for Edith. All these major life events – most of which have been shared by Edith and Robert – have led to increased marital tension.'

The letter goes on to detail the difficulties they are now experiencing in their sex life and some of the friction in their daily lives. It neatly sums up the key issues facing this couple as they entered therapy, and shows the kind of sensitive assesment work that can be done by GPs and community psychiatric nurses.

The following is a summary of the interventions with this couple.

Session 1

(1) The therapist explored their current difficulties, focussing on areas which they would wish to change. The therapist consistently ensured that Edith, who allowed Robert to speak for her, be encouraged to speak for herself; and that Robert be asked to speak about his feelings regarding their present situation.

Message

The couple were complimented for having agreed to seek joint treatment and for their directness in the session. The therapist expressed sympathy for their current difficulties, emphasising the normality of their additional emotional turmoil, at the time of the recent loss of Edith's mother and their second pregnancy.

(2) Because their sexual relationship was one in which Robert was pressurising Edith for more frequent sexual intercourse than she felt able to respond to, they agreed to a sexual timetable for one evening a week, with no intercourse on the other six evenings. Instead on the other days they were asked to explore alternative, non-sexual ways of showing affection to each other (see Section 10.10).

Session 2 (two weeks later) (part of this session has been described in detail in Section 8.2.1.)

(3) Both partners used the session to complain about the other's unreasonable behaviour, each assuming that the other could not change. The therapist used the framework of encouraging arguments over trivial issues; at the same time allying with Edith in order to assist her to be more assertive, and to reframe the complaints of both partners as positive requests for change. Robert continued to be loud and domineering while Edith was quieter and often in tears.

Message (Formulation)

We feel that you show determination to work on your relationship; but think that you need to help each other learn a model of gentle maleness and assertive femaleness. In order to help you do this we would like you to use a timetable for co-counselling. For 20 minutes on alternate days, you are each to spend time listening to the other. Spend the 20 minutes listening and not reacting, except to be supportive. Speak about the concerns you have regarding the difficulties you share.

Session 3 (three weeks later)

(4) Since the couple had done no homework, the therapist suggested that they should practise in-session, discussing one issue that was

important to them. With the therapist's help they chose the topic of how they would manage the birth of their second baby. The discussion took on the familiar pattern of attack and defence, by both partners, as they moved from the discussion of the birth of the baby to their sex life and finances. They had by now continued this discussion beyond the time they would usually stop; but the pattern of Edith in tears and Roger shouting angrily reasserted itself. The therapist intervened, encouraging Edith to be more assertive, and asking them both to stay with one discrete small area for negotiation. They were able to do this, and found some concrete examples in which Robert could support Edith. In particular, a request from Edith for help with their daughter Philippa, and the garden, was dealt with by an agreement that they could garden together with Philippa being looked after jointly.

Message (Formulation)

The message focussed on their lack of trust in each other, their determination to keep trying, and their stubbornness. They were given a split-team message, as follows: Some of the team thought the answer was to co-operate more together – for instance doing things together with Philippa, having daily conversations and planning together for the future. The other team members thought the only safe thing was, because you are both so sensitive, to keep your distance, rather like the cold war, never giving in and so keeping your own ends up, and avoiding the need to trust each other.

Session 4

(5) Robert reminded the therapist that this was likely to be the last session as the baby was due in six weeks' time and clinic holidays intervened. Since this was possibly the last session, the therapist reviewed with them remaining areas of discord. Their sexual life had improved to some extent, but each felt the partner was not sufficiently considerate. The therapist worked towards a compromise in which each would do something to please the other. Edith wanted Robert to go to bed early with her, as she felt this was comforting. He, however, was not ready for sleep and wanted to watch television in bed, which upset Edith, particularly if they had just made love. They were asked to discuss this, to see if they could reach a compromise, in which Robert could go to bed early but watch television if he needed to.

(6) They were also asked to discuss their individual needs in giving and receiving affection, and succeeded in doing this. Robert was by now gentler and not insisting on sexual intercourse, and Edith more able to state her needs. She was tearful only once in this session.

Final message (Formulation)

They were both given positive 'strokes' for the changes they had made:

We all noticed the improvement in communication between you, Robert showing gentleness and sensitivity and Edith being more in command of herself and less tearful. However, we thought that there were dangers in relying on words, which might trap you back into your old form of interaction (Robert becoming rather loud and outspoken and Edith crying and withdrawing). You can do much non-verbally for each other, for instance Edith cooking a good meal or showing physical affection, and Robert putting his arms around Edith in times of stress.

(7) We do have some specific things we suggest you can do. One night per week Edith could earn a 'husband token' by staying up late, and another night Edith could spend it by persuading Robert to go to bed early with her. He could then watch television in bed after she had gone to sleep if that becomes necessary.

This couple were given the opportunity to keep an appointment in the bank and return should they wish to have further therapy after the birth of the baby. Their relationship had improved and her depression had diminished by the end of treatment.

10.8.1 Discussion of the therapy

As already stated, this couple provide an example of reasonably straightforward interventions focussing on the key areas of: increasing the depressed spouse's assertiveness at (1), (2), (3) and (4) and the non-symptomatic partner's expressiveness at (1) and (5) (in their case greater expressiveness means for the husband to become gentler), putting the depressed partner into a caring position and encouraging positive rather than negative interaction at (6) and (7). As already described in Example 8A, because of the particular patterning of their interaction they were encouraged to argue over trivial issues.

With this particular couple, emphasis was placed on increasing their non-verbal interaction, thus interrupting the negative verbal communication patterns in which they were so well versed (Section 6.4.8). Edith's pregnancy also suggested to us that physical contact might be most reassuring to her and help the father to adjust to the presence of the unborn child.

10.9 Two further examples

We now present two somewhat more complicated examples. The first couple, Mr and Mrs D, were already living apart when therapy began and the therapist was faced with a series of dilemmas as to whether it was possible to work with them as a couple. Interestingly the couple also showed, besides the depression, two of the other patterns covered in this chapter, those of jealousy and conflicts over sex.

With the second case, Mabel and Christopher J, Mabel had a four and a half year history of psychiatric care, during which time little had changed except that her depressive mood had deepened. She was by this stage labelled by herself, her husband and the services as the sick partner.

Neither couple were simple to work with nor an outright success; they demonstrate difficulties encountered as well as areas of potential change. (For further examples of work done with couples where one partner is depressed, see Examples 9C, 9D and Section 10.10.1.)

10.9.1 Sydney and Beatrice D

Example 10E
Sydney D, aged 26 and unemployed and Beatrice, aged 24 and a housewife had been married for five years; before that they had lived together for three years. They had two children, aged 5 and 9. They were referred by their GP who wrote:

'Mrs D turned up yesterday with her husband, complaining of depression. She had apparently been crying most of the weekend. Within a few minutes it became evident that there were obvious marital difficulties. They had a trial separation last year; her husband seems keen to make this marriage work but she doesn't seem to know what she wants . . .

Neither of them seem to perceive the problem as a relationship difficulty and both feel she is depressed . . .'

Session 1
Two therapists worked with this couple (the female therapist in training and the male a more experienced therapist).

(1) By the time this couple came for their first appointment at the clinic they were again living apart. The session was opened by Sydney who said 'My wife is depressed'. Beatrice added 'Yes I'm depressed'. This first session focussed on their interaction and what kind of a relationship they would like to have now. Sydney still wanted to work at their relationship but Beatrice was uncertain. She felt nothing would change if she returned to her husband. 'He would still smoke a cigarette, sitting on the edge of the bed, first thing in the morning.' They described considerable difficulties with Sydney's family who disliked Beatrice and had shown in many different ways their dismay at his marriage to her. Beatrice also felt this could not be changed.

Therapists' interventions
Throughout the first session the therapists were mindful to interrupt negative interaction, to decentre themselves (Section 4.6.9) and to encourage Beatrice (the more silent partner) to speak about her needs in their relationship.

At the end of this session, the therapists pulled together much of what had been learned. The couple's feelings of rejection by Sydney's family, their sense of responsibility in seeking therapy and their concern to help each other with whatever they decided to do were all connoted positively.

Since they were living apart and could not yet agree about the future of their relationship, they were told that they were wise to choose to stay apart for the moment. They were asked to use some times, before the next appointment, to talk and to listen to each other.

Session 2

(2) Beatrice came without Sydney. They had agreed that Beatrice should sort herself out before they could work on their relationship.

Therapists' interventions
In discussion the team felt that this was a typical move on the part of the couple, that of putting forward the depressed spouse as 'needing to be sorted out' and the other partner withdrawing. With this couple it was doubly difficult because of the uncertainty about their future as a couple. She seemed to be somewhat more assertive about her needs, which the therapists wished to encourage, but the therapists did not want to accept the couple's suggestion that 'Beatrice needed to get sorted out first' since they wished to reframe the depression as shared. Our practice in such situations is to see the solitary partner for about ten minutes with the aim of giving support to find ways of including the other partner in the next therapy session, but also to remain flexible to the immediacy of the situation.

Beatrice explained that she was becoming increasingly interested in other relationships and worried about the impact of the uncertainties on the two children. She was quite desperate to talk on her own, and felt pressurised by Sydney's insistence that she move back to live with him.

The therapists reminded Beatrice that, whether she stayed with Sydney or not, the issues she wanted to talk about related to the future of their marriage and were common issues between Beatrice and Sydney. After consultation, it was agreed to offer both Beatrice and Sydney individual sessions at the next appointment, to be followed immediately by a joint marital session. Beatrice readily accepted. The therapists felt this equalised the situation and brought Sydney back into therapy so that the focus could be their interaction. A letter was sent to confirm the arrangement with both of them.

Session 3 (individual session with Beatrice and the female therapist)

(3) Beatrice was quite desperate to speak in confidence to the therapist, insisting that she did not want information shared with her husband. She was reassured. Beatrice explained her need to talk alone was because Sydney was like the 'gestapo' constantly asking questions. He was extremely jealous of any relationship she may have outside the marriage, suspecting her of having affairs, searching her drawers and diary for evidence of infidelity. He cross-questioned her. He

pressurised her for sexual intercourse, which she had agreed to over recent weeks, although living apart. She enjoyed sex occasionally, but found his approach crude and pressurising. He tended to 'grab' her, which she found off-putting. She described how she was 'interfered with' at the age of eight, which she felt made her sensitive to how she was approached sexually. She was upset if he stared at her when undressing. Regarding the future of their relationship she felt they were both undecided; Sydney occasionally mentioned divorce, and threatened to go back to his parents. He provided her with a picture of uncertainty which made her and the children suffer.

Session 3 (Individual session with Sydney and the male therapist)
Sydney was eager to explain that he had only learned recently that Beatrice was sexually abused when eight years old by a neighbour. He felt that this helped him to understand much of Beatrice's behaviour, why she disliked him watching her undress and did not like cuddles or physical contact. He wished that she could be more expressive of her feelings and more able to talk openly to him. He talked about his jealousy, but believed that his suspicions were well founded as Beatrice would meet certain friends late at night. Although living apart they had met to have sexual intercourse on several recent occasions.

Therapists' interventions
Both therapists used the individual sessions to allow the partners to express their feelings about their relationship, reminding each spouse that some of these issues could be worked at in the next joint session.

(4) The couple were seen together at the end of therapy so that a message could be given to them as a couple.

Message (formulation)
Although we are still uncertain as to what will happen to your relationship in the future, we would like you to use the following timetables.

(a) We would like you to agree to choose one day a week only on which to have sexual intercourse. Otherwise we would like you to make no sexual advances towards each other. Sydney is also to restrain himself from looking at Beatrice in a sexy way. (They agreed to this and chose Saturdays for sex.)

(b) For 15 minutes, once a week, Beatrice is to listen to Sydney's worries and his jealousy; after 15 minutes this should be reversed. Beatrice should then complain about his behaviour and Sydney should listen for a further 15 minutes. (They chose Sundays at 3.00 to 3.30 pm.)

Session 4 (joint session, three weeks later)
The couple had moved back into the marital home. They had used the sexual timetable which they felt had helped. On the first Satur-

day, Beatrice had had flu and Sydney had been so upset at missing out on sexual relations that Beatrice had agreed to have intercourse with him on Monday, which had been enjoyable for both. The following Saturday, Sydney had fallen asleep, so that sex had not taken place, but they had since used the timetable and enjoyed sex together. They had also used the Sunday timetable for discussion, and reported that they had 'argued' several times. Beatrice volunteered that Sydney had been a 'good boy' between times in that he had not been pressuring her for sex, which she had found relaxing.

Then followed an in-session discussion about many of the complaints raised in the individual sessions but never discussed together. After many of their criticisms of each other had been aired, the female therapist interrupted and asked them to talk about 'what pleases you about each other'. The aim of this intervention is to encourage the couple to move towards more positive ways of interacting. Beatrice said Sydney was reliable and made her laugh. Sydney responded with how much he enjoyed being with her.

(5) The therapist again intervened to ask them what they wanted from each other, and this led into a fruitful interchange in which they were quite positive towards each other. Beatrice eventually asked Sydney to help her with the children, as she felt that both partners were inconsistent and lacked discipline with them.

Again the therapists helped them to focus on a small issue, and they eventually decided together to be more consistent about the boys tidying up their room.

Summary of Sessions 5 and 6

Sessions 5 and 6 followed a similiar pattern to session 4. The couple had made some small advances between sessions, they used part of the session to express resentments about each other and they were then encouraged to work towards positive interaction and to find common areas for change.

The jealousy had by now subsided, the depression in Beatrice was less marked and the sexual issue was no problem. They had extended the sexual timetable to two nights a week: Beatrice was finding it more possible to say no if she did not want sexual intercourse, while Sydney no longer felt so rejected.

They were discharged after the sixth session.

The final message

We are going to ask you to continue with the same tasks. We want you to add one evening when you go out separately, and to continue with two evenings of 30 minutes for discussion of issues which are important to you. After discharge we will keep an appointment for you 'in the bank', so that you can contact us if you both agree that you need to. (See Section 4.8.2.)

(6) Meanwhile, although things are better between you, we do wonder if the tasks you want to do together, such as redecorating the house and possibly having another child, will help you cope with the boredom which we think you may experience if you settle down into being a sedately married couple.

10.9.2 Discussion of the therapy

If we review the interventions used by the co-therapists, we can see that the first major dilemma for the therapists, at **(1)**, was how to reframe the depression as interactional, since the couple were living apart and Beatrice was uncertain what she wanted from this relationship.

The therapists did not advise the couple about their future relationship. (We think this is very unwise, see Section 2.4.3.5.) However, since they were already living apart, a slightly paradoxical message, 'Continue living apart for the moment', was given. This was also supporting Beatrice as she was feeling very pressurised by Sydney to return home.

At **(2)** the therapists were given their second major challenge to reframing the depression as interactional, by Beatrice arriving without her husband for the second session.

The compromise offer of separate sessions, followed by a joint marital session, was used and seems to have freed both partners to raise some of their mutual concerns in the following joint session. It also balances the therapy, ensuring that the therapists are not sucked in to the couple's definition of the problem, which is, in this case, to label Beatrice as the person who needs therapy.

At **(3)**, during the individual session with Beatrice, the therapist might have been tempted to follow the individual dynamics of Beatrice, particularly since she revealed that she had been sexually abused at eight years of age. However, while hearing this and noticing its importance, the therapist kept the focus of the therapy on their interaction and the impact of this experience on their present relationship.

At **(4)**, although Beatrice and Sydney had been seen individually for the session, they were brought together to conclude the session and a joint message was given. This message addressed the two central issues which had arisen in both individual sessions: their sexual relationship and their jealous interaction. Once again keeping the focus on the interaction, and recognising Beatrice's need to develop a more secure ability to relate assertively to her pressurising husband, the two issues were woven together to fulfil an aspect of each partner's wishes.

At **(5)** the therapists began the process of finding joint domestic issues upon which they could build towards a more positive future relationship, thus encouraging positive interaction.

At **(6)** the therapists addressed the question of boredom, should they settle down to a more sedate marital relationship. We often use the notion of fear of boredom in couple relationships. We hypothesise that couples are often apprehensive about allowing themselves to relax into a relationship which may be perceived by one or other partner as boring.

By raising the issue we hope to reduce the expectations of the couple and anticipate difficulties they may face in the future. Finally, in the above case, Beatrice's depression seems to have acted as an umbrella covering other aspects of their relationship, in particular Sydney's jealousy (which was never discussed with the referring GP), their sexual difficulties and Beatrice's inability to assert herself adequately within the relationship. When these interactive issues were attended to the depression abated and the jealousy became less intense.

10.9.3 Christopher and Mabel J

Christopher and Mabel J (previously cited in Example 9D) are presented partly because of the intrinsic interest of the case and partly because their treatment was unusually long-term for this clinic. The therapy seems to have fallen into three distinct phases. Phase one took seven sessions, in which the therapist was working towards reframing the depression as interactional. This required tenacity and much support from other members of the therapy team. The second phase took seven sessions, in which the couple worked together to develop greater flexibility in their interaction, and phase three took three sessions, in which termination was dealt with.

This was a complex case, and although some major changes occurred in both the couple and the individuals, many questions still remain unanswered.

Example 10F
Christopher, aged 23, and Mabel, aged 22, had been married for five years and had no children. (They have already been described in Example 9D as an example of a couple who were seen by us as 'babes in the wood' and seemed to assume that 'married couples should not have fun together'.) Their therapy is described in greater detail here, to underline some particular problems which may be faced when working with couples where one partner is depressed.

Mabel and Christopher were referred by the emergency clinic at the Maudsley Hospital. They had attended the emergency clinic over the previous six months, following three overdose episodes by Mabel. She had been a patient at the Maudsley Hospital for the past four and a half years, having initially been referred for social phobia. She received a course of behaviour therapy and although some of the more severe symptoms had lifted, the therapy was said to have failed. Consequently she was referred within the hospital to be treated for depression with antidepressants, and was admitted to a ward on at least one occasion.

On each visit to the emergency clinic her husband Christopher accompanied her. It was noted that they were an immature couple and that much unspoken tension existed between them. As a result, they were referred as a couple to the Marital Therapy Clinic. The notes were now recording Mabel as follows: Her mood has declined, and she has become increasingly preoccupied with killing herself'; 'She lacks interest in anything, has insomnia, both initial and early waking'; Mabel herself had said that 'it doesn't work at home' and that she was 'losing interest in sex'.

During the year prior to referral, Mabel had thrice completed a Shortened

Beck Depression Inventory and was rated between 10 and 15 (16 is severe). For four and a half of the five years for which they had been married, Mabel had been treated for individual psychiatric problems. She was small and attractive. She rarely spoke. Her attentive husband immediately answered any question addressed to her. He was serious, humourless and dedicated to 'nursing' his 'sick wife'. He himself worked as a laboratory technician in a pharmaceutical firm and had much experience of hospital life. They were an anxious, solemn and isolated young couple.

Phase one of treatment: seven sessions over five months
 (1) The initial sessions were taken up with the slow and patient work of trying to break through the cycle in which Christopher answered everything for Mabel.
 (2) At the same time, we began the process of negotiating small reciprocal interactions, in which Christopher would give up caring for Mabel and she would do some caring of him. Christopher, while being very polite, took the view that marital therapy was not necessary, and that he did not understand why they had been referred.
 (3) The therapist accepted his scepticism, and went along with the notion that since no other treatment had been helpful they should not expect marital therapy to succeed either.
     By the third session some tiny gains had been made with regard to Mabel speaking for herself and taking responsibility for one meal each week. Previously Christopher had done all of the cooking.
 (4) However, they returned to the emergency clinic, complaining that they had not asked for marital therapy, and since the therapist was agreeing that marital therapy would not work they therefore requested an alternative treatment, telling us that they required no further marital work. The emergency clinic accepted their request, and were in the process of setting up further assessments when we requested a conference between emergency clinic staff and the marital therapy clinic. Following this, it was agreed that the couple should be given a sympathetic hearing on their visits to the emergency clinic, but should be told that, for the moment, they were to continue with Marital Therapy.
     Christopher was quite angry at the next marital session. They were therefore asked to discuss together, in the session, whether they would continue to come for marital therapy, and came to no agreement.
 (5) Between sessions 5 and 6 they again returned to the emergency clinic, and were reminded that their present treatment was through the marital therapy clinic.
 (6) The consultant to the marital therapy clinic also received an anxious phone call from Christopher's employer who was eager to know why the marital therapy clinic was asking his employee to attend for marital therapy when he had actually sought help for his wife's

depression. The consultant explained our method of working with a depressed person, and asked the employer to support Christopher to continue with the marital therapy.

(7) Subsequently, they both visited their GP, who after hearing their story and Christopher's concern that he did not need marital therapy, offered Mabel the opportunity to take a course of anti-depressant drugs.

Session 7

At the next appointment (their seventh), Mabel announced that they had been to the GP who had offered her antidepressant drugs; but she had herself refused. She was surprisingly assertive about this and for the first time talked openly about wanting to sort herself out, with the help of Christopher and the marital therapy clinic. This seemed to us to be the first breakthrough with this couple. Christopher expressed himself to be pleased with Mabel's decision, though he also said he did not see how marital therapy could possibly help.

It is instructive to look at session 7, as it seems to be the first session in which the couple were both prepared to work together. Until now, one or both of them wanted to look for an individual solution to Mabel's difficulties. For the first time, in this session, they voluntarily brought to the session detail of their relationship other than Mabel's depression. Where finances were concerned, Christopher controlled these in detail, keeping a daily book for household finances and giving Mabel money in £10 allocations as needed. Mabel described herself as very fastidious, liking everything to be perfect and disappointed when she failed her high standards. Christopher was described by Mabel as good at finances, housekeeping and cooking, as a result he tended to take responsibility for all of these areas. Christopher was reluctant to say that Mabel had any current skill.

A reciprocal task was negotiated whereby Mabel would cook a special Sunday lunch and Christopher would take Mabel for a long walk on Wednesday.

The message

(1) That we noticed how much Mabel wanted to change and how Christopher found this a relief.

(2) That Mabel must be warned that since she was a perfectionist she should expect to fail her own high standards.

(3) That Christopher, who had been caring for Mabel very intelligently, should help her now, by encouraging her to accept that it is fine to be occasionally messy. He should help her learn to be messy in some specific areas.

(4) That whatever changes they wanted to make should be made very slowly. 'We do notice that you are now both saying that you would welcome some changes.'

Phase two: sessions 8–14

This phase was characterised by a greater willingness from both partners to work together to improve their relationship. Mabel was encouraged to be more assertive about her needs. Christopher was encouraged to express his anxieties and fears to Mabel and she to be supportive towards him. The negative interaction in which Christopher constantly described Mabel as inadequate and incompetent was interrupted as frequently as possible by discussing in-session joint worries and by using simple joint tasks as homework.

(8) During the intervening eight weeks Mabel had cooked meals and they had taken walks together. Mabel was more animated in the session while Christopher admitted that he had been under quite a bit of strain over the past few weeks. Most of the session involved asking Mabel to help Christopher talk about the strain he was under and be supportive to him. They engaged empathically with this task.

(9) Since they were more relaxed and more able to discuss personal issues, their sex life was raised and discussed. They both felt that sex had become rather stale and infrequent. Mabel expressed interest in taking more initiative in their sex life. She said that she had always been shy about sex but felt it was time that she tried to become less inhibited.

(10) Eight weeks later they reported on a very mixed intervening period. They had had more enjoyable sex but not as frequently as Mabel had originally intended. Mabel also reported that she had had one month of misery in which she felt occasionally quite suicidal. She had, however, resisted any temptation to act on this feeling, except to visit their GP who had again offered her antidepressants which she had refused.

(11) The session was used to help them discuss together Christopher's feelings about Mabel's suicidal thoughts. He shared a great deal of anxiety about how to handle these situations. In session Mabel became very caring towards Christopher and reassured him in many different ways that she knew she would not take an overdose. Christopher described how desperate he felt if Mabel talked to him about her misery.

Message

At the end of this session we were able to connote Mabel very positively for her ability to care for Christopher and to praise Christopher for sharing with Mabel his intense anxiety about her moodiness. We also told Mabel that because she was now so strong as to be able to resist taking antidepressant drugs, and knew she could manage to survive her very miserable feelings, she must find ways to help Christopher be as strong as she was about this. We felt that Christopher needed to learn some of her courage in facing difficult emotions.

(12) During the next session they had an angry disagreement; Mabel flounced out of the session, leaving Christopher upset and despondent. After some time she returned. This proved useful material for the session, as they were able to discuss together how they usually manage their disagreements.

(13) Christopher talked of his discomfort with Mabel's tantrums and how he spent hours trying to placate her to no avail. Mabel was able to say that she would prefer it if Christopher could leave her alone when she was angry or in a mood, as she knew she could get over her moods on her own, if left for a while. Again, Mabel was able to be the carer, by helping Christopher to talk about his fears of leaving her on her own on such occasions. He expressed intense fear that she might take an overdose or damage herself in some way.

(14) Mabel was able to express her feelings for him and to reassure him that, even though she still had days on which she had suicidal thoughts, she knew she would not take an overdose. She became quite angry with him, that he did not trust her enough to let her manage on her own.

(15) The time between sessions was increasingly lengthened, as there was a tendency for the couple to become dependent upon the clinic, and any changes were very gradual. The couple were now bringing to therapy new issues. Christopher felt that Mabel was irresponsible with money, as she was beginning to want to go to town on her own to buy herself some new clothes. They negotiated a small budget for Mabel and she went with a friend on a successful shopping trip. They spent a long weekend away together at a conference at which Christopher was making a presentation. They had both been worried about how this would be, but they were able to discuss it together and to give each other support. Christopher also talked about his own worries at work where he felt he was overstretched and uncertain as to whether he had been promoted above his abilities. They revealed that Mabel had always felt Christopher's parents to be critical of her, feeling that she was not good enough for him. All of the above issues were discussed in-session prior to the event and on each occasion they were able to overcome their anxieties and to enjoy themselves. They grew together in confidence and in their enjoyment of each other's company. Mabel still had peaks and troughs in her mood, and would occasionally still have thoroughly depressing days. Christopher was still very apprehensive about leaving her on her own.

(16) In spite of several attempts to encourage them to find activities to participate in separately outside the home, they both said they preferred to spend most of their available time together.

By this stage it seemed that the couple had stabilised at a slightly more effective level of interaction. Mabel was more able to express her own needs without Christopher speaking for her. Christopher was more able to give her space to come out of a mood without his constant attention. They were able to share the caring role more equally, and discuss their similar levels of anxiety about social events, particularly where family members were involved.

Phase three: terminating therapy

(17) Unusually for the clinic, this couple had attended for a total of fourteen sessions at monthly or bi-monthly intervals. It was felt that the reason for referral, Mabel's depression, had subsided, and that since therapy had reached a plateau in which little else was changing and the couple were becoming dependent upon the therapist, it was necessary to terminate treatment. The therapist explained, during the twelfth session, that therapy would be ending soon. Christopher began the fifteenth session by asking if Mabel could be referred for individual psychotherapy, as they both felt she still had many issues to sort out for herself. This seemed both a useful suggestion and an attempt to stay attached to therapy.

The usual practice of the clinic is to discourage couples from individual therapy during couple work, as we feel it usually detracts from the joint work. We also felt that this couple were still so enmeshed that they should both seek alternative activities, which would enable them both to grow independently within their relationship, rather than Mabel being once more relabelled as the patient and Christopher being separated from the work being done.

Since, however, we had already decided that there was little more we could do, we agreed to refer Mabel for individual psychotherapy. We did also suggest that Christopher could take up an activity for himself (such as swimming or an evening class) to balance the psychotherapy, but so far as we know he did not do so.

In order to facilitate the ending of therapy they were offered an appointment at an interval of six months. They brought to this appointment intense worries about a family wedding which they must attend. After two more rather static sessions they were discharged from treatment.

In the final message we cautioned that Mabel was likely to change faster than Christopher and this might cause stress in their future relationship; and left an appointment in the bank in case they should want to refer themselves back for future joint work.

10.9.4 Discussion of the therapy

This couple were fascinating and difficult. Using the theoretical framework already outlined, the therapist began work at (1) by asking Christopher to encourage Mabel to be more assertive by speaking for herself. At the same time she attempted to put Mabel into the caring role (thus trying to unbalance the system) at **(2)**. At **(3)** Christopher's expression of their scepticism regarding the usefulness of marital therapy was acknowledged, in the hopes that this might work paradoxically. However, they took our statements quite literally and approached the emergency clinic.

These early interventions seem to have made Christopher in particular angry. As can be seen at **(4)**, **(5)**, **(6)** and **(7)**, Christopher made four attempts to return to individual treatment for Mabel; Mabel for her part seemed satisfied to come for marital work but did not challenge Christopher's insistence that her depression was the problem.

Spouses are sometimes disconcerted to discover that we involve them in treatment. In Christopher's case he was adamant that their relationship was wonderful and therefore there could be nothing marital therapy could do to help.

This is a complicated issue for the spouse and for the therapist. We do not either believe, or suggest, that the spouse has in any way caused the depression. However, we do suggest that modifications in their interaction may help ameliorate the more stressful aspects of the depression for both partners. We can usually engage the non-symptomatic partner in this work. As described above, the assistance of other professionals, including Christopher's employer, was needed before this particular couple could be jointly engaged in couple therapy.

Perhaps the therapist lacked empathy with their situation, or began challenging the system too early in treatment. On the other hand, one could hypothesise that because this couple had already received four and a half years of medical treatment for Mabel's 'illness', there was an inevitability about the difficulties faced in reframing the symptom as interactional. It may be significant that when both the emergency clinic and Christopher's employer co-operated with treatment, and Mabel herself said no to taking anti-depressants, then both partners began to work together in therapy and small changes occurred. One might cynically assume that the couple by then felt they had no alternative but to co-operate with the treatment offered.

Thinking systemically, an hypothesis about the non-symptomatic partner's behaviour might be that keeping the 'patient' in the depressive role protects the non-symptomatic partner from acknowledging his own vulnerability, and by implication keeps him in the position of being the 'strong' partner. If this is correct then the therapist may need to show higher levels of empathy with the non-symptomatic partner than this therapist seems to have done. In allying heavily with the symptomatic partner the therapist risked alienating the non-symptomatic partner. If the balance is not kept there is an obvious hazard of either losing the couple from therapy or being unable to push the system sufficiently to facilitate changes.

We have already stated that the non-symptomatic partner may need to make some adjustments in order to accept a more assertive spouse.

At **(8)**, **(11)** and **(13)** the interventions were consequently designed to increase Christopher's expressiveness and at **(9)**, **(10)**, **(12)**, and **(14)** Mabel's assertiveness.

At **(15)** the couple had learned quite a lot about reciprocity, and interventions were now focussed on the detail of negotiating small practical tasks.

At **(16)** the therapist was struggling to move the therapy into another phase, that of encouraging this enmeshed couple to become less dependent on each other. Both partners insisted that they preferred their current relationship. Although the therapist and the team still felt that there were many areas that the couple might work at to develop a more mature relationship, the couple felt this was unnecessary. An interesting conflict between the couple's view of a good relationship and the therapists' judgment!

At **(17)** the therapist had developed quite an attachment to this young couple and was in some ways reluctant to terminate treatment (see Section 4.8). The couple also seemed to feel that the work could go on indefinitely. Termination became difficult. Time between appointments was lengthened to discourage greater dependency and to assess how well the couple managed without treatment (see Section 4.8.2). Since the depression had become less intense and some adjustments had been made in their relationship, therapy was terminated.

At the termination of treatment many questions remained. Their request for individual treatment for Mabel left one with the dilemma as to what had been achieved by treatment. Did they as a couple still see Mabel as the 'patient' even though we had assumed an interactive stance?

Would the therapy have been more successful had a paradox been used at several points in therapy? There was a naive immaturity about this couple which made it difficult to find paradoxical messages which would have been received as anything other than punishing; but we also wonder whether the therapist had become too involved with this couple and was therefore not able to detach from their difficulties in order to challenge the rigidity of the system.

Could we have worked more creatively to speed up the process of change? Was it appropriate for Mabel to seek individual psychotherapy, or was this simply relabelling her as the patient? Had the modification in their interaction ameliorated her depression, or had time simply intervened and the depression diminished?

We are unable to answer these and many other questions satisfactorily, with regard to working with couples where one partner is depressed. However, we do hope that therapists might consider using the interventions described, bearing in mind that the objective is not 'cure', but modification and amelioration of the debilitating aspects of depression, through joint work with the couple. (See goals of treatment, Chapter 2.)

Sexual conflicts

10.10 *Working with marital conflicts involving male demands and female reluctance for sex*
(see also Section 11.4.3)

We have described this method of working in detail (Crowe and Ridley 1986) and therefore we only propose to present in an abbreviated form here the ideas presented in that article.

The combination of reluctance for sex in the female partner with continual demands from the male partner is a common one amongst referrals to marital and sexual clinics. General sexual unresponsiveness in women was the most common female presenting problem in two clinical surveys: Bancroft and Coles (1976) found the problem in 62% of women presenters, and Mears (1978) in 51%. Whether marital conflict over the frequency of sex was a feature in all these cases of unresponsiveness is not clear, but the present authors' experience suggests that this is so in a high proportion of such cases.

In some couples both partners may seek direct help for the wife's 'frigidity', a term which we prefer to discourage as it is imprecise and locates the difficulty in one partner rather than in the relationship. Other couples may present with generalised marital difficulties, included amongst which may be the pattern of a husband pressurising for sexual intercourse with a wife who is increasingly reluctant. See, for example, Sydney and Beatrice D. (Example 10E) who presented to the GP because of Beatrice's depression; it was only as the therapist explored their interaction that their sexual difficulties emerged. Many couples are highly sensitive about discussing their sexual relationship and wait until the therapist invites them to do so.

Characteristic of the relationships which we are now describing is that while the male partner has been pressurising for sexual intercourse, the woman has either found sexual intercourse distasteful while continuing to co-operate with her partner's demands, or else she has increasingly tended to resist his demands. Most women in this situation are, however, able to achieve an orgasm on occasion, and this makes the problem even more incomprehensible from the man's point of view. In some cases there are arguments and disputes about sex, but in others the woman is unassertive, shows low self-esteem and finds it difficult to express her own needs or develop independence within the relationship.

Many authors have either suggested that the problem in a woman is intractable or give few guidelines as to how to work with such couples. Masters and Johnson (1970) refer to marital problems, which they see as a poor prognostic influence on therapy for sexual dysfunction. Others have written extensively on the subject and prefer to emphasise the need to encourage the expression of resentments and anger in individual therapy before approaching the sexual relationship (Kaplan 1979).

Individual treatment to overcome fears (Jehu 1979) or sexual stimulation to increase sexual desires in the reluctant partner (Gillan and Gillan 1976) have also been advocated. Yet others have emphasised the need to develop communication skills in conveying positive and negative feelings. Bancroft (1989) recommends the open communication of feelings during sensate focus, as well as self-focus exercises and cognitive techniques to assist with the low self-image of the reluctant partner. Hawton (1985) cites marital discord as the single most common cause of sexual conflicts and uses reciprocity negotiation to reduce resentments which he sees as underlying the reluctance for sex in many cases.

Our approach assumes that the reluctance for sex in the female partner is an integral part of the marital relationship. It derives in part from reciprocity negotiation (Stuart 1969) and the 'love days' described by Azrin *et al.* (1973) and has some aspects in common with rituals prescribed in family therapy (Selvini Palazzoli *et al.* 1978).

We have hypothesised that 'sexual reluctance, or refusal, in the female partner might serve the function of balancing what is otherwise a male-dominated relationship' (Crowe and Ridley 1986). Our approach to this problem is centred on the negotiated timetable, which helps a couple presenting in this way to reduce the severity of the conflicts over sex and to clear the way for fruitful negotiations over resentments and other problems within the relationship.

The negotiated timetable is an intervention which suggests to the couple that they should experiment with a somewhat unusual idea, that of agreeing, in-session with the therapist, when they will make a date to have sexual intercourse on a regular basis, usually once a week.

These details are negotiated in the session with the couple and clear choices are made. In particular, a timetable is worked out including every day of the week so that each partner is sure both when they will, and when they will not, have sexual intercourse. The evenings when the woman will not be pressurised by the man for sexual intercourse must be emphasised and the man must agree to abide by this, so that if they wish to show affection in other ways it is clear, that on those days, this must not lead to sexual intercourse.

In introducing the timetable, the therapist has to respect the sensitivities of the couple. Many couples feel that sex should be spontaneous, and resist the idea of a timetable. However, if they can be induced to try it on an experimental basis, they often find that it has some significant advantages. These can be a reduction in tension within the couple, a re-emergence of sexual enjoyment, more freedom to show affection in other ways and a separation between resentments brought about by their general relationship and their sexual activity.

Since the negotiated timetable is a somewhat unconventional therapy the way it is introduced to the couple is important. For some couples it may be wise to introduce it as a somewhat crazy idea, for others it can be described and the couple asked to think it over, while with others it may be wisest to wait until more conventional methods have failed. However, we are increasingly aware that couples find it useful, and it can be introduced early in treatment.

Once a couple have begun using the timetable the previous two to three weeks can be reviewed in-session as to how they have experienced its use. Where the couple have adhered to the timetable there will usually have been some improvement in their sexual relationship and arguments about sex will have reduced. However, we often find that other resentments and disagreements may begin to emerge. These can be developed in the session and, if helpful, a separate timetable for discussion or arguments can be set as additional homework (see Section 9.11).

If arguments have continued about sex then this is good material to be discussed in-session. It may be helpful to revise the timetable, to elaborate the rules associated with the timetable and to bring in other suggestions for altered behaviour. Where the timetable has failed this can be therapeutic, as for example when the failure of the timetable precipitates an argument over resentments which have been kept hidden.

· A dilemma for the therapist with couples who have successfully used the timetable is whether to suggest they continue with the timetable or not. Some couples seem to be more comfortable with the regularity of the timetable, others choose to vary it or occasionally add another evening, and yet others choose to give it up, returning to it if they go through a bad time again. The therapist should probably counsel caution about ceasing to use the timetable and suggest that they return to the timetable should the frequency of sexual intercourse become an issue or if disputes return.

In many cases associated with sexual reluctance on the woman's part we find resentment about the partner's sexual approach as well as the way she is treated generally. These should be explored in detail and we find this is most easily achieved after some of the tension has gone out of the relationship by the use of the timetable.

This intervention, as mentioned above, is most useful when both partners can experience normal sexual function, but the woman is very reluctant to have sexual intercourse whereas the man is enthusiastic and exerts pressure. It may be moderately useful in cases of female anorgasmia, when this is associated with reluctance and demands as described. It can occasionally be used when both partners have a low sexual desire but wish to increase its frequency for other reasons (e.g. fertility). We are beginning to test out whether it can also be useful for couples where the man is reluctant to have sexual intercourse and has a critical and dominant wife (Example 8C) and where a device such as the negotiated timetable may help him to be more assertive within the relationship. Some evidence is emerging that this is so.

We now describe an example of a young couple whose marriage of one year was at a crisis point. When their sexual difficulties were understood to fit the above criteria the sexual timetable was used; then followed a series of sessions during which other aspects of their relationship were explored and moderated.

10.10.1 Roy and Janice F

Example 10G
Roy, aged 29, and Janice F, aged 30, had been married one year, with no children. On referral this couple said they were in a crisis situation wondering whether they 'can survive together'. Prior to their marriage Janice had been an independent, competent and sociable person with her own flat and circle of interesting friends. Her husband was a quiet, home-loving and practical person, less academic, less outgoing and earning less than his wife. Janice felt restricted by their shared marital home; she had bouts of depression, especially at the weekend when they were together, and regretted the loss of her separate existence in her own flat. Roy was puzzled and upset at Janice's reaction as he felt only the need to be with her in their own home.

Sessions 1 and 2
(1) The first two sessions were taken up with discussions of their many differences of background, work environment and friends. Therapy focussed on reciprocity negotiation seeking joint and separate activities which would lessen the tension at the weekends.

Session 3
During the third session sexual issues were emerging as central to their difficulties. Janice felt very pressurised by Roy for sex, and felt harassed if he approached her crudely or when she was not in the mood. She felt strongly about women's sexuality being abused by men and had prosecuted a colleague, and won her case, for sexual harassment at work. Roy was confused and defensive as he felt his approaches to be loving and appreciative. Janice, however, complained that she was his only friend and wished he had others.
(2) They both had enjoyed sex in the beginning of their relationship, but Janice was becoming increasingly disinterested and repelled by Roy's continual sexual advances.
(3) The sexual timetable was introduced to this couple in the following way. Since sexual harassment was such a central issue for Janice it was suggested that Janice could exert her feminist needs on six nights of the week when she would not be harassed by Roy for sexual intercourse; however, on one night of the week they would choose to have intercourse when Janice could be a compassionate and understanding wife. As Janice was sensitive about being used sexually the choice of evening was left to her. She selected Saturdays.
They were encouraged to find ways of making Saturday evenings a special and relaxing time, perhaps having an interesting meal, wine, candles, music or whatever as a couple they would enjoy and would make the evening more pleasant. They agreed to try this as an experiment for the next two weeks.

Session 4 (two weeks later)

(4) They both reported that the sex rota had worked well and had taken the pressure off both of them. Janice in particular felt freer and had enjoyed intercourse. The rest of the session was taken up by Janice and Roy exploring together how they related to each other socially. Janice felt that she had many resentments about Roy's anti-social behaviour to which Roy did not respond: instead he would become quiet and sulky. This left her feeling upset or complaining.

Message

(5) The message at the end of this session addressed both of these issues.

(1) They should carry on with the sex rota, having sex on Saturdays as agreed, thus enabling Janice both to fulfil her wish to be a caring wife and an emancipated woman, and enabling Roy to show both his self-control and his affection for Janice in non-sexual ways.

(2) Having seen their interaction in the session we felt that Roy was being very caring of Janice by letting her continually criticise him, otherwise Janice might become very depressed if she had no-one to criticise.

(3) We felt that Janice should continue expressing the anger for both of them and thus help Roy to avoid expressing his own anger.

Session 5 (one month later)

(6) They reported the sex rota still working. However, Janice had changed the evening for sex. It appeared that they had had a major disagreement about whether it was reasonable for a past boyfriend to arrange her birthday treat. The therapist asked them to rehearse their disagreement in-session, allying with Roy to help him state his viewpoint. He angrily said he was 'fed up with compromising'. Janice responded that she was 'fed up with so little excitement' in their social life. The argument was emotionally heated, both stating their positions firmly, and each being upset with the present state of their relationship.

(7) The therapist intervened to change the focus of the discussion, and asked them to consider whether there was an aspect of their social life about which they could develop an acceptable compromise.

Roy mentioned a request of Janice's, that of inviting several friends for Sunday lunch, which he had so far rejected as he preferred a quiet Sunday. They began work on this in session.

Message

(8) (1) To continue with the sex rota, having sex on Saturdays.

(2) To go ahead with planning Sunday lunch, even though we felt that both of them were very fragile at present, Janice about commitment to this relationship and Roy about whether he can share Janice with other people.

Because Roy was not very sociable we wanted Roy to pretend to be sociable during Sunday lunch, even though he may not be feeling so. On all other days he should be unsociable. Janice, for her part, should act lovingly on Saturdays when they were having their evening for sexual intercourse even if she was not feeling loving. For the rest of the time she should be sexually rejecting.

Sessions 6, 7, 8 and 9

The couple continued to use the sexual timetable, which was seen by Janice as freeing her from 'sexual blackmail' and by Roy as a 'good compromise'. The couple brought to these later sessions many issues which were unresolved between them: the question of how much they could share (since they had different earning abilities), different hopes for their social life, how to plan their garden, whether they could afford to have children since their standard of living would drop considerably as Janice was a high earner. On some issues they worked out an acceptable compromise as, for example, the garden where they agreed to divide up the responsibility for designing the layout with Janice designing the front garden and Roy the back garden; on some issues the fact that they were able to feel safe enough to discuss them seemed to be sufficient, and in particular the different earning power of Janice and her fears that Roy was resentful were safely aired.

On discharge they were considering whether to add a second night for sexual intercourse. At follow-up nine months later, Janice described their sex life as 'quite brilliant now'. They had spontaneous sex two or three times a week, which might drop off a little before or during her periods, or if she was feeling particularly low. Roy was very concerned to take her feelings into consideration about not wanting to be pressurised, which she appreciated a great deal. They both felt free to take initiatives which made sex more interesting.

Janice described their marriage now as 'good, a much steadier relationship. We talk to each other more, we seem to consider each other's point of view more and understand much more how the other person may feel or check out in discussion how we feel.' They both felt the relationship was much safer and they were thinking about starting a family in the near future.

10.10.2 Discussion of the interventions

The above case has been presented because it underlines some of the characteristic elements of couples which are suitable for the sexual timetable. It also demonstrates the timing and sensitivity with which the sexual timetable should be introduced to the couple.

This couple presented with severe marital difficulties. For the first two sessions these were treated in session with standard reciprocity negotiation interventions (at **(1)**). The aim was to stay with the problems as presented by the couple and find small immediate and positive ways of altering their interaction. As often happens with couples, the sexual difficulties did not emerge until session 3. In this case Janice herself introduced their difficulties, although with other couples the therapist may well have needed to initiate discussion about their sexual relationship, if it had not already been raised by the couple. As soon as the pattern of their interaction was understood, they were offered the option of using the sexual timetable.

The three key elements were present (see Crowe and Ridley 1986), namely a husband pressurising for sex, a wife increasingly finding herself reluctant to have intercourse and the fact that she had enjoyed sex in the past (at **(2)**).

It is important that the therapist feels confident about the usefulness of the sexual timetable. With most couples the idea of a timetable for sex is a foreign one; therefore the idea can be introduced initially in a tentative way, and it is occasionally best to wait until more conventional approaches have failed (see Sections 10.10 and 11.4.3).

With the above couple we were very aware of Janice's clear articulation of her concerns about the nature of women's sexuality, and wished to take this into account when presenting the idea of a timetable for sex to them both (at **(3)**).

The particular sensitivities of the woman must be taken very seriously into account when designing the approach. As soon as the couple began to use the sexual timetable, and no longer needed to spend time quarrelling about their sexual relationship, they were able to bring to the therapy sessions many of their resentments and unresolved issues (at **(4)** and **(6)**). This is a pattern which we have learned to expect when using the sexual timetable with such couples. It seems that the use of the sexual timetable reduces the tension experienced by the couple and allows for a greater flexibility to explore and find compromises in other areas of their relationship.

At **(5)** the message is used to address both the sexual relationship and the couple's other difficulties.

At **(7)** the therapist is moving away from encouraging expression of resentments towards simpler, more concrete compromises upon which they might build. This move within a session, and within the process of therapy, from expression of resentments to discussions of positive proposals for small concrete changes, entailing a move down the ALI hierarchy (see Section 3.4), should by now be familiar to the reader, but is an essential ingredient when working with couples.

At **(8)** notice again how the task is woven together with a message about their relationship, in this case Janice's commitment to the relationship and Roy's anxiety about sharing her with others. This seems to give meaning to tasks which otherwise might seem somewhat sterile and remote from feelings.

10.10.3 What are the uses of the sexual timetable?

Although controlled trials are only beginning to be carried out, cases such as the one described above have demonstrated a marked improvement in sexual function after the timetable was used.

It may be used as a brief holding measure, while other fundamental relationship problems are dealt with, and may become unnecessary as the couple develop better ways of solving their conflicts. It may also be used to break deadlocks in therapy and provide a face-saving method for the couple to put conflicts 'on ice' for a time.

The timetable is easily understood and quickly instituted. Perhaps it is a good model for learning how to compromise. Perhaps it redistributes power by giving a somewhat submissive woman an opportunity to say 'no'. The apparent power division within marriages presenting this problem may be inferred from the observation that the husband is more active and assertive whilst the wife is submissive and less able to state her needs clearly. In the pre-treatment phase the wife is often labelled frigid or depressed, and thus appears the weaker partner. However, by the wife's sexual reluctance she effectively controls the husband's freedom of action, not by openly confronting him, but by asserting herself within the sexual relationship through a symptom for which she is not able to be held personally responsible.

Thus the timetable can be seen as adjusting the balance of power by means of a jointly negotiated agreement in which the husband voluntarily restricts his sexual demands in return for more regular and predictable sexual relations. The wife increases her visible power within the relationship while allowing an increase in sexual frequency within a clearly defined contract over which they have equal power and control. This allows her to reduce the constant vigilance which the pre-treatment situation imposed on her. There is a consequent increase in mutual trust in most cases where the timetable is running successfully, and this often makes it possible for freer discussions and arguments to take place on other areas of disagreement. Resentments and other undeclared negative feelings now become accessible and their resolution more feasible.

It might be objected that the very fact of using sex as the subject of negotiation in these couples is a male-oriented approach, and that it would be preferable to focus on the female resentments and underlying problems. In answer to this one can only cite the difficulties encountered in couple therapy using resentments as the main focus, both by the present authors and in most of the literature on sexual dysfunction, compared with the relative ease of work using the timetable.

A more systemic hypothesis regarding the usefulness of the sexual timetable might focus on its distance-regulating function (see Section 1.3). Another systemic hypothesis which is often valuable in therapy is the concept that symptoms and problems help to stabilise the relationship or solve another problem which is seen as more threatening. For instance, it might be thought that the conflict over sexual frequency in these couples serves to reassure the woman about her continued attractiveness and the man of his sexual capacity. If they adopt a timetable, however, they have the advantage of conflict resolution without losing the sexual balance represented by the problem; that of the husband demonstrating he has a greater sexual capacity and the woman that she is much desired.

10.10.4 Difficulties encountered in using the sexual timetable

Therapists occasionally question the use of the sexual timetable, as it seems to run counter to the wishes of the woman who is expressly stating that she does not currently enjoy sexual intercourse with her partner. It therefore seems chauvinistic to suggest to her that she should agree to regular weekly sexual intercourse, and feminist therapists may feel that one is colluding with the man in asking the woman to submit to his requests. Our experience is that the female partner is usually ready to accept this suggestion and, perhaps surprisingly, the male may be the reluctant partner. Perhaps the explanation of this is that both are seeking help with sexual difficulties and the woman is liberated by the timetable from unacceptable pressures during the rest of the week, whilst the man is being asked to use restraint except on the sex days. Since they are both looking for ways of improving their sexual relationship, both will usually agree to experiment.

Others may feel that the sexual timetable might appear unnatural and a negation of the spontaneity which should be present in sexual activity. There are in fact many restrictions placed on sex from other sources. Almost all religions prohibit pre-marital and extra-marital sex and some, such as Hindu, Jewish and Muslim religions, put some restrictions even on marital sex according to the phase of the moon, the menstrual cycle or religious festivals. These restrictions are not all negative in their effect on sexual interest: when sex is freely available couples do not necessarily indulge more often, and indeed some couples who have had an active pre-marital sexual relationship may reduce the frequency of sex when it becomes respectable after marriage.

The knowledge that the opportunity for sexual activity is restricted may encourage both partners to relax and enjoy it in the knowledge that it is time-limited. We have already discussed in some detail (Section 9.4) some possible reasons why timetables for other activities may produce greater security for couples. A distant analogy is provided by the familiar psychotherapeutic notion that the restriction of the analytical session to a firmly limited hour permits a freer expression of fantasy and unconscious wishes. In a similar way, couples who have adopted a sexual timetable find that they have a safe time-structure in which both partners can explore their varying needs, and neither has to be on the defensive in case the other takes advantage of the situation to assert unilateral control.

10.10.5 Summary of the negotiated timetable

What has been presented here is a new way of addressing a particular problem within sexual and marital therapy. It is not a replacement for the well known techniques such as sensate focus (Section 11.6.5), marital negotiation (Chapter 5), open expression of feelings (Section 6.5) or systemic interventions (Chapters 7, 8 and 9). It is, however, particularly useful where there is a high male drive for sex and a corresponding reluctance on the female side, but may also be used as an adjunct to therapy of other sexual marital problems, including couples where the male partner is reluctant for sexual intercourse.

As already described in Chapter 9, the timetable has many other uses. The resolution of sexual conflict in these couples often seems to lead to an improvement in the general relationship, and it may be that in the process of negotiating a sexual timetable they have been practising a model for negotiating other difficulties. The compromises they reach in these other areas may be informed by a greater sensitivity to each other's needs, deriving from improved communication in the difficult area of sexual relations. If, as we have suggested, the husband in such couples is usually more dominant and pressurising, and the wife more passive and less able to state her needs, they will both have learned in their negotiations how to state their needs more clearly, to listen to each other more accurately and to take each other's needs more seriously.

Further research is clearly needed on aspects of the negotiated timetable and its efficacy within the field of marital and sexual therapy, and a controlled trial is currently in progress at the Maudsley Hospital comparing the negotiated timetable with sensate focus for couples with male pressure and female reluctance for sex. It is offered here as a new approach with some clinical validity and one worthy of consideration as an adjunct to established therapeutic techniques.

Other specific problems

10.11 Selecting strategies from the behavioural-systems approach for other specific difficulties faced by couples

Couples enter therapy with a great variety of problems. In this chapter so far we have described interventions with couples where one partner was either excessively jealous or depressed, or where the woman was reluctant to have sexual intercourse. These have been described in some detail so that the reader may understand more clearly how the behavioural-systems approach can be used to address these specific issues. There are, however, many other difficulties presented by couples which deserve attention, and for which some specific strategies are more likely to be effective than others.

We go on to indicate some basic guidelines for therapists who are working with couples with some of these other specific problems; these include:

- Couples where sexual or physical abuse has occurred within the family (Section 10.12).
- Possible ways of working with triangular situations (Section 10.13).
- The older relationship (Section 10.14).
- Couples with an alcohol or drug-abuse problem (Section 10.15).
- The separating or divorcing couple and remarriage or further relationships (Section 10.16).

We have not tried to describe ways of working with couples with all possible relationship problems. We have not, for example, described couples where gambling, lying or violence occurs, nor where shoplifting, fetishism or petty crimes are present. For these kinds of problems, as with all of our therapy, we feel that when the problems are under the influence of the relationship, couple therapy can be very helpful (see also Sections 3.4.7 and 3.4.8).

When making choices about how to work with each couple it is helpful to check through the characteristics described in the ALI hierarchy (Chapter 3). One is continually assessing and reviewing the couple's interaction in several key areas. These are

(1) The couple's ability to negotiate.
(2) The freedom with which they communicate or what communication difficulties they face.
(3) Whether their relationship is currently flexible and amenable to change or fixed and rigid.
(4) Whether a symptom is believed to be lodged firmly in one partner.

According to how these four key areas are assessed by the therapist or team, choices will be made about what level in the behavioural-systems hierarchy the therapist will choose to work in the session and what message, task or timetable will be given at the end of each session (Chapter 3).

From experience, the more rigid the couple's interaction and the more fixed the 'symptom' appears, the greater flexibility and creativity are required of the therapist. Because of the nature of the specific difficulty faced and because couples seem to share some common characteristics it is possible to suggest the following general guidelines for therapists when working with couples. However, each couple presents a unique set of circumstances and resources and the therapist therefore will need to adapt and modify his/her interventions according to each couple's actual relationship.

We acknowledge the lack of research regarding these interventions and therefore wish to be modest about any claims of their long term effectiveness.

10.12 *The treatment of couples where sexual (or physical) abuse has occurred with children of the marriage or relationship*

(We are aware that abuse may have occurred within a step-relationship and use the term parent to include step-parents. In order to avoid duplication we have focussed on sexual abuse here, but we think that the interventions described can equally well be used for therapy with couples where physical abuse of a child has occurred.)

The work of assisting the individual child who has been abused is outside the scope of this book. Both individual and group therapy seem to have some therapeutic value in helping the abused child in overcoming this traumatic event in his/her developmental history (see Bentovim and Furniss 1983, Furniss 1983; Will 1983).

With both sexual and physical abuse it is important to work with the full agreement of the court or social service department having responsibility for the case. One should not encourage the couple to think of being rehabilitated as a family unless there is agreement by the appropriate authority, but it might still be appropriate to work with the couple's relationship in its own right where the family cannot be reunited.

We are therefore concerned with work which can be attempted with the parents. There is often a wish by one or both partners to discover whether a reconciliation as a couple is possible. There may also be a desire on the part of one or both parents to work towards a real parental relationship with the abused child or with their other children, and to become 'good enough' parents. Both these aims are achievable in some families, but great care has to be taken to consult the other professionals involved to assess whether the aims are realistic.

One worrying aspect of such couples is often an alarming degree of denial or lack of awareness on the part of either parent regarding the psychological damage to the abused child. This denial or lack of a preparedness to acknowledge the damage to the child is an area which the therapist will be required to help the couple to think about and face up to.

It seems to require of the therapist an ability to convey to the couple a degree of scepticism about instant change, at the same time as working empathically with them and believing in their potential. Therapists are often bemused by such parents, finding it impossible to know whether the parents are being deceitful, are callous or have simply been unable to understand the seriousness of the offence for the child. Such questions cannot be answered, but it seems essential that the parents do become able through the process of therapy to acknowledge their own part in the events surrounding the abuse and to understand the seriousness of its impact on the family member, on their relationship and the total family. The focus of therapy is therefore upon two areas: first the couple relationship and second their ability to be responsible parents who ensure that appropriate boundaries are kept between them and their children.

10.12.1 Helping the couple discuss together the impact of the offence on family relationships in-session

For the couple to make progress it seems essential that they are enabled to talk together in-session and to use specific times together between sessions to discuss the impact of the sexual abuse upon their relationship and upon all family members. Other aspects of the couple relationship may also need to be reviewed and modified, for example in the case of the couple described below, where therapy included helping them with sexual difficulties.

Many such couples have rarely if ever discussed together the actual details of the sexual abuse and the impact of this upon their relationship, upon the child/ren in question, and the family members. Many therapists are themselves reluctant to bring these issues out into the open for honest discussion. Therapists and couples are faced with a possible collusion of 'not noticing' the offence because it is so painful and difficult to discuss. This is the main hurdle to be overcome in therapy: the therapist must find empathic, gentle but firm ways of ensuring that the couple discuss in detail and with feeling the impact of the sexual abuse on themselves and their children. This is likely to take some time and probably requires the therapist to take the lead in talking about the sexual abuse.

Our experience suggests that the offending parent may appear impervious or self-assured, insisting that any damage has already been repaired, for several sessions. When this happens the therapist will need to be patient, supportive and persistent in order to establish that both parents are appropriately aware of the enormity of the offence and the difficulties faced in rehabilitating the family. It is a complex position for the therapist because it requires both a non-censorial approach and an open ability to help the father (or the offending partner) to confront the nature of the abuse, and to understand its damaging impact upon all of their relationships.

Example 10H
(This couple have already been described in Example 7C in order to explain the concept of alliances, boundaries and hierarchies.)

Tim, the father, had previously admitted the offence of having had intercourse with Merryl, his 18-year-old daughter, over a two-year period, and of having a relationship of an intimate sexual nature with Sandra at about the same time, and had been in prison for one year.

Tim's attitude in the early therapy sessions with his wife was that he had 'paid his price', and the offence should be forgotten and the family should be allowed to get back to normal as quickly as possible. Tina, his wife, seemed to want to go along with this except for the fact that two of the daughters did not want their father to return to live at home.

The therapist, who had the support of an observation team, tried to keep constantly in mind the question of the sexual abuse, and its impact upon every family member. During the first few sessions progress was slow, but by the seventh session Tina was able to talk more openly and to tell Tim directly about her disbelief and bitter disappointment at his having had a sexual relationship with Merryl. She also expressed feelings of anger against her daughter who she felt had taken over her role. At the same time, Tina was very ambivalent about this as she had rarely enjoyed sexual intercourse with Tim. She expressed strong feelings of guilt about this, and said that she thought she understood why her husband had found the teenage daughter sexually attractive; and that she held herself partly to blame because of her inability in the past to enjoy sexual intercourse with Tim.

Tim for his part constantly reassured his wife that he did find her attractive and wished very much that she could see herself as he saw her, which was sexually desirable. He wanted her to take more care of her physical appearance and be more flirtatious and sensual in his presence. However, he would not enter into any discussion about his relationship with his daughter except to say that it could not happen again.

By now the therapist was beginning to feel more hopeful about the rehabilitation of Tim with the family. The observation team on the other hand were quite pessimistic as Tim did not seem to have yet accepted his personal responsibility for having sexually abused Merryl over a two-year period. When this was raised for discussion in the team the therapist, somewhat defensively, emphasised that he had been concentrating upon helping the couple with their relationship and in particular with their sexual relationship, which was improving.

Tim had been pressurising Tina for more frequent intercourse and the couple had agreed to use a sexual timetable whereby they would have sex on two agreed days at his probation hostel, and Tim accepted that he would not pressurise Tina during the rest of the week (see Section 10.10.3). They were also using sensate focus exercises (see Section 11.6.5), as well as a timetable for discussion (see Section 9.9). They had expressed some satisfaction that their relationship was improving as a result and it was clear that this was so.

The couple were now more able to share their feelings with each other, and their sexual relationship had begun to improve so that Tina was no longer so rejecting or passive during intercourse.

After discussion with the team, the therapist agreed that in spite of the many improvements in the couple's relationship, Tim was still quite flippant about the impact of his offence upon his daughters and he was still insisting that they could be a happy family again, if only the authorities would allow him to go back home. It was decided that the therapist should once more confront Tim with his offence, and ask him if he yet understood why we were all unhappy about his returning to the family home, even though his relationship with Tina was improving.

Session 8

The therapist approached this session by asking the couple to review what they felt had contributed to the situation in which Tim had turned to his daughter for sexual satisfaction.

After a little hesitation the couple discussed together how Tim had slowly become isolated from Tina and the children. Tim described how lonely and miserable he had felt as he became a stranger in the family. Tina said that after the birth of the children Tim had seemed not to understand her feelings, and rows over the children had become a regular feature in their relationship.

The therapist then asked Tim directly how he now felt about having had intercourse with his daughter over two years. He suddenly became very sad and said that he was still finding it hard to accept that he had indeed done this. He said that he could become very angry when he read about other fathers who had done the same, and felt puzzled that if he could be so angry with others, how could he have done this himself to his own daughter? For the first time in therapy he dropped his flippant approach and expressed remorse and sadness.

Having begun to talk in this more open way the couple went on to use the session less defensively to talk with the therapist about their difficulties, to share their very mixed and perplexing feelings of disbelief, guilt and shame, and to consider what needed to be done to build a new relationship with the children which would protect them (Section 10.12.3).Tim had also found a job, which gave him a renewed sense of his worth and hope that he could now contribute more to the stability of his wife and family.

After some months of therapy, and with the agreement of the court, the social workers and the children's hospital which was treating the two daughters, Tim was allowed to return home, with continued social work monitoring of the welfare of all the children.

After the team had ensured that the therapist did not collude with the couple's pretence that everything was fine simply because they could talk to each other about the sexual abuse, they were eventually able to discuss the changes which needed to be made in their joint parenting.

Therapists who also have difficulty in being both supportive and confronting the offence directly may obtain support and encouragement from an observation team or supervisor (see Chapter 12) and such supervision will also help the therapist to avoid being overpersuaded by the couple's optimistic denial of future problems.

Such couples seem most helped if there is a court order requiring that they seek marital therapy: otherwise there may be quite a high risk of their dropping out of therapy. Where couples persevere it seems that rehabilitation may be possible.

10.12.2 The couple as parents: helping them to find ways of ensuring that the sexual abuse will never occur again

This part of the therapy can either follow the work described above or be done in parallel. The therapist can assess how rapidly the couple are able to move towards more appropriate parenting.

The therapist should help the couple negotiate in-session what can be done by them both, as parents, to ensure that the offence will never occur again, and set homework tasks which will continue the work done in-session. This may involve discussion of their daily routines, their communication patterns, their joint parenting skills, the alliances which need to be changed within the family, the role allocation between the couple, their authority, and so on. Each couple may have a particular pattern of interaction which must be modified to ensure the safety of the child; one is trying to encourage the couple to adopt the role of 'watch-dog' to safeguard their children.

As already mentioned, Tim and Tina were asked to spend one evening regularly together discussing how they could continue to co-operate in parenting their four children even though Tim was still living at a probation hostel. Often intensive work is needed between them as a couple in order to help them become more able to act as a united parental pair (see Section 7.3.6). Powerful resentments and fears are likely to be uncovered; their sexual life may well have become non-existent or indeed may always have been difficult. Sensate focus, sexual timetables, etc., are available for work in this area (see also Chapter 11).

There is a delicate balance to be kept between, on the one hand, ensuring that the offence and its implications are openly discussed and understood by both partners, and on the other hand focussing on the couple's own needs to develop a more intimate and trusting relationship which will help them become a more united and effective parental pair. In our experience, both of these areas are essential if progress is to be made. The therapist's attitude of scepticism and empathy is an important ingredient.

10.12.3 Involving family members

Additional therapeutic work may be necessary between the parents and their children which can be attempted by bringing children into therapy for a while. (See also Sections 2.2.4 and 7.3.6.)

10.12.4 Messages, tasks and timetables

Take-home tasks should make clear distinctions between their joint role as parents and their own relationship as a couple. Helping the couple to work on their relationship, keeping firm boundaries, finding time to discuss, to relax together, to give each other space, as well as encouraging mutual sharing of emotion, may all be part of helping such couples become more adequate as a couple and as parents. These may first be rehearsed in-session, then used as take-home tasks which are reviewed in the next session (see Chapter 9).

10.12.5 Involving the social worker and other agencies

Usually there are other agencies working with the couple and the family members. Where this is happening it is essential that they should be closely involved in the work being done and should be in general agreement with it. This may mean being available to attend case conferences and requires some degree of commitment by all concerned to ensure that regular contact is kept. It is particularly important to prevent any splits or disagreements between family members being reflected in the way the various therapists and agencies work together (Furniss 1983).

10.12.6 Outcome of therapy

Experience suggests that many such families are desperate to keep the family intact and are prepared to work hard to do so. At the same time a high level of denial, or lack of awareness of the impact of abuse on a child, leads us to be cautious about any rapid results. We feel it is necessary to be tentative, among ourselves and in discussion with the couple, about the long term outcome even where we think we have seen some considerable improvement in parenting skills and in the couple's own relationship. It has to be remembered that for many families in the end rehabilitation proves impossible, and the only solution is for either the offending parent or the abused child to remain away from the family. At present the criteria for making this decision are rather unclear, and we have to look at each case on its own merits. Often the decision can only be made after an attempt at rehabilitation has been made and the results reported back to a case conference involving social workers, probation officers, therapists and others. Rehabilitation remains perhaps the ideal outcome, if the goals described in Sections 10.12.2 to 10.12.5 can be achieved, and it is hoped that the long-term outcome for the child may be improved by this approach.

10.13 Triangles

Triangles include a wide range of phenomena presented by couples in which a third party is involved as part of the difficulty (including child sexual and physical abuse, see Section 10.12, which have been treated separately here). Triangles can involve a real or imagined affair; one partner's deep involvement with work; a loyalty to parents or children in which 'leaving home', in either family of origin or of procreation, has not been successfully accomplished (Haley 1980); an exclusive relationship with children or a friend; or indeed any interaction in which a third party is inappropriately competing or intervening in the relationship of the couple or is resented by one partner.

Of course what is inappropriate is impossible to define. A new-born baby may appropriately take much of the mother's time and attention; one couple may find this acceptable, for another it may become a source of distress. Regular weekend visits by a husband to his aged mother may be accepted by one wife and be a source of intense irritation to another. Many couples are aware of the discomfort triangular situations may cause their relationship, but are uncertain as to what, if anything, can be done.

Occasionally one partner may be involved in an affair which has not been declared to the partner (see Section 11.4.6) but still seeks therapy to improve the couple relationship and asks that the therapist keep this information confidential. This does present the therapist with some ethical difficulties. Even so, given the preparedness of both partners to work on their relationship some improvements may be possible.

As already stated, couples vary a great deal in how they respond to the possibility of one partner being deeply involved with another person in a triangular situation. One woman, whose husband had become involved in a relationship with another man, did not seem to mind the other relationship but was greatly upset that her husband had ceased to find time to be with her. When, as a result of therapy, he made a greater effort to be with her and to show her he enjoyed her company her worry about his relationship with the other man diminished.

Other partners have extreme difficulty in coping with an affair and are unable to sleep, eat or concentrate and may lose any sense of their own worth. They may worry a great deal about what the partner is doing in the affair, or feel guilty that they themselves must have done something to make this happen. Yet others may choose to pay the partner back by going off and deliberately sleeping with one or several partners in an attempt to 'make it equal'. Jealousy, rivalry, depression or a wish to get back at the rival may all play a part in the response of the partner.

Where the person or persons triangled in are family members or outside activities the responses are likely to be complicated (see Section 10.12). Felicity was able to say to Frank (Example 9C) that she thought that the union Frank worked for was his mistress, and therapy helped this couple to make choices between the competing demands which took them away from each other. With Penny and Paul (Example 9A), Penny felt that Paul had only married her in order to provide a home for his son Roger and consequently felt very excluded by Paul and Roger's relationship. She had then become depressed and had expressed suicidal ideas. For Alan and Jemima (Example 10B), Jemima's involvement with her own parents and their children had contributed to his intense feelings of jealousy in which he accused her of having sexual relationships with many of their friends.

Thinking systemically and looking for the positive function of the triangular relationship one can hypothesise a variety of functions. It might be that of a 'distance regulator' maintaining emotional or physical intimacy within the couple at a 'safe' level, or on the other hand it might bring excitement into a somewhat stale relationship as occasionally seems to happen with affairs. It may be being used as a lever which enables the partners to review their commitment to each other and make choices as to whether they want to continue in a permanent relationship together. When the triangle includes parents it can be said to be maintaining links with the family of origin at the expense of the couple; others might wish to hypothesise unresolved oedipal wishes.

Triangular elements of some sort are almost inevitable in most relationships, and it is only when they interfere seriously with a couple's relationship that they require therapy.

10.13.1 Redrawing the boundaries around the triangulated couple by focussing on their interaction in-session

Whatever type of triangle is present, an essential focus of therapy will be to attempt to draw a clearer boundary around the couple's relationship, so that they develop a greater sense of joint identity. This process should be seen as gradual. Interventions which are likely to assist are:

- In-session discussion of things they share in common (see Sections 8.5 and 9.8).
- In-session discussion of what would need to change in their relationship to distance them from the third party, followed by negotiations for some small positive changes.
- In-session discussion about what is an acceptable relationship with the third party.
- In-session discussion about what is missing in their relationship and how this can be changed (ensuring that the third party is not brought into the discussion).
- In-session discussion about how they would each manage if their present relationship were to end.

10.13.2 Messages, timetables or tasks for use with triangular situations
(see Chapter 9)

As already described, there are many ways in which messages, timetables and tasks can be used in therapy. When working with triangular situations the following guidelines may be helpful. (Although we have used examples of extra-marital affairs in this section, the guidelines are also relevant in other situations where triangles exist, such as where one partner has an intrusive mother or is overinvolved with a child.)

- Emphasise the couple's interaction rather than the third party.
- Design a message which reframes the affair as having a positive function in their relationship, such as:

  We think that Susan's affair with Trevor has been very useful to you both because it has alerted Michael to the fact that Susan has felt very isolated because of his being away from the house so much. It has reminded Susan just how hard Michael works in order to provide the family with security and material comfort.

- Where the third party may be hypothesised to be protecting the couple from discord, depression or an unhappy relationship this may need to be underlined in a paradoxical message to the couple.
- Other hypotheses may involve the need to protect the couple from boredom, or to provide excitement or a distraction from other pressing problems.
- Design tasks which bring into the couple relationship some of the elements which may be found in the affair, such as excitement, secrecy or seduction: the couple may be asked to make a plan for an activity or trip which the involved partner will keep secret from his/her lover.
- Where letters have been exchanged as part of the affair, it may be helpful to include the writing of letters between the couple which are to be kept secret from the lover.

A guiding principle is then to refocus the work on the interaction of the couple and find creative ways to explore their difficulties and enhance their relationship. A key to the missing elements of the couple's relationship may well be found in the nature of the impact of the triangular relationship upon the couple. For example if the mother is triangled in and is felt to be more caring of the husband than the wife, then the couple may need to find ways of being more attentive and caring towards each other.

10.13.3 Grieving over their mutual loss

Where an affair has had a major effect upon the life of the couple, and as part of the renewing of the relationship the third person is to be 'given up' this may be experienced as a severe loss to the involved partner, whilst for the other partner the loss induced by the affair may be that of trust in the erring partner or of an ideal such as the innocence or exclusiveness of the couple's relationship.

Where a partner has been too involved in work to share the early upbringing of children, or where a mother was so involved with children that the couple relationship was sacrificed, these are losses which can be openly discussed and the feelings of disappointment or regret can be shared. In this way the therapist can help the couple to recognise the mutuality of their losses.

10.13.4 Using the paradox for affairs

It would appear that couples often expect therapists to chastise the partner who has had the affair, and it may be for this reason that the paradox sometimes has a major impact upon such couples. A paradox which outlines the benefits the couple may have experienced from the triangular relationship and a suggestion not to change might therefore be considered.

10.13.5 A word of caution

Therapists must be careful not to impose upon the couple their own value judgements about affairs or over-close involvement of relatives and other third parties in their relationship (see Section 2.4.3.5). If sufficient effort is put into assisting the couple to discuss the detail of their relationship they may work towards a compromise solution which fits their own needs and value orientation (see also Chapter 12).

10.14 Issues facing the older relationship

This is an area of work presenting new challenges as increasing numbers of older couples seek therapy. Their difficulties often revolve around the response to a particular life event, and may include:

* Children leaving home and the impact this has upon the couple's relationship (the empty nest, see Section 9.7).
* The need to make decisions about how to support elderly relatives in their old age, or how to cope with the death of a close relative.
* Concerns over grown-up children, their circumstances and the impact of these upon the older relationship.
* Changes relating to advancing years such as sexual adjustments, illness or work related concerns.
* Retirement or redundancy and its impact upon the couple.
* Anxieties about facing the future together as an 'old couple'.
* Questions regarding the nature of older relationships and whether they are experienced as boring by the partners.

10.14.1 Interrupting the ritual dances of older relationships

Many couples seem to have developed a comfortable relationship which has been satisfactory for the child-rearing years, but as they begin to face the future without their children and with responsibilities of a different nature, their pattern of interaction no longer seems adequate to the task. One can conceptualise the situation as one in which the couple ask themselves whether they want to 'remarry' and face the future together. In order to do this, however, they must first find out more about each other. It is as though they have coasted along on the knowledge derived from their early relationship which is no longer adequate, or has become ritualised and rigid. Alternatively, they may have seen less of each other during the years when the children were at home, and the absence of the children can throw them more into each other's company. The same change may result from retirement, and both situations can put a strain on the couple's relationship because of more time being spent together.

Because of the ritualised nature of such relationships it is often useful to:

- Prescribe time together in a new environment.
- Suggest tasks in which they surprise each other with something new every day.
- Suggest they should 'catch each other doing something nice'. These should be small everyday things, such as a wife saying to her husband 'I did notice that you gave me a hug when you came in from work', or a husband saying 'I like the way you have tidied up the store cupboard, it means I can find things more easily'.
- Ask the couple to identify their own rituals and find ways of varying them. For example, if the woman notes that the man always made the morning cup of tea, then she should occasionally initiate making morning tea.
- Suggest a timetable for discussion in which the couple agree not to go over old ground.

Most couples quickly catch on to rituals which they have developed and, although often blind to their own rituals, are also keen observers of each other's. This can be turned into a helpful game between them, making it easier to break the mould. By the time such couples come to therapy they are usually very ready to make modifications. However,

- Where a couple have developed a very rigid way of interaction a paradoxical message may be necessary in which good reasons should be given for them to 'stay just as you are'.

10.14.2 The sexual life of the older couple
(see also Section 11.5.1)

Much could be written about the sexual life of older couples (Masters and Johnson 1970). Suffice it to say here that couples may need help to make adjustments to the changing tempo of their sexual life. Discussion, negotiation and experimentation seem to be the key to greater satisfaction in the older couple's sexual life. Some couples need the therapist's support to acknowledge their needs sexually. Standard Masters and Johnson techniques can be considered, but there may be a wish to bring greater excitement and novelty into their sex life. Ideas such as taking a bath or a shower together, mutual massage with scented oils, having sex in front of a warm fire, or exploring each other's bodies using body paints can all be considered as helpful and possible for the older couple. Sex and age are sometimes seen as incompatible, but these taboos can be modified by a creative therapist. However, if a couple feel that they are both unenthusiastic about sex then it may be necessary to help them adjust to the lack of sex in their lives by encouraging them to find other satisfying ways of showing their affection for each other.

Where illness or disability is evident, then couples should be helped to express any sadness they feel about these changes and then to explore what adjustments are necessary. Whatever the specific problem, the sexual needs of the older couple should not be ignored; a change in tempo, approach, or who takes the initiative may all enhance an older couple's sexual life.

10.15 Couples with an alcohol or drug-abuse problem

Alcohol or drug abuse present a therapist with some particular difficulties. The first, and in some ways the most necessary, one may be to help the couple to assess the nature and severity of the dependency upon alcohol or drugs. Where the dependency or addiction is considered to be extreme and relatively uninfluenced by the couple's interaction, it may be necessary to refer the couple to an appropriate agency such as Alcoholics Anonymous or Alanon, or to a local unit specialising in drug dependency. Couple therapy is not likely to be effective if one or both partners is heavily involved with drugs or alcohol. Couple therapy can commence after the dependency has moderated.

Where the dependency is mild to moderate it is useful to work with any other agency who may be helping the couple or individual, and a mixed approach involving both individual and relationship therapy may have the best chance of being effective.

In other couples, alcohol or drugs play an important part in their relationship. These couples often seem to have a complementary relationship of the saint and sinner or the nurse and patient; there is often an intense (almost passionate) though painful relationship between the couple (see Example 4C). The therapist may well need to work from a systems perspective and consider:

- What positive function the symptom performs in the relationship.
- How the complementary nature of the relationship can be connoted positively.
- Whether conflict avoidance is an issue within this couple, and what would happen to the couple if the symptom was removed (i.e. the feared consequences).
- Whether the alcohol or drugs are performing a similar function to that of an affair (see Section 10.13.2).

Therapy with such a couple may well revolve around finding ways for the couple to change their relationship into one which is good enough without the symptom. This is likely to mean altering the complementary nature of their relationship. It might mean helping the submissive partner to become more assertive and independent, at the same time helping the dominant partner to be less aggressive and accept some support from the partner (see Examples 8A and 10D).

They may also need to learn to argue over trivial issues (Section 8.2), to find activities, some of which they can share (Section 9.8), and to find others which they encourage each other to pursue separately (see Section 9.9). The therapist may have to put quite a lot of energy into this work in the beginning stages to reframe the problem as joint and the solution for which can best be shared.

10.16 Separating and divorcing couples and couples in second relationships

We would encourage therapists to be careful about accepting statements from couples that their relationship is over until their difficulties have been explored in some depth in the therapist's presence. Some couples do seem to use the question of separation as a means of seeking help for their relationship, and we have experience of seeing couples move back from the brink of separation to develop a more viable relationship (see Section 8.4.6). It is equally important that the therapist does not make any decision for the couple, no matter how hard one or both partners seek his/her advice (see Section 2.4.3.5).

Therapy with couples who are thinking about separation usually means helping the couple to negotiate and communicate effectively with each other, and the skills outlined in Chapters 5 and 6 become very necessary for both therapist and couple. If a couple can negotiate from a position of some willingness to listen to the other's viewpoint and to offer some alternative ways forward, then the couple are likely to be able to make their decision.

If it becomes clear that the couple are genuinely on the verge of separation or divorce, help can be given in some key areas which are a little similar to bereavement counselling (Parkinson 1986). When there are children, then the focus can be how they will continue to be good enough parents to their children after they have split up.

Example 10I
Adrian and Grace P, both in their late thirties, with three children Alan (14), James (12) amd Susan (10), had been separated for four years. They presented the main problem as Grace's difficulty in getting on with their middle child, James. The marriage had broken due to Adrian's affair with a female colleague, with whom he was now living. He visited the children conscientiously each week and maintained quite a strong parental interest. He took almost too much responsibility for Grace's wellbeing as Grace was increasingly taking on a 'patient' role while Adrian became the therapist. Grace remained angry with

him for his desertion and the three children had taken up different positions on the issue. Alan refused to meet father's girlfriend or to visit his flat; James was a regular visitor there and seemed to act as father's advocate when mother criticised father; and Susan visited father's flat occasionally, but did not take sides between her parents.

Therapy involved the whole family (but not father's girlfriend) on the first two visits and the couple alone on the final visit. After some structural moves confirming the parental pair as the source of authority, suggestions were made for Grace to organise the children's activities, such as a dishwashing rota and bedtime, more tightly. This also had the effect of helping the elder son, Alan, to relinquish some of his role as a husband-substitute supporting Grace. The therapist supported mother in controlling James' sometimes disruptive behaviour in the session, and suggested that she and James could find something they would enjoy doing together: they chose painting and wallpapering as the joint activity they had previously enjoyed. Susan was praised as the diplomat and peacemaker.

By the third session, when most of the behaviour problems had settled and a new acceptance was occurring, Adrian began to complain of Alan's negative attitude to him and his new partner. The therapist then suggested that Alan, at 14, should have the right to make his own independent decision on where he spent his time and discouraged Adrian from pressurising him. Grace talked about her earlier 'over-dependence' on Adrian, and her new-found self-reliance. Adrian emerged from this last session in less of a 'helper' role and more able to live his own life while taking appropriate levels of parental responsibility for the children.

10.16.1 Discussion of the above case

This case illustrates a number of points with regard to couples who are separated but continue a co-parenting relationship.

(1) If the parents can negotiate and reach a successful agreement on managing the children's behaviour, that behaviour will usually settle down, and the 'parental child' can take a more age-appropriate role.
(2) The task of therapy at one level is to redraw the boundaries of both couple relationships (the co-parenting one and the father's new relationship) and to make it clear where responsibilities begin and end.
(3) If the 'incompetent' partner can become more self-reliant the couple can reduce the excessive interdependence.
(4) Children should not be pressurised to visit or not to visit the absent parent.
(5) Older children should be allowed more freedom to make decisions than younger children.
(6) The therapist should not make value-judgments supporting any member of the family in their individual views of the rights and wrongs of what other family members are doing.

10.16.2 Other interventions which can be used with separating couples

- Review the good and bad times they had together as an aspect of the bereavement process of separation.
- Facilitate any grieving which needs to be done over the loss of this relationship.
- Discuss in-session, and timetable meetings between the partners, to consider their future joint parenting.
- Help them to discuss finances, property, custody and access.

Experience suggests that focussing on these three key areas of ongoing parenting, reviewing the 'good times' and grieving for the loss of the relationship may facilitate a separation which minimises the rancour and resentment and may encourage the couple to continue their joint parenting more successfully.

10.16.3 Difficulties in couples who are in second marriages or similar relationships

Where one or both partners have had previous marriages or partners and the current relationship has run into difficulties, the specific work which can be done may be similar to working with triangles (see Section 10.13). Boundaries must be clarified around the present couple and consideration given to what factors may be affecting the present relationship. From a systemic viewpoint, the timescale of the previous relationship may be interfering with the present relationship and this may need to be highlighted. For example, in a marriage of seven years' duration where the previous marriage ended after seven years, anxiety about the current relationship may be heightened. Such hidden agendas can be approached through the formulation given to the couple at the end of therapy.

Other factors such as how often the previous partner is seen, fantasies about the past relationship, links with the children from the earlier relationship, holidays together, financial arrangements, may all need to be reviewed in-session (preferably by a decentred therapist) in order to restructure these relationships and to help those involved to be realistic about each other.

The pace at which the new relationship can develop may depend upon how the couple negotiate the management of such relationships with children and previous partners (see Example 10I). There may also be a general reluctance or hesitancy about any commitment to a new relationship because of the fear that things will go wrong again.

Work with such couples is often better in a decentred mode (see Chapter 4) where these emotional and practical questions can be faced. See for example Paul and Penny (Example 9A), a second marriage for Paul who had a son Roger from his first marriage. Penny, his second wife, who had not been married before, began to feel that the marriage was merely a convenience for Paul which allowed him to provide a home for Roger at the weekend. Paul and Roger were very close and Penny became increasingly depressed about feeling pushed out and used by her husband. Much of the therapy revolved around helping Paul to allow Penny to develop a good relationship with Roger at the same time as encouraging Penny to become more assertive within the relationship. Paul, who had kept Penny at a distance by joking and teasing, was also helped to allow her to come closer to him by taking her more seriously.

10.17 Conclusion

We have described some specific problems in detail and others in broader outline in order to show how the behavioural-systems approach can be used. We hope to encourage therapists to consider alternative ways of intervening if their usual approach does not effect any change. In particular we suggest that therapists can select specific strategies from different parts of the ALI hierarchy to match the particular relationship difficulties observed, and can also vary the intervention style as the couple relationship changes: moving up the hierarchy where the couple seem more rigid and unresponsive to therapy and down the hierarchy as the couple develop greater flexibility.

Chapter 11

Sexual relationships: disorders of interest, arousal and orgasm

11.1 Introduction

We have included a chapter on sexual dysfunction in this book, partly because it is something that all couple therapists should have a basic understanding of, and partly to counteract the frequent tendency in other writing and teaching for sexual problems to be treated separately and differently from general relationship problems. We are not attempting here to give an authoritative and full account of the nature and treatment of sexual dysfunctions, such as can be found in Bancroft (1989) and at a more practical level in Hawton (1985) and Gillan (1987). Our aim is to make those who deal mainly with the general relationship aware of the importance of sexual aspects, and the ways in which the two areas interact, so that they may develop greater confidence in using a more integrated approach to therapy with couples.

In Chapter 3 we described the hierarchy of interventions in the therapy of relationship problems, beginning with the simpler forms of negotiation and ending with more ingenious systemic or paradoxical interventions. While we are working on the general relationship in a couple with a sexual problem we would follow the hierarchy of interventions as in any other couple, according to the degree of individual focus and the difficulty in producing change. Thus, the more a problem is defined as 'his problem' or 'her difficulty' with sex, the more the therapist has to use ingenuity to move the couple's thinking to focus on the relationship, and this is best done by the use of systemic interventions. However, sexual problems are also to some extent and in some cases physical in origin, and in that way they resemble the kinds of illness which we have to accept as unable to be helped by couple therapy (Section 3.4.14). Our approach then has to be one which advances on two fronts, and in this work we have to be constantly aware of both individual and relationship aspects of the problem.

11.1.1 The sexual relationship

The sexual relationship is a central aspect of many intimate relationships, whether these involve marriage, cohabitation or other looser forms of tie. Our clinic is available to all sorts of couples, and we would make little distinction as to the kind of couple we are ready to treat. The presence of psychiatric illness, physical handicap or mental impairment would not make it impossible to treat a couple complaining of a sexual problem. We have also helped gay couples of both sexes, although this is rather a rare type of referral. As the typical couple we see is hetero-sexual and non-handicapped we will be writing mainly with reference to this type of case, but the whole chapter may be read, *mutatis mutandis*, as referring to the other, non-typical cases.

The sexual relationship is usually thought of as consisting of three components, those of desire, arousal and orgasm, each of which con-tains both physical and emotional responses. There is, however, a wide range of variation in the way that individuals respond within each of these elements and to the varying needs of the partner. Misunder-standings can easily arise when the physical and emotional aspects of sexual arousal are out of phase between the two partners. For example, a man may find a woman particularly desirable when she is angry with him and therefore become more aroused; whilst the woman's anger may prevent her from becoming aroused and his advances may therefore be rejected. Another may prefer sex to be passionate and serious whilst the partner may feel that sex should be fun and light-hearted. One such couple had great difficulty in coming to terms with their differences in desire and arousal. It was only after the woman had had an affair with another man and the couple entered therapy that she began to be prepared to take sex more seriously and the husband was able to be more light-hearted about it.

It is equally quite common for individuals to vary in pace and intensity in experiencing orgasm, and indeed statistics suggest that 40% of women do not experience orgasm during intercourse, though they may well experience orgasm through other forms of stimulation (Sanders 1985).

In spite of these great variations between individuals and couples there are many social, religious and moral pressures which suggest that individuals should conform to stereotypes. We try in the clinic to help people to resist this pressure from society, but we have to work within the limits imposed by reality, and some (especially religious) pressures have to be respected in the way we can help individual couples. In par-ticular, the ban on masturbation in some religions will modify the degree to which we can use this activity as a homework exercise in sexual therapy.

11.1.2   The interaction between sex and the general relationship

Not all emotionally intimate relationships are necessarily sexual in nature, but for the majority of couple relationships sex is important, for many reasons. Sex is often part of the initial attraction and the sexual urge may remain as a cohesive force holding them together. Indeed, when things go wrong in the general aspects of the relationship, sex can often have the effect of putting them right, at least temporarily.

Good sex, however, may also depend on the quality of the relationship, and many relationship problems can damage sex, as we will be illustrating in this chapter. Resentment, lack of trust, anger (especially if it is suppressed) and tension can all tend to spoil sex. More subtle alterations in the balance can also upset the sexual side, for example when a man is afraid of his partner and does everything to placate her, or when a woman lives in fear of her husband's uncontrollable temper.

On the other hand, the lack of good sex can affect the rest of the relationship, and many men and women become irritable and frustrated under these circumstances. The physical expression of warmth may become increasingly inhibited, perhaps because each partner feels that physical contact brings the sexual difficulties to the fore, and a damaging spiral may ensue in which each attempt to make physical contact is rebuffed because of sexual difficulties, which in turn increases the level of frustration and dissatisfaction within the relationship.

Couples often find great difficulty in talking about sex, and this general 'no-go' area can lead to poor communication in which each builds up untested assumptions about the other's attitude to it. Thus vicious circles develop in which the sexual problem becomes perpetuated, and with the poor communication produces a problem from which the couple cannot extricate themselves. Sex then interacts with other aspects of the relationship, and each can adversely affect the other.

11.1.3 Sex: a physical event

Sex is a physical event which involves complicated physiological functions in both partners. The mechanisms of erection and ejaculation, of lubrication and orgasm, are part of the physiology of the individual, and can be interfered with by various medications, or by diseases which affect nerves or blood vessels (see Sections 11.5 to 11.5.6).

11.1.4 Sex: a psychological event

Sex is also an individual psychological event, and the attitudes of the individual, his/her earlier experience, anxiety, tiredness and overwork can all have a major damaging effect on sex. A woman who has been sexually abused as a child may anticipate sexual intercourse with varying degrees of anxiety or horror. One man who had been beaten regularly by his mother had difficulty in having sex with his wife if she touched him with her hands, so that sexual therapy had to be centred round developing sexual approaches in which the wife's hands were not involved.

Many women at the present time are insisting that they be seen as whole persons rather than sexual objects and such a woman may experience her partner's demands as sexual harassment (see also Sections 11.3.2 and 11.3.3).

11.1.5 Integrated approach

For these reasons it is important to consider sex in the context of both the relationship and the individual partners. It would obviously be just as wrong to work only on the physical side of sex in a couple whose sexual problem is based on resentment and lack of trust as it would be to work exclusively with the relationship if a man has impotence caused by nerve damage. An integrated approach is what we try to practise and teach, and in it we use treatment methods which involve both the relationship and the individual.

11.1.6 The language of sex: matter-of-fact presentation

The material in this chapter is deliberately presented in a direct and explicit way. We often find that the sexual aspect of a relationship is avoided by both therapist and couple for a variety of reasons, not least of which may be the therapist's own lack of confidence in understanding and talking about the sexual relationship. We present the material explicitly so as to encourage therapists to familiarise themselves with the physical and psychological aspects of the sexual relationship. In this way we hope to help them to feel comfortable using the language, whether in exploring the couple's sexual relationship or explaining details of sexuality or sexual homework exercises to couples.

It is particularly important that the therapist should be able to help the couple overcome any embarrassment they may feel in talking about their sexual relationship. Inhibitions in this regard can be hidden by couples for many years, and the therapist should feel both comfortable and competent in helping them to explore this sometimes forbidden territory. In this way the therapist can move between working with the couple's general relationship and their sex life with greater ease, and is in a better position to help them to communicate together on this vital and intimate area.

11.2 The distinction between problems of desire and problems of arousal and orgasm

When Masters and Johnson (1970) produced their pioneering classification of sexual dysfunctions, they were mainly concerned with problems of function: thus they described impotence (loss of erection), premature and delayed ejaculation, anorgasmia (absence of orgasm), vaginismus (muscle spasm preventing penetration) and dyspareunia (pain during intercourse).

Kaplan (1974, 1979) wrote about disorders of desire, arousal and orgasm, and suggested that disorders of desire (loss of sexual interest) were for the most part caused by individual problems or blocks requiring intensive psychotherapy. We would go along with Kaplan's classification

Table 11.1 Classification of sexual dysfunctions

Aspect of sexuality affected	Women	Men
Interest	Impaired sexual interest	Impaired sexual interest
Arousal	Impaired sexual arousal	Erectile dysfunction or impotence
Orgasm	Orgasmic dysfunction	Premature ejaculation Delayed ejaculation Ejaculatory pain
Other types of dysfunction	Vaginismus Dyspareunia Sexual phobias	Dyspareunia Sexual phobias

for the most part, but where she advocated individual psychotherapy to get rid of the blocks to sexual desire and satisfaction, we would in most cases look first to the relationship for the origins of the lack of interest.

Probably the most satisfactory practical classification of sexual problems is that of Hawton (1985), shown in Table 11.1. We will be covering all these forms of dysfunction in this chapter, but the priority here is to make a distinction between the two main types of sexual problem, namely problems of interest and problems of actual function. Clearly many of those with sexual problems will complain of both specific dysfunction and loss of desire. However, it is useful in therapy to distinguish between the two aspects, since their management is often rather different. Thus in general a man who says 'I have normal erections, but somehow I don't fancy my wife' can be said to have a problem of interest, while a man who says 'I desire my partner and I feel sexy, but I can't achieve an erection' is likely to have a problem of function. Similarly, a woman who says 'I can't climax in intercourse, but I'm usually ready for sex and enjoy it' can be said to have a problem of function, whereas a woman who says 'I always avoid sex if I can, but if it happens I usually climax' can be said to have a problem of desire.

When the two aspects are both present in a couple, as for instance in the man who has throughout his adult life had difficulty with premature ejaculation and has recently developed impotence and lack of desire, the therapist has to take all the factors into account in assessing the case, including of course the partner's attitudes and wishes.

11.3 Problems of sexual interest or desire

We are dealing with this area first, as the problems of loss of interest are more closely related to relationship problems, the main subject of this book. We will be dealing with problems of function later in the chapter. However, it should be remembered throughout that the two areas do in fact overlap considerably, and when we specify a causal factor leading to lack of desire, that factor may also lead directly or indirectly to lack of function (see Section 8.4).

Problems of sexual interest may present in either partner, and many of the factors leading to them are common to men and women. These may be divided into physical causes, psychological factors originating in the individual's development, factors in the individual's present life circumstances and problems arising from the relationship itself. In particular, the relationship factors may be circular in nature, as for instance when the woman's reluctance for sex is accompanied by a clumsy and demanding approach in the man, and the severity of the problem is increased by her reluctance and his clumsiness. Table 11.2 illustrates some of the causative factors which may lead to loss of sexual interest and may also disturb sexual function (see Section 11.5)

As can be seen from Table 11.2, there are many possible factors leading to loss of sexual interest. Some of these can be discovered by careful

Table 11.2 Factors leading to a loss of sexual interest

Factor	Men only	Both sexes	Women only
(1) Physical factors (*see Section 11.5*)			
Low testosterone (castration or pituitary disease)	Usually		
Menstrual cycle	May affect men indirectly		Interest may vary with the cycle
Oral contraception			Rarely
Tranquillisers and hypnotics		Quite frequently	
Most drugs of addiction		Frequently	
Alcohol		Short-term increase, but usually decrease with long-term use	
Coffee, tobacco, etc.		May occur rarely	
Any debilitating physical illness		Frequently	
Aging	Loss of drive		Possible loss of drive

Table 11.2 (cont.)

Factor	Men only	Both sexes	Women only
(2) Current life circumstances and reaction to these *(see Section 11.3.1)*			
Stress and overwork		Quite frequently	
Sleep loss		Quite frequently	
Depression and anxiety		Quite frequently	
Pregnancy and childbirth	Rarely		Frequently
(3) Past experiences *(see Section 11.3.3)*			
Traumatic sexual experiences		Quite frequently	
Sexual attitudes of parents, etc., leading to inhibition and ignorance		Quite frequently	
Poor self-image		Quite frequently	
Deviations in one or other partner		Variably	
(4) Relationship aspects *(see Section 11.4)*			
Excessive politeness and consideration		Quite frequently	
Hostility, threats and violence		Quite frequently	
Volatile woman, conciliatory man	Quite frequently		
Dominant man, silent resentful woman			Quite frequently
'Parent/child' or 'patient/nurse' relationships		Quite frequently	
Inability to 'close the bedroom door'		Quite frequently	
Extra-marital affairs		Variably	

history taking, while others can only be deduced from observing the couple's interaction in therapy. We will be giving further examples in the specific sections dealing with treatment. The only caution to be raised here is that sometimes lack of desire can be masked by a functional problem such as lack of arousal or anorgasmia, and may only emerge in its own right when the couple's motivation seems to be poor, as shown by failure to progress in sex therapy for the functional problem which they first presented.

The next few sections will give further details of some of the situations listed in Table 11.2, selecting especially those which are of greater importance to the therapist dealing with marital or relationship problems.

11.3.1 Stress and overwork

This is a common factor in causing loss of desire. It occurs in both men and women, and one often hears from couples with this problem that sex is very good on holiday or when they can get away from stress for a time.

Example 11A
For example, a couple who had a poor sexual relationship due to the man's tension, withdrawal and lack of interest reported that when they went on holiday he remained tense and withdrawn for four to five days, but thereafter he relaxed, joined in the family activities and became more interested in sex.

Example 11B
Another young couple found that the husband's absorbing business life as a broker, with millions of pounds risked every day in the foreign exchange markets, left him tired and uninterested in sex at the end of the day. Again, the couple found that when they went on holiday his sexual interest revived.

Example 11C
A woman with teenage children complained that her sex interest was very low, and also reported that she spent many hours each day worrying about her children's school work and helping them with their homework. Her husband was persuaded to help one of the children in place of his wife, to listen to her worries and to worry with her about the children. In addition this couple were given a negotiated timetable for sexual intercourse once a week (see Chapter 10 and Section 11.4.3) and their sexual satisfaction and frequency increased.

Other stresses which affect sexual desire adversely are bereavement, redundancy, debt, eviction, burglary of the home, worry about family members and difficulty with neighbours (see Section 11.4.5). Most of these problems can only be tackled in their own right, and if they cannot be resolved the lack of desire in the affected partner may remain.

11.3.2 Problems during pregnancy or following childbirth

It is very common for couples to reduce their sexual activity in the last three months of pregnancy, perhaps because of fears of damaging the baby, although medical opinion differs as to whether intercourse at this time would have an adverse effect on the baby. For some couples their sexual relationship is affected throughout the duration of the pregnancy, particularly in those where infertility has been a factor or illness has affected the pregnancy. After delivery, most couples continue to abstain for a month or longer, although sexual interest may recover more quickly than this and there seems to be a wide variation in how couples manage this period and whether they have full sexual intercourse or use other ways of giving each other sexual or physical pleasure.

Some couples take much longer to recover their sexual activity and some may never do so. Various possible explanations are put forward to account for this, including the possibility that the vagina has been damaged during delivery or that some permanent hormonal changes have occurred as a result of the pregnancy. These have never been convincingly demonstrated, except for a now rare complication of severe post-partum haemorrhage in which the pituitary gland is damaged causing hormonal failure, and in the great majority of cases some other explanation has to be sought. Some possible explanations are:

(1) The woman centres her satisfaction on baby care and finds her partner's requests for sexual satisfaction inappropriate or ill-timed.
(2) Worry about the welfare of the baby, leading to an inability for either partner to relax and make sex enjoyable for both.
(3) Simple tiredness in either partner.
(4) The woman feeling overwhelmed with the demands of the baby, so that the man's sexual demands seem to be yet another drain on her reserves of tolerance.
(5) The man finding his partner less sexually attractive while pregnant or as a mother (and perhaps seeking other sexual outlets).
(6) A wish on the man's part to protect the woman from his needs for sex which he now finds difficult to request from her (leading again perhaps to his seeking other outlets such as an affair).
(7) Resentment by the woman that the man is not taking his fair share of household and baby care; probably accompanied by resentments in the man that the woman no longer pays so much attention to him.
(8) The husband, in his impatience to recommence sexual activity again, may adopt a clumsy and insensitive approach, leading to resentment and rejection.

Thus, many of the difficulties couples have in their sexual relationships at this time may present as sexual reluctance in women, but are likely to be accompanied by a corresponding attitude in the man of impatience and demands, an overprotective approach or the possible emergence of either casual or more permanent sexual relationships with a third person. These problems, although arising mainly from the physical events of pregnancy and childbirth, can be seen as being connected directly or indirectly to family or relationship factors, and couple therapy is an appropriate way to approach the problem.

11.3.3 Traumatic sexual experiences

Many women report having been sexually molested either as children or in adolescence. The proportion of adult women who report sexual molestation in earlier life is now thought to be over 7% (Fritz *et al.* 1981). How many of such women have sexual difficulties is not clear, but in Fritz's study 23% of those who had been molested as children reported sexual dysfunction. The difficulty in interpreting this is that we have no very good figures on the prevalence of sexual dysfunction in those women who have never been molested, so that the influence of such experiences on later sexual adjustment is hard to assess.

Therapeutic approaches (Douglas *et al.* 1989) have involved intensive counselling of the woman by a female therapist, with some reliving of the earlier experience, followed by conjoint therapy with her and her sexual partner. Clinical impressions suggest that this combination of approaches is better than either form of treatment alone.

The effects of rape and other sexual assaults on later sexual function are also being investigated (Feldman *et al.* 1979) and the general conclusion is that after a rape the victim may be put off some of the sexual activities involved in the rape itself, e.g. intercourse and touching male genitals, while other forms of sexual arousal such as normal foreplay and self-masturbation remain unaffected.

Our clinical experience suggests that sometimes a man whose partner was either abused as a child or has been raped may become extremely sensitive to the fact of these damaging sexual experiences and find it difficult to feel confident that his sexual advances will not be rejected by the woman as either rape or abuse. This leads to a mutual hypersensitivity towards their sexual relationship. As with those sexually abused as children, some kind of combination of individual and couple therapy would seem the best approach.

11.3.4 Sexual attitudes of parents leading to inhibition or ignorance

We obtain our knowledge of sex from many sources, and much of it is informal, either from schoolfriends, the media or from sexual partners. Often, however, parents themselves are not simply uninformative about sex, but positively discourage their children from learning about it. One result of this general inhibition about passing on information about the sexual development of children or discussing sexual relationships in an open and informative manner is that many couples do not have an adequate vocabulary for conversations about their sexual relationship. Some may find it painfully embarrassing to use any language which refers to their own or their partner's sexuality or gender. The more assertive and exploratory children may ignore this, but the more shy, passive or inhibited children can be strongly influenced by such parents to remain in considerable ignorance about sexual matters.

Example 11D
In one case a young couple attended our clinic with a problem of non-consummation, and yet on examination of the woman there was no vaginismus, nor did the man have any loss of erection. They had simply not realised that some pressure was needed in order to achieve penetration, and the discomfort she experienced at first attempt was interpreted as meaning that she was abnormal. Once their misunderstanding had been cleared up, they rapidly resolved the problem.

Example 11E
Another couple in their thirties complained that after intercourse the woman was 'ejaculating' and expelling the semen, and that this had made conception impossible. On further questioning it transpired that the penis was only able to penetrate about one centimetre into the vagina owing to vaginismus (see Section 11.5.3) and the semen had never actually entered beyond the entrance of the vagina. Therapy involving progressive relaxation of the vaginal entrance was successful, and the couple conceived.

Sometimes difficulties in sexual function can be more directly traced to negative parental influences. For example, sex may be satisfactory while it is kept secret, but as soon as the engagement is announced or the couple are married, one partner may become averse to sex.

One such woman explained this as being due to embarrassment that her mother 'knows that we are doing it'. Therapy with this couple involved the 'empty chair' technique, in which the woman confronted her mother in imagination and assertively told her that their sex life was their own business.

Another alternative is a paradoxical gesture in which the couple can put the photograph of the intrusive parent in the bedroom or deliberately think of the parent during sex as a way of separating from and gaining independence from him or her.

11.3.5 Poor self-image

It is quite common, especially among people who are prone to depression or other psychiatric symptoms, to have a very poor or negative self-image. One essential prerequisite to experiencing sexual pleasure is the ability to allow oneself to enjoy things, and this is often lacking in those whose self-image is poor. Depressed patients will often complain that they have not enjoyed anything for a long time, but such lack of enjoyment is also found in those who make few demands of life and expect a rather dull and unexciting existence.

Example 11F
It is often the partner rather than the patient who complains of this situation, as in the case of a husband whose wife was rather depressed, and who expected

her to need and enjoy sex as much as he did. In therapy we helped her with the depression by methods based on cognitive therapy (Beck 1979), but therapy also included an attempt to change the husband's expectations and to help him to reduce his demands.

In general, the presence of low self-esteem in people makes it harder to help them with sexual problems, and they may need some individual therapy to enable them to gain a better view of themselves, and as a result respond better to sexual therapy. It may also be possible for couple therapy to focus on helping the partner with low self-esteem to become more assertive and the other partner to be more able to share his/her own feelings. This preliminary work may enable both partners to become more expressive of their own needs and have an impact upon their sexual relationship (see Section 10.7).

11.3.6 Deviation in one partner

(We use the words deviant and deviation here as the most practical way of describing sexual activities or desires which are seen as deviating from a norm, but we do not intend to imply a pejorative sense by their use.)

Many types of sexual deviation or variation are compatible with continuing a heterosexual relationship. Kinsey found that about 40% of the male and female population had both heterosexual and homosexual experience or desire, mostly in adolescence. The fact that the majority of such people are in stable heterosexual relationships speaks to their ability to suppress or live with these urges which society deems to be deviant, to a greater or lesser extent.

This ability for a deviation to exist side by side with a more 'normal' relationship seems to occur most of the time in transvestism, fetishism, exhibitionism and voyeurism. Although some people with deviant desires are only capable of being aroused by those desires, many have the ability to be aroused by either the deviant activity or by 'normal' heterosexual attraction.

In such situations occurring in a couple, there may be sexual problems, either because of loss of interest on the part of the deviant partner or because the other partner is offended by the deviant behaviour and is either refusing sex or threatening the relationship. In therapy one has to work around the deviant urges and try to improve the dysfunction in the couple by conjoint psychosexual therapy; but it is often also necessary to take a more active approach to the deviation itself. This may take the form of more strictly behavioural therapy to reduce the deviant urges (e.g. covert sensitisation or orgasmic conditioning, Bancroft 1989) or an attempt to persuade the other partner to be more flexible in his/her attitude to the deviation, and perhaps to incorporate it in some of the occasions on which the couple are together sexually.

11.4 Relationship factors leading to a loss of sexual interest
(see Table 11.2)

There are many ways in which couple relationships can affect sexual life adversely, and some are so subtle that they are easily missed by therapists not alerted to the problem. What is generally agreed is that poor marital relationships are associated with a poor sex life, and may make sexual therapy more difficult. This was clearly stated by Masters and Johnson (1970) and was also noted by Crowe *et al.* (1977) and by Kaplan (1979).

In Chapter 1 (Section 1.2.2) we reviewed some of the findings which describe differences between distressed and non-distressed couples. There is an emphasis here on the presence of non-verbal aspects of eye contact, touch and attentiveness (Schaap and Jansen-Nawas 1987) or tenderness and good communication (Hahlweg *et al.* 1984) which are found more in the non-distressed couples and predict successful outcome of therapy. These are useful indicators for assessment of couples and possible areas on which therapy might focus.

However, there is otherwise a lack of a convincing classification of relationships and their problems; it is only possible at this point to highlight some of the patterns we regularly observe in connection with loss of sexual interest.

11.4.1 Excessive politeness and consideration

In couples in which both partners show this characteristic it is not unusual for the sexual problem presented to be that of non-consummation. Whether the non-consummation is associated with vaginismus (see Section 11.5.3) or with impotence (see Section 11.5.1) or both, there is often in these couples a strong ambivalence towards sexual intercourse by both partners. There is also a great reluctance on both sides to cause or experience discomfort. Such couples seldom if ever have rows, and they are often cautious and unassertive in their relationships with each other and with outsiders. Whether these characteristics are responsible for the non-consummation is not clear, but it is often helpful in therapy to encourage these couples to have rows over trivial issues, and it is possible to speculate that if they had had a more robust attitude to conflict or physical discomfort they might have consummated the marriage unaided (see Section 8.1 and Example 8A).

It is a common experience for sexual therapists to have to use considerable encouragement in couples being treated for vaginismus to complete their homework exercises.

Example 11G
One typical couple had progressed quite well in progressive relaxation and dilatation of the vagina, with the wife carrying out most of the treatment for herself, and the husband helping her to pass the dilators in the later stages of

treatment. However, when it came to attempted penetration with the penis, both seemed highly reluctant, and for about four sessions they returned without having attempted it, even though the dilator being used at that stage was of a similar size to the penis. It took a great deal of persuasion to get them to the stage of penetration, including some fairly heated discussions between them and the therapist. When they had finally overcome the problem, however, they both enjoyed the sexual intercourse greatly.

11.4.2 Continual hostilities

Couples who spend most of their time together in hostile verbal confrontation may never experience a sufficiently long period of truce to have the time or the inclination for sex. This applies equally to those who have 'symmetrical' arguments and to those in which the hostility is one-sided and the response is passive withdrawal. Once again we encounter the point made in Section 11.4 that poor marital adjustment often goes with a poor sex life. Therapeutically the most useful approach is often to attempt to explore the resentments and to see if the couple may unite to overcome these by negotiation and compromise. Failing this, timetables for arguments (Sections 8.2, 8.4 and 9.10) or a paradoxical prescription for continual arguments would be possible lines to follow (Section 9.13).

Closely allied to verbal hostility are threats and physical violence in the relationship. In some couples, physical violence is a sexually stimulating thing for both partners, and one sometimes sees 'battered' wives returning, for motives which are not clear, to the men who have ill-treated them. The violence may, however, get out of hand; it is often cited as the grounds for divorce and may also have dangerous consequences. In a very violent relationship sex is usually in any case an infrequent event.

Example 11H
The connection between sex and violence in some relationships is illustrated by the case of a woman who had had a stormy and violent, but sexually satisfying, first marriage to a fellow artist. After the divorce she had married a caring and unassertive civil servant. They were quite contented in most ways, but sex was far too infrequent for the wife, partly because of the husband's lack of motivation, but also because when he did make a tentative approach the wife tended to pick a quarrel with him which put him off. She on her side seemed to be expecting him to respond assertively, and to be hoping that good sexual interaction which would satisfy them both would follow the row.

11.4.3 Inequalities in dominance or assertiveness

This can often be associated with a problem of sexual desire. Various patterns of sexual difficulty can be found in this situation, but the most common is that the unassertive partner is less interested in sex. We would hypothesise that this is connected with resentment on the part of that partner over the apparent control which the more assertive partner exerts, for example in initiating joint activities, in taking the spokesman role, in overruling the quieter partner and in expressing feelings openly. In contrast, the quiet partner sees him/herself as being passed over, being controlled, giving in for the sake of peace and not expressing emotions.

Such inequalities may, of course, exist without adversely affecting sexual function or desire; but if one partner comes with a complaint of lack of sexual desire it is usually worthwhile exploring the couple's non-sexual relationship.

There seem to be some regular differences between men and women in the ways in which dominance and assertiveness may be shown in their relationship. We have described two such cases in some detail in earlier chapters: Example 8C (the 'toilet seat couple'), in which the man was unassertive and disinterested in sexual intercourse, and Example 10G, in which the woman was reluctant to have sexual intercourse. An hypothesis which may be appropriate to both of these cases is that where the quieter partner finds it difficult to be assertive within their social interaction there may be a tendency to take control within the sexual sphere which reveals itself as sexual reluctance.

We have also considered in Chapter 1 some of the factors currently influencing men and women in their inter-relationships where questions such as the changing role of women, the search for greater equality and the demand that men moderate their attitudes have meant that issues of dominance and assertiveness in some couples, and indeed also in discussions within therapy teams, can become highly sensitive. In describing couples within this chapter we are aware of this ongoing debate, but do not wish to enter into it except to describe couples as we observe their interaction and show how the inequalities in dominance and assertiveness seem to affect their sexual relationship.

When the woman is the overtly dominant partner she will often be volatile and outspoken, socially confident but prone to lose her temper at times. She will often criticise her husband for quite trivial 'offences', even in front of third parties, and the male partner, even though he is quite competent and effective in his work, will go along with his wife's wishes and 'give in for the sake of peace'. Such men seem to present frequently in the clinic with a loss of interest in sex within the marriage; they may in some cases have a normal sex drive as expressed in masturbation, while in others they may also experience erectile impotence.

Example 11I
In one such case the husband had been very passive and placating towards his dominant wife, but in therapy was encouraged to be more assertive towards her (an approach which she in fact welcomed) and his sexual potency improved in response. He said in one of the later sessions that he had finally realised that his sex life was 'too serious to be taken seriously', which appeared to imply that

when he was trying too hard to please his wife sexually he was in fact defeating his own object because the anxiety caused failure.

If the man is the overtly dominant partner, he is usually more articulate than the woman. He often appears even-tempered on the surface and seems to have an unruffled enjoyment of what is often an active life. He is usually the undisputed spokesman for the family, and if there is sexual reluctance on the part of the woman it will probably be labelled by both partners as her problem. Both will often find the problem quite inexplicable, and they may both use the word frigidity (a term that we tend to avoid in the clinic because it is both imprecise and puts a rather judgmental label on one partner). The woman will often also complain of depression and low self-esteem, and she may find it difficult to express any resentment. However, it is often quite easy to uncover areas of potential conflict in the conjoint session on which the partners have opposing views, and it may well become clear that the depression and the sexual reluctance can be traced to the same unspoken resentments (see Section 10.10).

Example 11J
A characteristic case is given by a couple who had been married for 18 years and presented with the wife's reluctance for sexual relations. She had also experienced some depression, and felt that she was in most ways inferior to her husband. At badminton, for instance, he was in the top group, while she was in the lower one, and she felt rather jealous of some of the more competent women, who played in the top group with him, and seemed to be so much more self-confident than she. In therapy they explored some of these differences and it emerged that the husband had some insecurities which he had never mentioned to her, and that she herself could be much more competent than he in relation to their children's illnesses. This 'equalisation' and the temporary imposition of a sexual timetable (Section 10.10) helped them to reach a much better adjustment both maritally and sexually.

In both types of relationship, whether male or female dominated, the balance can be redressed. This may at first be a temporary phenomenon, but if it is accompanied by a marked improvement in sexual adjustment the couple may see it as desirable in the long term, and in some couples the greater equality can become a permanent feature of the relationship. The therapist, in trying to bring about these changes, will need the full range of skills described in Chapter 4, including problem definition, reframing the problem as interactional, decentring and encouraging good empathy and communication.

In addition, it is often revealing as well as therapeutic to ask the couple to argue about a trivial matter such as toilet rolls or toothpaste (see Chapter 8) in order to help them to become comfortable with the process of arguing without risking an altercation on important or threatening areas. Having argued about these more trivial areas, the couple may feel confident to have open discussions about more serious issues, perhaps with more constructiveness and less fire, but the therapist should make sure, as in the more trivial arguments, that the quieter partner has the chance to express his or her views and to be taken seriously.

In most male-reluctance cases the above approaches are the mainstay of therapy, but in female-reluctance cases, and also in the occasional case of male-reluctance, the negotiated timetable (Crowe and Ridley 1986) can be very effective, both as a temporary holding technique to take the heat out of the sexual issue, and in some cases as a long-term solution. This approach is fully described in Section 10.10, but it is of such usefulness that it is worth giving a brief résumé here. The couple are asked to negotiate a compromise on frequency of sexual intercourse, between, for example, the woman's preferred frequency of once a month and the man's preferred frequency of three times weekly. If once weekly is the compromise frequency decided upon, the couple are then asked to decide on which day of the week sex will occur. They pledge themselves to have intercourse on that day and never to have intercourse on any other day. The woman is thus relieved of pressure on six days of the week, the man is guaranteed his once-weekly satisfaction. On the 'non-sex' days the couple can express whatever physical affection they wish without the man assuming that it will lead to sexual intercourse and the woman getting anxious on the same account.

It is often found that when a negotiated timetable has been arranged other issues become easier to discuss, perhaps because when the heat is taken out of the sexual conflict, discussion of other issues can take place without leading back to the previously central issue of sex.

11.4.4 'Parent/child' or 'patient/nurse' couple relationships where sex seems to have a low priority

Another kind of inequality which can lead to sexual difficulties is that of a partner who is psychiatrically or physically ill, or who is seriously irresponsible (e.g. a gambler or an alcoholic). In most of these couples there is a problem with the sexual relationship, but it is not usually one of conflict or refusal. Instead, both partners are often agreed that sex is fairly low among their priorities (see Section 1.2.5, sexual closeness). It is as if there is an over-responsible kind of parenting going on between them, and any sexual relationship is limited by the kind of taboo that usually prevents incest between parent and child. The acceptable involvement with their partner in attaining mutual sexual satisfaction is in these couples somehow inhibited. This can in many cases be rationalised as being because the ill partner would not enjoy sex if it took place, and the caretaking partner would not wish to impose a unilateral exploitation on the other. Another, more systemic, formulation which may be used in some of the couples where the illness is more in the nature of illness behaviour is that it suits both partners to have a highly complementary relationship since this reduces the possibility of conflict of which both partners are afraid (see below, this section, and Section 7.3.2).

In many such couples presenting to our clinics, sex as such is not an issue. They do not have a sexual relationship, but neither is particularly bothered by this. In others, the well or the ill partner may be keen to resume sexual relations, but the issue is never discussed, and therefore neither takes any initiative on the matter.

If the problem in the ill partner is a physical one such as cancer, the aims of therapy may have to be quite limited, and the restoration of the sexual relationship may be neither possible nor desirable. This is not to say, however, that sex is impossible in all such cases, and if both partners are willing, sex may take place within the limitations imposed by the illness. Particularly in the case of coronary heart disease, the patient should not be overprotected in relation to sex. Assuming that the acute phase is over (e.g. after the first three months) and subject to medical advice in the individual case, the gentle exercise involved in sex may do no harm, and indeed may improve the outlook by reducing frustration (see Section 7.4.1).

Other couples may be suffering not so much from illness in one partner as from the adoption of the sick role. The avoidance of sex in these couples may in some way be balancing the system, or may be a continuation of an earlier disinclination for sex in one or both partners which is lent legitimacy by the label of illness. If the couple are uninterested in altering their sex life, there is probably no purpose in attempting to pursue the issue. However, it is quite possible, especially in couples where one partner is depressed, to help the ill partner to be more assertive, and thereby to improve both the depression and the sex life (see also Examples 10D and 10E).

Where illness is a factor in the relationship it is possible to help the couple have a more satisfactory relationship, both sexual and social, as in the following example.

Example 11K

A couple came for therapy in association with the husband's diabetes. It is not unusual for a man with diabetes to have a degree of impotence due to nerve or artery damage, but in this case he also suffered loss of sex interest because of his attitude to his illness, which was to see himself as an invalid; in addition his wife was overprotective, taking over many of the jobs which had been his, and he also experienced performance anxiety during intercourse itself. This couple were encouraged to discuss their fears about his illness in-session and were given timetabled discussions at home to discuss what practical adjustments they would need to make to accommodate his diabetes (Section 9.10).

As a consequence of these discussions they both became more confident about his diabetes and the husband resumed many of his activities while the wife became less protective. They were also given some standard relaxation exercises combined with a Masters and Johnson programme to increase their sexual pleasure and reduce their anxiety and eventually adopted a sexual timetable. Both their sex life and their relationship improved while he made some necessary adjustments to his diabetic treatment.

In many cases, however, including both those with serious illnesses and those where there appears to be a sick role element, there is no way round the sexual problem, and even if one partner is interested in sex it may have to be concluded that the lack of a sex life is inevitable.

11.4.5 Inability to close the bedroom door

Some very practical problems can prevent a couple from having the sort of sexual relationship they want. One common difficulty is the presence of children in the house at the time when they are attempting to have intercourse. Whether the children are small or whether they are teenagers, the problem can be similar. It is the difficulty that many couples have in 'closing the bedroom door'. With young children the problem is often that the parents are worried that they will get into mischief or danger if they are not under supervision. With teenagers the couple may be worried that the children will suspect that they are having intercourse, and this leads to embarrassment, inhibition and often complete avoidance.

There are other ways in which the children may inhibit their parents' sex life. Sometimes one parent may be so worried about the children that there is never an opportunity to relax and enjoy sex. The case (Example 11C) of the mother with teenage children is a good example of these problems and their treatment.

What is true of children can also be true of other relatives. Many couples find that their sex life is diminished if an elderly mother, father or other relative comes to live with them. Worry about the person's health, or irritation with their habits or their interference, can inhibit one or both partners. They can also be inhibited by the possibility that their relative is able to hear them having sexual relations, just as under similar circumstances they might be worried about teenage children.

Some couples have the same problem with dogs. One particular couple found that whenever they attempted sexual relations, their three dogs insisted on coming into the bedroom, and it became impossible to continue. Other couples seem to have difficulty in removing the family pet from the couple's bed, a little like the couple who seem to bring a younger child into bed with them which acts as a form of protection against having sexual intercourse.

Physical circumstances such as overcrowding can cause great difficulty for some couples. Sometimes it is the presence of young children sleeping in the marital bedroom that causes difficulty, and at other times the couple have to sleep on a couch in the living room or in separate beds.

Example 11L
In one extreme case a couple were living in a basement flat, and the landlord had to come through their flat whenever he wanted to get to the back yard. The husband had erectile problems under these difficult conditions, and they were

only able to overcome their problem when they moved to another town and obtained a council house.

Management of problems to do with children and the inability to close the bedroom door can sometimes be along simple and practical lines, helping the couple to take steps such as planning safe activities for young children and securing all dangerous equipment so that they cannot come to harm while the parents are otherwise occupied. Alternatively, they may need help in being tougher and insisting that a child is returned to his/her own bed, or by making more reasonable bedtimes rather than letting the children stay up to watch television until late. With older children it may simply be necessary to declare the parental bedroom off-limits, and literally lock the children out when sex is on the agenda.

It is not always as simple as that, however, and in some couples the practical solutions are undermined by their own unwillingness (perhaps in one partner only) to draw acceptable boundaries between themselves as a couple and other people. This difficulty in being exclusive, and only being comfortable in triangular relationships, has been discussed already (see Section 10.13) and may be associated with difficulty in separating from one's family of origin and adopting a position of autonomy. For such couples or individuals the very idea of an exclusive sexual and 'co-parental' relationship can be difficult to sustain. (See also Section 10.12 for a case example where sexual abuse had occurred within the family.)

In many situations in which this triangulation with other family members occurs the therapist will almost certainly have to move to a more indirect and inventive way of working, by choosing a systemic approach (see Chapters 3 and 7 to 9). It may even be useful at different stages to ask for the children to attend for a session or two to deal with issues of parental control and the negotiation of bedtimes, etc. The therapist, whether in marital or family sessions, will need to use many of the techniques outlined in the descriptions of systems therapy, including becoming decentred and giving paradoxical messages.

11.4.6 Extra-marital affairs and sexual therapy
(see also Section 10.13)

Not infrequently we are presented with a sexually dysfunctional couple in which one partner has had, or is still involved in, an outside sexual relationship. This is, in a sense, the most unstable form of triangle. Society seems to expect the involved partner to make a choice between spouse and lover, so that the situation will resolve itself. If this does not happen, however, there are few positive aspects to the situation as seen from the uninvolved partner's point of view. The outside relationship has the effect of diluting both the emotional and the sexual bond which makes a marriage or long-term relationship an exclusive and stable relationship. Guilt, recriminations, jealousy, forgiveness, insecurity, heightened emotional levels and pressure are all present in large measure in many such situations. In some cases, however, the affair, if it is declared, can bring the couple closer together and even make their sexual relationship more exciting and open.

This situation, more than most others in sexual therapy, taxes the judgment and conscience of the therapist, and it is the situation for which theory has fewest satisfactory answers. The one thing the therapist cannot do is to make decisions on behalf of the partners, despite the fact that, in cases where the affair has been admitted, the uninvolved partner often puts pressure on him/her to castigate the other partner or to decide their future (see Section 2.4.3.5).

It is, moreover, very difficult to carry out therapy designed to help a couple with their sexual problem when it is not clear whether both partners are committed to the relationship. Where it is the involved partner who has lost his/her sexual interest, therapy can be very slow and often quite fruitless.

Experience suggests that therapy can be a little easier if either the affair is clearly over and both partners are fully persuaded of this or the affair remains a secret from one partner. If the affair is over, there may be a good deal of residual resentment, the uninvolved partner being angry because of the affair and the involved partner because of having to give it up. However, there is in this situation considerable hope that the couple might reconcile and retain or redevelop their sexual feelings for each other.

If the affair remains undisclosed to the other partner, one is faced as therapist with a secret known to oneself and one partner but not to the other. If the therapist can live with this secret, despite the strains involved, it may be possible to help the couple to improve their sexual relationship, and it may be that, as the couple's sexual relationship improves, the importance of the affair will lessen and the couple will strengthen their alliance. Even if the affair continues, it is possible that in some cases a permanent triangle can exist, whether known to the uninvolved partner or not, and thus for both relationships to continue in parallel.

It is clear that this presents therapists with complex questions regarding ethics and confidentiality; however, one can bear in mind that 'blunt or brutal honesty is seldom a disclosure of intimacy' (see Section 6.3) and that the couple should be the ultimate judges of what degree of sharing they wish to have in the relationship.

Example 11M

An example of this is given by a couple in their early thirties. The husband was working abroad, and spent one to two months at a time away from his wife. She worked in this country and the couple had no children. She presented the problem as one of sexual unresponsiveness to her husband, to whom however she was devoted and whom she respected. She also disclosed to the therapist early in therapy that she was having a sexually successful affair which she neither wanted to confess to her husband nor to give up. The husband was devoted to her, and felt that despite the sexual problem he wanted the marriage to continue.

They worked together on the sexual relationship, and made some progress with a combination of the Masters and Johnson approach and a timetable, and at the end of therapy they were enjoying a limited but fairly satisfying form of sexual relationship when they could get together. The affair, as far as was known to the therapist, was still continuing. The future of the marriage remains uncertain in the long term, but the improvement in the couple's sexual relationship probably had the effect of strengthening the marriage.

The important lesson from this case is that the therapist is not in a position to make moral judgments, and although some therapists might have refused to take the couple on under these conditions, the therapy that was done probably helped the marriage more than a forced disclosure of the affair or refusal to treat would have done.

11.5 Problems of function (erection, arousal, penetration, orgasm and ejaculation)

Sexual function is a very complicated emotional and physical process (as mentioned already in Section 11.1) even when considering one individual alone. When, as in sexual intercourse, it involves two people taking complementary roles the complications are multiplied. Inhibitions, taboos, fears and fantasies become entangled in the search for mutual enjoyment of intimacy, tenderness or passion. Perhaps it is more surprising that the majority of couples enjoy their sexual life sufficiently well to take it for granted than that for others it may go wrong and cause problems.

Sexual dysfunctions are often treated in specific clinics devoted to these problems, and as this book is not a specialised text on that subject we will not deal with these disorders of function in as much detail as disorders of desire or motivation for sex (Sections 11.3 and 11.4). However, we believe that all couple therapists should have at least a basic knowledge of sexual function and be aware of the physical and emotional problems involved and of the treatments available, so that they can be more effective in their treatment of couples and make appropriate referrals when necessary.

11.5.1 Disorders of erection

The process of erection is initiated by impulses along the fibres of the pudendal nerve, which runs from the sacral segments of the spinal cord to the genital area. These impulses activate a neurotransmitter in the blood vessels of the penis (probably vasoactive intestinal polypeptide) causing the arteries of the penis to supply a greatly increased amount of blood to the inside of the penis (the corpora cavernosa), as a result of which the organ swells and becomes stiff. It is also almost certain that other, inhibitory, impulses along the sympathetic nerve fibres are normally acting to keep the penis in a flaccid state, and that these impulses have to be suppressed to allow erection to occur. Both types of nerve stimulation may have to be involved in erection, and it is of course necessary for the blood supply to be intact for erection to occur.

Loss of erection may be total, but many variants of this are seen. For example, a man may begin by experiencing an erection when sexually aroused and then lose it before he can have sexual intercourse. In other men, erection does not happen during sexual involvement with his partner, but may occur normally in sleep or when he is masturbating: this is termed 'situational impotence'. In other men the loss of erection may be incomplete, and this is usually called 'partial impotence'.

The process of erection can be interfered with by various physical diseases, for example those which damage the nerves (multiple sclerosis, diabetes, etc.) or the spinal cord (paraplegia or spinal cord compression) or those which prevent a normal blood supply (diabetes again, and blockage of the aorta or large arteries by atheroma). Some medications such as antidepressants and diuretics can also interfere with erection, probably by increasing the influence of the inhibitory nerve impulses (see above). Alcohol has a complicated influence (see below) which has physical and psychological aspects.

The effects of aging are somewhat complicated, and involve a reduction of the desire for sex as well as a general slowing of the erectile response. Erection is slower to develop and needs more physical stimulation to develop and maintain it than in the younger man, but this is unlikely to cause problems if the man remains calm about it, and if the partner has learned to participate in sexual foreplay by caressing and stimulating the penis. Some men develop performance anxiety as a result of this slowing down in their sexual responsiveness and they may reach the erroneous conclusion that they are impotent.

One of the most common inhibitors of erection is in fact anxiety. This can be anxiety about ordinary everyday worries, such as those involving family or job, but very commonly so-called performance anxiety is added. This is the fear that sex will go wrong, and may be felt by either or both partners during sexual activity. It is a powerful factor in inhibiting sexual responsiveness, and is an almost universal accompaniment of sexual dysfunctions, especially erectile impotence.

As mentioned in Section 11.3, most of the factors leading to loss of desire can also result in poor erections, and some of those mentioned there are especially prone to affect erections. These include stress, overwork, debilitating physical illnesses and the various relationship factors mentioned there, especially the 'volatile woman and conciliatory man' combination (see Section 11.4.3).

The effect of alcohol on potency is complex. As mentioned in Section

11.3, alcohol taken regularly can lead to a loss of desire, but it also leads to inability to obtain an erection, by mechanisms which are not fully understood, but may involve damage to both nerves and arteries. One unfortunate aspect of the problem is that giving up alcohol does not usually restore the ability to have an erection, at least in the short term, perhaps partly due to the partner's lack of encouragement after negative experiences of sex during the period of drinking. The drinker may well feel highly aroused sexually but be both clumsy and unable to sustain an erection long enough to give his partner any kind of satisfaction. Other offputting characteristics of the man under the influence of drink may be the smell of drink on his breath, his occasional bouts of vomiting or indeed violence and his general lack of sensitivity towards the partner. All of these difficulties, as well as the probable physical effect of alcohol in producing loss of erection, combine to produce in many cases a problem with sexual function which may require a considerable period of abstinence and relationship therapy to solve.

(For treatment of erectile problems see Section 11.6 *et seq.*)

11.5.2 Problems of ejaculation

The mechanism of ejaculation is not fully understood, although it is clear that it is a reflex usually stimulated by rubbing or stroking of the penis. It is divided into two stages, in the first of which the semen is moved from the seminal vesicles to the prostate gland. In nocturnal emissions (wet dreams) the semen then slowly emerges through the urethra, while in ejaculation itself the semen is expelled forcefully by the co-ordinated contraction of the muscles at the base of the penis, which is repeated about eight times over a period of about eight seconds. This is accompanied by an acute sense of pleasure. There is usually a rapid loss of erection immediately after ejaculation, and a variable period of time (from a few minutes to several hours) during which a further erection cannot be obtained. This period of unresponsiveness after ejaculation becomes rather longer with advancing age.

Premature ejaculation is a very common problem, and at its widest definition (for example if a man ever ejaculates before he would have wished to, with a sense of loss of control) probably affects at least 50% of the male population. These mild cases do not pose a major problem, or need anything other than reassurance, but for others premature ejaculation can be severe enough to prevent intercourse because ejaculation occurs before penetration. In other cases it causes extreme frustration to both partners and can lead to secondary impotence.

There are probably no specific physical disorders leading to premature ejaculation, although there is clearly a wide variability among the male population from those who are most prone to premature ejaculation to those whose ejaculation is retarded or never happens. This implies some sort of constitutional factor in the regulation of ejaculation, but there is as yet no understanding of how this might work. One thing, however, is quite clear and that is that, as with impotence, anxiety has an important part to play in worsening premature ejaculation.

Delayed ejaculation is much less common than premature ejaculation. There is a similar spread of severity, between those who have only an occasional problem in ejaculating and those who have never ejaculated under any circumstances. Some can experience emissions while asleep but be unable to ejaculate in the waking state, while others can ejaculate in masturbation but not in intercourse ('situational failure to ejaculate'). Most of the cases have no clear cause, but some forms of medication such as antidepressants or tranquillisers can cause delayed ejaculation. The problem sometimes only comes to light when the couple ask for help with infertility. Since intercourse is often quite prolonged, the woman may climax easily, but will often feel emotionally dissatisfied because her partner is unable to experience a climax himself.

Premature and delayed ejaculation are the most important disorders of ejaculation, but other problems with ejaculation include pain (often associated with inflammation of the prostate gland or urethra) and a lack of pleasure in ejaculation (usually in men who are rather self-absorbed and perfectionist).

(For treatment of ejaculatory problems see Section 11.6 *et seq.*)

11.5.3 Problems with penetration

The therapist is often faced with couples complaining of non-consummation. This may be associated with impotence (see Section 11.5.1) or with an unusually tough hymen at the entrance of the vagina, but is most commonly associated with vaginismus, a condition in which the muscles round the entrance of the vagina go into involuntary spasm when penetration is attempted. The woman often shows fear, which in some may amount to a phobia, either of penetration itself or of pregnancy and childbirth. There is usually quite a normal response to sexual arousal, as long as this goes no further than petting, and clitoral orgasm is usually experienced. In such couples the male partner is often unassertive and dislikes causing discomfort, and in therapy one may have to work as hard in modifying his attitudes as in helping the woman to relax. Usually vaginismus is psychological in origin, but it sometimes occurs after childbirth (e.g. following painful stitches) or after sexual assault.

Dyspareunia refers to pain experienced during sexual intercourse. This may be superficial (i.e. in the vagina) when it is often associated with local infections such as thrush, or with mild vaginismus (see above) or with lack of arousal and lubrication.

Alternatively, the dyspareunia may be deep (i.e. in the pelvis) and it is then often associated with various physical diseases including endometriosis, tube infection, cysts or tumours in the ovary or womb. Sometimes deep dyspareunia is due to inability to relax, but until the physical causes have been excluded it is better not to assume a psychological origin.

Occasionally men may complain of pain on intercourse, and this is often connected with having a very tight foreskin, or an associated tear in the foreskin.

(For treatment of problems of penetration see Section 11.6 *et seq.*)

11.5.4 Problems of female arousal

The process of female arousal and lubrication is physiologically equivalent to that of erection in the male. There is an increase in blood supply to the walls of the vagina, probably under the same excitatory and inhibitory nerves as in the male (see Section 11.5.1). The increased blood flow stimulates glands in the vaginal walls to produce considerable quantities of lubrication. At the same time the clitoris becomes stiff and is drawn back under its 'hood', the labia become swollen and darker in colour, and the vagina becomes enlarged or 'tented' at the inner end near the neck of the womb. As in men, these changes can be inhibited by anxiety. Similarly, drugs such as antidepressants and diuretics, which interfere with erection, may also interfere with female arousal. Diseases such as diabetes, multiple sclerosis, paraplegia and blockage of blood vessels may also have a negative effect on arousal, as they do in men, but it is not usually as radical a disturbance as in men, and the number of women complaining of these problems is proportionally smaller.

Aging in women has a specific effect on arousal, in that the reduction of oestrogen after the menopause may lead to a thinning and weakening of the vaginal walls and a reduction of the glands producing vaginal lubrication. This can cause dryness, discomfort and sometimes bleeding during sexual intercourse. It can be overcome either by the use of lubricating jelly or by hormone replacement therapy, either by mouth or in the form of a vaginal cream.

(For treatment of female arousal problems see Section 11.6 *et seq.*)

11.5.5 Female anorgasmia

The mechanism of female orgasm is no better understood than that of ejaculation. It is physiologically quite similar, having the quality of a reflex stimulated by stroking the clitoris or the entrance of the vagina, and being associated with an acute sense of pleasure and repeated contractions of the muscles of the floor of the pelvis. The period of unresponsiveness following this is, however, usually shorter than in the male, making it easier for women than men to experience multiple orgasms.

Lack of orgasm can be total or situational. It may for instance be possible in some cases for a woman to achieve an orgasm using a vibrator or her hand on the clitoris, but not during intercourse. In fact, a considerable proportion of women in a steady relationship or in marriage experience this form of situational anorgasmia and are unable to achieve a climax during intercourse (Sanders 1985). Lack of orgasm has no effect on fertility, and as the great majority of women can climax in some way it is often only necessary to reassure the couple who suffer from situational anorgasmia.

(For treatment of anorgasmia see Section 11.6 *et seq*.)

11.5.6 General aspects of dysfunction

Although the specific types of dysfunction have been presented separately, they often exist together. It is quite possible, for example, for a couple to be experiencing erectile difficulties in the male and loss of desire in the female partner; in fact the two may be inter-related, each problem amplifying the other.

Some other fairly common combinations are impotence following premature ejaculation, premature ejaculation with loss of female interest and anorgasmia and primary impotence with vaginismus and non-consummation.

Similarly, with causative factors, the problems found in any one couple seem to have several apparent causes. For example, it is not unusual in many forms of sexual dysfunction for performance anxiety to convert a little functional difficulty, such as loss of erection, into a major dysfunction such as complete impotence (fortunately usually reversible, see Example 11K).

Thus the sexual and marital therapist has to be continually aware of the coexistence of other sexual problems, of other relationship factors and of individual responses to the dysfunction in addition to the main presenting problem.

Example 11N
The case of Ernest and Frances T will be presented here to illustrate the interaction of various factors in the origins of sexual problems and the methods used to explore and deal with them. The presenting problem was Ernest's partial loss of erection, which had been there since the couple first attempted sexual intercourse two years before. They were both in their fifties and both had been widowed during the last five years. Indeed, in earlier years the two couples had known each other quite well, and Ernest and Frances had been friends for many years. After their marriage, which had been about a year before referral, they had decided to live in the house which Frances had shared with her late husband, and sell Ernest's house. They each had two daughters, and all the children also knew each other and got on quite well.

At the beginning of therapy it was necessary to help the couple to come to a realistic assessment of what to expect in terms of sexual frequency and performance. Both had at first assumed that they would have the same kind of sex together as they had had with their previous partners at the beginning of those marriages, but were prepared to accept a more realistic expectation after discussion. There was, however, a residual tendency for Frances to feel jealous about the kind of sex life which Ernest had had with his first wife.

In therapy the couple responded quite well to non-genital sensate focus, and Ernest was getting quite good erections at this stage. However, Frances felt that it was left to her to choose when to do the homework exercises, and complained in general that Ernest was too passive and left too many decisions to her. He explained that he was rather afraid to decide things in case she disagreed, and this was partly related to the fact that they were living in her house and he felt in some ways like a lodger.

The therapist asked them to discuss something they disagreed about: he chose the way that her daughters appeared to get away with things which his daughters were not allowed to do, and an argument ensued in which she lost her temper and threatened to end the relationship. The couple went on to agree on some rules for their children in what was now acknowledged as 'their' house, and after settling this difference were able to go on to genital sensate focus, with Ernest taking more initiative.

Towards the end of therapy, Frances was not willing to attend joint sessions any more, but Ernest continued and reported that he was functioning much better sexually, and that Frances had been pleased both with this and his increased readiness to take responsibility in the house.

This case illustrates the use of sensate focus exercises in helping to reduce performance anxiety, the need for middle-aged couples to reduce their unrealistic expectations, the use of trivial arguments in redressing the balance in a relationship and the importance of territorial considerations in determining the dominance hierarchy of a relationship.

11.6 Assessment and treatment of sexual dysfunctions

11.6.1 Assessment

Assessment of a couple presenting with sexual problems begins with taking a history of the problem, of the individuals and of the relationship. This may be done by seeing them both together, but we usually prefer to see each partner alone for at least part of the time. We concentrate on the problem itself, its duration, the factors which make it better or worse, the attitudes of both partners to the difficulties and the quality of the sexual relationship apart from the aspect which is dysfunctional. We then look at other facets of the relationship, including communication, resentment, stresses, inhibitions and positive strengths. We then take an individual sexual history with an emphasis on all the factors contributing to the problem, and on what the partners have done right in the past which they are perhaps doing less right at present. The biographical and family history we have already obtained by asking the partners to fill in a history sheet before coming to the clinic (see appendix).

In some cases we also do a physical examination of the dysfunctional partner, but this is more or less confined to two conditions, erectile impotence and vaginismus. In the case of impotence the examination is to find out if there are any organic illnesses which might be contributing to the problem, and in the case of vaginismus it is to confirm if muscle spasm is indeed there and to begin the process of therapy with relaxation and dilatation.

11.6.2 General treatment principles

Although we do not adhere strictly to the approach initiated by Masters and Johnson (1970), their work is still in many ways the mainstay of sexual therapy, as in most centres. The variations that have been introduced have been largely in order to make the treatment more acceptable to National Health Service patients and additionally in the case of our own clinic, to increase the emphasis on the relationship and communication in therapy.

The work of Masters and Johnson represented a breakthrough in the treatment of sexual dysfunctions. These had hitherto been understood as individual illnesses, either physical or psychological, with little or no reference to the relationship in which they occurred. Masters and Johnson began the practice of treating both partners together, which has now been adopted by nearly all sexual and marital therapists, and most therapists still use, in a modified form, the general method initiated by them.

The main features of their approach are (a) anxiety reduction, (b) work on communication, (c) education and permission-giving, (d) exercises encouraging physical contact without demand and (e) specific techniques for specific problems. These are placed within a context of the total environment in which the couple are interacting sexually, so that questions about the comfort of the room, warmth, personal hygiene and attractive oils, talcum powder or perfumes, gentle lighting, soft music, a locked door, perhaps a bottle of wine and a good meal together are all considered when using the following exercises.

11.6.3 Relaxation exercises

Although Masters and Johnson did not specifically recommend these exercises for couples with sexual dysfunctions, we have found that they are generally helpful, and at the Maudsley sexual dysfunction clinic most couples are taught relaxation (Jacobson 1938) on their first visit. Progressive relaxation of different muscle groups, preceded by tensing the muscles, is accompanied by deep, slow breathing and a mental image of a peaceful scene or a flower. The pelvic muscles in particular are tensed and relaxed, as in the Kegel exercises (Kegel 1952), since control of these muscles can be helpful in dealing with some problems such as anorgasmia.

11.6.4 Communication and permission-giving

In this process, which continues throughout most of the therapy and usually takes place in the conjoint sessions, the therapist should follow all the guidelines in the chapters on couple therapy (Chapters 4 to 10). A particularly useful technique in this regard is decentring (Section 6.4.1). It is also important to keep a sense of purpose in the sessions, so as not to drift into simple support for the couple; however, this should not lead to an over-serious approach, and lightness of touch and some use of humour are important components of therapy (Section 4.3.4). It is often necessary to bring out some quite painful emotions in therapy (Section 6.5) and an atmosphere in which these are accepted without seeming the most important thing in the world will help considerably. It may at times be necessary to use reframes (Section 9.13.2), timetables (Section 9.4) and even paradox (Section 9.13) in dealing with the communication problems that couples bring to therapy, and it is always useful to have these techniques available when dealing with sexual problems.

The concept of permission-giving relates to the difficulties which some couples and individuals have with knowing what is acceptable. Their parents may have had very strict views on masturbation, for example, and taboos about sexual touching may inhibit many couples from healthy experimentation. The therapist can take the role of a benign 'second parent' in the therapy, whatever the relative ages of therapist and couple, and thus assist them to achieve the goals of therapy.

11.6.5 Sensate focus (non-genital)

Sensate focus (Masters and Johnson) is a series of homework exercises designed to help couples to become more comfortable with physical contact and closeness. They are encouraged to learn to communicate by touch, although speaking is not forbidden. What is forbidden, however, is any touching of breasts or of the genital areas (at least at first) and sexual intercourse. The ban has an anxiety-reducing effect, since performance anxiety is present in most forms of dysfunction, and the ban on performance can liberate the inhibited urges. Indeed, it sometimes has the paradoxical effect of leading the couple to break the ban and have intercourse, although the therapist should not allow them to become complacent if this occurs, but should predict failure the next time they break the ban.

The exercises begin with non-genital sensate focus. The couple should ensure that they have a warm and comfortable place to practise, using extra heat in the bedroom if necessary. They should then undress and, having carried out the relaxation exercises, stroke and caress each other's bodies in turn, using body lotion or oil on the hands (or talcum powder if preferred). The emphasis is on physical communication through the hands of the active partner and the body of the recipient, and they are encouraged to talk only about their emotional responses to what is happening ('I liked that feeling' or 'I feel warm and relaxed') and requests for other types of touching ('I liked that, but I would like you to use the palm of your hand rather than the tips of your fingers because that makes me feel more sensual').

11.6.6 Genital sensate focus

From this the couple can move on after a week or two to genital sensate focus. At this stage the touching of breasts and genital areas is permitted, but the ban on intercourse remains, and they are encouraged not to aim to maintain an erection or achieve arousal in the woman. Instead, they should use a 'teasing' technique, with pauses between periods of genital contact to allow the excitement to abate. They may be encouraged to use a vibrator at this stage, or to use other aids such as the spray from a shower head to stimulate themselves. The advantage of breaking off from stimulation from time to time is that it avoids the idea that they are expected to have successful intercourse immediately, and if they can reduce and then regain the excitement, they will not panic if in future the erection is temporarily lost or the woman loses her arousal.

It is quite useful, in those couples to whom it is acceptable, to recommend some oral-genital stimulation at this stage. It provides a good transition between manual or vibrator stimulation and full intercourse.

11.6.7 Self-focus

Some couples can be helped at this stage by self-focussing. The partners are asked to have homework sessions alone in which they can examine themselves, perhaps with the use of a hand-mirror, to explore their own anatomy and responsiveness. It may be very useful to recommend the use of a vibrator at this stage, either for men or women: many women in particular can achieve orgasm more easily by this means than most others.

11.6.8 Other general techniques

After using relaxation, sensate focus and perhaps self-focus, the couple may be ready to proceed to attempt penetration, which should be tried as an extension of a sensate focus session. The woman-above position is a good one to recommend, since (a) it gets away from conditioned anxiety experienced in the more usual positions, (b) it involves less manoeuvring by the man to achieve penetration and (c) it gives the woman more freedom of movement. (For greater detail see Comfort (1972) or Kaplan (1981).)

It may be useful at this stage of therapy to recommend the couple to read explicit books or magazines or watch explicit videotapes to stimulate their sexual fantasy. Research has shown (Gillan 1987) that both men and women respond with physiological and emotional arousal to this kind of material; but the therapist should be careful not to recommend it to those who might find it offensive.

11.6.9 Management of impotence

For men with erectile failure the basic approach used is sensate focus, with both self-focussing and teasing in the genital stage. Many men respond well to this, especially if they have high anxiety levels. Another good prognostic sign is if the man reports erections either spontaneously in the daytime or on waking at night and in the early morning. The problem is also helped if the man has a high sex drive, and if his partner is an enthusiastic, but not too critical, participant in the homework exercises. From non-genital sensate focus the couple are encouraged to proceed to genital sensate focus and then to experiment with penetration in the woman-above position.

Impotence was the condition which Masters and Johnson found to be the hardest to treat successfully, and that is still the experience of most sexual therapists today. Whether the cause seems to be organic (diabetes, multiple sclerosis, etc.) or psychological, the number of successes is still probably below 50%. In those who fail to improve with psychosexual approaches there are four more or less promising forms of physical treatment available.

The first is the use of medication by mouth. The drug yohimbine, which antagonises the alpha action of adrenaline, has been shown recently to have useful effects in some cases of impotence, especially in helping men to obtain erections by self or partner stimulation (Riley *et al.* 1989), and we have seen some men with partial or situational impotence greatly helped when other methods have failed. The response rate is, however, quite low, and better drugs may well be developed.

The second is the use of papaverine injections directly into the penis. The man has to learn to inject himself, as the effect only lasts for an hour or so, but this drug, which acts by dilating blood vessels, can produce a full erection in most men who are impotent, whether the cause is psychological or due to nerve damage. It is particularly useful in men who are paraplegic, for whom it can provide a sex life and the possibility of having children, which are otherwise almost impossible. The effect is, however, usually poor in those who have impaired blood supply, including many elderly men. The method is of course quite unacceptable to some men and to some of their partners, but to others it can offer a reliable substitute for a natural erection, and ejaculation can occur during intercourse. There are some risks, the most serious of which is that the erection may last too long and cause permanent damage to the penis, but with good technique these can be minimised (see Crowe and Qureshi 1989 and Brindley 1983).

The third approach is the surgical implantation of teflon rods into the penis, which produce a semi-permanent erection which can be bent to shape as required. This radical treatment is not for the squeamish, but many patients, especially in the USA, appear to have found it acceptable. It can be very valuable in cases where because of disease the penis has become deformed and normal function is completely impossible.

The fourth approach is the use of a semi-rigid condom. When the air is sucked out of this through a tube, the penis enlarges passively, and intercourse can take place.

None of these physical solutions are completely satisfactory, as they merely provide a mechanical or pharmacological substitute for normal male arousal.

11.6.10 Management of premature ejaculation

Some degree of control of ejaculation can be achieved by the 'stop-start' technique first described by Semans (1956). The man is encouraged, as part of his homework, to obtain an erection and then masturbate as if to produce ejaculation. At the moment of 'ejaculatory inevitability', but before ejaculation occurs, he is told to stop touching himself and allow the urge to abate. The penis then becomes unresponsive, and when he begins to stimulate himself a minute or so later, he finds that quite vigorous stimulation is possible without ejaculation. The cycle can be repeated several times, using the stop-start technique each time, and we suggest continuing for 15 minutes without ejaculating before proceeding to the next step.

The next step is to carry out the same exercise with body-oil on his hand, to make control more difficult, and the experience more like that of intercourse. The third and fourth steps are for his partner to stimulate the penis with a dry hand and then with body-oil on her hand. Eventually control can be achieved by using the technique in oral sex and in full intercourse.

We usually emphasise to the couple that the stop-start technique is not a cure for premature ejaculation, but rather a means of controlling and circumventing what may well be a lifelong tendency to ejaculate early. In some refractory cases, the drug clomipramine (an antidepressant) can be given to the man 30 minutes before intercourse, and may produce a delay in ejaculation: this makes use of one of clomipramine's side effects.

11.6.11 Management of delayed or absent ejaculation

The management of delayed ejaculation is somewhat similar to that of premature ejaculation. The Masters and Johnson technique of 'super-stimulation' is used, in which the penis is rubbed very vigorously with the hand lubricated with body-oil until ejaculation occurs. There is then a progression from self-stimulation of the penis to stimulation by the partner and then to intercourse. It is very much easier to help those men who can at least ejaculate in masturbation, and for some of those who can only have nocturnal emissions it may be impossible to achieve ejaculation in the waking state. However, when ejaculation does occur in the successful cases, it is as if a taboo has been broken and the man can feel more confident about doing so in future.

11.6.12 Management of vaginismus

In the treatment of this problem the main emphasis is on gradual retraining of the muscles surrounding the vagina to relax. This is achieved by the use of graded dilators (smooth tapered tubes of different sizes) or by the use of fingers. It is always possible for a woman with this problem to be examined internally using one finger, and after the doctor has done this the woman, and then the partner, is usually asked to follow suit.

The subsequent homework involves the insertion by the woman, and then by the man, of one, two and then three fingers or of the graded dilators into the vagina over a period of several weeks. Eventually the couple can allow penetration, slowly and carefully, by the erect penis, with the woman on top. Most couples with this problem eventually consummate the relationship, but difficulties are often encountered at the stage of penile penetration, with both partners being equally resistant to progress (see Example 11G).

11.6.13 Management of female lack of arousal and anorgasmia

The treatment of this problem follows the general course of therapy outlined in Sections 11.6.1 to 11.6.4. Sensate focus, genital sensate focus, self-focussing techniques and communication are all important in these problems, and it is especially important to explore two areas of the relationship. The first is whether there are any unspoken resentments and the second is to explore in depth the couple's love-making to find whether there are any approaches by the man which could be improved to be more acceptable to the woman.

In treating anorgasmia various self-stimulation techniques can be recommended, which might include more conventional approaches such as the use of the fingers or more unconventional ones such as the spray from a shower head or a soft sponge in the bath. Vibrators are very useful, and it has been claimed that 95% of women can achieve an orgasm with the help of a vibrator, whereas a much lower proportion do so regularly in sexual intercourse. It is this last finding which suggests that a couple may often have to settle for a less than ideal relationship in which the woman achieves her climax separately from the act of intercourse.

11.7 Conclusions

There are now many ways of helping couples with problems of both sexual motivation and sexual dysfunction. Many of the motivational difficulties (problems of sexual desire) can be dealt with in couple therapy without any special experience of sexual dysfunction work. Problems of function, however, are best treated in a sexual dysfunction clinic, where specialist advice is available and where physical examination and treatment can be carried out.

One important reservation should be repeated here, and that is that therapy in this field can help couples and individuals to improve their functioning and their interest in sex, but is in no way to be understood as 'curing' a condition or disease. If they can incorporate the new ideas they have learned, they may well go on through the rest of their relationship without further problems, but the possibility will remain that the problem may recur, at times of stress or when illness or other adversity comes on them to make them more vulnerable.

Chapter 12

Training of therapists

12.1 Introduction

Behavioural-systems couple therapy is not intrinsically very difficult to learn, especially in the more behavioural aspects, but does require of the therapist an ability to understand and use different theoretical approaches. It also requires a preparedness to alter interventions according to the needs of the couple. We have included some basic exercises which can be used in training or supervision to help therapists begin to learn and use this approach.

The exercises are designed to help the trainee therapist to use the current relationship of the couple and their interaction as the focus for therapy. This is an essential starting point. Should trainees wish to adapt any of these skills for use in their regular work with couples it is preferable that this should be accompanied initially by suitably qualified and experienced supervision.

Case illustrations presented in earlier chapters are referred to as material for many of the exercises; each exercise will therefore require some additional preparation by trainers or supervisors who will need to familiarise themselves with the relevant chapter, case description and details of the exercise being used.

Guidelines have been given for the amount of time which may be required for some of the exercises. Trainers are advised to ensure that sufficient time is also available for discussion and review of each training session. Times stated in [ ] are the minimum recommended.

It is also recommended that best use can be made of this chapter if a series of training or supervision sessions is set up so that trainees can digest the material and return for further exploration.

Trainers should also be aware of the need to provide adequate space, time and comfort for training and a supportive environment in which trainees can experiment in order to extend their repertoire of skills.

12.2 Requirements for those wishing to train as couple therapists

Before training as a couple therapist, trainees should have a basic knowledge and understanding of the following areas:

- The dynamics and sociology of marriage and family interaction.
- The phases of human development.
- The potential impact on the individual and the family of life events.
- Knowledge of sexual function and behaviour and their interaction in couple relationships (see Chapter 11).
- Some knowledge of mental and physical illness and the interaction of these with couple and family relationships.
- Some knowledge of socio-cultural norms and variations in couple relationships.

In addition to the above, a potential couple therapist should already have basic counselling skills to be able to begin and sustain relationships with couples, to be empathic while maintaining a level of objectivity, to be able to be flexible enough to develop new knowledge and skills, and to learn from direct observation and feedback. Individual attributes are difficult to define but the personality, integrity and commitment of the individual play a significant part in the therapeutic process.

(See *Marriage Matters* (1979) for further discussion of the basic requirements for trainees wishing to become couple therapists.)

12.3 Getting away from bias in the therapist

Because the Maudsley Marital Therapy Clinic participates in the Hospital's post-graduate training programme, over the years many trainees have attended the clinic. They have come from diverse cultures, and have varied in their theoretical orientation, skills, sensitivity and interests. This has usually added to the understanding and perception of the team, and the trainees and the whole therapy team have also been able to extend their own views of what is normal. An essential aspect of training is to assist the trainee to be aware of and to draw upon his/her stored knowledge when observing and working with couples. In spite of this diversity of culture, knowledge and skills, trainees usually find areas of common ground which can be built upon in using the be-havioural-systems approach.

Many trainees have strong personal views about couple relationships. As outlined in Chapter 1, the current climate of opinion is one of fluidity and controversy. Gender and sexuality, child-rearing practices, power and control within the family and where it should rest are all matters about which the therapist, as well as the couple, may hold opinions. No therapist can ever be completely free from cultural and social attitudes. What is important in training is how these opinions and attitudes affect the therapist's ability to observe, understand and intervene into the couple's interaction.

A practical initial solution to this dilemma is to help therapists to acknowledge that most couples are the arbiters of their own require-ments. This means that the therapist learns to concentrate on the re-quirements and concerns which the couple bring into therapy (rather than assumed difficulties which are derived from the therapist's own values and theoretical preferences), and ensures that the couple's agenda is the focus of therapy (Section 4.6.3).

There are of course many situations in therapy where the agenda of the couple and therapist are necessarily different, for example some cases of child physical or sexual abuse (Section 10.12), depression in one partner (Section 10.7) or jealousy (Section 10.3). However, for training purposes it seems essential to begin by focussing on the problem presented by the couple.

Where there is a clash of ideals between the therapist and the couple this should be taken to supervision for open discussion. Regular supervision is an integral part of training, and provides a forum for exploration and sharing of attitude and experience between therapists. A section on supervision has been included at the end of this chapter, and many of the training exercises can also be used in group supervision.

12.4 Training issues

Areas which have been selected as beginning points in learning how to use the behavioural/systems approach are:

- Focussing on the interaction by using role-play (Section 12.6).
- The use of current case material in role-play situations (Section 12.6.9).
- Decentring (Section 12.7).
- Moving in and out of the interaction (Section 12.8).
- Exercises relating to the worker's feelings of helplessness (Section 12.10).
- Appropriate use of empathy, and feedback from co-therapists (Section 12.11).
- Thinking about a relationship systemically (Section 12.12).
- Formulating messages (Section 12.13).
- Training in dealing with sexual issues (Section 12.14).
- Supervision (Section 12.16).

12.5 Focussing on the interaction
(see Sections 4.4.1 and 4.6.5)

In order to focus on the interaction between the couple, the therapist must find ways of helping the couple to talk together in-session about an aspect of their relationship which has brought them into therapy. They should be kept to the topic in gentle but firm ways so that the therapist has the opportunity to observe how they communicate together.

Therapists may find three areas difficult.

(1) How to interrupt the couple and take control of the use the couple make of the session (see Sections 4.3.3 and 4.4.2).

(2) How to be persistent and supportive while asking the couple to 'stick to the topic' (see Sections 4.6.2 and 6.4.3).

(3) Decentring: how to continue to ask the couple to talk to each other rather than to the therapist (see Sections 4.6.8 and 6.4.1).

Many therapists have been trained to listen and to allow the client to associate freely, and are discouraged from interrupting the flow of material from the client. Possibly, too, general good manners and etiquette in Britain suggest that it is discourteous to interrupt while someone is talking, particularly while describing difficulties. In order to use the behavioural-systems approach a more interventionist style is often required. From a behavioural perspective one needs to develop these skills in order to change the observed behaviour in the session; from a systems perspective, to interrupt and take control of the session is a useful way of 'challenging the system'.

12.6 Using role-play to practice focussing on the interaction

Role-play is an effective learning tool. It allows therapists to practise with colleagues, to receive feedback as to how they were experienced as therapists and to learn how it might feel to be a client, whether male or female partner, in a particular situation. It is therefore helpful if therapists can practise the four roles of therapist, husband, wife and observer in a training session (Morry van Ments 1983; Manor 1984; Priestley and McGuire 1978).

We suggest that the following guidelines should be followed by trainers until they have acquired greater experience and become more confident with the material. Then the guidelines can be implemented more flexibly.

12.6.1 Setting up a role-play

(1) Select a suitable couple. When setting up a role-play the trainer should be clear about what work is to be attempted. Examples quoted in the text can be used, beginning with couples who are neither too rigid nor too difficult, and using the guidelines for setting up and learning from role-play (Sections 12.6.1–12.6.7).

For example, Caroline and Douglas (Example 5A) may be used in order to *develop skills in reciprocity negotiation and to make a simple request of each other* (see Sections 5.2 to 5.7). (When using other case material the group or trainer should decide the focus of the exercise and alter this statement accordingly.) If Caroline and Douglas are used it should be noted that they tend to make requests which are vague; therefore those role-playing the couple should be ready to talk to each other but should be somewhat hesitant about *making a simple request of each other*.

(2) Divide into groups of four.

(3) Decide who will play the role of husband, wife, therapist and observer.

(4) Each participant should spend about two minutes thinking about the role, reading the available details and thinking about the attitude of the person.

(5) Designate one chair for each role, so that participants change chairs as they change roles (as in diagram).

H   W

                    T

          O

(6) The therapist must be clear about what s/he will attempt to do, and explain this to the observer.

12.6.2 Guidelines for the therapist in the role-play

In this role-play the therapist's task is to ask the couple to *make a simple request of each other*, and to continue to work towards achieving this. (When using other examples the specific task will be inserted here.) The therapist should be patient, supportive and sensitive to how the couple respond to the request, but not give in, certainly not before more than four or five attempts have been made to enable the couple to work together on the task. The therapist can feel free to explain, use humour, accept that his/her manner may be somewhat like that of a school-teacher, acknowledge any embarrassment the couple may feel, but should not give up.

It is also important to try to ensure that the interaction is reciprocal and that each partner is about equally involved. If, for example, one partner is taking a long time to make a simple request of the other, the therapist can suggest that this is 'put on the back burner' for the moment and the other partner is brought in to make a simple request. In such a way the interaction is kept as reciprocal as possible.

Any anxieties about being persistent and the impact of this on the couple should be kept until the role-play is being reviewed.

12.6.3 The use of the observer in the role-play

The observer's role is that of assistant to the therapist, resembling the team behind the screen in our therapy clinic. For this reason the therapist should tell the observer what work is being attempted. It is important that the observer is attentive, and makes any critical comments positively and in such a way that the therapist feels supported. Giving supportive but useful feedback is one of the essential ingredients in training. The role of the observer mirrors some of the work the therapist does with the couple, and the observer should be able to pass the control back to the therapist after any interruption, in the same way as the therapist does with the couple.

12.6.4 Time-limited role-play

When setting up role-plays the trainer should be clear about how much time is to be used, and whether or not the role-play will be interrupted. As a general rule, trainers should be strict about timekeeping.

If using Caroline and Douglas (Example 5A), take five to ten minutes for the role-play. The observer may interrupt to talk to the therapist, then proceed with the role-play and stop after ten minutes. Do not run over time. The trainer has an overall responsibility for the exercise and in doing so can model the behaviour of stepping in, taking control and then giving it back to the participants. [5–10 minutes]

12.6.5 Learning from the role-play by reviewing the experience

(1) Ask each partner in turn to say what it felt like to have a therapist who, in this role-play *kept them to the topic*. (In alternative role-plays substitute here the therapist's task.) Allow time for each partner to contribute equally.
(2) Now ask the observer to comment about the therapist's interventions.
(3) Give the therapist time to say first how it felt, and second what has been learned from the experience.
(4) Do not hurry this reviewing and discussion, and do ensure that each participant is given adequate time to speak about the experience. Each person should say something about how it felt and what was learned, both in role and out of role. Much valuable learning takes place in these review sessions. As a general rule of thumb, if the roleplay takes ten minutes, the reviewing will take at least 20–30 minutes.

As the trainer gains more experience of the material and of the training group these can be used more flexibly.

12.6.6 Rotate

Using the same case material, rotate three more times so that each trainee can experience each role. The scenario will change slightly and each role-play will build upon earlier suggestions.

12.6.7 Derole

It is sensible to make a regular habit of deroling after each exercise. A simple method is for pairs to talk together about (a) something they did yesterday and (b) something they anticipate doing later in the day. Another way is to state your name and what you are doing in the training group and that you are not the person you have been role-playing.

Such an exercise enables trainees to move between roles and to set down the feelings associated with a previous part. Deroling should not be ignored: it is of itself a useful learning experience and may help therapists to think about issues such as overinvolvement with clients, and the development of empathy with a wide range of clients. [3–5 minutes]

As each role-play progresses, the trainee should become a little more confident about focussing on the interaction by interrupting and taking control of the use the couple make of the session, gently and firmly keeping the couple to the topic and decentring.

12.6.8 Additional examples from the test

(1) Ken and Louise, Example 6D. In this example Ken is being asked to *say something positive* about his wife Louise. The therapist can use this example to develop skills in communication training by *encouraging an increase in positive interaction* (see Section 6.4.8). The therapist can work with Ken and Louise to encourage Ken to say something positive to Louise. After this has been achieved the therapist should intervene to make the interchange reciprocal by asking Louise to say something positive to Ken.

Each role play should last for 5–10 minutes followed by each player giving feedback about the experience. Follow the procedure set up in the preceding example from Section 12.6.1 to 12.6.7.

(2) Ken and Louise can also be used for a role-play in which couples are requested to *say something positive about each other without adding a sting in the tail* (see Section 6.4.7).

(3) Ian and Jenny, Example 6C, had never discussed together whether they really wanted to move out of Brixton and needed the therapist's help to do so. Use this in another role-play in which the task of the therapist is *to assist Jenny and Ian to have this discussion*.

(4) When trainees are ready for more challenging material, Tony and Jane M (Example 7A) can be used as role-play material. Since it took an experienced therapist at least three sessions before this couple were prepared to set aside years of ritual arguments, the trainees should expect to meet negative responses. This case *can be used for discussion and experimentation of work with more rigid couples*.

12.6.9 Using case material from current work load

Many therapists find it helpful to use cases known to them as learning material. In selecting cases for training purposes start with simpler problems, and be quite specific about what skills are being practised. The group can be asked to discuss together couples known to them and to choose one couple to be used for a role-play, bearing in mind the two principles of beginning with a simpler couple and being specific about what skills are being practised. Experience suggests that both trainee and trained therapists enjoy role-playing difficult clients and 'giving the therapist hell'. This tendency should be avoided if possible, for example by the trainer warning the trainee of the danger before the role-play.

One caveat here is that the person who introduced the case which is being role-played must relinquish the right to make factual corrections to the role-players. Statements such as 'the real George wouldn't have been as dogmatic as that' are not helpful, and divert the group from the task of learning how to carry out couple therapy. The accuracy of the details of the case is irrelevant in an exercise mainly focussed on technique.

12.6.10 Other uses of role-play

Once trainees have become familiar with using role-play to focus on the interaction, then current case material can be used in practising other skills. Exercises using role-play could focus on any of the following:

- Encouraging arguments (see Section 8.2).
- Keeping up the momentum by asking for short interactions (see Section 6.4.9).
- Using the silent partner as facilitator (see Section 4.6.6).
- Encouraging discussion about small issues (see Section 8.3.4).
- Encouraging discussion of resentments (see Section 6.5).
- Changing or reframing the issue so that:
  a) complaints become wishes (see Section 5.5),
  b) a sting in the tail becomes a positive comment (see Section 6.4.7),
  c) mind-reading becomes an 'I' statement (see Sections 6.4.5 and 6.4.6),
  d) the past is related to the present (see Section 6.4.9.2).

12.7 Decentring

In order to ensure that the couple talk to each other and not to the therapist, the therapist must be firm and ensure that s/he is not continually interrupting the couple or being brought back into the interaction. Some of this work has already been started in the above examples, as each time the couple work together in the session and the therapist does not intervene we can say that the therapist is decentred (see Sections 4.6.9 and 6.4.1).

The following role-play can be used as practice material.

Example 12A

Pam and Peter T have been married for five years and have no children. Peter had a 'one-night stand' while working in San Francisco nine months ago. Ever since he told his wife about this (six months ago) their marriage has deteriorated. Pam no longer feels that she can trust her husband, no matter what he does to reassure her that this was in no sense a meaningful relationship. Peter feels that he has been sufficiently penitent for his 'sins' and is irritable with his wife. Both Peter and Pam want the therapist to agree that they are personally justified in their viewpoint. They constantly ask the therapist to agree with them, and to tell the spouse that s/he has misbehaved. For example:

PAM
He is completely untrustworthy. Don't you agree? Don't you think that he had no right to treat me like he has done?

PETER
I've tried and tried to make it up to her, I've apologised, I've begged and pleaded with her. Can you make her see reason?

The therapist's task is to not get drawn in to answer any of these questions, but to help the couple address their questions to each other. The therapist should be particularly aware of non-verbal interaction between him/herself and the couple. It is often useful to look at the non-speaking partner, but not to make eye contact. (See also Section 4.6.9 for helpful phrases which make it easier to decentre.) A neutral position in relation to both partners should be sought. [10 minutes]

Follow the outline for learning from the role-play in Section 12.6.1 and ensure that sufficient time is available for reviewing and discussion. Rotate roles as in Section 12.6.6 where useful.

12.8 Moving in and out of the interaction

As the therapist gains confidence in being decentred, similar role plays can be used to gain experience in 'moving in' or 'staying out' (decentred) of the interaction. Bearing in mind that one is asking the couple to work on their relationship, the therapist only interrupts to find alternative ways of helping them continue with their work. The therapist has a range of options to consider, and may wish to move in to the interaction in order to:

- Balance the interaction (see Section 6.4.1).
- Ask the speaking partner to seek help from the non-speaking partner in some way (see Section 4.6.7).
- Challenge the pattern that is developing in the session, e.g. the therapist constantly allying with one partner (see Section 8.3.3).

- Stay with the issue (Section 8.3.5).
- Decide to ally with one partner in order to take a discussion further (Sections 10.7.3 and 10.7.4).
- Ask the couple to check out the meaning of each other's non-verbal behaviour (Section 6.4.2.1).
- Suggest that the couple 'reverse role-play' the discussion which has just taken place, each taking the other partner's attitude and words (see Section 10.5.2).
- Stop the action and discuss how it felt for each partner (see Section 9.10.2, David and Marcia T, at point 12).
- Introduce a topic mentioned earlier in the session but not resolved (see Section 8.3.5).

All of the above interventions can be practised in training sessions with the use of role-play and current case material.

12.9 Summary of the use of role-play for training purposes

When using role-play to develop greater skills in any of these areas it is most helpful if the therapist states clearly which intervention is being attempted before the role-play begins. The other participants can then feed back to the therapist their experiences of how s/he worked.

Note should be made of the pacing of interventions from the therapist as well as the degree of confidence and empathy showed.Feedback from role-play is usually helpful to the inexperienced therapist as risks can be taken in an experimental but supportive environment, and feedback is necessary so that the trainee can learn from such experiments. Therapists who have been trained in a more reflective style and may be reluctant to experiment with an interventionist approach are reassured to learn that the role-play clients usually perceive the more active therapist as supportive. The role-play couple often express surprise that they are asked to work together in the session and go on to express ways in which they found it helpful. Discussion of the various interventions and how they were experienced by each player should be encouraged.

Role-players may feel that they have been expressing in the role-play their own personality and biases; or they may feel that they have been temporarily taken over by the part they have played. The trainer should encourage open discussion of any area of difficulty experienced by the participants and ensure that all participants have been adequately de-roled.

Others may be reluctant to try role-play and question how accurately any role-play can reflect the life experiences of couples; this must remain an open question. However, from our own experiences in training we suggest that it is one of the better training resources available at present.

Role-playing thus provides a format for training which allows experimentation and feedback in a supervised situation, encourages participants to experience what it might be like to be on the receiving end of therapy and encourages flexibility in the worker.

12.10   Exercises relating to the worker's feelings of helplessness

One of the difficulties therapists encounter is that, when faced with the couple's distress, if they seem to be in a rigid or uncompromising relationship, the therapist may begin to feel a personal sense of helplessness. Rather than working gently in the session to facilitate small changes of the kind we recommend,therapists may become either too passive or too active. These may be natural reactions to being overwhelmed by a sense of the apparently irreversible nature of the couple's difficulties. It may also reflect something of how the couple are feeling. Within the psychoanalytical field such feelings experienced by the therapist might be used to understand the projected and possibly denied feelings of the couple.

We are not, however, only concerned to understand the dynamics of the situation, but to assist the therapist to find resources to overcome this feeling of helplessness and ensure progress in therapy without overcompensating in either direction. This could take the form of being overactive in that the therapist begins to give advice or lecture the couple on how best to solve their problem, or being passive and simply letting the session drift aimlessly.

12.10.1   Exercise in which the observer's task is to assist the therapist to overcome feelings of helplessness

Use Example 6J: Pat and Theresa K (see Section 6.4.6). Pat and Theresa K are extremely concerned that their marriage might be at an end, and want desperately to see if there is any possibility of saving their marriage for the sake of the children. Pat seems more anxious than his wife to continue the relationship. Theresa describes their difficulties as longstanding. They each have many complaints against the other and continue their battling in the session.

12.10.2   Setting up the 'helplessness' role-play

Set up the role-play with husband, wife, therapist and observer; follow the guidelines in Sections 12.6.1 to 12.6.7. The guidelines for the observer and therapist are altered as follows.

12.10.3   Guidelines for the observer in the 'helplessness' role-play

The observer's task is to support the therapist in the following manner. When the observer senses that the therapist is being either too active or too passive, the observer is to interrupt the role-play and make a suggestion as to how the therapist might intervene to help the couple make a small change in their interaction. Some suggestions might be non-verbal changes (see Section 6.4.2), role reversal (see Section 10.5.2), proposals of topics to be discussed (see Section 6.4.3) or changes in communication such as asking each couple to take the 'I' position (see Section 6.4.5). If the therapist is being too active s/he can be reminded to stay decentred as much as possible and to keep up the momentum of the couple's interaction (see Sections 4.6.4, 4.6.5 and 4.6.9).

12.10.4 Guidelines for the therapist in the 'helplessness' role-play

For this exercise the therapist has to trust the observer and accept the observer's suggestions as a way forward. For example, the couple in role-play may be complaining about each other and saying that nothing can be done. The therapist may be allowing the interaction to drift, feeling similarly that nothing can be done. The observer might interrupt and ask the therapist to choose to:

(a) feed back to the couple that they are good at complaining about each other, and suggest that they stop complaining and instead say something that pleases each about the other's character; or
(b) sympathise with their powerful feelings that as a couple it is hard to change, but suggest that each make a simple suggestion of something they could do which would contribute towards change, starting with the phrase 'I suggest I could . . .'.

The therapist's task is to choose one of these suggestions (even if in disagreement) and practise this intervention in the role-play.

Where the therapist has been too active then s/he should accept the suggestion of the observer to stay decentred and to focus on the couple's interaction.

12.10.5 Timespan

To allow time for interruptions and discussions between the therapist and observer, each role-play can run for 20–30 minutes.

12.10.6 Discussion of the interventions

Discussions should follow the process outlined in Section 12.6.5. The therapist's feelings of being helpless and what was learned by being asked to change the tempo of the interventions should be explored.

12.10.7 Rotate and derole

This exercise can be continued until each participant has practised each role. The repetition allows trainees to observe a wider range of alternative intervention as well as experiencing being a client. Trainers should ensure that participants de-role at the end of these exercises (see Sections 12.6.6 and 12.6.7.)

12.10.8 Using case material from current work load to assist trainees overcome feelings of helplessness

Following the use of the above role-play, therapists may benefit from role-playing couples from their current work load who bring up similar feelings of helplessness when working. The observer should continue to be responsible for initiating interventions when the therapist becomes either passive or overactive, as in the above guidelines.

12.10.9 Summary of 'helplessness' role-play

The use of the observer in the above exercises is analogous to the use of the telephone in our setting where the team is behind the one-way screen and may telephone and make suggestions to the therapist while in the session. Occasionally the therapist may be called out of the room to discuss alternative strategies. This break is often enough to interrupt the feelings of being helpless, and enables him/her to go back into the session with a more patient or a more positive approach.

Therapists often wish to discuss together reasons why these feelings occur and concepts such as transference or projection are often used as a possible explanation of the therapist's feelings. Another, more systemic, explanation is that the couple are in some way finding that the current situation stabilises their relationship in the face of a life event or a life cycle transition, and are therefore happier with the status quo, including the symptoms, than any alternative.

The aim of this exercise is to give the trainee an experience of finding alternative interventions which can help with feelings of helplessness that are generated by some more rigid or uncompromising couples.

12.11 Training in the appropriate use of empathy in the context of a more active therapeutic approach

The appropriate use of empathy is an exceptionally difficult area, and should be included in regular supervision (see also Sections 6.4.2.1 to 6.4.2.5). When working with couples one is often learning about intimate relationships and complex emotions and these may generate in the trainee intense personal responses. Such reactions may be both a help and a hindrance to the therapist, but it is often quite difficult for therapists to be aware of how such strong emotional responses affect the way they work. A trainee can learn more about how s/he is experienced by others by receiving regular, appropriate and supportive feedback from co-trainees, who have observed each other's work. This is best achieved in small training groups where trainees can learn to trust each others' judgment and respect each others' feelings.

12.11.1 Checklist of therapist skills in empathising

When such training groups are focussing on appropriate empathy the following feedback regarding the trainee's ability to pick up the feelings of the two partners and communicate with them is useful:

- Sensitivity to the feelings of both partners in-session.
- Non-verbal communication with the couple.
- Ability to pace any intervention to the seriousness of the situation.
- Ability to be supportive without rescuing.
- Ability to stay decentred and avoid being pulled in on the side of one partner by differentially empathising with them.
- Ability to 'stay with' the feelings of the moment.
- Ability to use the therapist's empathy to increase the partners' empathy with each other.
- Ability to help the couple to talk about intimate and personal issues without embarrassment.
- Ability to accept the occasional negative or hostile comment without retaliating.

Training group members will need to develop an open and accepting approach to each other's difficulties and be supportive when giving feedback.

12.11.2 Format for feedback sessions

Where therapists feel they need to have further training on any of the above topics a useful format is as follows.

(1) Choose the topic area to be considered; for example *a trainee's difficulty in staying with the expression of anger between the partners.*

(2) Discuss in pairs the difficulties you personally encounter when working with this characteristic.

(3) Move into a small group (no more than six members) to discuss together the concerns surrounding the issue. Ensure that each worker has time to speak about him/herself.

(4) Set up a role-play which highlights a couple who present this particular difficulty for the therapist. Additional observers can be used where available. (In this particular role-play the couple might be asked to escalate the behaviour which has been identified as difficult for the trainees: for example if the topic is *working with the expression of anger between partners* those role-playing the couple might be asked to escalate their anger in order to give the trainee experience of this.)

(5) The therapist should be supported by the observers and encouraged to go beyond a situation in which s/he would have intervened to avoid the expression of anger.

(6) Stop the role-play for discussion as necessary. Allow the role-play to restart several times before concluding. [20 minutes]

(7) Learning from the role-play; use the format described in Section 12.6.5. In this case the feedback is to focus upon the therapist's ability to empathise with the couple, even though finding the interaction difficult. Give feedback using the checklist in Section 12.11.1.

(8) Since this is a training session the group should be encouraged to be experimental and replay the role-play several times with different interventions in order to explore the whole issue more thoroughly, stopping for discussion of feelings and reactions, and to give feedback to the person playing the role of therapist.

(9) All participants should have the chance to be the therapist and to receive feedback.

12.11.3 Other problems for which the approach can be used

The above process can be used to help trainees with any attitude, prejudice or embarrassment which they feel in relation to couples and should help them to empathise more accurately with these couples. Trainees may wish to consider their difficulties with any of the following:

- Ethnic and cultural issues.
- The language of a particular sub-group or culture.
- Gender questions and sexual functioning.
- Child physical abuse.
- Sexual abuse and incest.
- Intuitive feelings of dislike, disgust or sympathy with one spouse.
- Concerns regarding current topics such as AIDS, abortion, drug abuse or alcoholism, or other emotive areas with which clients and therapist are dealing.

12.12 *Thinking about a relationship systemically*

As described in Chapter 7, thinking about a relationship as a system requires a reformulation of conceptual thinking from linear to a circular pattern of interaction. Hypotheses are then developed to explain the possible positive functions of these circular interactive patterns. These hypotheses are used during therapy. To develop these hypotheses data are collected from many different sources.

The following exercises are designed to help trainees make this shift and to begin to conceptualise the data from a systems perspective.

Should trainees wish to take these exercises further when working with clients it is advisable for them to be in supervision with someone who understands the systems orientation.

12.12.1 Exercise in thinking systemically about a relationship

[Allow one to one and a half hours for the complete exercise.]

(1) Trainers should provide the following information about a couple: the personal history of each partner, the history of their relationship and that of their families of origin, a letter outlining the reason for referral and information about any current life events.

It is preferable if trainers can provide material known to them and therefore more immediate. (Where case material is not readily available the following couples from the book might be used: Diana and Samuel S, Example 8C; Derek and Sylvia B, Example 8D and David and Marcia T, Example 9E.)

(2) *In pairs* Divide the training group into pairs so that trainees will know with whom they will work.

(3) *Individually* Browse through the material noting as many interacting patterns as possible (see Sections 7.3.1 to 7.3.6). Each time you recognise a pattern in one partner's situation, look for a possible complementary or symmetrical aspect in the partner: e.g. if the man has a repeated pattern of angry outbursts, to what behaviour from the woman might he be responding? Note down any patterns you think are emerging. [15 minutes]

(4) *In pairs* Come together with your partner and share your observations. [10–15 minutes]

(5) Check together whether you have found interacting patterns in any of the following areas. [10–15 minutes]

Age: for example the ages of either spouses coinciding with the age of a significant family member when a distressing event occurred, such as the man who is now 45 and depressed having experienced his own father dying at 45 years; or a wife having difficulties with a daughter who is now the same age as she was herself when she ran away from home.

Developmental stages and life events: are there any developmental stages or life events which seem to interact, such as children being born, starting or leaving school, leaving home, marrying or divorcing? Are there events such as a bereavment or illness affecting the couple? What about such difficulties as retirement, redundancy, affairs or criminal offences occurring in any part of the family constellation?

Think widely about the varied aspects of the developmental stages, consider aspects such as anniversaries, retirement, or children leaving home. Consider factors such as the woman's wish to work after the children leave home and the husband's hope that his wife will be a companion to him during his impending early retirement.

Previous experiences: take into account previous experiences by either spouse of abandonment, neglect, sexual abuse, changing homes or changing countries and how they impinge upon their present relationship.

Previous significant relationships: are there any previous relationships in which there was a pattern of violence, drinking, gambling or separation, or other difficulty which can be seen as interacting with the present relationship in a repetitive way? For example, does each partner still have a commitment to a previous relationship? Does a previous relationship in which there was much marital violence affect the present relationship so that for example the husband is extremely sensitive to the wife's needs and does not request anything for himself?

Can you spot any patterns symmetrical, complementary or a combination of both which seem to be operating to maintain the relationship in its present state (see Section 7.3.3)?

(6) From your list of interacting patterns or repetitive sequences see if you can choose two which seem to fit the data best. [10 minutes]

(7) Using the two repetitive sequences which you have selected see if you can answer the following three questions. [10–15 minutes]

(a) 'Why worry?' i.e. what is the problem in terms of the interaction, the symptom or reciprocal behaviour? What might have precipitated it?
(b) 'Why now?' i.e. what is it about the present moment which precipitates the crisis and makes the couple seek therapy?
(c) 'What for?' What positive functions do the repetitive patterns serve in the relationship of the couple at present? (See Kraemer 1986)

(8) Take the final step and think about what the feared consequences might be if things changed. [10–15 minutes]

With the whole training group
(9) Come together in a larger group and share your findings. Can you come to a consensus as a group in the following areas? (Write a list of the main points made by the group. There may be a consensus or there may be a divergence of views. Where there are divergent views when answering the following questions ensure that alternatives are openly discussed, remembering that there is usually no 'right' answer.) [20 minutes]

(a) Repetitive sequences or interacting patterns which you have noted.
(b) Positive reasons for these regular interacting patterns.
(c) Possible feared consequences should things change.

(10) *Conclusion* Ask the members to say what they have learned from the exercise.

12.12.2 Summary of exercise in thinking about a relationship systemically

This exercise is designed to help trainees develop the ability to think systemically and understand the basis on which hypotheses are formulated. It is offered as an introduction to thinking about a couple from a systems perspective. Any therapist wishing to take these ideas further might consider seeking appropriate training and regular supervision.

12.13 Formulating messages or tasks
(see Chapter 9)

The above exercise on systemic thinking is a useful introduction to the formulation of messages and should have been completed before attempting to use this exercise. (Trainees should also be familiar with Chapter 9, particularly Sections 9.1 to 9.5.2.) Again we wish to emphasise that these are training exercises to familiarise therapists with the behavioural-systems approach; if therapists wish to begin to use this approach in therapy, adequate training and good supervision are advisable.

12.13.1 Case material

Trainers may prefer to use material known to them. Alternatively the following examples given in Chapter 9 can also be used: Tom and Evie B (Example 9B, Section 9.6) Frank and Felicity C (Example 9C, Section 9.7) or Christopher and Mabel J (Example 9D, Sections 9.8.2.1 to 9.8.2.5). In selecting which couple will be used for this exercise, if an example is taken from the text, do not at this stage reread the messages given to each couple. The message used in the text can be used at the end of the exercise for comparative purposes.

12.13.2 Role-play

If time allows, in order to help the material come alive for the trainees, set up a role-play of the couple as if it were a first session in which the therapist is finding out about the couple (see Sections 12.6.1 to 12.6.7). [About 30 minutes for the whole exercise including role-play and feedback]

12.13.3 Formulating a message

The following exercise will take a minimum of one hour.

(1) *In pairs* Where role-play is not used ensure that the trainees have had time to read about and understand the couple chosen. Using the details

available discuss what message, timetable or task might be given to this couple. [15 minutes] Write this down, choosing words, metaphor or symbolism which is appropriate to the couple. Take time to select each word with care. [15 minutes]

(2) *Join together with another pair* Share together the content and wording of the message. [10 minutes]

(3) *Feedback* Each pair should take turns in giving feedback to the others about their message for the chosen couple. The following checklist can be used when giving feedback.

(4) *Checklist*

- Simplicity: Was the message sufficiently brief and understandable? (see Section 9.5)
- Formulation: Was there a formulation? Did it make sense to you? (see Section 9.2)
- Task: Was a task used? Did it seem to relate directly to the problems of the couple? Was it small and achievable in the time available? (see Section 9.3)
- Timetable: Was a timetable used? Did it seem to fit with the needs of the couple? (see Section 9.4)
- Language and metaphor: Were the language and metaphor appropriate to the couple? (see Section 9.2.3)
- Balance: Was there a balance between what was asked from both partners or did the message favour one partner over another? (see Section 9.5.2)
- Empathy: In general did you feel that the message was empathic with the difficulties presented by the couple? (see Section 4.4.1)
- Paradox: If a paradoxical element was introduced into the message did this seem rejecting or supportive? (see Section 9.14)

The above checklist is not exhaustive but should be used by the two pairs as a guide to their joint discussion. [20 minutes]

(5) If an example from Chapter 9 was used, now compare the messages with those given in the text. What are the differences?

(6) If an example from the text has been used examine the message given, and use the checklist to help you to discuss what amendments you might make to the messages. Pay particular attention to the language and to the metaphor used. [10 minutes]

12.13.4 Summary of formulating messages

Messages, formulations, tasks and timetables are used to continue the work done in the session and to stimulate further work on the relationship in the period between sessions. Each message should be appropriate to the couple and their difficulty. It should use language and metaphor taken from the couple's own dialogue as much as possible. In most circumstances it should be framed so as to have an impact on changing the system, whether given as part of a message containing a timetable or as a paradoxical message. There are, however, some situations where only a caring and sympathetic message would be appropriate. Above all, it should be simple and understandable. On reviewing the messages given as examples in the text we would expect the trainee to suggest that some of these messages may be too complicated. With increasing experience we feel that messages are most effective if quite simple. The above exercise is designed to give trainees practice in formulating such messages.

12.14 Training in dealing with sexual issues

We include a brief section on sex therapy as trainees in general couple therapy need to develop a sense of confidence in dealing with sexual matters so as to help couples, who may themselves be somewhat self-conscious about discussing intimate sexual details, to feel more at ease with their own sexuality.

This is not intended as a training for sexual therapy as such, for which see other textbooks such as Bancroft (1989) and Hawton (1985).

12.14.1 Naming the parts of the body

As a beginning exercise to help trainees relax and enjoy the training, the trainees' own experience can be used as follows:

(1) *In pairs* Ask the pairs to find out from each other what words were used in their family of origin to describe parts of the body and in particular the genitals and erotic zones. These should be written down. [10 minutes]

(2) Ask the pair to see if they can extend this list by including additional words which each has learned as they got older. [5 minutes]

(3) *The training group* Come together and make a common list of all the terms used. Ensure that colloquial or pet names are included. [30 minutes for the whole exercise.]

12.14.2 Where do babies come from?

Again, using the trainees' own experience:

(1) *In pairs* Ask the pair to discuss together their very first experience of learning about 'where do babies come from?' (For example a first experience might have been learning that Mummy had gone to hospital to buy a baby sister.) [10 minutes]

(2) *The training group* Discuss together:

(a) how each first learned about 'where babies come from' and
(b) what further information they were given as they got older.

[30 minutes]

Beginning warm-up exercises such as these described should be followed by a combination of didactic input and ongoing exercises to help the trainees become increasingly comfortable with the whole area of sexual development and interaction.

12.14.3 Knowledge: didactic input

It is important to include some teaching about the following areas:

- Knowledge of sexual anatomy and physiology.
- The varieties of sexual experience (including cultural influences and sexual variations).
- Myths of sexuality (Zilbergeld 1980).
- The Masters and Johnson approach.
- Physical treatments for sexual inadequacy.
- Relationship problems and their relevance to sexuality (Chapter 11).

The above didactic input should be given in such a way that allows for discussion and exploration of trainee attitudes.

12.14.4 Attitude

In order to help trainees understand their own attitudes to different aspects of sexuality, it may be helpful to hold group discussions based on their reactions to films such as those which have been developed for training purposes by organisations such as Sexual Attitude Restructuring (SAR) or the Institute of Sex Education and Research. These are best used by trainers who are already familiar with the material and who are able to facilitate the group discussion.

As trainees become more acquainted with the material they may wish to discuss the impact of this knowledge upon themselves and their relationships. This can be taken up in supervision where more personal questions of this nature are best considered. Although personal therapy is not the province of supervision, it is likely to be helpful for trainees to feel that they can discuss the impact of the training on sexual matters within the context of supervision.

12.14.5 Observation of practice

Perhaps one of the best ways for trainees to become more confident in dealing with sexual issues is to spend some time as an observer sitting in on sessions with an experienced sexual and marital therapist. (Because of the very personal nature of the difficulties experienced it is less likely that the one-way screen will be used for sex therapy). Following the session the trainee will have the opportunity to discuss alternative interventions with the therapist, and can often be helpful to the therapist by bringing another view of the relationship.

12.14.6 Summary of training in dealing with sexual issues

To become comfortable in discussing this area requires some additional knowledge and training, particularly in helping the trainee understand his/her own attitudes and knowledge of the physical as well as relationship aspects of sexual functioning.

12.15 *Conclusion of the training section*

We have outlined several exercises which can be used to help trainees begin to understand and practise some of the skills which are necessary when using the behavioural-systems approach. We have suggested that the trainee should begin by focussing on the current relationship and the interaction of the couple as the focus of therapy and have offered some exercises which are designed to assist in learning some skills in this area. Two exercises outlining ways in which trainees can be helped to make a shift into thinking systemically and the formulation of messages have also been included.

A brief section on the sexual component of relationship difficulties is included as our aim is to develop well rounded therapists who are comfortable working with both sexual and relationship difficulties.

We have not attempted to cover all aspects of training for the behavioural-systems approach, partly because this would make the book repetitive, and partly because it may be more helpful for trainees to seek additional training or supervision directly from someone familiar with the behavioural-systems approach.

We have therefore left out large areas relating to the choosing and setting of tasks at the end of a session and the reviewing of these at the beginning of the next session. The delivery of messages (and in particular the delivery of paradoxical or split-team messages) has also not been included here (see Sections 4.6.12, 9.5.1 and 9.13). The question of when and how to write letters as part of therapy is not included, nor is the use of consultation breaks. These have, however, been described in other parts of the book (see Sections 9.5.3 and 9.10.4). Many of the systemic interventions described in Chapter 8 have not been included, nor the specific strategies described in Chapter 10. We hope, however, to have described sufficient exercises to enable trainees to begin to understand and feel comfortable with the use of the behavioural-systems approach.

12.16 Supervision

Adequate supervision of therapists is an important subject, too complex to cover in a brief section such as this. Training and supervision should go hand in hand, and too many therapists are working in isolated positions without adequate support, training or supervision. Much supervision is carried out in a one-to-one relationship (or one supervisor to two trainees), with the trainee using written or spoken reports to convey to the supervisor how s/he is working and any areas of concern. This provides a setting in which the trainee can deal with many of the more personal worries which occur while learning a new therapy; increased knowledge and experience of dealing with sexual and inter-personal difficulties may raise anxieties in the trainees which can be most appropriately dealt with in one-to-one (or one-to-two) supervision. Care must be taken to ensure that a clear boundary is drawn between supervision and personal therapy by keeping the focus of supervision on the trainee's ability to develop as a couple therapist.

The British Association of Counselling and the Association of Sexual and Marital Therapists have both been engaged in setting standards for adequate supervision, and guidelines are now available. Individual (or one-to-two) and group supervision are the basic forms of supervision recommended. Although these are the traditional forms of supervision they do have some drawbacks, not least of which is the second-hand nature of the supervision (Wijnberg and Schwarz 1977; DHSS 1978; Gizinski 1978).

We suggest that live supervision adds a dimension of immediacy and may lead to better supervision. Traditional supervision is still valid and necessary, but as a supplement to the more immediate methods below.

12.16.1 Live supervision

By observing therapists through a one-way screen, one becomes in-creasingly aware that some aspects of the interaction are not noticed by even the most experienced therapists. This seems an inevitable con-sequence of the spontaneous interaction between a therapist and a couple.

It does, however, underline the fact that on-the-spot observation is a useful aid to both therapy and supervision. The ability to interrupt the session by phoning through, or to speak directly to the therapist who is wearing an earphone, makes it possible for supervision to concentrate on how the therapist is now working in this session. It also allows the supervisor and therapist to participate together in the work, rather than being in a remote and often hierarchical relationship.

Where, for example, a therapist is being tentative about following through with an intervention, s/he can be asked to go back to the particular intervention and try again in the session. Additionally, therapists are often unaware that they are, for example, being tentative and so would not necessarily report this as a difficulty to the supervisor in one-to-one supervision. Where a therapist is not noticing that s/he is having a conversation with one partner while the other sits bored and withdrawn, the supervisor can interrupt to point this out and to make a suggestion which would enable the trainee to bring the passive partner into the interaction.

Sometimes trainees may wish to leave the session and consult with their supervisor or the supervisor may wish to call the trainee out of the session in order to discuss what is happening. In such ways supervision has a direct impact upon the trainee and the therapy, the trainee feels supported and guided while working and alternative ways of intervention can be more easily attempted. Since the supervisor is working side-by-side with the trainee, s/he is less remote and supervision becomes more of a shared task.

The benefits tend to increase when several trainees are trained together, as they can observe each other working through the one-way screen and provide a supervision group for each other. This obviously helps to cut the costs of training and make the use of a one-way screen more economical. Particularly valuable is the encouragement and creative environment which a training group offers and which can, for example, galvanise a therapist who has been feeling hopelessly stuck (see Section 12.10). Working as we do with couples who have had longstanding relationship difficulties, the support and inventiveness of the team and training group are much appreciated.

Although there are initial additional costs in installing a one-way screen, the benefits would seem to justify this (Heilveil, 1984; Manor 1984).

12.16.2 In-session observation

An alternative to live supervision is that of using an observer to sit in and observe during therapy sessions; this is useful if a one-way screen is not available (we use this method when the observation room is being heavily used or we have several additional trainees). In such a situation the therapist informs the couple that, for example, 'Mr John Jones will sit in and observe the session in order to give me some assistance' and that there will be a break in the session after about 30 to 40 minutes, after which the therapy will be resumed. The observer can sometimes speak to the therapist in the session, to make the kind of suggestions which in the one-way screen situation would be made by intercom.

During the break the observer and therapist will discuss together what has occurred in the session, what other work might usefully be done in the remaining part of the session and a message, timetable or task is formulated together.

In-session observation has many of the advantages of one-way-screen supervision in that there is the immediacy of the observation. It is usually a good learning situation for the observer who is able to experience at first hand the quality of the interaction in the session.

Though time-consuming, therapists who work alone might usefully pair up with a therapist who works locally and exchange at least one session per week in which they sit in on each other's therapy sessions. Time could be set aside on a regular basis for feedback, discussion and supervision. In this way isolated therapists could support each other, learn together and extend each other's repertoire of alternative interventions. Often, as we have described, therapists get locked into the couple's rigidity, and an outside observer can help identify ways of freeing the therapist.

It would be sensible to define a clear contract between the two workers; areas of strength and weakness might be drawn up by each participant and goals of supervision established. The supervision would then have a focus and a purpose and this should prevent the supervision session from deteriorating into a social chat. In this way, valuable support can be given to therapists who feel both pressurised and isolated.

12.16.3 The use of video or audio recording

Many therapists are hesitant about using a video recorder, either because of personal embarrassment or in order to protect the couple. Our experience is that couples usually feel encouraged to learn that therapists take the trouble to think about them in detail. If recording is used, confidentiality must be respected by asking for the couple's permission to use the film or tape for training or supervision purposes, and a suitable form provided for their signature.

The video, particularly with the replay facility, enables the therapist to study in great detail both the couple's interaction and his/her interventions. Bad habits can be checked, non-verbal interaction noted; the specific words, the voice tone or general demeanour can all be examined at leisure. If a video is not available regularly a system can be hired for occasional use. What applies to video can also apply to audio recordings of sessions. They are usually experienced by both the trainee and couple as less intrusive. They are also cheaper and easier to manage. Trainees should be encouraged to use either video or audio recording as much as possible throughout training (and where possible as part of ongoing work).

12.16.4 Group supervision

Group supervision can be carried out in a variety of forms. The standard form of supervision is for a group of therapists (or trainees) to come together once a week (for one to one and a half hours) for supervision with an experienced worker. Cases may be presented verbatim, by audio or video recorder, and they are discussed within the group with the supervisor making comments or suggesting alternative treatments. The disadvantage of this method is that the worker is not seen at the same time as the work is being done, and suggestion can only be introduced into future therapy.

It is the usual form of supervision for working with sexual problems and as such is perfectly adequate. However, as therapeutic interventions which focus on the sexual life of couples become more a standard part of the couple therapist's repertoire of skills, it should be possible to do more supervision of therapy involving sexual problems by the use of the one-way screen or video, thus making it possible for the supervisor's assistance to be used directly in treatment.

To compensate for this lack, it is helpful if role-play is used to focus on particularly difficult clients, or particular concerns of the trainees. (This is possible in group supervision but is impractical in one-to-one supervision for obvious reasons.) Role-play allows the worker to practise alternative styles of working and to get a sense of their usefulness. It also allows the group and the supervisor to observe and to guide the trainee on the spot. Voice tone, body posture, eye contact and the use of language all become available for direct supervision within the role-play. Though role-play cannot take the place of live supervision, it does bring an increased awareness of the therapist's style of working (Morry Van Ments 1983; Jaques 1984).

12.16.5 Supervision during the session break

Where therapists are accustomed to taking a break in therapy the workers can come together for supervision in the break. It can be difficult to co-ordinate the breaks between sessions which are taking place in parallel, but if it is possible it can provide another opportunity to have supervision while work is in progress.

12.16.6 Questions which are likely to arise in supervision of behavioural-systems couple therapy

Supervisors should be alert to some of the specific areas which trainees may need to discuss in supervision arising out of behavioural-systems couple therapy. These may be, for example, the short-term nature of therapy and how to end both the session and the therapy satisfactorily. The focus on the interaction, rather than on the relationship between the partners and the therapist, may mean that the trainee does not feel as rewarded for the work as in other methods. In-session breaks and how they can be managed may be discussed. Ethical, legal and moral issues arising out of specific aspects of couple interaction may cause difficulties, and trainees may have problems in treating the relationship rather than the symptom.

Supervision, whether in groups or one-to-one, and with or without a one-way screen, is an ideal place in which to raise the questions which arise as a result of training. Working as one does within the behavioural-systems approach for much of the time from a decentred position, supervision becomes a place in which one can explore questions and also gain a great deal of personal support. The open expression of questions and concerns in supervision facilitates the giving and gaining of both the knowledge and the support which is required.

12.16.7 Supervision as an integral part of training

Supervision goes hand in hand with, and in many ways is an integral part of, good training and has therefore been included in this chapter. Many of the exercises described in the training section can equally well be used within supervision and vice versa. We have advocated that, where possible, trainees should find situations where they have direct access to supervision while working and have suggested alternatives if this is not possible. We have not touched upon the training of supervisors, but it goes without saying that supervisors should themselves be competent and well qualified therapists, who are conversant with and sympathetic to the behavioural-systems approach as well as feeling comfortable with an experiential model of training. Ideally they, too, should have regular access to their own form of supervision or support from colleagues for their therapy and their supervision work.

Chapter 13

Summary, reappraisal
and prospects

13.1 A summary of the main ideas discussed in this book

Our purpose in this book has been to describe and put in context the behavioural-systems approach to couple therapy, and we would like now to highlight those aspects of the work which we feel deserve special comment, taking each chapter in turn.

13.1.1 The increasing demand for couple therapy

In the first chapter we pointed out that marriage and similar relationships are seen as being of great importance in the present time, partly in response to the decline in importance of the extended family and partly in view of the idealisation of 'love' relationships. At the same time, marriage and couple relationships are under attack from several quarters, including the high and increasing divorce rate, the growing awareness of the existence of physical and sexual abuse within families, the greater economic freedom of women, the increased prevalence of one-parent households and the continued debate about the relative roles of men and women in relationships. In the context of all these influences it is not surprising that it seems that the demand for understanding and help for couple relationships is growing.

13.1.2 Goals of therapy

In the second chapter we explored the various goals which might be set for couple therapy. After outlining some ways of defining these goals, both in general terms and in the context of other approaches to couple therapy, we defined the goals which we would try to achieve in behavioural-systems couple therapy. We concluded that these were primarily improved interaction and ability of the partners to take each other seriously, accompanied by increased flexibility within the relationship. Along with these goals, in those couples in which one partner has a symptom or behavioural problem, we would hope that the symptom would become less severe, that the labelling of that person as 'sick' would be reduced and that any improvement would be reasonably lasting.

13.1.3 The ALI hierarchy

In Chapter 3 we looked at the indications for couple therapy, both in relation to individual problems and to family and sexual problems. We also presented our view of how to choose the best kind of intervention within the behavioural-systems approach, in the form of the hierarchy of alternative levels of intervention, or ALI. In this the different interventions are matched to the presenting problems in an ascending series of steps. The more the couple appear to be inflexible or rigid and the more they tend to place the problem in one partner only, the more ingenuity the therapist has to show in devising interventions and the further s/he has to depart from the problem as presented by the couple. Therapy is more behavioural and literal in approach when couples present problems defined as belonging in the relationship, and more systemic and meta-phorical when they blame the individual and find difficulty in altering the relationship. To put it another way, the therapist has to be more flexible in response to greater rigidity on the part of the couple, whereas in couples who are quite flexible s/he can work quite successfully 'by the (behavioural) book'.

13.1.4 The process of therapy: maintaining the momentum

In Chapter 4 we presented our suggestions for engaging the couple in therapy, for structuring the therapy session and for managing the beginning and end of therapy. We work with the couple in a room with a one-way screen and an observation team, and will often start therapy by a team discussion about the couple before seeing them. We then concentrate in the session on the problem presented and the observed interaction, and we would emphasise that the first session is not simply an exercise for making introductions and gathering information, but also the place in which the process of change begins. As a part of this process the couple are helped to take each other more seriously, while at the same time we suggest that the therapist uses a light touch and even humour in order to soften the approach in therapy.

We have elicited much of the background information by correspondence before meeting the couple, and an important element of the first therapy session is to keep the momentum going. There are many ways to do this, but probably the most helpful and successful is to ask the partners to talk to each other, with the therapist in the decentred position. In this way the therapist can focus on the interaction, cut short unhelpful monologues, encourage more effective negotiation, improve communication and also, by improving the momentum of their interaction, give the couple the experience of actual change in the session itself. Various other techniques are described, both for keeping up the momentum for change and for managing the process of therapy, and the chapter ends with advice on how to end both the session and the therapy.

13.1.5 The range of alternative interventions

The next four chapters (5 to 8) go into considerably more detail about the techniques used in the behavioural-systems approach. The practical aspects of reciprocity negotiation and communication training are described in Chapters 5 and 6 with large numbers of case examples. These techniques are not, of course, original to the behavioural-systems approach, but we believe that the decentred position of the therapist in these behavioural approaches is a useful innovation of ours which helps to increase the immediacy of the experience for the couple, and makes these well-tried techniques even more effective.

In Chapter 7 we discuss systems theory in more detail, since a basic understanding of it is a prerequisite for the construction of hypotheses and messages to use with couples who present problems which are not amenable to negotiation or communication training. Our acceptance of the theory is not, however, completely uncritical and we tend to adopt only those aspects which we find of most practical use in helping couples with the less straightforward difficulties.

In chapter 8 we describe our modification of various structural family techniques and non-verbal communication techniques derived in part from gestalt therapies. These are particularly useful where there is a tense but polite relationship in which argument and the open expression of feeling are inhibited. One of the most common interventions we use is that of encouraging arguments on trivial issues. The presenting problem in these couples is often depression or sexual reluctance in either partner.

13.1.6 Timetabled tasks

In Chapter 9 we give an account of another of our innovations, in the use of timetables for homework tasks. The use of tasks is, of course, a common type of intervention in systemic work, but in our clinic we tend to ask the couple to agree in the session on which days and at what time they will carry out their homework tasks, and we feel that this tends to increase the likelihood that the tasks will be completed. The chapter also has some helpful suggestions for the framing and delivery of messages at the end of the session, and for the use of paradox, either alone or as part of a 'split-team' message.

13.1.7 Therapy for some specific problems

In Chapter 10 we refer to some of the specific problems we have been able to improve by behavioural-systems couple therapy, in particular jealousy, depression and sexual reluctance. These are unusually difficult problems to tackle in couple therapy, and in all three the therapist is having to exercise a good deal of ingenuity in reframing the problem as one of relationship, in the knowledge that such a reframe may produce a new perspective on it and the hope of a more lasting solution. The interventions used are all those which have been described in earlier chapters, but in using them we have introduced refinements to adapt them to these rather complicated presenting problems. In Chapter 10 we also mention briefly the use of couple therapy in such problems as child physical and sexual abuse, triangular relationships, the older couple, alcohol and drug abuse, divorce and remarriage.

13.1.8 An integrated approach to sexual problems

In Chapter 11 we give a rather brief account of sexual problems within relationships and their management. We feel that couple therapists should not be ignorant about sexual function and the things which can go wrong with it, and we would also commend to sexual therapists the need for their therapy for sexual dysfunction to take full account of the non-sexual relationship and of the couple's communication.

13.1.9 Training and supervision

Chapter 12 deals with training for this kind of work, and emphasises the importance of experiential exercises and role-play in learning how to carry out couple therapy. Some suggestions for supervision are made, both supervision in the traditional sense and live supervision by one-way screen.

13.2 *The innovations in our approach*

Many of the interventions we advocate in the behavioural-systems approach to couple therapy are derived from other types of therapy. The well known and effective techniques of reciprocity negotiation and communication training (Chapters 5 and 6) have been taken over by us from behavioural marital therapy, but with one refinement which has proved exceptionally useful, and that is the technique of decentring. The traditional way of carrying out these approaches is for the therapist to ask each partner what they would like, to repeat that to the other partner, and then to carry out a three-way negotiating process using the therapist as mediator. This three-way process is clearly part of most of the case descriptions of Jacobson, Segraves, Mackay and others. Our way of doing therapy in the behavioural mode is to remain decentred and to ask the couple to negotiate or talk together while the therapist listens and comments as necessary. This offers a much more naturalistic view of the couple's own communication process, and improvements may be perceived by the couple as occurring in the relationship itself rather than in the triangle including the therapist. Some therapists may dislike this way of working at first, as it can give the impression of the session being out of control. It is also less easy than in the usual form of behavioural marital therapy for researchers to be clear about the process of therapy in the session. The advantage is, however, that by moving in and out of an ongoing interaction which quite closely resembles the couple's way of relating at home, the therapist has a much better chance of effecting a lasting change in the real relationship, and this outweighs any disadvantages.

We have extracted from structural therapy what we regard as the most useful technique for couples, and that is the initiation and maintenance of arguments (Chapter 8). Structural therapy is full of other moves which serve to alter the power structure in families, to weaken or strengthen alliances, to support the parental pair and to help younger members to escape from enmeshment with a parent. Some of these are quite useful at times with couples, but the use of arguments is the one we find most constantly effective. Once again we have made a refinement in this move, in that we now usually invite the couple to choose a specific and trivial issue to argue about, rather than use, as in structural therapy, whatever subject they happen to be talking about at the time. As stated in Chapter 8, the reason for this is that the outcome of such a trivial argument is unlikely to cause severe consequences to the relationship, and yet the experience of arguing, especially if they are not accustomed to it, is often of great benefit. Having had such a trivial argument and finding the experience less dangerous than they expected, they may then feel able to have heated discussions more frequently, and thus open up a rather inhibited relationship. Indeed, the experience of becoming accustomed to an activity which they previously feared is rather similar to the process of desensitisation for phobias, and thus makes an interesting link between structural and behavioural methods. In order to generalise their improvement to the home setting, we will then often suggest timetabled arguments for homework (see next paragraph).

The use of timetables (Chapter 9) is quite widespread in many forms of systems therapy. In our work, however, the timetable has taken a central position, and we seldom give homework activities without some type of timing attached. Conversation and mutual counselling sessions, arguments and the discussion of jealousy can all be timetabled. One important aspect of such timetables is the fact that we suggest not only a starting time but also a finishing time for the activities, so that, for example, an argument or a discussion of jealousy will be able to be terminated rather than dragging on all night.

More traditionally, we also timetable 'fun' activities for couples, such as outings to cinemas or country drives. But the most important, and probably original, use of timetables in our work is the 'negotiated timetable' for sex (Chapter 10), which has transformed the lives of many couples locked in the struggle produced by a strong sexual urge in one partner (usually the male) and great reluctance in the other.

Timetables of all sorts extend the therapeutic influence from the session into the home, and we feel that a timetabled task is more likely to be remembered and carried out than a task which is given with no specific time commitment.

The use of paradox in our work is in many ways similar to its use in many other settings where systemic work is done with couples or families (Chapter 9). We probably put less faith in the 'truth' of our hypotheses than some systemic workers, and more in their utility as agents of change, but we try to give the messages with respect for the feelings and aspirations of the clients, and in no sense as 'throw-away' or dismissive comments on the couples' problems. We will sometimes, as Perrotta (1986) advocates, express the paradox in the form of a 'split-team' message, but in some really stuck situations we recognise that a purely paradoxical message is the only intervention which may have the potential to unblock the system and relieve the patient of the symptom.

Another innovation of our clinic, if indeed the linking of two pre-existing forms of therapy can be called an innovation, is our approach to the treatment of sexual problems in the context of the relationship (Chapter 11). The work of Masters and Johnson (1970) did address this issue to some degree, but in spite of the strong emphasis on communication in their work, the technique they used was rather formalised, and there were some rigid rules about who could talk to whom in the therapy session. In more recent texts on sexual dysfunction there has been a tendency for sexual issues to be split off from relationship ones, and Kaplan (1974) even invited a guest author to write her chapter on marital problems and therapy. Our clinic, in contrast, places the general relationship at the centre of the sexual therapy, as well as making sure that sex is discussed openly at some stage in all couples coming to the clinic with non-sexual problems. Whereas sex has physical and medical aspects which mean that it must at times be treated by physical or other individual approaches, the sexual relationship is also very central to most intimate relationships and, especially in its motivational aspects, cannot be separated from the couple's general pattern of communication and interaction.

The uniting element in the behavioural-systems approach, which brings together the disparate techniques as a coherent therapeutic method, is the hierarchy of alternative levels of intervention (Chapter 3). The matching of different interventions to different presenting problems means that the therapist has to show more ingenuity in devising interventions the more the couple show either rigidity in their interaction or an individual focus in their presentation of the problem. The therapist can be very flexible in using the method, and merely has to remember to be aware of the level of difficulty of the presented problem before selecting from the hierarchy the best approach to use.

13.3 The advantages of behavioural-systems couple therapy

The type of therapy we have been describing in this book is thus partly original and partly a refinement of other approaches, useful for a wide variety of problems presenting both in terms of the relationship and in terms of individual symptoms. The ALI hierarchy is a useful clinical guideline to indicate which approach to use for which problem. The fact that we work in a predominantly psychiatric setting does not invalidate the method for other settings such as marriage guidance; it merely indicates that those who work in other settings may not need such a wide range of intervention strategies as we do. One might hope, however, that the use of this method in non-medical settings could encourage those counsellors to take on with greater confidence cases for which they previously felt that they had little to offer.

There are in our view many advantages to the method which we have evolved. First it is adapted to the short-term timescale, which for reasons of cost alone is an important consideration. However, it is not only the cost to the therapy team which is important, but also the amount of time which the couple must invest in therapy in order to be helped. Most couples would probably agree that it is better to be helped in ten sessions than twenty or a hundred, especially as there is little evidence from couple therapy research or indeed in any form of psychotherapy that long-term therapy gives better results than short-term therapy.

If one is looking for results in the short-term, it is consistent to use an approach which keeps the momentum of therapy going and, as we made clear in Chapter 4, the behavioural-systems approach aims to do that at all stages of the process. The momentum is maintained by cutting through long outbursts of complaint and by reducing monologues by either partner. It is also maintained by the 'businesslike' approach of the therapist and the insistence on focussing on what will be happening in the immediate future rather than what the couple are complaining of in the past.

The use of the decentred position (Sections 4.6.9 and 6.4.1) by the therapist is seen as another advantage of our approach. This results in the couple having to work rather closely as a team to resolve their problems, and we observe that the changes they are able to bring about in this way seem to be more durable than changes produced by the therapist as either an intermediary in the negotiations or an interpreter of their feelings. The experience which they have in the session of working on the problem, with interventions from the therapist designed to help them to stick with the point at issue, can make it easier for them to apply the same sort of tactics to problems encountered at home. We have speculated as to whether this process represents the equivalent of a kind of 'behavioural insight', whereby the couple have learned not so much what internal conflicts their problems are related to, but rather what to do about them if they recur. Another aspect of the approach which resembles traditional behavioural therapy is the way in which the couple are asked to proceed by small and achievable steps towards their goals, for example by arguing about trivial matters before trying to tackle the more important ones.

Behavioural-systems couple therapy is a versatile type of therapy, which can be adapted to many kinds of problem. It is quite good for the couples who present conflicts in their relationship as the main problem, as it gets away from blame and side-taking (except where deliberately choosing to ally with one partner, as described in Section 8.2) and focusses on the immediate future. It is equally good for couples where the problems of behaviour are located by them in one partner, since by delabelling the labelled partner and focussing on the interaction it makes it possible to work on the relationship. Having encouraged this, it is then possible to help each partner to develop an increased repertoire of responses within the relationship, and we believe that this will contribute to the resolution of the problem. This versatility is particularly useful in a psychiatric setting, but may be an advantage also in other areas of work.

One of the most useful aspects of the method is the way in which, having worked systemically to resolve a problem previously regarded by the couple as an individual symptom, the therapist can then move down the ALI hierarchy (Chapter 3) to a negotiating mode in order to solve the relationship problems which may emerge after the system becomes more open and flexible. We may even at times use interventions which have both behavioural and paradoxical elements. For example, we may suggest a behavioural task for a couple while at the same time predicting that they will not be able to complete it. At another time we may say 'don't change too quickly' during a predominantly behavioural prescription. The flexible mix of systemic and behavioural elements is creative and quite often very effective (see Chapter 10 for further examples of the use of such creative messages).

The approach is also compatible with many other forms of treatment. There are very few types of treatment which cannot be given either concurrently or as part of behavioural-systems couple therapy. Most psychiatric medications, medical treatment, most forms of behavioural therapy and individual counselling are compatible with the therapy. It is very suitable for combining with the Masters and Johnson approach for sexual problems, and indeed both forms of therapy are integrated in our treatment of these problems. The only slight reservation we have is about intensive dynamic psychotherapy, with its rather different emphasis on exploring internal conflicts and understanding meanings. We have in some cases been able to do successful couple therapy concurrently with such psychotherapy, but we usually advise postponing the start of dynamic therapy if possible until the couple therapy is over.

Another advantage of the approach is its suitability for 'emergency' situations in couples presenting in a crisis, with their inherent risks of separation or violence. What is usually needed in such situations is an approach to conflict resolution, which reciprocity negotiation and communication training can certainly provide. However, we are not only concerned with conflict resolution and may in fact initiate conflict in some couples who appear to be afraid of conflict. Our approach does not necessarily see the reduction of conflict as a desirable goal, even in couples who seem to be in a state of crisis due to conflict, and we can often help them tolerate such conflict until a more acceptable type of interaction emerges.

Although the behavioural-systems approach is a combination of various different forms of therapy, it is not in practice particularly difficult to teach, given a gradual introduction to the way of working and adequately skilled supervision. In trainees who have had some experience in work with couples (for example Relate counsellors) the addition of other techniques can be accommodated without much difficulty. Junior doctors who have only had experience with individual patients may at first find the transition to couple work a little difficult, but the general problem-solving approach is in some ways quite compatible with the medical model, and they soon learn to adapt to the couple situation. The same applies to other professionals such as psychologists, social workers and nurses.

A last, but by no means minor, advantage of the method is that it is highly suitable for the evaluation of results in research work. This has already borne considerable fruit in the field of behavioural marital therapy, and we hope that the clear-cut goals and well identified techniques of the behavioural-systems approach will enable similar research work to be done on the outcome of therapy.

13.4 The evidence for the efficacy of couple therapy

We have written little so far in this book about the efficacy of couple therapy. We do not intend to write a great deal about it, mainly because the book is intended to be primarily a practical guide to the types of therapy described. However, it is ultimately on the demonstration of its efficacy that any therapy depends for its long-term acceptability. Without this it will remain something of unproven value, maintained by nothing more than the enthusiasm of its practitioners.

Fortunately, a good deal of outcome research has been done, especially on the behavioural approaches of reciprocity negotiation and communication training, although much less has so far been carried out on systems therapy. A number of pioneering reports on behavioural marital therapy (BMT) were produced in the early 1970s. The first group (for example Ely 1970; Cardillo 1971; Azrin *et al.* 1973) showed that BMT in various forms was useful in improving marital adjustment, and was more effective than other types of intervention to which it was compared, including forms of therapy designed to bring out feelings in the session.

Liberman (1976) gave couples counselling as a group, and showed that if they had behavioural tasks they did better in therapy than if they were simply asked to discuss their feelings.

Crowe (1978) carried out quite a large-scale study on 42 moderately distressed couples, divided into three cohorts of 14 each. The first 14 couples had a behavioural (directive) form of treatment with reciprocity negotiation, communication training and some Masters and Johnson therapy (see Chapter 11), the second 14 had a type of therapy (interpretative) based on interpretation of the unconscious conflicts underlying their problems, and the third 14 were allowed to sit with the therapist and talk about their problems, but the therapist did little but sympathise with what was said by each partner (the supportive approach). The results were quite surprising, in that all three cohorts of couples showed significant improvement, especially on the 'target problems' of which they were mainly complaining. In many ways, however, the first group did best, improving their sexual adjustment and their target problems more than those in the other two groups. This advantage was also seen at 18 months after the end of treatment, especially over the third group. The second group, which had shown no superiority at the end of therapy over the third group, became superior on marital adjustment at nine months after treatment.

The conclusions of this study were that the directive approach was the most effective of the three, but that the interpretative approach was perhaps more likely to help couples in the longer term rather than immediately. Contrary to what might have been expected, the behavioural approach was effective not only at the end of the treatment period, but also in the more long-term timescale, and therefore produced more than simply a transient change in behaviour. The fact that the supportive approach produced significant changes, even though these were less striking than those of the directive approach, suggests that there are a number of non-specific factors in treatment which are present irrespective of the particular technique used. We can use this finding in one way to reassure trainees who seem daunted by the complexities of couple therapy, in that it seems that, even if the therapist just sits with the couple and allows them to discuss things in a general way, some improvement results.

Since these pioneering studies, other research studies have been carried out on the outcome of marital therapy (Baucom and Mehlman 1984; Jacobson *et al.* 1984), and most of it has again focussed on the behavioural approaches. In all of the reported studies the behavioural approach has been effective compared to other forms of treatment or to no-treatment controls (Hahlweg & Jacobson 1984).

Less research has been done on other forms of couple therapy. One interesting study by Emmelkamp *et al.* (1984) compared three forms of therapy: contingency contracting (reciprocity negotiation), communication training and 'system-theoretic' therapy. All three approaches produced significant improvements, but none was superior to any of the others.

In a thoughtful analysis of the research on outcome in marital therapy, Jacobson *et al.* (1984) commented that, although couples in most outcome studies showed improvement as a group, of those who began therapy in the 'distressed' range (the more severe types of problem) less than half improved sufficiently to place them in the 'non-distressed' range at the end of treatment. These authors also commented that the studies such as those of Emmelkamp and Crowe (see above), which compared different approaches to couple therapy, showed only minor differences between the behavioural method and the active comparison treatment. Thus although the behavioural treatment was clearly superior to no treatment, or to a 'control' activity as in Crowe's study, its superiority to all other forms of couple therapy has not been proved beyond all doubt, and the improvements produced are worthwhile but do not completely resolve the problems complained of. This we feel to be a research-based confirmation of our clinical decision to extend the use of behavioural couple therapy by the addition of systemic techniques for the more disturbed couples.

In a rather ingenious study carried out at the Maudsley Marital Clinic, Bennun (1985) found that it was possible to give behavioural couple therapy by seeing only one partner. He divided his couples into two groups and deliberately saw only one partner in half of the couples, giving the other half conventional couple therapy. The results of treatment were similar in both groups of couples, thus showing that it is the homework exercises rather than the work with the couple in the session which is the important ingredient of this form of therapy.

Another question was asked by Crowe *et al.* (1981). This was whether it was necessary, as stated by Masters and Johnson (op. cit.) to have two co-therapists of opposite sexes for couples in sexual therapy. The answer was that this is not so, and that one therapist produces as much improvement in sexual therapy as two. This finding is consistent with those of a number of other research studies in both sexual and marital therapy.

The measures for assessing marital and sexual adjustment, used in many of the above outcome studies, have been reviewed in Section 2.1.3.

13.5 Where behavioural-systems couple therapy stands in relation to psychiatric problems, addictions, family work, divorce and remarriage

In Chapter 3 we described the limits of couple therapy in terms of what sort of problem is unsuitable for this kind of work. Couple therapy can be of considerable benefit in relation to such problems as abuse of alcohol and drugs, psychiatric illness in general, marital violence, divorce and abuse of children. However, this benefit is most obvious in those cases where the problem is of a relatively minor degree and is somehow still amenable to the influence of family dynamics.

In our earlier discussion of the indications for couple therapy we stated that we see this kind of therapy as being only one of many options for dealing with problems. Whereas some family and marital therapists would see all these problems as arising from the 'system' and seek to treat them by a systemic approach, we would prefer to be flexible as to whether to offer conjoint therapy for the couple or some more specific kind of treatment for the individual.

Couple therapy can often be a useful way of treating psychiatric problems (Chapter 10) and problems of addiction (Section 10.15) in individuals who are part of a marriage or similar close relationship, but this depends on a number of factors. Some of these patients seem to be in a situation in which the problem has taken over their whole life (for example if a man is drinking alcohol more or less continuously, or a psychiatric patient is judged to need compulsory admission to hospital for her own protection). At that stage there seems to be no way in which the relationship can affect the problem either positively or negatively, and couple therapy would be seen as irrelevant. However, when the acute phase is over, or the dependency or illness has become less extreme, it would be quite appropriate to offer some help to the couple, since there may then very well be interpersonal factors which could increase or decrease the likelihood of relapse. Some examples of these are given in the discussion in Section 3.4.14 about the ways of helping relatives to prevent a schizophrenic patient from relapsing by showing 'low expressed emotion'. Any couple therapy in such cases should, of course, be given in parallel with individual help and in consultation with the psychiatric team or Alcoholics or Narcotics Anonymous (see Sections 3.3 and 13.3).

The partner of such a patient may also need a good deal of support, in view of the pain and distress caused by the problem. It is to be hoped this will be available from the services looking after the patient in the acute phase, but when the couple enter conjoint therapy it may be possible to help the patient to provide some of that support for the 'well' partner, and this may redress some of the inequality in the couple and thus make recurrence of the problem less likely (see Chapter 10 for examples of this).

With problems involving other family members, particularly children, couple therapy can be carried out alongside family therapy, with a fairly flexible commitment to sessions for the whole family or the couple alone. In cases of child abuse, whether physical or sexual (Section 10.12), it is important for the couple or family therapist to be in regular consultation with social workers, probation officers and the courts to ensure that there is adequate control over the legal and related aspects of the case and, especially where family rehabilitation is being attempted, that the abused child is being properly protected.

In relation to separation, divorce and remarriage, couple therapy again has a central role to play (Section 10.16). The situation is often more complicated than in therapy with intact couples, and the therapist has to take into account divided loyalties, triangles of various sorts, shifting boundaries and coalitions and the difficulty the couple have in separating from each other but remaining 'co-parents'. Some very delicate negotiations may be necessary to deal with the conflicting interests of, say, a first wife who is looking after the children of the marriage, her ex-husband who visits them and the second wife who feels undermined by the loyalty which her husband shows to his children and first wife. These complexities should not, however, deter therapists from taking these couples on (as in conciliation work, Parkinson 1986): the emphasis is often on the ability of the separated partners to take joint responsibility for their children.

13.6 Difficulties which might be encountered by therapists or trainees using this approach

The approach we have been describing in this book is one which has been developed and refined in the couple therapy clinic at the Maudsley Hospital. Our trainees have a gradual exposure to the type of work described through observation via the one-way screen and through role-play exercises, and may be expected to be fairly familiar with the philosophy and the therapeutic moves by the time they come to see their first couple. However, others who attempt the work without participation in such a supportive setting may find the transition more difficult (see Chapter 12).

We anticipate that therapists who have been used to allowing the couple's problems to emerge in their own time may have difficulty in keeping the momentum going in a behavioural-systems approach, and may feel that important issues which might otherwise have emerged are being passed over. They may also feel uncomfortable with the relative lack of emphasis on the past, whether of the individual or of the relationship. We usually suggest that the trainee should try the approach first, since they will often be surprised at the way in which the kind of information they are seeking does in fact emerge in the course of de-centred discussion by the couple or in circular questioning, if indeed it is not already there in the biographical history sheets. We believe that in most couples there are more benefits to be gained from the experience of change in the session itself than from understanding of the past.

Another kind of objection may come from a completely different point of view, that of the medically trained therapist who sees a couple in which one partner is suffering from, say, depression which might respond easily to antidepressant medication. This therapist might feel that it is unethical to try to reframe the problem as arising from the relationship and treat it by couple therapy. Our approach to this sort of case would usually be to encourage the 'patient' to consult another doctor (psychiatrist or general practitioner) about the symptoms, and if appropriate to receive medication, while we continue to work concurrently with the couple. However, the concept of illness behaviour, and the idea that we may be able to formulate a depression as an 'optional' series of symptoms arising from the relationship is, we think, a valuable one which may help many depressed individuals to control their otherwise intractable symptoms without the need for long-term medication.

13.7　*Prospects for future developments*

13.7.1　Therapeutic developments

The current state of behavioural-systems couple therapy is one of constant development and experimentation. There are some problems which we now feel fairly confident in treating, including sexual reluctance (especially in the female partner), general communication difficulties, problems defined as relationship ones and some milder cases of depression. We still see less favourable outcomes with more severe depression, with jealousy (although the outcome in jealousy is probably better with couple therapy than with many other approaches) and with couples who are already in the early stages of separation or in which one partner is having an affair.

We may hope that for these more difficult problems we will be able to develop better types of intervention. It should be remembered that, until recently, problems of sexual reluctance were considered much more difficult to treat than problems of function, and yet we now see them as being relatively easy and rewarding. The possibility exists that approaches may be found to help those with more severe depression to be helped by increasing assertiveness within the relationship, thereby reducing the need for the depressive symptoms and for long-term medication. The approaches of Leff, Falloon and Goldstein to schizophrenics and their families may be able to be extended to work with depressives, who are known to be, if anything, more sensitive to expressed emotion than schizophrenics.

Jealousy is another problem in which we may expect some more progress with our approach to the couple. The compulsive nature of the symptom suggests that a more paradoxical approach may be particularly useful in this condition. There may also be some advantage in the addition of cognitive therapy techniques to the couple therapy in jealousy, since this therapeutic approach has shown hopeful results in non-delusional cases.

The difficulties in helping couples who are on the edge of separation will probably remain, although it may be possible, as couple therapy becomes more widely accepted, that such couples will come for help at an earlier stage of the problem and so make it easier to be helped.

Thus we hope that in the future we will be able to help more difficult clients, and do better for those with whom we can already make considerable progress. However, we have always to remember that what we offer is not a 'cure' for relationship problems, but an improved adjustment to the relationship, which in turn may make the symptoms (if there are any) less prominent. The goals are therefore still fairly modest, but we would also hope that if each partner can improve their flexibility by, say, five per cent, the couple can improve their relationship by ten per cent, and that that may make sufficient difference to them to stabilise the relationship and perhaps avoid the real dangers and disadvantages which both would suffer by divorce or by the continuation of the invalidism of one partner.

13.7.2 Developments in research

As stated earlier in this chapter, much research on the outcome of therapy has been done in relation to behavioural marital therapy. We are now in a position to extend the research effort to other forms of therapy, and in particular to assess whether our addition of systemic interventions really improves the outcome of therapy. Probably this will not be done by the type of study reported in Section 13.1, in which a number of couples had one type of therapy and a similar number had another, with comparison of the outcome as between the two groups. It would be more appropriate to carry out single case studies to test the specific effects of different interventions, and thereby to build on the creative and experimental work already being done in our clinic. In addition to outcome research we need much more work to be done on the basic understanding of how relationships begin and develop (see discussion in Chapter 1). In particular, the importance of non-verbal communication is only slowly being recognised, and greater knowledge on this subject should help us as therapists in both the behavioural and the systemic aspects of our work.

Another useful area for research is the question of how couples can best adjust to the changes brought about by the family life cycle (see Chapter 7). It would be very useful to have data on which to base our advice to couples, rather than relying on our own experience or intuition.

The other largely unknown territory in the field of couple relationships is sexual behaviour. Some data are available, but the Kinsey reports are now over 30 years old and were carried out in the USA, and surveys such as those of Sanders (1985 and 1987) are rather weak because they relied on self-selected responders filling in questionnaires sent out in magazines. There is in fact very little that we know in a real sense about sexual behaviour within relationships, beyond our own experience and what our client couples tell us.

13.7.3 Developments in the provision of therapy

In view of the large numbers of couples and individuals who refer themselves for counselling, both to centres like ours and to national organizations like Relate Marriage Guidance, it seems that there could be some advantages in a more rapid and cost-effective form of therapy becoming widely available. If the approach we have been describing becomes more acceptable to therapists and counsellors, it may be that couples will be able to be helped more rapidly than hitherto, and either the waiting lists for therapy will be reduced or more couples, who now find it impossible to get help, will be able to be taken on for therapy.

13.7.4 Developments in the prevention of relationship problems

As the knowledge about the development and maintenance of relationships grows, it may be possible to help couples who are in the early
stages of their problems to take steps to improve the situation without
outside help. Two techniques which would be well suited for use in a
'do-it-yourself' fashion are reciprocity negotiation and timetables. A
couple with difficulties could simply buy a manual with instructions for
self-help counselling and apply them. Of course in many cases the
couple's inherent power struggles would prevent co-operation on the
instructions and would invalidate the exercise, but if even five per cent
of disturbed couples could help themselves in this way it would reduce
some of the pressures on the overstretched counselling and therapy
services of the country.

There will probably never be a situation in which all relationship
problems can be prevented or even successfully treated, but if it becomes
possible to reduce some of the unhappiness caused by this kind of
difficulty, both to adults and to their children, some useful purpose will
have been served.

Appendix

Explanatory letter sent to couples who have been referred for therapy

We have received a request to send you an appointment for our Family and Marital Therapy Clinic. We can offer you an appointment on _____ at 1 45 p.m. and should be grateful if you could return the attached slip by _____ indicating whether or not you will be able to attend on this day.

Owing to the nature of our work it is important you attend as a couple or family. If it is mainly a marital problem we would expect to see husband and wife together. If it is primarily a problem in a son or daughter living with their parents, then we would expect to see all the family members who live together, at least on the first occasion.

The way we work involves the assigned therapist being assisted by a team of colleagues using a one-way screen, at least on the first visit. In our experience this is the best approach for family and marital difficulties.

In order to help us assess the problem we should be grateful if both you and your partner could complete and return the attached History Sheets before you come for the appointment. Please fill in as much as you can on these forms, but if there are any problems you can contact my secretary on . . .

It would be helpful if you could let us have a telephone number where we can contact you if we have a cancellation and are able to offer you an appointment at short notice.

Yours sincerely

Psychiatric history sheet, (Marital & sexual problems clinic)

Try and be brief in your answers. If in doubt, put down something quickly and pass on to the next question.

Name   *Age*   *Sex*   *Marital status*

Occupation

Main problems (in your own words)

How long have you had this problem?

Write the names of your parents and your brothers and sisters (names, ages, married or single, occupations).

Do any of your relatives suffer from nerves? Give details.

As a child how did you get on with your parents and your brother(s) and sister(s)? Mention any special difficulties.

Previous health
Have you had any serious illness or operation?

Have you had any treatment for your nerves? Give details of hospital admissions and treatment (if known)

Personal history
Where were you born?

As far as you know, were you a normal baby?

Did you have any nervous habits as a child, e.g. sleep-walking, nail-biting, wetting the bed, any special fears?

What age did you start and finish school?

Did you enjoy school? If not, why not?

Did you pass any exams (e.g. CSE, 'O' Level?) Give details of further education if any, e.g. college degrees etc.

Work
What age did you start work? Give list of jobs with dates and reasons for change (e.g. promotion, more money, the sack).

Social

How much do you drink (e.g. social, heavy, too much)?

How many cigarettes do you smoke a day?

How do you spend your leisure time as a couple?

How do you spend your leisure time alone?

Do you take any medicines or pills prescribed by a doctor (give details if known)?

Do you take any drugs which are not prescribed?

What contraception do you use as a couple?

Do you live in a house, flat, bedsitter? Rent or mortgage?

What do you consider your living conditions to be like?

Do you have any special money problems?

Marriage and children

How long have you been married to your present partner?

How long (if at all) did you live together before marriage?

How many children do you have in the present marriage? (give names, sexes, ages and state if any have nervous problems) (please state if any of your children are adopted, and if so at what age).

Have you at any time separated from your present spouse? (please give times and details)

Have you been married before? (please give details, reasons for ending the relationship, number and ages of any children and who is now looking after them)

Personality
How would you describe yourself as a person?

How would your worst enemy describe you?

Present state
Do you feel depressed or anxious? Give details.

Do you have any special fears or phobias, e.g. animals, going out alone, strangers, social occasions, dirt, germs, illness?

Do you check things (e.g. the front door when going out) more than once?

Have you ever heard voices or noises that other people cannot hear?

Is your concentration good?

Have you been crying lately?

Is your memory reasonable for your age?

Do you have difficulty in getting to sleep?

Do you wake often in the early hours of the morning?

Is your appetite poor at present?

Have you lost weight recently? If so, how much and in what length of time?

Has your sexual drive been reduced recently?

References

Ackerman N. (1968) *Treating the Troubled Family*. Basic Books, New York.

Ainsworth M. & Bell S. (1970) Attachment, exploration and separation: illustrated by the behaviour of one-year olds in a strange situation. *Child Development*, **41**, 49–67.

Azrin N.H., Naster B.J. & Jones R. (1973) Reciprocity counselling: a rapid learning-based procedure for marital counselling. *Behaviour Research and Therapy*, **11**, 365–382.

Bach M. & Wyden P. (1969) *The Intimate Enemy. How to Fair Fight in Love and Marriage*. Morrow, New York.

Bancroft J. (1989) *Human Sexuality and its Problems*. Churchill Livingstone, Edinburgh.

Bancroft J. & Coles L. (1976) Three years experience in a sexual problems clinic. *British Medical Journal*, **1**, 1575–7.

Barker P. (1986) *Basic Family Therapy*. BSP Professional, Oxford.

Barnes H. & Olson D.H. (1985) Parent adolescent communication and the circumplex model. *Child Development*.

Bateson G. (1955) A theory of play and fantasy. *Psychiatric Research Reports*, Nos 1, 2, 39–51.

Bateson G. (1958) *Naven*. Stanford California University Press.

Bateson G. (1971) *Steps to an Ecology of Mind*. Ballantine Books, New York.

Bateson G. (1979) *Mind and Nature*. Wildwood House, London.

Bateson G., Jackson D.D., Haley J. & Weakland J. (1956) Towards a theory of schizophrenia. *Behavioural Science*, **1**, 351–64.

Baucom D.H. (1984) The active ingredients of behavioural marital therapy: the effectiveness of problem-solving/communication training, contingency contracting, and their combination. In *Marital Interaction* (Ed. by K. Hahlweg & N.S. Jacobson). Guilford Press, New York.

Baucom D.H. & Mehlman S.K. (1984) Predicting marital status following behavioural marital therapy: a comparison of models of marital relationships. *Marital Interaction* (Ed. by K. Hahlweg & N.S. Jacobson). Guilford Press, New York.

Beavers W.R. (1976) A theoretical basis for family evaluation. *No Single Thread: Psychological Health in Family Systems* (Ed. by J.M. Lewis, W.R. Beavers, J.T. Gossett & V.A. Phillips). Brunner/Mazel, New York.

Beavers W.R. (1985) *Successful Marriage. A Family Systems Approach to Couple Therapy*. W.W. Norton, New York.

Beavers W.R. & Voeller M.N. (1983) Comparing and contrasting the Olson circumplex model with the Beavers systems model. *Family Process*, **22**, 85–98.

Beck A. (1967) *Depression: Causes and Treatment*. University of Pennsylvania Press.

Beck A. (1976) *Cognitive Therapy and the Emotional Disorders*. International Universities Press, New York.

Beck A. (1979) *Cognitive Therapy of Depression*. Guilford Press, New York.

Belliveau F. & Richter L. (1971) *Understanding Human Sexuality*. Hodder and Stoughton, London.

Bennun I. (1985) Prediction and responsiveness in behavioural marital therapy. *Behavioural Pyschotherapy*, **13**, 186–201.

Bentovim A. & Furniss T. (1983) *Workshop on Sexual Abuse and the Family*. Institute of Family Therapy, London.

Bergmann M.S. (1987) *The Anatomy of Loving*. Columbia University Press.

Berkowitz R. & Leff J. (1984) Clinical teams reflect family dysfunction. *Journal of Family Therapy*, **6**, (2).

Berne E. (1964) *Games People Play*. Grove Press, New York.

Bion W. (1962) *Learning from Experiences*. Heinemann, London.

Bion W. (1970) *Attention and Interpretation*. Basic Books, New York.

Birchler G.R. (1972) *Differential patterns of instrumental affiliative behaviour as a function of degree of marital distress and level of intimacy*. Doctoral dissertation, Oregon University.

Birchler G.R., Weiss R.L. & Vincent J.P. (1975) A multi method analysis of social reinforcement exchange between mentally distressed and nondistressed spouse and stranger dyads. *Journal of Personality and Social Psychology*, **31**, 349–60.

Birtchnell J. (1986) The imperfect attainment of intimacy: a key concept in marital therapy. *Journal of Family Therapy*, **8**, (2), 153–72.

Birtchnell J. (1987) Attachment–detachment, directiveness–receptiveness: A system for classifying interpersonal attitudes and behaviour. *British Journal of Medical Psychology*, **60**, 17–27.

Birtchnell J. (1989) *Understanding marital relationships in terms of the styles of relating of marital partners*. Paper at Symposium on Family Therapy and Family Research, Institute of Psychiatry, London.

Blake D. (1982) Handicap and Family Therapy. *Family Therapy*. (Ed. by A. Bentovim, G.G. Barnes and A. Cooklin). Academic Press, London.

Bott E. (1971) *Family and Social Networks*, revised edn. Tavistock, London.

Bowlby J. (1969) *Attachment and Loss*, **1 & 2**. Hogarth Press, London.

Brannen J. & Collard J. (1982) *Marriages in Trouble: The Process of Seeking Help*. Tavistock, London.

Brecher R. & Brecher E. (1968) *An Analysis of Human Sexual Response*. Panther, New York.

Brindley G.S. (1983) Cavernosal alpha-blockade: a new treatment for investigating and treating erectile impotence. *British Journal of Psychiatry*, **143**, 332–7.

Briscoe M.E. (1982) Sex differences in psychological wellbeing. *Psychological Medicine Monograph*, Suppl 1.

Briscoe M.E. (1986) Identification of emotional problems in post-partum women by health visitors. *British Medical Journal*. **292**, 1245–7.

Briscoe M.E. (1987) Why do people go to the doctor? Sex differences in the correlates of G.P. consultation. *Social Science and Medicine*, **25**, 507–13.

Brown G.W. & Harris T. (1978) *Social Origins of Depression*. Tavistock, London.

Brown G.W., Brochlain M. & Harris T. (1975) Social class and psychiatric disturbance among women in urban populations. *Sociology*, **9**, 225–54.

Brown P. & Faulder C. (1977) *Treat Yourself to Sex*. Penguin, Middlesex.

Burgess E.W. & Locke H.J. (1953) *The Family from Institution to Companionship*. American Book Co, New York.

Byng-Hall J. (1980) Symptom bearer as marital distance regulator: clinical implications. *Family Process*, **19**, 355–65.

Byng-Hall J. (1982a) Grandparents, other relatives, friends and pets. In *Family Therapy* (Ed. by A. Bentovim, G.G. Barnes & A. Cooklin) Academic Press, London.

Byng-Hall J. (1982b) Family legends: their significance for the therapist. In *Family Therapy* (Ed. by A. Bentovim, G.G. Barnes & A. Cooklin). Academic Press, London.

Byng-Hall J. (1985) Resolving distance conflicts. In *Casebook of Marital Therapy* (Ed. by A.S. Gurman). Guilford Press, New York.

Campbell D. (1982) Adolescence in families. In *Family Therapy*, (Ed. by A. Bentovim, G.G. Barnes & A. Cooklin). Academic Press, London.

Caplan G. (1984) *Principles of Preventive Psychiatry*. Tavistock, London.

Cardillo J.P. (1971) The effects of teaching communication roles in interpersonal self-perception and self-concept in disturbed marriages. *Dissertation Abstracts International*, **32**, 2392–3.

Casement P. (1985) *On Learning from the Patient*. Tavistock, London.

Cecchin G. (1987) Hypothesising circularity and neutrality revisited: An invitation to curiosity. *Family Process*, **26**, (4), 405–414.

Chadwick B.A. & Jones J.K. (1976) *Social Exchange Theory. Its Structure and Influence in Social Psychology*. Academic Press, London.

Chester R. (1973) Marital satisfaction and stability in the post parental years. *Marriage Guidance*, **14**, (11), 338–48.

Chodorow N. (1978) *The Reproduction of Mothering*. University of California Press.

Clare A. (1976) *Psychiatry in Dissent*. Tavistock, London.

Clare A.W. & Jenkins R. (1985) Women and mental illness. *British Medical Journal*, **291**, 1521–2.

Cobb J.P., McDonald R., Marks I.M. & Stern R. (1980) Marital vs exposure therapy, Psychological treatments of co-existing marital and phobic-obsessive problems. *European Journal of Behavioural Analysis and Modification*, **4**, 3–16.

Comfort A. (1972) *The Joy of Sex*. Quartet Books, London.

Cooklin A. (1982) Changes in the here and now system vs systems over time. In *Family Therapy*, **1** (Ed. by A. Bentovim, G.G. Barnes & A. Cooklin). Academic Press, London.

Crisp A.H. (1980) *Anorexia Nervosa Let Me Be*. Academic Press, London.

Cronin V.E., Johnson K.M., & Lannamann J.W. (1982) Paradoxes, double binds and reflexive loops: An alternative theoretical perspective. *Family Process*, **21**, 91–112.

Crowe M.J. (1978) Conjoint marital therapy: a controlled outcome study. *Psychological Medicine*, **8**, 623–36.

Crowe M.J. (1982) The treatment of marital and sexual problems. A behavioural approach. In *Family Therapy*, **1** (Ed. by A. Bentovim, G.G. Barnes & A. Cooklin). Academic Press, London.

Crowe M.J. (1985) Marital Therapy – a behavioural-systems approach. *Marital Therapy in Britain*. (Ed. by W. Dryden). Harper & Row, London.

Crowe M.J. (1988) Indications for family, marital and sexual therapy. *Handbook of Behavioural Family Therapy*. (Ed. by I.R.H. Falloon). Guilford Press, New York.

Crowe M.J. & Ridley J. (1986) The negotiated timetable: a new approach to marital conflicts involving male demands and female reluctance for sex. *Sexual and Marital Therapy*, 1, 157–173.

Crowe M.J. & Qureshi M. (1990) Cavernosal unstriated muscle relaxant injections (CUMRI) as a maintenance treatment for erectile impotence: a report of 41 cases. *Sexual and Marital Therapy*, in press.

Crowe M.J., Czechowitz H. & Gillan P. (1977) *The treatment of sexual dysfunction: a report of 75 cases*. Paper presented at V1 World Congress of Psychiatry, Honolulu.

Crowe M.J., Gillan P. & Golombok S. (1981) Form and content in the conjoint treatment of sexual dysfunction: a controlled study. *Behaviour Research and Therapy*, 19, 47–54.

Daniell D. (1985) Marital therapy, the psychodynamic approach. *Marital Therapy in Britain*, 1. (Ed. by W. Dryden). Harper and Row, London.

Dare C. (1982a) Families with school going children. In *Family Therapy*, 2 (Ed. by A. Bentovim, G.G. Barnes & A. Cooklin). Academic Press, London.

Dare C. (1982b) The empty nest: Families with older adolescents and the models of family therapy. In *Family Therapy*, 2 (Ed. by A. Bentovim, G.G. Barnes & A. Cooklin). Academic Press, London.

Dell P.F. (1981) Some irreverent thoughts on paradox. *Family Process*, 20, 37–51.

Dell P.F. (1982) Beyond homeostasis: toward a concept of coherence. *Family Process*, 21, 21–41.

Dell P.F. (1986) Why do we still call them paradoxes? *Family Process*, 25, 223–34.

de Silva P. (1987) An unusual case of morbid jealousy treated with role reversal. *Sexual and Marital Therapy*, 2, 179–82.

DHSS (1978) Social service teams, the practitioner's view. In *Supervision and Accountability*. HMSO, London.

Dicks H.V. (1967) *Marital Tensions*. Routledge and Kegan Paul, London.

Douglas A., Matson I.C. & Hunter S. (1989) Sex therapy for women incestuously aroused as children. *Sexual and Marital Therapy*, 4, 143–60.

Elton A. (1982) Birth of a baby and the pre-school years. In *Family Therapy*, 2 (Ed. by A. Bentovim, G.G. Barnes & A. Cooklin). Academic Press, London.

Ely A.L. (1970) *Efficacy of training in conjugal therapy*. PhD thesis, Rutgers University.

Emmelkamp P.M.G. (1983) *Phobic and Obsessive-compulsive Disorders: Theory, Research and Practice*. Plenum Press.

Emmelkamp P., van der Helm M., MacGillavry D., & van Zanten B. (1984) Marital therapy with clinically distressed couples: a comparative evaluation of system-theoretic, contingency contracting and communication skills approaches. *Marital Interaction: Analysis and Modification*. (Ed. by K. Hahlweg & N.S. Jacobson). Guilford Press, New York.

EOC (Equal Opportunities Commission) (1980) *The experience of caring for elderly and handicapped: community care policies and women's lives.*

Erickson M. (1967) In *Advanced Techniques in Hypnosis and Therapy* (Ed. by J. Haley). Grune and Stratton, New York.

Falloon I.R.H. & Liberman R.P. (1983) Behavioural family interventions in the management of chronic schizophrenia. *Family Therapy in Schizophrenia.* (Ed. by W.R. McFarlane). Guilford Press, New York.

Falloon I.R.H., Boyd J.L. & McGill C.W. (1984) *Family Care of Schizophrenia: A Problem Solving Approach to the Treatment of Mental Illness.* Guilford Press, New York.

Family Policy Studies Fact Sheet (1985) Family Policy Studies Centre, London.

Feldman L. (1976) Depression and marital interaction. *Family Process,* **15,** (4).

Feldman L. (1979) Marital conflict and marital intimacy. An integrative psycho-dynamic-behavioural-systemic model. *Family Process,* **18,** 69–78.

Feldman M.P. & MacCulloch M.J. (1971) *Homosexual Behaviour: Therapy and Assessment.* Pergamon Press, Oxford.

Feldman M.P., Summers S., Gordon P.E. & Meagher J.R. (1979) The impact of rape on sexual satisfaction. *Journal of Abnormal Psychology,* **88,** 101–5.

Franks H. (1988) Get it together. *The Guardian,* 26 July.

Fredman N. & Sherman R. (1987) *Handbook of measurements for Marriage and Family Therapy.* Brunner/Mazel, New York.

Freud S. (1917) Mourning and Melancholia. *The Standard Edition of the Complete Psychological Works of Sigmund Freud.* (1957), **14,** Hogarth Press and the Institute of Psychoanalysis, London.

Friedman A.S. (1975) Interaction of drug therapy with marital therapy in depressive patients. *Archives of General Psychiatry,* **32,** 619–37.

Fritz G.S., Stoll K. & Wagner N. (1981) A comparison of males and females who were sexually molested as children. *Journal of Sex and Marital Therapy,* **7,** 54–9.

Furniss T. (1983) Family process in the treatment of intrafamilial child sexual abuse. *Journal of Family Therapy,* **5,** 263–78.

Gillan P. (1987) *Sex Therapy Manual.* Blackwell Scientific Publications, Oxford.

Gillan P. & Gillan R. (1976) *Sex Therapy Today.* Open Books, London.

Gilligan C. (1977) In a different voice: women's conception of self and morality. *Harvard Educational Review,* **4,** 481–517.

Gilligan C. (1982) *In a Different Voice.* Harvard University Press.

Gizinski M. (1978) Self awareness of the supervisor in supervision. *Clinical Social Work Journal,* **6.**

Glick I. & Kessler D. (1980) *Marital and Family Therapy,* 2e. Grune and Stratton, New York.

Gordon T. (1975) *Parent Effectiveness Training.* New American Library, New York.

Gottman J. et al. (1976) *A Couple's Guide to Communication.* Champaign Illinois Research Press.

Gottman J., Markman H. & Notarius C. (1977) The topography of marital conflict: A sequential analysis of verbal and nonverbal behaviour. *Journal of Marriage and the Family,* **39,** 461–77.

Graaf B. (1988) Men in marital therapy. *Handbook of Counselling and Psychotherapy with Men.* (Ed. by B. Scher). Sage Publications, New York.

Grinker R.R. Sr (Ed.) (1967) *Towards a Unified Theory of Human Behaviour.* Basic Books, New York.

Gurman A.S. (1973) The effects and effectiveness of marital therapy: a review of outcome research. *Family Process,* **12,** 145–70.

Gurman A.S. (1978) Contemporary marital therapies: a critique and comparative analysis of psychoanalytic, behavioural and systems theory approaches. *Marriage and Marital Therapy* (Ed. by T.J. Paolino & B.S. McCrady). Brunner/ Mazel, New York.

Gurman A.S. (1979) Dimensions of marital therapy. A comprehensive analysis. *Journal of Marital and Family Therapy,* **5,** 5–16.

Gurman A.S. & Kniskern D.P. (1977) *Marital Enrichment Programmes.* Brunner/ Mazel, New York.

Gurman A.S. & Kniskern D.P. (1981) *Handbook of Family Therapy.* Brunner/Mazel, New York.

Guthrie L. & Mattinson J. (1971) *Brief Casework with a Marital Problem.* Institute of Marital Studies, London.

Hafner J. (1984) Predicting the effects on husbands of behaviour therapy for wives' agoraphobia. *Behaviour Research and Therapy,* **22,** 217–26.

Hahlweg K., Schindler L., Revensdorf D. & Brengelmann C. (1984) The Munich Marital Therapy Study. In *Marital Interaction* (Ed. by K. Hahlweg & N.S. Jacobson). Guilford Press, New York.

Haley J. (1963) *Strategies of Psychotherapy.* Grune and Stratton, New York.

Haley J. (1973) *Uncommon Therapy: The Psychiatric Techniques of Milton E. Erickson.* W.W. Norton, New York.

Haley J. (1976) *Problem Solving Therapy.* Harper and Row, New York.

Haley J. (1980) *Leaving Home.* McGraw-Hill, New York.

Hampson R.B., Beavers W.R. & Hulgus Y.F. (1988) Commentary: comparing the Beavers and circumplex models of family functioning. *Family Process,* **27,** 85–92.

Harrison T. (1970) *The Loiners.* Fulcrum Press.

Harrison T. (1984) *Selected Poems.* King Penguin, Middlesex.

Hawton K. (1985) *Sex Therapy. A Practical Guide.* Oxford Medical Publications, Oxford.

Heilweil I. (1984) *Video in Mental Health Practice.* Tavistock, London.

Henwood M. & Wicks M. (1984) *Forgotten army: family care and elderly people.* Briefing paper, Family Policy Studies Centre.

Henwood M., Rimmer L. & Wicks M. (1987) *Inside the family: Changing roles of men and women.* Occasional paper, Family Policy Studies Centre.

Hoffman L. (1971) Deviation-amplifying process in natural groups. In *Changing Families* (Ed. by J. Haley). Grune and Stratton, New York.

Hoffman L. (1981) *Foundations of Family Therapy.* Basic Books, New York.

Hops H., Wills T.A., Patterson G.R. & Weiss R.L. (1972) *Marital Interaction Coding System.* Eugene: University of Oregon Research Institute.

Hunt P.A. (1964) Responses to marriage counselling. *British Journal of Guidance and Counselling,* **12,** (1), 72–83.

Hunt P.A. (1985) *Clients' responses to marriage counselling*. Research Report No 3, The National Marriage Guidance Council.

Im W.G., Wilner R.S. & Breit M. (1983) Jealousy: interventions in couple therapy. *Family Process*, **22**, 211–19.

Jackson D.D. (1965) The study of the family. *Family Process*, **4**, 1–20.
Jackson D.D. (1968) *The Mirages of Marriage*. W.W. Norton, New York.
Jackson S.W. (1986) *Melancholia and Depression from Hippocratic to Modern Times*. Yale University Press.
Jacobson E. (1938) *Progressive Relaxation*. University of Chicago Press.
Jacobson N.S. (1979) Increasing positive behaviour in severely distressed marital relationships: the effects of problem solving training. *Behaviour Therapy*, **10**, 311–26.
Jacobson N.S. & Martin B. (1976) Behavioural marriage therapy: current status. *Psychological Bulletin*, **83**, 540–66.
Jacobson N.S. & Weiss R.L. (1978) Behavioural marriage therapy: The contents of Gurman *et al.* may be hazardous to our health. *Family Process*, **17**, 149–161.
Jacobson N.S. & Margolin G. (1979) *Marital Therapy: Strategies based on Social Learning and Behavioural Exchange Principles*. Bruner/Mazel, New York.
Jacobson N.S. & Hahlweg K. (1984) The modification of cognitive processes in behavioural marital therapy: integrating cognitive and behavioural intervention strategies. In *Marital Interaction*. Guilford Press, New York.
Jaques D. (1984) *Learning in Groups*. Croom Helm, London.
Jehu D. (1979) *Sexual Dysfunction. A Behavioural Approach to Causation, Assessment and Treatment*. John Wiley and Sons, New York.
Jenkins R. (1985) Women and Mental Illness. *British Medical Journal*, London, **291**, 1521–2.

Kaplan H.S. (1974) *The New Sex Therapy. Active Treatment of Sexual Dysfunction*. Brunner/Mazel, New York.
Kaplan H.S. (1979) *Disorders of Sexual Desire, and Other New Concepts and Techniques of Sex Therapy*. Bruner/Mazel, New York.
Kaplan H.S. (1981) *The illustrated Manual of Sex Therapy*. Granada, London.
Kaplan H.S. (Ed.) (1985) *Comprehensive Evaluation of Disorders of Sexual Desire*. American Psychiatric Association, Washington D.C.
Kegel A.H. (1952) Sexual function of the pubococcygeus muscle. *Western Journal of Surgery, Obstetrics and Gynaecology*, **60**, 521–4.
Kiely G.M. (1984) Social change and marital problems; implications for marriage counselling. *British Journal of Guidance and Counselling*, **12**, (1), 92–100.
Kraemer S. (1986) *Why worry, Why now, What for*. Tavistock Clinic Paper No 45.
Kubler-Ross E. (1970) *On Death and Dying*. Tavistock, London.
Kuipers L. & Bebbington P. (1985) Relatives as a resource in the management of schizophrenia. *British Journal of Psychiatry*, **147**, 465–71.

L'Abate L. (1977) Intimacy is sharing hurt feelings. *Journal of Marriage and Family Counselling*, April, 13–16.

L'Abate L. & McHenry S. (1983) *Handbook of Marital Interventions*. Grune and Stratton, New York.

Lask B. (1982) Family therapy in paediatric settings. *Family Therapy*, 2 (Ed. by A. Bentovim, G.G. Barnes & A. Cooklin). Academic Press, London.

Lee C. (1988) Theories of family adaptability: Toward a synthesis of Olson's circumplex and the Beavers systems models. *Family Process*, **27**, 73–85.

Leff J.P. (1976) Schizophrenia and sensitivity to family environments. *Schizophrenia Bulletin*, **2**, 566–74.

Leff J. & Vaughn C. (1985) *Expressed Emotion in Families*. Guilford Press, New York.

Leff J.P., Kuipers L., Berkowitz R., Eberlein-Vreis R. & Sturgeon D. (1983) A controlled trial of social intervention in the families of schizophrenic patients. *British Journal of Psychiatry*, **141**, 121–34.

Liberman R.P. (1970) Behavioural approaches in family and couple therapy. *American Journal of Orthopsychiatry*, **40**, 106–118.

Liberman R.P., Levine J., Wheeler E., Sanders N. & Wallace C. (1976) Experimental evaluation of marital group therapy: Behavioural vs interaction-insight formats. *Acta Psychiatrica Scandinavica*, suppl 266.

Lieberman S. & Black D. (1982) Loss, mourning and grief. *Family Therapy*. (Ed. by A. Bentovim, G.G. Barnes and A. Cooklin). Academic Press, London.

Locke H.J. & Wallace K.M. (1959) Short marital adjustment and prediction tests: their reliability and validity. *Marriage and Family Living*, **21**, 251–255.

Mackay D. (1985) Marital therapy: The behavioural approach. In *Marital Therapy in Britain* (Ed. by W. Dryden). Harper and Row, London.

Manor O. (1984) *Family Work in Action*. Tavistock, London.

Mansfield P. & Collard J. (1988) *The Beginning of the Rest of Your Life*. Macmillan Press, London.

Martin J. & Roberts C. (1984) *Women and Employment*, DE/OPCS. HMSO, London.

Maruyama M. (1968) The second cybernetics: deviation amplifying mutual causal processes. *Modern Systems Research for the Behavioural Scientist*. (Ed. by W. Buckley). Aldine, Chicago.

Maruyama M. (1983) The second cybernetics: Deviation amplifying mutual causative processes. *American Scientist*, **51**, 164–79.

Masters W.H. & Johnson V.E. (1966) *Human Sexual Response*. Little, Brown and Co, Boston.

Masters W.H. & Johnson V.E. (1970) *Human Sexual Inadequacy*. Little, Brown and Co, Boston.

Mattinson J. & Sinclair I. (1979) *Mate and Stale Mate*. Tavistock Institute, London.

McLean P.D. (1976) Therapeutic decision making in the behavioural treatment of depression. *The Behavioural Management of Anxiety, Depression and Pain* (Ed. by P.O. Davidson). Brunner/Mazel, New York.

McLean P.D. & Hakstian A.R. (1979) Clinical depression. Comparative efficacy of outpatient treatment. *Journal of Consulting and Clinical Psychology*, **47**, 818–36.

McLean P.D., Ogston K. & Graner L. (1973) A behavioural approach to the treatment of depression. *Journal of Behaviour Therapy and Experimental Psychology*, **14**, 323–30.

Mears E. (1970) Sexual problem clinics: an assessment of the work of 26 doctors trained by the Institute of Psychosexual Medicine. *Public Health (London)*, **92**, 218–223.

Mehrabian A. (1972) *Non Verbal Communication*. Chicago Aldine Atherton.

Meissner W.W. (1978) The conceptualisation of marriage and family dynamics from a psychoanalytic perspective. *Marriage and Marital Therapy*. (Ed. by T.J. Paolino and B.S. McCrady). Brunner/Mazel, New York.

Metcalf A. & Humphries M. (1985) *The Sexuality of Men*. Pluto Press, London.

Miller S. *et al.* (1975) Minnesota Couples Communication Programme. *Small Group Behaviour*, **6**, 57–71.

Minuchin S. (1974) *Families and Family Therapy*. Tavistock Publications, London.

Minuchin S. & Fishman C.H. (1981) *Family Therapy Techniques*. Harvard University Press.

Minuchin S., Rosman B. & Baker L. (1978) *Psychosomatic Families*. Harvard University Press.

Morry van Ments (1983) *The Effective Use of Role-play. A Handbook for Teachers and Trainers*. Kogan Page, London.

Mountjoy P. (1972) *The Experimental Analysis of Social Behaviour*. Appleton-Century-Crofts, New York.

Oakley A. (1974) *The Sociology of Housework*. Basil Blackwell, Oxford.

O'Brien M. (1988) Men and fathers in therapy. *Journal of Family Therapy*, **10**, 109–122.

O'Leary K.D. (Ed.) (1987) *Assessment of Marital Discord*. Lawrence Erlbaum Associates.

O'Leary K.D. & Turkewitz H. (1978) The treatment of marital disorders from a behavioural perspective. In *Marriage and Marital Therapy: Psychoanalytic, Behavioural and Systems Theory Perspective* (Ed. by T.J. Paolini & B.S. McCrady). Brunner/Mazel, New York.

Olson D.H. (1976) *Treating Relationships*. Graphic Press, New York.

Olson D.H., Russell C.S. & Sprenkle D.H. (1983) Circumplex model of marital and family systems. VI Theoretical update. *Family Process*, **22**, (1), 69–84.

Olson D.H., McCubbin H.I., Barnes H., Larsen A., Muxen M. & Wilson M. (1983) *Families: what makes them work*. Sage Publications, Los Angeles, California.

Orbach S. & Eichenbaum L. (1983) *Understanding Women*. Penguin Books, London.

Orden S.R. & Bradburn N.A. (1968) Dimensions of marriage and happiness. *American Journal of Sociology*, **73**, 715–31.

Pahl J. (1980) Patterns of money management within marriage. *Journal of Social Policy*, **9**, (3), 313–35.

Paolini T.J. & McCrady B.S. (1978) *Marriage and Marital Therapy*. Brunner/Mazel, New York.

Papousek H. & Papousek M. (1974) Mirror image and self recognition in young human infants: a new method of experimental analysis. *Developmental Psychobiology*, **7**, (2), 149–57.

Parker G. (1985) *With due care and attention*. Occasional paper No 2. Family Policy Studies Centre, London.

Parkes C.M. (1972) *Bereavement*. International University Press, London.

Parkinson L. (1986) *Conciliation in Separation and Divorce*. Croom Helm, London.

Patterson G.R & Hops H. (1982) Coercion, a game for two: Intervention techniques for marital conflict. In *Handbook of Affective Disorders* (Ed. by R.E. Ulrich & E.S. Paykel) Churchill Livingstone, New York.

Paykel E.S., Myers J.K., Dienelt M.N., Klerman G.L., Lindenthal J.J. & Pepper M. (1969) Life events and depression. *Archives of General Psychiatary*, **21**, 753–60.

Perrotta P. (1986) Leaving home: Later stages of treatment. *Family Process*, **25**, 461–74.

Piaget J. (1929) *The Child's Conception of the World*. Harcourt, Brace and World, New York.

Piaget J. (1951) *Play, Dreams and Imitation in Childhood*. Heinemann, London.

Piaget J. (1955) *The Child's Construction of Reality*. Routledge and Kegan Paul, London.

Pincus L. (Ed.) (1960) *Marriage: Studies in Emotional Conflict and Growth*. Institute of Marital Studies. Methuen, London.

Pincus L. & Bannister K. (1965) *Shared phantasy in marital problems*. Institute of Marital Studies, London.

Pines M. (1989) Mirroring and Child Development. *Self and Identity*. (Ed. Hones T. and Yardley K.) Routledge, London.

Priestley P., McGuire J. Flegg D., Hemsley V. & Welham D. (1978) *Social skills and personal problem solving*. Tavistock Publications, London.

Quinton D. & Rutter M. (1976) An evaluation of an interview assessment of marriage. *Psychological Medicine*, **6**, 577–86.

Rajeki D.W., Lamb M.E. & Obsmacher P. (1978) Toward a general theory of infantile attachment: A comparative review of aspects of the social bond. *Behaviour Brain Sciences*, **1**, 417–64.

Rappoport R. (1965) Normal crises, family structure and mental health. In *Crisis Intervention*. (Ed. by H.R. Parad) F.S.A.A. New York.

Rappoport R., Rappoport R.N. & Strelitz P. (1977) *Fathers, Mothers and Others*. Routledge and Kegan Paul, London.

Riley A.J., Goodman R.E., Kellett J.M. & Orr R. (1989) Double-blind trial of yohimbine hydrochloride in the treatment of erection inadequacy. *Sexual and Marital Therapy*, **4**, 17–26.

Rimmer L. (1983) *Families in focus*. Occasional paper, Study commission on the family. London.

Robinson M. (1982) Reconstituted families: some implications for the family therapists. *Family Therapy*. (Ed. by A. Bentovim, G.G. Barnes and A. Cooklin). Academic Press, London.

Rosenblatt D.B. (1980) Play. In *Developmental Psychiatry* (Ed. by M. Rutter). Heinemann Medical Books, London.

Rossi A.S. (1981) On the Reproduction of Mothering: a Methodological Debate. *Signs: Journal of Women in Culture and Society.* University of Chicago Press.

Rowbotham S. (1983) *Dreams and Dilemmas.* Virago Press, London.

Ruesch J. (1957) *Disturbed Communication.* W.W. Norton and Co, New York.

Rust J. & Golombok S. (1985) The validation of the Golombok-Rust inventory of sexual satisfaction. *British Journal of Clinical Psychology,* **24**, 63–4.

Rust J., Bennun I., Crowe M. & Golombok S. (1986) The Golombok Rust Inventory of Marital State (GRIMS). *Sexual and Marital Therapy,* **1**, 55–60.

Rutter M. (1980) *Scientific Foundations of Developmental Psychiatry.* Heinemann Medical Books, London.

Sanders D. (1985) *The Woman Book of Love and Sex.* Sphere Books, London.

Sanders D. (1987) *The Woman Report on Men.* Sphere Books, London.

Satir V. (1964) *Conjoint Family Therapy.* Science and Behaviour Books, Palo Alto, California.

Schaap C. & Jansen-Nawas C. (1987) Marital interaction, affect and conflict resolution. *Sexual and Marital Therapy,* **2**, 35–51.

Scharff D.E. (1982) *The Sexual Relationship.* Routledge and Kegan Paul, Boston.

Scharff D.E. & Scharff J.S. (1987) *Object Relations Family Therapy.* Jason Aronson, Northvale, New Jersey.

Schindler L. & Vollmer M. (1984) Cognitive prospectus in behavioural marital therapy: some proposals for bridging theory, research and practice. *Marital Interaction.* (Ed. by K. Hahlweg and N.S. Jacobson) Guilford Press, New York.

Segraves R.T. (1982) *Marital Therapy: A Combined Psychodynamic-Behavioural Approach.* Plenum Medical, New York.

Selvini Palazzoli M. (1989) *Family Games: General Models of Psychotic Processes – the Family.* Karnac Books.

Selvini Palazzoli M., Boscolo L., Cecchin G. & Prata G. (1978) *Paradox and Counter-Paradox.* Jason Aronson, New York.

Selvini Palazzoli M., Boscolo L., Cecchin G. & Prata G. (1980) Hypothesising, circularity, neutrality, three guidelines for the conductor of the session. *Family Process,* **19**, 3–12.

Semans J.H. (1956) Premature ejaculation, a new approach. *Southern Medical Journal,* **49**, 353–7.

Shepherd M. (1961) Morbid jealousy: Some clinical and social aspects of a psychiatric symptom. *Journal of Mental Science,* **107**, 687–753.

Skynner A.C.R. (1976) *One Flesh: Separate Persons; Principles of Family and Marital Psychotherapy,* Constable, London.

Skynner A.C.R. (1982) Framework for viewing the family as a system. *Family Therapy,* **1** (Ed. by A. Bentovim, G.G. Barnes & A. Cooklin). Academic Press, London.

Skynner A.C.R. (1987) Recent developments in marital therapy. *Journal of Family Therapy,* **2**, 271–96. Reprinted in *Explorations with Families: Group Analysis and Family Therapy.* Methuen, London.

Sluzki C.E. (1978) Marital therapy from a systems perspective. In *Marriage and Marital Therapy* (Ed. by T.J. Paolini & B.S. McCrady). Brunner/Mazel, New York.

Spanier G.B. (1976) Measuring dyadic adjustments. New scales for assessing the quality of marriage and similar dyads. *Journal of Marriage and the Family*, **38**, 15–28.

Spiegel J. (1957) The resolution of role conflict within the family. *Psychiatry*, **20**, 1–15.

Spinks S.H. & Birchler G.R. (1982) Behavioural-systems marital therapy: dealing with resistance. *Family Process*, **21**, 169–185.

Stern D. (1983) Self, Other and 'Self and Other'. *Reflections on Self Psychology* (Ed. by J.D. Lichtenberg and S. Kaplan). N.J. Hillsdale, Analytic Press.

Sternberg R.J. (Ed.) (1988) *The Psychology of Love*. Yale University Press.

Storr A. (1971) *Human Aggression*. Penguin Books, London.

Stuart R.B. (1969) Operant interpersonal treatment for marital discord. *Journal of Consulting and Clinical Psychology*, **33**, 675–82.

Stuart R.B. (1980) *Helping Couples Change*. Guilford Press, New York.

Teisman M.W. (1979) Jealousy: systematic, problem-solving therapy with couples. *Family Process*, **18**, 151–60.

Thibault J.W. & Kelly H.H. (1959) *The Social Psychology of Groups*. Wiley, New York.

Thornes B. & Collard D. (1979) *Who Divorces?* Routledge and Kegan Paul, London.

Vaughn C.E. & Leff J. (1976) The influence of family and social factors on the course of psychiatric patients. *British Journal of Social and Clinical Psychology*, **15**, 157–65.

Vaughn C.E. & Leff J. (1976) The measurement of expressed emotion in the families of psychiatric illness. *British Journal of Psychiatry*, **129**, 125–37.

Vincent J.P. (1972) *The relationship of sex, level of intimacy, and level of marital distress to problem solving behaviour and exchange of social reinforcements*. Doctoral dissertation, University of Oregon.

Walsh M.R. (1987) *The Psychology of Women*. Yale University Press.

Watzlawick P., Beavin J.H. & Jackson D.D. (1967) *Pragmatics of Human Communication: A Study of Interactional Patterns, Pathologies, and Paradoxes*. W.W. Norton, New York.

Watzlawick P., Weakland J. & Fisch (1974) *Change: Principles of Problem Formulation and Problem Resolution*. W.W. Norton, New York.

Weeks G.R. (1978) A bibliography of paradoxical methods in psychotherapy of family systems. *Family Process*, **17**, 95–98.

Weeks G.R. (Ed.) (1989) *Treating Couples, The Intersystem Model of the Marriage Council of Philadelphia*. Bruner/Mazel, New York.

Weeks G.R. & Hof L. (1988) *Integrating Sex and Marital Therapy*. Brunner/Mazel, New York.

Weiss R.L. (1978) The conceptualisation of marriage from a behavioural perspective. In *Marriage and Marital Therapy* (Ed. by T.J. Paolino & B.S. McCrady). Brunner/Mazel.

Weiss R.L. & Birchler G.R. (1978) *Adults with Marital Dysfunction in Behaviour Therapy in the Psychiatric Setting*. Williams and Williams, Baltimore.

Weissman M.M. & Paykel E.S. (1974) *The Depressed Woman: A Study of Social Relationships*. University of Chicago Press.

Weissman M.M., Paykel E.S. & Klerman G.L. (1972) The depressed woman as mother. *Social Psychiatry*, **7**, 98–108.

Whitehead A.N. & Russell B. (1910) *Principia Mathematica*. Cambridge University Press.

Wijnberg M.H. & Schwarz M.C. (1977) Models of student supervision. The apprentice, growth and role systems models. *Journal of Education for Social Work*, **13**, (3), 107–113.

Wilkinson G.D. (1988) Depression, *Family Doctor Guide*. British Medical Association, London.

Will D. (1983) Approaching the incestuous and sexually abusive family. *Journal of Adolescence*, **6**, 229–46.

Wills T.S., Weiss R.L. & Patterson G.R. (1974) A behavioural analysis of determinants of marital satisfaction. *Journal of Consulting and Clinical Psychology*, **42**, 802–11.

Wilson E.O. (1975) *Sociobiology, The New Synthesis*. Harvard University Press.

Wing J.K. (1978) *Schizophrenia. Towards a New Synthesis*. Academic Press, London.

Winnicott D.W. (1965) *The Maternal Process and the Facilitating Environment*. Hogarth Press, London.

Winnicott D.W. (1971) *Playing and Reality*. Penguin Books, London.

Winnicott D.W. (1975) Primary maternal preoccupation (1956). *Through paediatrics to Psycho-analysis*. Hogarth Press, London.

Working Party on Marriage Guidance (1979) *Marriage Matters*, a consultative document, HMSO, London.

Wynne L.C. (1988) *The state of the art in family therapy: controversies and recommendations*. Family Process Press, New York.

Wynne L.C., Ryckoff I.N., Day I. & Hirsch S.I. (1972) Pseudomutuality in the family of relations of schizophrenics. *Psychiatry*, **21**, 205–20.

Young M. & Willmott P. (1973) *The Symmetrical Family*. Routledge and Kegan Paul, London.

Zilbergeld B. (1980) *Men and Sex*. Fontana, London.

Association addresses

Association of Sexual and Marital Therapists, P.O. Box 62, Sheffield S10 3TS.
British Association of Counselling, 37A Sheep Street, Rugby, Warwickshire, CV21 3BX.

Index

Index of cases